INFORMATION
ASSURANCE
ARCHITECTURE

802.1X Port-Based Authentication
Edwin Lyle Brown
ISBN: 1-4200-4464-8

Building an Effective Information Security Policy Architecture
Sandy Bacik
ISBN: 1-4200-5905-X

CISO Soft Skills: Securing Organizations Impaired by Employee Politics, Apathy, and Intolerant Perspectives
Michael Gentile, Ron Collette and Skye Gentile
ISBN: 1-4200-8910-2

Complete Guide to Security and Privacy Metrics: Measuring Regulatory Compliance, Operational Resilience, and ROI
Debra S. Herrmann
ISBN: 0-8493-5402-1

Computer Forensics: Evidence Collection and Management
Robert C. Newman
ISBN: 0-8493-0561-6

Cyber Forensics: A Field Manual for Collecting, Examining, and Preserving Evidence of Computer Crimes, Second Edition
Albert Marcella, Jr. and Doug Menendez
ISBN: 0-8493-8328-5

Digital Privacy: Theory, Technologies, and Practices
Alessandro Acquisti, Stefanos Gritzalis, Costos Lambrinoudakis and Sabrina di Vimercati
ISBN: 1-4200-5217-9

How to Achieve 27001 Certification: An Example of Applied Compliance Management
Sigurjon Thor Arnason and Keith D. Willett
ISBN: 0-8493-3648-1

Information Assurance Architecture
Keith D. Willett
ISBN: 0-8493-8067-7

Information Security Management Handbook, Sixth Edition
Harold F. Tipton and Micki Krause
ISBN: 0-8493-7495-2

Information Security Management Handbook, Sixth Edition, Volume 2
Harold F. Tipton and Micki Krause
ISBN: 1-4200-6708-7

Information Security Management Handbook, 2008 CD-ROM Edition
Harold F. Tipton and Micki Krause
ISBN: 1-4200-6698-6

Insider Computer Fraud: An In-depth Framework for Detecting and Defending against Insider IT Attacks
Kenneth Brancik
ISBN 1-4200-4659-4

Mechanics of User Identification and Authentication: Fundamentals of Identity Management
Dobromir Todorov
ISBN: 1-4200-5219-5

Official (ISC)2 Guide to the SSCP CBK
Diana-Lynn Contesti, Douglas Andre, Eric Waxvik, Paul A. Henry and Bonnie A. Goins
ISBN: 0-8493-2774-1

Oracle Identity Management: Governance, Risk, and Compliance Architecture, Third Edition
Marlin B. Pohlman
ISBN: 1-4200-7247-1

Software Deployment, Updating, and Patching
Bill Stackpole and Patrick Hanrion
ISBN: 0-8493-5800-0

Testing Code Security
Maura A. van der Linden
ISBN: 0-8493-9251-9

Wireless Crime and Forensic Investigation
Gregory Kipper
ISBN: 0-8493-3188-9

AUERBACH PUBLICATIONS

www.auerbach-publications.com
To Order Call: 1-800-272-7737 • Fax: 1-800-374-3401
E-mail: orders@crcpress.com

INFORMATION ASSURANCE ARCHITECTURE

KEITH D. WILLETT

CRC Press
Taylor & Francis Group
Boca Raton   London   New York

CRC Press is an imprint of the
Taylor & Francis Group, an **Informa** business
AN AUERBACH BOOK

Auerbach Publications
Taylor & Francis Group
6000 Broken Sound Parkway NW, Suite 300
Boca Raton, FL 33487-2742

© 2008 by Taylor & Francis Group, LLC
Auerbach is an imprint of Taylor & Francis Group, an Informa business

No claim to original U.S. Government works
Printed in the United States of America on acid-free paper
10 9 8 7 6 5 4 3 2 1

International Standard Book Number-13: 978-0-8493-8067-9 (Hardcover)

Library of Congress Cataloging-in-Publication Data

Willett, Keith D.
   Information assurance architecture / author, Keith D. WIllett.
       p. cm.
   Includes bibliographical references and index.
   ISBN 978-0-8493-8067-9 (hardback : alk. paper) 1. Computer security.
   2. Computer networks--Security measures. 3. Information resources
   management. 4. Information technology--Management. 5. Business
   enterprises--Communication systems--Management. 6. Data protection. I.
   Title.

   QA76.9.A25W5487 2008
   005.8--dc22   2008010630

Visit the Taylor & Francis Web site at
http://www.taylorandfrancis.com

and the Auerbach Web site at
http://www.auerbach-publications.com

Dedication

To opportunity! *Luck* is preparation meeting opportunity. I dedicate this book to those who provided me with the opportunity to put into practice many, many years of preparation:

- My father, Louis Willett, for teaching me what discipline is as he learned from his grandfather Henry Cochran, and for living the example that education and success are never further away than a commitment to hard work.
- My mother, Mary Elizabeth Willett, for always being there in every situation.
- My wife, Terri Meyer Willett, for her unwavering encouragement and patience during the writing of this book, and for being a shining example of perseverance and showing me a strong spirit gets you through the challenges.
- My teacher, Joyce Currie Little, for inspiration in forward thinking and turning thoughts into action; I never told her this in person and I am only sorry it took me 20 years to express my appreciation.
- My first technical manager, Doris Fell, for her ability to express complex issues in understandable terms and her patience in repeating many examples many times.
- My first commercial hiring manager, John Parkent—thanks for the opportunity; it was a first step on a long and winding career path.
- Mich Kabay for an example of truest professionalism and energy. Mich sets a new standard for vision, execution, and results. Mich's hard work in developing the Norwich University Master of Information Assurance (MSIA) program provided the forum to develop the initial version of this work as a master's thesis.
- Peter Stephenson for introducing me to the excellent people at Auerbach Publications who afforded me the opportunity to write this book.

Contents

SECTION II APPLIED IA²

SECTION III   IA² ENTERPRISE CONTEXT

Author's Note

If I have seen further it is by standing on ye shoulders of Giants.

—**Isaac Newton**

This work is a continuation on a long path of knowledge, and my greatest hope is to take another step forward in the professions of information assurance and enterprise architecture.

Information assurance architecture (IA²) will evolve into an ever-more refined discipline that promotes practical and efficient information assurance (IA) solutions to effectively address business risk. Please feel free and encouraged to supply any comments or input to kwillett@ia2.info. Also, look for IA² updates, clarification, and supplemental tools on www.ia2.info. You may need a copy of this book handy to find the passwords that grant access to the extras for those of you kind enough to have purchased this book.

This book may make reference to vendors, products, and services. These are for examples only and do not constitute an endorsement of any particular vendor, product, or service for any particular purpose.

Scope and Objective

Information Assurance Architecture introduces a new way to think about IA. The IA services and IA mechanisms herein are not new; however, IA² provides a method to identify, select, and arrange IA services and mechanisms that find root in business needs and provide for the effective management of business risks. This work provides the security industry with a formal *information assurance architecture* (IA²) that complements enterprise architecture, systems engineering, and enterprise life-cycle management (ELCM). For many readers, this book will be an introduction to the disciplines of enterprise architecture (EA) and systems engineering (SE). There are many excellent books on these subjects (see Appendix L, "Reading List") and the details regarding EA and SE herein are merely an introduction to give context to IA².

IA² itself consists of an IA² Framework, IA² Process, and many supporting tools, templates, and methodologies. The IA² Framework provides a reference model for the consideration of security in many contexts and from many various perspectives. The IA² Process provides direction on how to apply the IA² Framework. There are many tools that may be used individually or together to address IA issues. IA² provides you with the tools for a disciplined approach to think about, plan for, implement, and operate IA solutions that integrate with the enterprise.

Security for its own sake, like technology for its own sake, is not good business practice. If security or technology is a hobby, then by all means pursue them to the delight of your intellectual satisfaction. However, when introducing IA services or IA mechanisms into a business environment, there must be sound business reasons to do so. Therefore, this book conveys many non-IA aspects with the understanding that a discussion about a business process, business service, technical infrastructure, or technical application is incomplete until there are discussions about risk and how to address that risk. Therefore, it is critical to integrate IA into the processes, planning, and implementation of business governance, management, and operations.

The objectives of *Information Assurance Architecture* include:

- Introduce the disciplines of enterprise architecture and systems engineering
- Introduce the concept of IA architecture
- Introduce the IA² constructs: the IA² Framework and the IA² Process
- Provide a business context for IA²
- Align IA² with the discipline of EA
- Explain how to use IA² Framework and IA² Process as tools for business risk management
- Introduce a series of frameworks to provide the IA architect with an effective approach to manage the complexity of enterprisewide IA

Target Audience

This book is primarily for security engineers, security architects (information assurance architects), security management, and other security personnel with interest in identifying and addressing business risk in a disciplined, repeatable, and comprehensive manner. The book is also useful for enterprise architects and systems architects who desire to integrate information assurance in their solutions. Business managers, project managers, program managers, and many others will find this book useful to understand information assurance in context of the enterprise, including business need, business fit, and business justification for IA.

The book is written to address the information assurance architect. You may take this term to imply any individual who desires a disciplined, repeatable approach to identify, enumerate, articulate, understand, and address business risk, or in other words, understand the enterprise context of IA.

This work covers many information assurance (IA) subjects, like disaster recovery, firewalls, etc. However, the goal is *not* to instruct in the mechanics of these areas; rather, the objective is to present security services and security mechanisms in context of IA², architectural considerations, and in an enterprise context of managing business risk. The reader should have at least intermediate knowledge of information technology and information assurance to derive the most benefit from this book.

Goals for the Reader

We all start out life not knowing that we do not know. As we go along, most of us learn *about* many things; that is, we become aware of them. There is a big difference between *knowing about* something and *knowing* that something. We decide what subjects to pursue in more depth according to our personal interest, economic need, and many other motivations. We then discover varying degrees of aptitude and fluency with what we pursue. The learning progression is from awareness to understanding, understanding to use, and varying degrees of use, including *appropriate* use, *effective* use, and even *secure* use (Figure 1).

As an IA architect, you need the right tools to accomplish your mission of generating an IA architecture and integrating IA with enterprise architecture. *Information Assurance Architecture* is an IA architecture toolkit. A toolkit is a collection of tools, a tool is a device for a specific purpose; a hammer drives in nails, or the other end of the hammer can pull out nails. Moreover, there is an appropriate use for each tool; a hammer can insert a screw, but a screwdriver is a better choice so the threads grip the wood more effectively. Experience and skill provide for appropriate tool selection and effective tool application.

At the end of studying this material, you should have an understanding of IA², the IA² Framework, and the IA² Process, and how to apply them in an enterprise

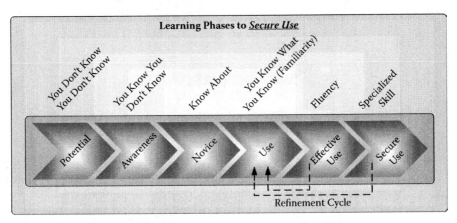

Figure 1   Learning phases to secure use.

context. You should have an awareness of what EA is and the need to integrate information assurance with EA. Moreover, you should understand how to use IA^2 to determine IA requirements and align those IA requirements with business drivers. You should understand an approach to develop an IA quantification scheme.

This book provides you with a disciplined approach to learn the variety of contexts and perspectives for IA, and how to view and think about IA in various contexts and from various perspectives. Fluency in IA^2 only comes from study, application, and hard work. IA architecture is not easy, but is critical for cost-effective risk management.

Preface

When teaching at Towson University in 1984, a student asked, "What is the purpose of college?" My answer was that college should teach you two things: how to think, and if you do not know the answer, where to find it. A subsequent question was, "How do you teach someone to think?" My answer was, "Hmmm...well, I don't know." More than 20 years later, I still do not know, but I have some ideas. Many of those ideas are herein.

Information Assurance Architecture does not provide answers to conventional questions regarding security. You will not learn how to perform a risk assessment, design a secure network, or configure a firewall. You will learn *how to think about* these and many other aspects of information assurance. *Information Assurance Architecture* is more a philosophy of IA than a how-to for IA—a philosophy that provides insight on how to think about IA in context of the entire organization (the enterprise). This IA thought process will help you discern and define the problem (the risks), identify and enumerate options on how to address the problem, identify constraints on determining the best solution, and how to select the best solution and move forward to design, implement, test, deploy, and operate that solution.

Will this book teach you how to think? Well, if you do not know how to think, it may point you in the right direction. If you already know how to think, *Information Assurance Architecture* will help you think better.

Acknowledgments

I wish to gratefully acknowledge Elizabeth Templeton, the administrative director of the MSIA program at Norwich University in Vermont. Elizabeth provided invaluable support as an editor for this book. Elizabeth's technical and editing experience enabled her to provide thoughtful input with challenges as necessary and encouragement when needed. Thank you!

IA²

Chapter 1

Foundational Concepts for IA²

1.1 Introduction

Information Assurance Architecture (IA²) is a book on how to think about security in terms directly related to the core reasons for the existence of the organization. In general, the core objective of a commercial organization is to make a profit for investors, the core objective of a government organization is to provide service to citizens, and the core objective of a military organization is to defend national interests. The accomplishment of these core objectives is a complex of constantly evolving strategic and tactical objectives, strategic and tactical planning, projects, acquisitions, implementation, and ongoing operations and maintenance. Each layer, phase, stage, and step must consider organizational risk, including risks to the existence of the organization, risks to fulfilling core objectives, and risks to assets, employees, and infrastructure. IA² offers a discipline to identify, enumerate, articulate, and address risks at every organizational level in business and technical terms, and to describe those risks in both subjective narrative and objective quantification.

A key objective of this book is to make IA² practical, useful, and usable as a tool to effectively identify and address organizational risk. The tone of this book will fluctuate in and out of lofty academic discourse and just plain conversational expressions. The lofty discourse is necessary at times to express complex ideas in concise terms, like taxonomies and ontologies.* Plain expressions often help make these lofty terms understandable.

Moreover, *Information Assurance Architecture* provides many frameworks and processes, but also presents a philosophical perspective on IA and IA architecture. This philosophy attempts to get at root principles of why. As an architect, you are very interested in why. Why IA. Why this is a risk. Why addressing this risk is a priority.

1.2 Objective

The objective of this chapter is to introduce foundational concepts and definitions fundamental to IA^2, the IA^2 Framework, and the IA^2 Process. These concepts include:

- Enterprise architecture (EA)
- Systems engineering (SE)
- Services
- Mechanisms
- Information assurance (IA)
- Information assurance architecture (IA^2)
- IA architectural framework ($IA^2 F$)
- IA architectural process ($IA^2 P$)
- Ontology
- Taxonomy
- Hierarchy

Why *architecture*? If one were to say, "I've engaged an architect!" you would likely picture a building construction project. A building architect provides guidance to a builder in the form of blueprints. To produce the blueprints, the architect works closely with the owner or sponsor for the building. The architect discovers the owner's goals and desires. These goals and desires include functional aspects of the building as well as aesthetic aspects. Moreover, the architect considers the environment in which the building will reside, including the climate, sunrise, and sunset, all with the intent to create a useful, efficient, aesthetically pleasing structure. The architect creates elevations, models, and finally blueprints that describe the relationship among the building site and the building's floors, walls, light, and space, all of which have been designed to meet the owner's requirements.

What if the construction project were to build a business, a nationwide enterprise, or a global enterprise? Initial thoughts would be to engage accountants, lawyers, and business professionals in marketing, supply line management, and other

---

* See glossary.

such expertise. Although this is good, how do these people know that they are doing the right things in the context of a larger plan? Is there such a thing as a business architect? Yes, and they are referred to as *enterprise architects*; enterprise architects develop *enterprise architectures*. So, now there is this enterprise architecture that describes the complexities of the business, assets, people, technology, relationships, and operations. How do you safeguard these assets? How do you ensure continuity of operations? Maintain organizational viability? The answer resides in the services of an architect for security.

What will a security architect design? If organizational wealth is physical assets like currency or gold, a prudent security architecture includes safes, vaults, door locks, and surveillance equipment. In the contemporary business environment, most organizational wealth is now largely bits* on a hard drive. The transfer of organizational wealth (e.g., employee payroll via direct deposit and interorganization transactions) is bits traveling across a wire. Physical buildings and land no longer represent the largest portion of organizational value; instead, most organizational assets are intellectual property in the form of either employee knowledge or documents and information—most of these are in the form of bits on electronic media (e.g., a hard drive).

The mission of the information assurance architect is to develop an information assurance architecture and align IA with the enterprise architecture (EA) to ensure appropriate safeguards that maintain the organization's operational integrity and long-term viability.

An effective IA² practitioner must have a breadth and depth of experience with technology, security, and business. The intent of this book is to provide the IA² practitioner with a disciplined thought process for IA planning and integration of IA in the enterprise.

1.3   Foundations of Successful Architecture

Foundations of any successful architecture, be it enterprise or information assurance, include:

- Lexicon
- Standards
- Means
- Method
- Motivation
- Mission

---

* The term *bit* is a contraction of the phrase *binary digit*. The value of a binary digit is either 0 or 1.

A **lexicon** is a dictionary of the words and phrases pertaining to a particular subject. A lexicon ensures that all stakeholders with an interest in a project interpret and use the same language consistently. For example, *risk* means different things to different people and may mean different things to the same person in different situations. The debate on whether a definition is right or wrong can go on ad infinitum. The important point is for everyone to agree that for now the working definition is as the lexicon states.

Standards provide a baseline upon which to build a successful IA architecture. Using an industry standard means that the approach, the details, or both can be vetted against an accepted reality. Rarely will any one standard address all organizational needs. However, using standards within an architecture removes the perception of arbitrariness and provides a credible reference point from which to customize the organization-specific solution.

Means are the available resources and include people, expertise, time, material, and budget.

Method is a prescribed manner to proceed. The IA² Framework and IA² Process together provide the IA architectural method.

Motivation is a set of reasons. The root motivation for IA architecture is to recognize the presence of business risk and address it appropriately.

Mission is a specific focus. The specific focus for IA² may be a system, a business function, a technical service, a group of people, or the overall IA posture of the enterprise.

1.3.1 Architecture Terminology

Architecture is the art of consciously forming a coherent structure. In a technical environment, an *architecture view* is a "representation of a system from the perspective of related concerns or issues,"* "a collection of logically related models."† An *architectural framework* is "a standard for the description of architectures."‡ Architecture addresses not only structure, but also behavior of systems and data, as well as behavior of people in terms of relationships, actions, and cognition.

An architecture is a unifying structure using a set of design artifacts and descriptive representations to describe an entity such that it can be produced to requirements and be maintained over its life cycle. An entity may be physical, logical, system, cyber, or a combination of these. An architectural process provides a disciplined methodology to promote repeatability, consistency, high quality, and complexity management.

---

* IEEE 1471.
† Maier and Rechtin.
‡ Maier and Rechtin.

1.3.1.1 Enterprise Architecture and Systems Architecture

Architecture is a multidimensional practice. Challenges facing the architect include paradox, dichotomies, balancing a multitude of tasks, deadlines, conflicting premises, constraints, uncertainty with existing information, and missing information. Critical architectural decisions may include many assumptions (a professional euphemism for *guesses*). A structured approach to architecture provides a method to minimize assumption uncertainty. An effective architectural approach addresses enterprise architecture (the big picture) as well as systems architecture (the pieces comprising the big picture).

GEAO* describes *enterprise architecture* as follows:

> The way in which an enterprise vision is expressed in the structure and dynamics of an Enterprise. It provides, on various architecture abstraction levels, a coherent set of models, principles, guidelines, and policies, to translate, align, and evolve the systems that exist within the scope and context of an Enterprise.

An EA process is a methodology that aligns solutions (business, technical, operations, etc.) with organizational core mission and strategic direction in terms of *to-be*, target architecture; *as-is*, current architecture; and *transition*, migration plan from *as-is* to *to-be*.

Understanding that systems comprise the greater enterprise, there is a distinction between enterprise architecture and systems architecture. A system may or may not be a computer system, but is by definition an entity that accepts input, performs a process, generates output, and reacts to feedback (e.g., nervous system, economic system, or computer system). Based on the GEAO definition of enterprise architecture, *system architecture* is defined as follows:

> Systems architecture refers to the way in which a system vision is expressed in the structure and dynamics of the system and often in context of a collection of systems. It provides, on various architecture abstraction levels, a coherent set of models, principles, guidelines, and policies, used for the translation, alignment, and evolution of the components that exist within the scope and context of a system.

Enterprise architecture and system architecture are complex practices of abstraction that provide guidelines to develop business solutions without regard to specific services or mechanisms. Information assurance architecture is itself a complex practice of abstraction requiring a melding of architectural concepts, information

---

* Global Enterprise Architecture Organization (www.geao.org).

assurance concepts, and the development of new terms to describe nuances of the IA² practice.

Most people in technology think in terms of the technology they are familiar with and the operations that technology supports. Although this is not bad, it is not enough. The architect needs to think in abstract terms of hierarchies, taxonomies, and principles that emphasize the business perspective and guide the mechanisms that support operations. A business driver of secure communications between the Internet and the internal network results in IA services and IA mechanisms to support that business driver. The size, complexity, type, and notoriety of the organization drive the breadth and depth of these IA services and mechanisms. A small Midwest insurance agency is unlikely to be a direct target of international cyber terrorism; however, it may be an indirect victim of a cyber virus in the wild. A prudent precaution is for this small Midwest company to install anti-malware on servers and desktops to protect itself from incidental infection. A government organization of military and political significance is more likely to be under *direct* attack from not only conventional malware, but also unique malware specifically targeted at that organization. This government organization requires a significantly larger investment in defense, monitoring, and response with respect to malware. The architectural process assists in discerning these differences and providing the appropriate safeguards to balance operational effectiveness, security, and cost.

1.3.2   Information Assurance: A Working Definition

An abstract organizational mission statement reads: Provide the people we serve with quality products and services on time, within budget, and within specified service level agreements (SLAs). The ultimate focus is on stakeholder value. Stakeholder value may be shareholder value in the private sector or constituent value in the public sector. Whatever the mission, it requires operational integrity—operations must continue despite incidents that may interrupt, information must be accurate despite incidents that may corrupt, and information critical to mission success must be kept confidential from competitors, enemies, or other opposition despite incidents that may disclose. Many factors, including buildings, utility services (i.e., power and water), personnel, and information technologies, support the mission. *Information assurance defines and applies a collection of policies, standards, methodologies, services, and mechanisms to maintain mission integrity with respect to people, process, technology, information, and supporting infrastructure.*

Information assurance addresses information, not just information technology. A chief information officer (CIO) is responsible for information, not just information technology. Information assurance provides for *confidentiality, integrity, availability, possession, utility, authenticity, nonrepudiation, authorized use,* and *privacy* of information in all forms and during all exchanges.

Figure 1.1 Mission integrity boundary model.

1.3.2.1 Mission Integrity versus Mission Entropy

To maintain *mission integrity*, all relevant operations are working toward the fulfillment of the mission within an acceptable level of deviation. When operational levels exceed deviation parameters, operations have entered a state of *mission entropy*.* Deviation parameters define a fuzzy line separating mission integrity (successful mission fulfillment) from mission entropy where mission success is in jeopardy (Figure 1.1).

The goal of IA is to keep operations within acceptable deviation from that ever-elusive goal of perfection; that is, IA attempts to keep operations within acceptable mission integrity boundaries. When mission entropy threatens, corrective action is required to move operations back in line. It is possible to introduce too much security and introduce mission entropy (e.g., shutting down external Internet access is very secure but unacceptable when the E-commerce site generates 80 percent of revenues). IA must balance the right amount of security with the right amount of freedom to operate.

The need for corrective action to maintain mission integrity emphasizes the importance of knowing how to anticipate, defend, monitor, detect, alert, respond, and correct such deviations. *Information Assurance Architecture* presents many frameworks, processes, services, and mechanisms to ensure corrective action. Note the purpose of IA² is not to teach these security services and mechanisms; there are many excellent references on security operations, firewalls, intrusion detection systems (IDSs), disaster recovery planning, etc. Rather, IA² presents various ways to think about security services and mechanisms, and how to apply them to design and implement IA to achieve optimum effectiveness in context of business drivers and business risk.

1.3.2.2 Melding Architecture and Information Assurance

Using the definitions for architecture and information assurance, Table 1.1 presents IA architectural terms critical to understanding IA architectural concepts.

---

* *Entropy* implies disorder, chaos, compromise, impairment, or random activity that takes operations outside acceptable operating parameters.

Table 1.1   Information Assurance and Derivative Terminology

IA Term	Definition
Information assurance (IA)	Defines and applies a collection of policies, standards, methodologies, services, and mechanisms to maintain mission integrity with respect to people, process, technology, information, and supporting infrastructure
Information assurance architecture (IA^2)	The art of consciously forming a coherent structure of information assurance services and mechanisms
IA^2 Framework	The basic conceptual structure for defining and describing an IA^2 solution
IA^2 Process	The steps required to generate an information assurance architecture

The discipline of architecture uses terms of particular nuance. This book attempts to use these terms in a manner widely accepted; however, given the nature of the topic, this book introduces new terms surrounding IA architecture. The glossary provides a lexicon to distinguish the nuances among these terms. Understanding these terms is essential to understanding the IA architectural concepts herein. This book is internally consistent in the use of the terms as defined in the glossary.

1.3.3   Systems Engineering

A system is a collection of entities (real or virtual) that interact to produce an objective or result. Systems engineering (SE) is a discipline to plan for and ultimately produce a system. Systems engineering may follow the guidance provided by an enterprise architecture to implement the intent of that architecture. This may include the information assurance services and mechanisms in the appropriate context of managing business risk. IA^2 is a discipline for IA that also applies to the requirements engineering aspect of SE.

The traditional use of SE is to produce a system of known and definable operation. The environment within which the system will work is known, inputs are well defined, and the interactions of the system are known (the providers of inputs and the consumers of outputs). There is an emerging need to provide an engineering discipline to systems or solutions that must operate today, but may operate in an environment where the expectations of that solution are not predictable. For example, a Web service may be used in manners completely unexpected by the developer. There becomes a need to define the environment very well and prescribe the rules necessary to operate in that environment. That environment may be a technical environment or it may be the enterprise. The enterprise environment looks at combining services in as many ways as it takes to produce results effectively. Therefore, there is an emerging need for a discipline of enterprise systems engineering.

1.4 Ontologies, Taxonomies, and Hierarchies

An **ontology** is an orderly classification; an ontological class represents an abstract ideal. An instance is a specific example of something within that class; IA² is an instance of an ontology for addressing information assurance from an enterprise architecture perspective. A **taxonomy** is an orderly classification to define relationships between classes; IA² uses taxonomies in process flow descriptions to establish relationships between classes. A **hierarchy** is a top-down structure that denotes superior–subordinate relationships. A hierarchy may represent a control structure, a classification structure, or an organizational structure.

1.5 Context and Perspective

This book uses the terms *context* and *perspective* a lot. **Context** is the environment within which something exists or resides. An enterprise context is the entire organizational environment; an organizational structure context is the environment of the hierarchical relationships within the enterprise. **Perspective** is a point of view. For example, an executive (CEO) perspective on a project looks for the benefit to stakeholders in terms of return on investment; the system administrator perspective looks for the benefit to users in terms of providing the capabilities and performance they expect. The appropriate application of architecture is context dependent. Moreover, the architect must see things from the perspective of many different people and must look at things from a business perspective and technical perspective.

1.6 Identify, Enumerate, Articulate, and Address

The main theme in this book is IA² as a discipline to identify, enumerate, articulate, and address risks. To **identify** risk is to discern the characteristics of the risk, those distinguishing features that provide identity to that risk. To **enumerate** risks is to list all the relevant risks. To **articulate** risks is to elaborate on the characteristics, to give them business meaning, an enterprise context, and make them understandable. To **address** a risk is to acknowledge its existence and state how to deal with it in terms of accept, ignore, transfer, share, or mitigate.

An important distinction is that to address risk is not necessarily to spend money to mitigate that risk. A perfectly legitimate manner of addressing risk is to state that the organization chooses to accept that risk and provide a rationale as to why.

1.7 Summary and Conclusion

The IA architect needs a framework, a process, and a set of tools, templates, and methods to produce an IA architecture. These IA² constructs provide the ability to address IA comprehensively in terms of business risk as well as in technical terms meaningful to developers, implementers, and operations. These IA² support artifacts also provide a repeatable, consistent methodology for producing IA architectures. Caveat: No matter the supporting frameworks, tools, templates, etc., architecture can never be a cookie-cutter, rote process performed by anyone who reads the manual and follows a checklist. Architecture is an art that uses the discipline of science to help guide the architect through the methodology.

The fundamental concepts in this chapter provide a basis for understanding the IA² Framework and IA² Process. The next chapter uses these concepts to define an IA² Framework.

Chapter 2

The IA² Framework

2.1 Introduction

The Federal Enterprise Architecture (FEA) is one approach to developing an enterprise architecture. The FEA is based on a commercial model, the Zachman Framework.* The Department of Defense Architecture Framework (DoDAF) is based on FEA. All of these EA approaches offer views that include business architecture, data architecture, application architecture, and technology architecture. A common construct within EA is the reference model. FEA provides reference models for *performance, business, services, technology,* and *data.* These reference models provide templates to capture the line of sight from the business to the technology that supports the business.

The IA² approach is exclusively for information assurance. You may use IA² to integrate IA into FEA, Zachman, DoDAF, or other enterprise architecture approaches to effectively identify and address business risk. All too often security is an afterthought that causes service delays and increases organizational risk by not integrating with business processes, performance goals, and technical solutions. Identifying risk and inserting appropriate risk mitigation throughout the EA process and overall enterprise life cycle management (ELCM)† is more effective than after-the-fact bolt-on of IA. IA integration from inception is far more efficient from the perspectives of development and implementation cost, operations, and overall performance value. The enterprise architect or the IA architect should apply IA² throughout the enterprise architecture (EA) process.

---

* http://www.zifa.com/ (accessed July 2007).
† See glossary.

This book prepares you to address information assurance from an enterprise architecture perspective that includes a holistic IA perspective. This requires deferring technical specifics to abstract thinking, or taking specifics and abstracting them to principles or rules that apply in a broader sense. These abstractions take the form of frameworks, hierarchies, taxonomies, and ontologies. Hierarchies define top-down relationships similar to parent–child or manager–subordinate. A taxonomy is an orderly classification that align classes in a particular relationship such that any member of one classification may relate to any member of another classification according to the relationship defined. Ontologies provide for definitions of class, instances, attributes, relationships, and communications.

Chapter 1 introduced concepts and terms of architecture, enterprise architecture, information assurance, and information assurance architecture (IA^2). The material in this chapter introduces the IA^2 Framework, the flow through the framework as a line of sight linking the abstract IA architecture to IA operational constructs.

The technical and physical specifics (e.g., IA services and IA mechanisms) are still important; however, an architect reaches specifics by way of generalities. If the architect designs the solution to accommodate X technology, the life cycle of the solution is limited to the life cycle of technology X. For example, if the design for a solution focuses on network components from a particular manufacturer (no names to hide the guilty), the solution is as good as that manufacturer's components. If the solution design is on the *capabilities* necessary for enterprise communications, then various manufacturers may provide that capability. Yes, there are benefits to having network components from a single manufacturer (see chapter 9 for a discussion of homogeneous versus heterogeneous technical environments). However, *the point is to design the solution to the business capability and not to the technology.*

2.2 Objectives

Chapter objectives include the following:

- Introduce the IA^2 Framework (IA^2 F)
- Walk through the details of the IA^2 F
- Present the details of the IA^2 F architectural views
- Present the nine IA core principles
- Introduce the IA operations cycle (IA ops cycle)
- Discuss the IA^2 line of sight

Your objectives include learning about the IA^2 Framework as the core of IA^2. There are many supporting and complementary aspects to the IA^2 Framework. Each is another tool in the IA toolkit. A tool to be applied in the craft of IA architecture. A tool to be applied by you, the IA architect. What to apply? The craftsperson draws upon the right tool for the right job. When to apply? The craftsperson draws upon the right tool at the right time. Where to apply? The craftsperson draws upon the right tool for the right application. When to apply? The craftsperson draws upon the right tool at the right time. How to apply? The craftsperson is on a never-ending quest to develop expertise and fine-tune that expertise.

How do you learn what tools to draw upon for the right application? Experience. How do you get experience in applying the right tools in the right place at the right time? Part of the answer is applying the wrong tools in the wrong place at the wrong time. The other part of the answer is using a disciplined approach to assist in making the right choices and learning from the wrong choices. IA² provides that disciplined approach. Your objective is to learn this disciplined approach starting with the IA² Framework.

2.3   IA² Framework Details

A framework is a basic conceptual structure. A framework provides the ability to describe a subject using a predefined set of descriptive terms and concepts. A framework is not the solution itself, but a way to define and describe the solution. An EA framework is a basic conceptual structure of an enterprise architecture.* The IA² Framework is the basic conceptual structure for defining and describing an information assurance architecture.

The IA² Framework (Figure 2.1) starts with IA architectural drivers that include both business drivers and technical drivers. The root driver behind IA is risk—risk that may be expressed in terms of business risk and technical risk. The IA² Framework then presents six architectural views: *people, policy, business process, systems and applications, information/data,* and *infrastructure.* The IA² views provide for a more granular† perspective on the IA architectural drivers. There are nine IA core principles. Each IA² view considers each of the nine IA core principles (Figure 2.3) for each IA architectural driver. What starts as a single statement of risk may now be stated from the perspective of nine IA core principles, each from one of six different IA² views, or 54 perspectives on that single risk.

Consideration of how to address risk may be within the bounds of organizational discretion. That is, the organization may examine a risk and determine how to address that risk drawing upon organizational experience and organizational objectives. IA² also provides a filter through IA compliance requirements. IA compliance requirements may include externally imposed requirements like legislation, and IA compliance requirements may include internally imposed requirements like adherence to an industry security standard. Each of the 54 cross sections between

---

* To clarify, this book refers to EA as a practice, a process, and a document. There is such a document as an enterprise architecture, there is an enterprise architecture process to assist in producing that document, and there is a greater professional practice of enterprise architecture.

† Granular means a finer grain, the ability to see more detail from the component parts.

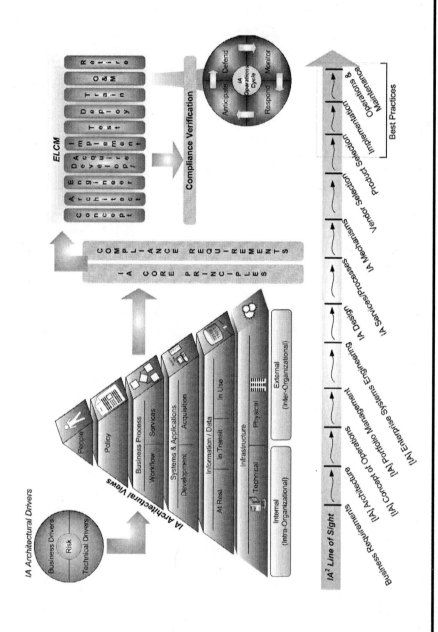

Figure 2.1   IA² Framework overview.

IA² views and IA core principles may have influences* from these external and internal compliance requirements.

Subsets of these apply in varying degrees to the current phase of the enterprise life cycle management (ELCM). The ELCM phases provide for the *conception, architecture, engineering, development or acquisition, implementation, testing, deployment,* and *retirement* of a solution. A solution may be a business service, technical service, or system. Finally, there is compliance verification to assure the IA preparations actually work as intended. Compliance verification ensures the final solution satisfies compliance requirements. Figure 2.1 shows the ELCM operation and maintenance (O&M) phase in more detail as an expansion of one ELCM phase. O&M is a large part of a solution's total cost of ownership. The details of O&M warrant particular attention.

An underlying taxonomy† within the IA² Framework is the IA² line of sight (IA² LoS). The IA² LoS begins with business requirements and then aligns subsequent classes with increasing technical focus and narrowing of detail. Business requirements drive architectural specifications, which are often in abstract terms, that include principles and philosophies that describe the best way to satisfy the business requirements. O&M requires actual products and services that perform tasks and produce results. The IA² LoS provides a detailed alignment from abstract business requirements and architectural specifications to the tangible constructs of O&M. The discipline of applying the line of sight as part of the IA² Process ensures a traceable alignment between solution investments and business requirements.

The following describes the IA² Framework (IA² F):

- IA architectural drivers
  - Business drivers
  - Technical drivers
- IA² views
  - People
  - Policy
  - Business process
    - Workflow
    - Services
  - Systems and applications
    - Development
    - Acquisition
  - Information or data
    - At rest
    - In transit
    - In use

---

* See glossary.
† Ibid.

- Infrastructure
  - ■ Technical
  - ■ Physical
  - Intraorganizational (internal)
  - Interorganizational (external)
- ■ IA core principles
  - Confidentiality-integrity-availability (CIA)
  - Possession-authenticity-utility (PAU)
  - Privacy–authorized use–nonrepudiation (PAN)
- ■ Compliance requirements
- ■ Enterprise life cycle management (ELCM)
  - Supporting constructs*
    - ■ For example, IA operations framework
- ■ Compliance verification
- ■ Line of sight

The following sections elaborate the IA² F.

2.4   IA² Architectural Drivers

The root motivation behind technology is business need. Business risk is a direct outgrowth of business need, and is the root driver behind IA. The two macro-level IA² architectural drivers are *business drivers* and *technical drivers*. Technical drivers are distinct from business drivers; however, both find root in business need. Two good architectural principles are *no business need, no technology* and *no business risk, no IA*.

2.4.1   Business Drivers

Business drivers come out of mission statements, organizational strategies, and compliance requirements†; organizational policies convey business drivers to the organization in everyday language. Enterprise architecture must align business requirements with services and mechanisms that will fulfill those requirements. IA² must align business risks with the IA services and IA mechanisms that mitigate those risks.

Two of the many ways to characterize business drivers are in financial terms and in terms of enterprise need. Chapter 12 contains additional details on the ROI framework and the enterprise perspective of an IA (EPIA) framework. These frame-

---

* See glossary for definition of construct.
† See Section 2.8 for an elaboration on compliance requirements.

works assist the architect in characterizing business drivers in terms of finance and enterprise need, respectively.

As an example, the following ROI framework may characterize business drivers in terms of revenue and cost:

- Revenue
  - Increase revenue
    - Increase in sales
      - Existing product line
      - Add to product features
      - Add products
  - Revenue acceleration
    - Increase time to revenue realization
      - Accelerate time to market
      - Increase cash flow
  - Sustain revenue
    - Mission realization/mission integrity/mission assurance
      - Service level agreements (SLAs), e.g., uptime SLAs for E-commerce site
    - Customer satisfaction; contract renewal
- Cost
  - Reduce cost
    - Increase in profit; manage cost of goods
    - Higher productivity per employee
    - Higher productivity per hour
  - Avoid cost
    - Legislative compliance; avoid fines
    - SLA penalties; operate within agreed upon parameters

Figure 2.2 summarizes the ROI framework in terms of currency in and currency out of the enterprise.

IA² assists to identify, enumerate, articulate, and address risks to revenue and costs. For example, if an E-commerce solution provides a new sales channel to increase sales, IA² addresses the risks of implementing, sustaining, and growing that new sales channel. When legislation (e.g., Sarbanes–Oxley Act of 2002) introduces IA requirements, there is business risk (jail time for officers and fines to the

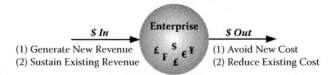

Figure 2.2   ROI framework summary.

organization) if compliance is insufficient. Business drivers for IA in terms of ROI include legislative compliance for cost avoidance.

The business perspective addresses business need, business fit, and business justification. The technical perspective addresses the technical fit, technical development and delivery, technical mechanisms, and the use of the technical mechanisms. Similarly, an IA perspective includes the business need for IA, the business fit for IA, the business justification for IA, the technical fit of IA, the technical acquisition/development and delivery of IA, the O&M of IA technical mechanisms, and the use of IA.

2.4.2   Technical Drivers

Technical drivers may be enablers of or constraints upon operational constructs. For example, the introduction of local areas networks (LANs) enabled the sharing of expensive resources, one common printer on the LAN versus 20 printers, and one per personal computer (PC). Pre-wireless LANs were constrained to wired links and physical limitations of cable lengths; e.g., working from the picnic bench in the courtyard was highly unlikely due to the need to stretch a 100-foot cable from the building. Business drivers provide the root motivation for action and technical drivers enable or constrain a subset of those actions. Technical drivers include information, applications, and information technology; for example:

- Information/data
  - Bits (dynamic, in transit, in use)
  - Creation
  - Acceptance
  - Collection (static, at rest)
    - Imminent use
      - Hard drive
    - Backup
      - Tape, floppy, compact disk (CD), digital versatile disc (DVD), universal serial bus (USB) device, etc.
    - Archive
      - Tape, floppy, CD, DVD, USB device, etc.
  - Collective organization of bits into data and information
- Applications
  - In-house versus outsource development
  - Common off-the-shelf software (COTS) and government off-the-shelf software (GOTS)
- Technology
  - Clients/servers; personal computers (PCs)
  - Medium

- ■ Wired, wireless
- ■ Transmission (e.g., Ethernet, Frame Relay [FR], Asynchronous Transfer Mode [ATM])
- – Infrastructure
  - ■ Information technology (IT) (e.g., routers, switches, Frame Relay access devices [FRADs])
  - ■ Information assurance (IA) (e.g., firewall [FW], virtual private network [VPN], anti-virus [AV], and intrusion detection system [IDS])

IA addresses risk to data, application, and technology, including technical services, network communications, and technical infrastructure.

2.5 IA² Views

A technical focus often limits traditional IA thought; however, the IA architect should by no means restrict IA concerns solely within technical bounds. Hence, the IA² Framework architectural views include nontechnical aspects like people, process, and physical infrastructure. One definition of architectural view is "a representation of a system from the perspective of related concerns or issues."* IA² defines an architectural view as a perspective on the architecture that isolates and focuses attention on a specific class of concerns. The IA² F defines six architectural views: people, policy, business process, systems and applications, information/data, and infrastructure.

Among the architect's audience are executives and high-ranking managers. On rare occasions, they will want to hear about bits and bytes; mostly, they want to hear about solving business problems, managing business risks, revenue streams, or cost containment. The breadth of the architectural views provides a wide window through which to view the organization's business needs.

Traditional IA thought also often resides in third-party, external security mechanisms providing after-the-fact *bolt-ons* (e.g., firewall, virtual private network, intrusion detection system, and anti-virus). Effective IA requires *integration from inception*, including software development, operating system design and selection, aligning IA policy with business goals and operations, physical security, personnel security, administrative security, operations security, and concentration on the most critical aspect of a successful security program: people.

2.5.1 People

The constant factor throughout IA² F is people. IA success depends on appropriate architecture, design, implementation, executive backing, and the IA profes-

---

* IEEE 1471.

sional's ability to articulate the philosophies, practices, policies, and technologies in terms readily understood by the audience. However, even the most elegant IA architecture is worthless unless people are aware of IA, understand IA, and use IA effectively.

The IA[2] people view addresses individuals as well as groups of people. The people view, as the capstone to the framework, is the key to failure or success of information assurance. People must be aware of and actively involved in IA from inception through implementation, operations, and maintenance to ensure awareness, understanding, and buy-in. From executive buy-in to customer acceptance, people are the key factor. An outline of the people view includes:

- Internal
  - Sponsors
    - Executive
  - Decision makers/approvers
    - Business manager/line manager
  - Operations
    - Administrators
    - Network operating center (NOC)/security operating center (SOC) operators
  - Users
    - Everyone receives awareness training
  - Legacy system owners
    - Manage perception of IA plus the process of introducing IA or potential violations of existing IA with introduction of new solutions that interface to legacy systems
  - Project team
    - Developers
      - Inserting IA in the planning, design, and implementation phase of the systems development life cycle
    - IA professionals
      - Managing, leading, training—turning them into champions of IA
- External
  - Customers
    - Perception management (e.g., privacy)
  - Stakeholders
    - People with a vested interest in organization's effective use of IA
  - Public
    - Perception management
  - Investors/shareholders
    - Benefits to shareholders and would-be investors on IA adding to the bottom line

- Constituents
  - ■ Benefits of taxpayer investment in IA in government
- ■ Personalities and relationships
  - Interactions, dependencies, expectation management

The IA² architect cannot ignore ethics, personal psychology, group dynamics, politics, and professional development when constructing the people view. Each of these areas is a complex discipline that requires much effort and study to master, and each is widely addressed in the current business, technology, and IA literature.

Chapter 12 presents an Enterprise Context Framework (ECF). The ECF is a hierarchy of enterprise constituents, that is, a hierarchy of elements that make up the enterprise. One constituent element of the enterprise is collectives, or groups of people. Collectives consist of individual people that act alone or in groups. The IA² F people view provides an IA perspective of people and collections of people by looking at the risks inherent with individuals, groups, group relationships, group actions, and group motivations. People within the organization possess certain trust levels, typically more trust than those outside the organization. The IA² people view assists in characterizing external threats, internal threats, and how to address those threats.

2.5.2 Policy

Policies specify appropriate and desired behavior. Employees use policies to guide decisions that affect the organization. The IA² F policy architectural view looks at risks within business policies and produces policies to guide IA activities and decisions across the enterprise. Examples of IA policies include continuity of operation plan (COOP), business continuity, disaster recovery, privacy policies, and technical policies, including firewall policy, access control, and incident response.

2.5.3 Business Process

One constituent element is the business process. The IA² F business process view provides an IA perspective of business processes. The IA² F business process view looks at risks within a business process, workflow, and services to assist the IA architect in addressing those risks.

A business process is an activity that consists of one or more workflows. A workflow consists of one or more procedures. The successful completion of a workflow fulfills a business service. A human may provide a service, or technology may provide a service. For example, a business function may be accounting. Accounting consists of business processes that include accounts receivable, employee expense reimbursement, and statements and ledgers. Accounts receivable consists of workflows that include inputs, trigger events for action, processing of inputs, production of some result, and the delivery of some output; procedures (formal representation of a process) assist with the performance of the workflow. Procedures consist of prescribed tasks, either automated or assigned to personnel. A person may then perform a manual task (carry out a routine procedure) or a cognitive task (e.g., decide upon an action). An automated service may substitute for a person, or enhance manual and cognitive tasks performed by a person. The IA^{2}F provides a discipline to identify risks associated with business processes by reviewing each business process and the elements of each business process with respect to the nine IA core principles.

2.5.4 Systems and Applications

The IA^2 development view addresses the software development process. Many information technology implementations require custom software. IA^2 ensures that development takes place in a controlled manner and that the final product provides secure operations. The goals inherent in the IA^2 development view include minimizing the effects on software quality by such development errors as buffer overflows, Trojans, backdoors, and memory leaks. During application development, IA^2 practices integrate security measures from inception, as opposed to safeguards bolted on as discrete mechanisms after the fact.

An example of secure development methodology is SEI-CMMI, http://www.sei.cmu.edu/. Included in the Carnegie Mellon philosophy is preventive security management through software development quality control. This philosophy treats application security holes like any other software bug, bugs that could be prevented by sound development practices.

The IA^2 acquisitions view addresses the purchase of or otherwise acquiring secure solutions. What makes a solution secure? What makes a solution secure enough? These are all contingent upon the organization and its tolerance for risk. Some considerations for secure acquisition include:

- Secure development environment; controlled environment for coding, testing, producing final product
- Solution development country of origin; known adversary of the government
- Solution development organization; known adversary of your organization
- Proof of secure development process that includes software quality assurance (SQA)

Addressing IA in solution acquisition is ever more critical given the number of hardware and software components of foreign development. Foreign development is of course a relative term and applicable to all countries. If you work for a national government, consider the consequences of acquiring and using technology developed in another country whose government is on less than friendly terms with yours. If you work for any high-visibility commercial company (e.g., a major world bank), consider consequences of acquiring software from a source that may wish to subvert your operations. The systems and applications view helps the IA architect consider these issues and determine the possibility of risks and the probability of risks.

2.5.5 *Information or Data*

Strictly speaking, data is raw details, whereas information implies some collection of data that conveys a particular meaning. The IA² view information/data considers them both in a similar manner and distinguishes information/data (or just data) from the perspectives of being at rest, in transit, and in use.

Data at rest resides on a server, workstation, or PC. Data at rest may also reside on mobile or long-term storage media such as universal service bus (USB) drive, CD, DVD, tape, removable hard drive, PDA, laptop, or cell phone. Data at rest may be ready for imminent use like on a server or PC hard drive, as well as in long-term storage like backups or archives. Data at rest safeguards apply to data in a car, truck, or otherwise being sent through the mail or private transport service.

Data in transit includes any data traversing a network. The network may be wired or wireless, private or public, or local, regional, or wide area.

Data in use refers to data that is currently in use on a PC, workstation, server, mainframe, etc. This is data currently being processed by an application, and it resides in random access memory (RAM) or in some other temporary storage location during processing (e.g., page swap space). Good security practice requires clearing memory of sensitive data; otherwise, another application may access that same storage space and retrieve that data inadvertently or subversively.

2.5.6 *Infrastructure*

Infrastructure is an underlying foundation. Enterprise infrastructure consists of a physical infrastructure and a technical infrastructure. Both technical and physical infrastructures may introduce business risk; therefore, the IA² infrastructure view addresses the risks of technical and physical infrastructure.

The technical infrastructure includes information technology (IT) services and mechanisms like routers, switches, voice servers (PBXs*), and voice adjuncts (e.g.,

---

* Private branch exchange (more commonly becoming known as a *voice server* on the data network).

Table 2.1 Physical Infrastructure

Infrastructure Category	Physical Infrastructure Considerations
Campus	Entry, exit, interbuilding transport, interbuilding communication, parking, lighting, safety, perimeter protection
Building	Entry, exit, presence, parking, lighting, safety, perimeter protection, intrabuilding transport
Floors	Lobby areas (main, per floor), loading dock, elevators, stairs, monitoring, safety (fire exits)
Rooms	Labeling, extra security (locks, pass cards, PINs)
Workstations	Access, visibility, lockable storage, standard configuration, standard labeling scheme

voice mail). The IA^2 technical infrastructure view addresses IA services and IA mechanisms to defend and monitor the technical infrastructure.

Physical infrastructure includes campus, building, floor, room/office, utility and communications services, and work areas. It also includes access to these components and areas. The IA^2 view physical infrastructure addresses IA services and IA mechanisms to defend and monitor the physical infrastructure. Some examples include property entry management (e.g., driveway gates, video), building entry management (e.g., guards, badges, radio frequency identification [RFID], biometric authentication), power backup, environmental controls for temperature and humidity, and much more. Table 2.1 provides example physical infrastructure considerations.

2.5.7 Intraorganizational/Interorganizational

Intraorganizational refers to within the organization. **Interorganizational** implies between or among organizations. IA^2 F intraorganizational refers to people, relationships, processes, communications, connectivity, data transport, infrastructure, etc., inside the organization. IA^2 F interorganizational refers to the same, only between your organization and other individuals, groups, or organizations.

The IA^2 book also uses *endo-* and *exo-* prefixes to distinguish between the domains of inside the organization and outside the organization, respectively. IA^2 uses the prefixes *intra-* and *inter-* for relationships, connectivity, or interactions. The difference between internal and external, and intraorganizational and interorganizational, with respect to IA^2 can be seen when examining the scope of control. The scope of control framework (chapter 12) consists of the following:

- Direct control
- Indirect control
- No control
- Influence
- Control response

The organizational risk exposure varies according to scope of control. The organization has *direct control* over the intraorganizational environment, systems, processes, and people. Outside the organization, there may be direct control, but far less than internally. The organization may exert external direct control in partnerships where it has a majority interest, or in situations where vendors derive a large percentage of revenue from the organization; it is true that money talks and money can control. More often, the organization may not have direct control but may have considerable *influence*. The organization may request or even suggest certain actions, but really does not exert direct control. In many cases, the organization has *no control*, e.g., hurricane, ice storm, or power outage. Although the organization cannot stop a hurricane, it can control its response to a hurricane by preparing business continuity and disaster recovery plans.

2.6   IA Core Principles

A threat is an expression of intent to inflict damage, or circumstances that provide opportunity for unintended damage. A vulnerability is a weakness that may be exploited to cause loss or injury. Risk is the possibility of loss or injury. The likelihood of a threat exploiting a vulnerability is one expression of risk. The IA core principles define the fundamental objectives of information assurance by identifying vulnerabilities and safeguarding against threats; in other words, the IA core principles provide fundamental objectives for managing risk. Figure 2.3 shows the IA core principles* of *confidentiality-integrity-availability* (CIA), *possession-authenticity-utility* (PAU), and *privacy–authorized use–nonrepudiation* (PAN). See chapter 12, Table 12.2 for a summary of business motivations behind the IA core principles.

Confidentiality ensures the disclosure of information only to those persons with authority to see it. Encryption is one method to ensure confidentiality of information in transit. Access controls ensure confidentiality of data at rest; you cannot see the information if you cannot get on the system that contains it.

Integrity ensures that information remains in its original form. During transmission, information may be corrupted either inadvertently or with intent. Inadvertent corruption may occur due to transmission errors. A cyclical redundancy

---

* Derived in part from the Donn B. Parker model as presented in *Toward a New Framework for Information Security.*

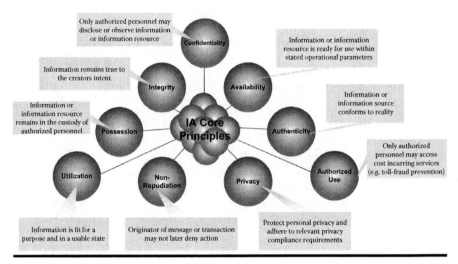

Only authorized personnel may disclose or observe information or information resource

Information remains true to the creators intent

Information or information resource remains in the custody of authorized personnel

Information or information resource is ready for use within stated operational parameters

Information or information source conforms to reality

Only authorized personnel may access cost incurring services (e.g. toll-fraud prevention)

Information is fit for a purpose and in a usable state

Originator of message or transaction may not later deny action

Protect personal privacy and adhere to relevant privacy compliance requirements

Figure 2.3   Information assurance core principles.

check (CRC) is one method to ensure the integrity of transmission. Intentional corruption may occur by changing key aspects of the data—perhaps adding a zero to a bank transfer request, or modifying map coordinates for a military mission. The use of encryption assists with integrity, especially the use of hashing. A hash algorithm generates a numerical representation of the original message prior to transmission. Upon receipt, the same hash algorithm generates a numerical representation and is compared against the original. Any difference is a clue that the integrity of the message is in question.

Availability ensures that information or information technology is ready for use. A denial-of-service attack may target a server or application. If successful, this attack renders that server or application unavailable.

Possession ensures the physical protection of an asset. Loss of possession may be through carelessness (e.g., leaving the laptop on the train) or from theft. Physical safeguards help to ensure possession.

Authenticity ensures that information actually conforms to reality, that the information is not misrepresented as something it is not. Ensuring authenticity is a safeguard against deception, falsehood, or imitation; for example, downloading software that looks like it is from a reputable software vendor when indeed it is a modified version that introduces malware to the organizational network.

Utility ensures the continued use of the information or information technology. Though you remain in physical possession of the asset and the information on the asset remains confidential, in its original form, and is available for use, the asset may not be usable. For example, the use of hard drive encryption is growing in popularity. Upon system start-up, the user enters a password that decrypts the information on the hard drive. This safeguards against the disclosure of data if the hard drive is stolen or lost. However, if the hard drive is encrypted and the password forgotten, the information on the hard drive is unusable. This same principle applies to individual documents, databases, backups, archives, etc.

Although **privacy** is traditionally absorbed under confidentiality, it deserves its own consideration due to the sensitivity of the issue (e.g., identity theft). Personal privacy concerns will continue to increase as technology becomes even more pervasive in our daily lives and awareness of privacy issues increases. There is little difficulty in gathering the personal information of name, address, SSN, financial records, educational and professional backgrounds, and purchase histories. There are many valid uses for this information; however, there are many opportunities to use this information in an exploitive manner. One example is to manipulate unwanted advertising toward an individual's purchasing patterns. Moreover, there is need to protect personal information the disclosure of which may cause person harm. For example, medical tests that may disclose genetic predisposition to heart attack or cancer may affect the ability to get insurance coverage or pass a job interview. Privacy management is indeed a critical IA element. Appendix J contains an outline for a privacy management program. A privacy management program is supplemental to a security management program (appendix E).

Authorized use is the antithesis to theft of service (e.g., toll fraud). Toll fraud costs businesses worldwide billions of dollars per year. Adding Transmission Control Protocol/Internet Protocol (TCP/IP) connectivity to phone systems (e.g., IP telephony or Voice-over-IP [VoIP]) creates potential new mediums to perpetrate toll fraud: the LAN, wide area network (WAN), and the Internet. A core principle of IA is to safeguard access to services that incur cost to the organization.

The IA core principles include **nonrepudiation** due to the increasing use of online transactions and legal agreements. Nonrepudiation provides means that the initiator of a transaction may not later deny having initiated that transaction. Including details that support nonrepudiation in logs is an essential part of trust in online transactions. Transactions may be of a commercial nature (e.g., buy/sell), or a transaction may be one of requesting a service in a service-oriented architecture (SOA) environment. The nonrepudiation safeguard ensures that a service requestor may not later deny having requested that service. The integrity of audit logs, establishing a chronology of activities, ensuring the validity of those activities, and of the identity of the people or entities involved in those activities depends in part on nonrepudiation.

2.7   IA² Principles

An *objective* is a goal. A *principle* is a fundamental edict or underlying faculty that describes a characteristic of the objective or the accomplishment of the objective. The IA Core Principles define the fundamental objectives of information assurance. The design of the IA² framework itself, as well as the application of the IA² framework, follows a set of information assurance architecture principles; Table 2.2 provides a list of fundamental IA^2 principles.

2.8   IA Compliance Requirements

Compliance requirements include legislative, regulatory, and other mandates on the organization. These mandates may be externally imposed (e.g., legislation) or internally imposed (e.g., selection of an industry standard to guide organizational practices, like ISO 9001 for quality management). Both the externally imposed legislation and the internally imposed standard become part of a compliance management process. A Compliance Management Framework consists of the following categories:

- External
  - Explicit
  - Implicit
- Internal
  - Explicit
  - Implicit

External explicit compliance requirements include those directly applicable to the organization. For a health care organization, this may include the Health Insurance Portability and Accountability Act (HIPAA). For a publicly traded company in the United States, this may include Sarbanes–Oxley (SOX). An example of an external implicit requirement is chapter 8 of the Federal Sentencing Guidelines, "Sentencing of Organizations." Following the specifications in this guideline can reduce organizational culpability in the event of litigation. Reducing culpability means reducing potential fines and potential jail time for officers. Understanding and including the details from the Federal Sentencing Guidelines in the compliance management program is good business practice to reduce the potential effects of litigation.

Internal compliance requirements are those requirements the organization generates itself or imposes upon itself. These may be internal SLAs, contractual obligations, or a self-imposed security standard (e.g., ISO 27001 or ISO 27002*). A comprehensive compliance management program identifies, enumerates, and articulates all relevant compliance requirements whether externally or internally imposed.

IA compliance requirements include legal and regulatory requirements, local policies, and project-specific documents related to the creation of an information assurance solution. IA^2 compliance requirements consist of documents that include requests for proposal (RFPs); laws, regulations, and guidelines (e.g., FISMA, NIST,

---

* ISO 27002 is the new reference for the standard formerly known as ISO 17799.

Table 2.2   IA² Principles

IA² Principle	*Definition*
Actionability	The resulting IA architecture guides or otherwise supports actions to implement.
Adaptability	Adaptable to align with many enterprise architecture methodologies, e.g., Federal Enterprise Architecture (FEA), Department of Defense (DoD), EA, etc.
Agility	Strategic agility to accommodate evolving business and compliance requirements, operating environments (e.g., world economy); also, tactical agility to adapt to dynamic nature of threat sources, motives, means, methods, and opportunity.
BG²E	*Best, good, good enough principle;* consider that any solution may take the form of best, good, or good enough, and that the customer may be completely happy with any of these depending on business goals and budget.
Business focus	IA promotes and supports focus on business requirements and business drivers; technology supports business need, not business adapts to technology du jour.
Complexity management	Provide the ability to organize and deal with hard-to-understand concepts, services, and mechanisms inherent in enterprise solutions.
Consistency	Provide a framework and process that produce consistent results across multiple projects by multiple architects.
Divisibility	Divisible to segregate those aspects needed for the current situation; note: similar to modular only modular addresses the initial construction of IA² where divisible supports the need to decompose modules into more granular parts.
Extensibility	Extensible to accommodate unforeseen business requirements; tomorrow's targets may not exist today; the IA² F may encompass tomorrow's targets in existing classifications and be flexible enough to take on additional classifications.

Continued

Table 2.2 IA² Principles (Continued)

IA² Principle	*Definition*
Flexibility	Flexible to apply to private and public sector and to align with various SLCM, SDLC, and ELCM standards and practices.
Harmony	To reach a state of optimality by way of integration; e.g., IA in harmony with business operations implies an integration of both, with the result being optimal business operations that are also optimally secure.
Implementation agnostic	The IA² Framework is independent from services and tools that provide the operational solution; the selection of services and tools should align with the architecture, but the architecture is not dependent on specific services or tools.
Integrate from inception	Insert IA considerations as part of the innovation process and through the ELCM.
Modularity	Separate the IA² Framework into discrete parts and provide the ability to apply a subset of IA² parts to fit the needs of the current situation.
Pragmatism/practicality	Architecture is often abstract in nature to accommodate principles of modularity, extensibility, and agility. However, there is need to map abstract architectural concepts to business requirements and ultimately to a final solution including product selection, implementation, and operations; that is, provide a line of sight between architectural abstraction and product implementation. Fiscally optimize commercial-oriented shareholder value (SHV) or public-oriented constituent value (CV), which may also be considered citizen value.
Provide for IA elements	Protect information and information technology with respect to core IA principles: confidentiality, possession, integrity, utility, availability, authenticity, authorized use, privacy, and nonrepudiation; in keeping with the extensible principle, IA² may accommodate additional IA elements.
Repeatability	Provide a framework and process that are repeatable.

Table 2.2 IA² Principles (Continued)

IA² Principle	*Definition*
Results oriented	Establish and maintain focus on the end product, service, or deliverable to keep the architectural process focused on results.
Scalability	Able to accommodate single systems or large, complex solutions; that is, if it can work for 1 or 2, it can work for 100 or 200.
Traceability	Link business requirements to services to mechanics to vendors to products to implementation best practices to operations; formal recording of the IA² line of sight.

C&A, COOP)*; enterprise architecture's current state and desired state, plus transition states; business process architecture; and technical process architecture. See appendix F for an example of the NIST compliance documents for information and information technology security.

To achieve a well-rounded perspective on business drivers, good business practice is the complement to compliance requirements. Compliance requirements describe the minimum (do at least this much to adhere to laws, regulations, etc.). Good business practice requires additional activity to meet business objectives.

2.9 Aligning IA with ELCM

The ELCM† applies across the enterprise for business functions, workflows, and services as well as technology. Each of these has a conception, a design, an implementation, an operation, and an ending. The specifics of architectural drivers, architectural views, IA core principles, and compliance requirements will vary according to the current phase of the ELCM. For example, the ELCM design and development phases find the IA² systems and applications development view more prevalent than during the operations phase.

Figure 2.4 shows a taxonomic alignment between the ELCM and IA. A taxonomic alignment is not a direct one-to-one relationship; rather, it is a many-to-many relationship, where any one phase in the ELCM may align with any aspect of IA. IA² views assist to guide IA considerations. Each ELCM phase may have different IA considerations that are entirely situation dependent. The differences in IA considerations are what categories and elements of IA to consider (breadth of

---

* See glossary for an expansion and explanation of acronyms.

† ELCM is a more abstract but similar view of solutions life cycle management, systems life cycle management (SLCM), or system development life cycle (SDLC).

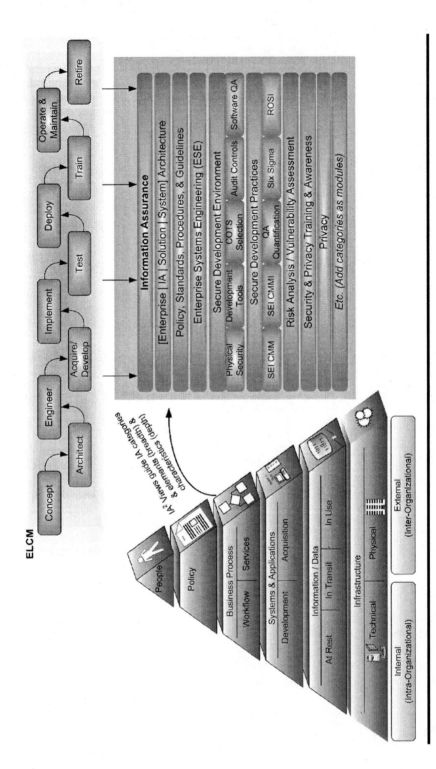

Figure 2.4 Aligning information assurance and ELCM.

IA), as well as the characteristics of IA elements (depth of IA). Appendix D presents more detail on IA categories and IA elements.

The following sections elaborate on the ELCM phases as they relate to IA².

2.9.1 Concept

Any idea starts with conception, which is the first phase in the ELCM. Chapter 12 presents an innovation framework to assist in determining the need for business change and what about the business needs to change. The innovation framework provides a discipline for idea conception. The intent of considering risk in the concept phase is not to dissuade pursuit of the idea. To the contrary, early consideration of risk raises awareness of important realities. IA² provides a disciplined approach to deal with these risks in a rational manner that becomes part of the solution.

2.9.2 Architect

The ELCM architect phase guides the enterprise fit of the concept. This includes enterprise architecture and information assurance architecture. The architect phase looks at the business fit of the concept and begins to shape the concept in the form of a solution or series of solutions, where solution may involve a technology, a process, or people. The solution may be entirely new, or the solution may be to modify existing enterprise elements.

The architect phase is the primary focus of the IA architect and the primary application of the IA² Framework and IA² Process. The architect phase segues into the engineer phase, which looks at the technical fit of the solution.

2.9.3 Engineer

Engineering looks at the technical details behind the business focus of the architecture. The focus of the ELCM engineer phase is on the technical fit of the solution in the enterprise. Engineering may include systems engineering for a discrete system or for a system of systems. The engineering phase may also include enterprise systems engineering where the engineering approach must accommodate an environment of complexity; e.g., initially unknown requirements that will emerge with use of the system. The ELCM engineer phase provides additional details to development and acquisition of features to ensure technical fit of the final solution.

2.9.4 Acquire/Develop

A good principle in acquisition/development decisions is *outsource before buy and buy before build*. In-house development and operations is expensive. Many organizations today desire to focus on their core competencies. A manufacturer of small engines does not necessarily know about IT or IA. The expense of recruiting, hiring, and maintaining an in-house workforce with this expertise may not be worthwhile. Outsourcing to a service provider may be a more cost-effective solution.

For example, the service provider may run IT and IA operations from off site, or locally on site depending on the organizational specific requirements. A managed security service (MSS) is an option for handling IA issues. Effective use of an MSS or any kind of outsourcing service still requires in-house expertise to understand what the organization needs and to ensure the service provider actually fulfills those needs. Using an MSS does not eliminate the need for in-house IA expertise, but it does reduce it.

2.9.5   Implement

Implementation is the initial insertion of the solution into the organizational environment, e.g., a pilot application. Whether the solution is acquired or developed, implementation will determine the solution's fit with the organizational culture, business environment, existing processes, and technology. This is the first step to determine if the solution works at all.

2.9.6   Test

The test phase determines first if the solution works at all, then how effectively the solution works, and how securely the solution works. Testing the solution in phases is a wise idea, including a test environment with appropriate data that ensures accurate and effective processing that mirrors reality. Use the IA^2 views when developing the test environment to ensure the right people are involved, the appropriate policies exist for the secure creation and maintenance of a test environment, and to ensure the secure use of test data.

Test data should reflect production data as closely as possible. The best test data is excerpts from production data. As such, there may be sensitive information in the test data such that the test data warrants the same protection (confidentiality and privacy) as the production data.

Beyond the test environment is the pilot environment. A pilot environment enables the discovery and resolution of many procedural and technical issues prior to investing in enterprise deployment.

2.9.7   Deploy

When implementation and testing are complete, there remains enterprisewide deployment of the solution. Deployment may be to a single location or to all enterprise locations, ranging from a couple/few to thousands. Each scenario brings a different set of risks and IA requirements.

2.9.8   Train

Personnel need education and preparation for using the new solution to fulfill the business objectives. Training occurs concurrently or immediately follows deployment. Training (including awareness, training, and education) includes management, operations, and the user community. Part of the personnel preparation is security awareness, training, and education.

2.9.9   Operate and Maintain

Architects, builders (see the Organizational Context Framework in chapter 11), and project managers are the key players up through deployment. Concurrent with deployment is a transition from building the solution to the operations and maintenance (O&M) of that solution. O&M is now the custodian of the solution and is responsible for solution performance, service level agreements (SLAs), and security.

Aligning business requirements with technology is good practice for projects as well as for the enterprise. Projects come and go, where the enterprise lives on. The IA² LoS is an enterprise tool as well as a project tool. The enterprise use of IA² LoS is to maintain an ongoing relationship between O&M and the business drivers behind O&M. Business requirements will change over time, and there is need to periodically revisit operational constructs to see if they still align with valid business drivers. If a tactical operation, service, or mechanism is not traceable to a business driver, then that operational expense is no longer necessary. With no traceable business justification for X, X is a wasted expense.

2.9.10   Retire

The final phase of ELCM is the retirement of the system. This includes knowing when to retire the system, who the retirement affects, and how to retire (phase out versus cut off). Knowing when to retire a system is problematic. If the business driver goes away, there is no longer a need for the continuance of the solution. So, elimination of the business driver is one motivation to retire a solution. However, the reason for the existence of a system may be lost with personnel turnover. System retirement is a useful context to convey one benefit of the IA² LoS.

Effective use of the IA² LoS aligns business drivers with the O&M of solutions. The use of IA² LoS produces a traceability document that captures the details of the business driver to O&M alignment. The IA² LoS document records and maintains enterprise knowledge of the motivations behind the creation and operation of a system. The IA² LoS provides a point of reference for intelligent decision support on retiring a system.

2.10 IA² Compliance Verification

IA² compliance verification ensures the solution works as intended and satisfies legal requirements, policy directives, accepted or mandated standards, and the business and technical drivers behind the solution. Compliance verification may be measured using a very formal industry-accepted process, like the Department of Defense Information Assurance Certification and Accreditation Process (DIA-CAP), or compliance verification may be against an organization's internally generated test plan. An independent party may perform a compliance verification, or the organization may perform compliance verification itself. The variety and depth of compliance verification is organization and situation specific.

Technical mechanism (e.g., server) compliance verification may use a formal certification and accreditation (C&A) process. Application (software) verification through careful unit, system, and user testing validates that business capabilities (including information assurance) are indeed present, functional, and effective. A tabletop exercise is one administrative way of verifying the effectiveness of a continuity of operation plan (COOP). Business process verification checks to see that X is [consistent | extensible | scalable | auditable | agile | process oriented | as simple as it can be | no more complex as it needs to be | etc.], where $X \in$ (policy, process, procedure, plan, tool, intelligence gathering, intelligence processing, end-user interface, end-user data collection, etc.).

2.10.1 IA Compliance Verification: A Sample Resource

According to the Federal Information Security Management Act (FISMA) 2002, the National Institute of Standards and Technology (NIST) is heavily involved in establishing cyber-security compliance requirements and verification for federal systems. The NIST information assurance process consists of *categorize* information and information systems; select, specify, and *apply security controls*; and *verify* the effectiveness of the security controls. NIST provides verification guidance in *Verification of Security Control Effectiveness* (SP 800-37 and SP 800-53A).

2.10.2 IA Operations Cycle

The purpose of IA architecture is to create a line of sight from business and technical drivers to IA services, IA mechanisms, and IA operations. The IA² Framework specifically calls out an IA operations cycle (IA ops cycle) that consists of anticipate, defend, monitor, and respond (Figure 2.5). The IA architecture process includes consideration of IA services and IA mechanisms in light of the operational objectives they will fulfill.

To *anticipate* is to give advance thought to and foresee certain situations, actions, and needs. IA services that support this phase of the IA ops cycle include risk analysis, threat analysis, vulnerability assessment, business impact assessment, compliance assessment, and compliance audit.*

To *defend* is to protect, to safeguard. IA defense includes deterrence, preemption, prevention, and mitigation. The

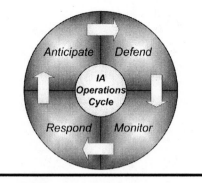

Figure 2.5   IA operations cycle (IA ops cycle).

IA philosophy of defense in depth adds defenses at various operational layers to force an attacker to overcome many obstacles to reach an objective. Each obstacle to overcome requires additional time and expense on the part of the attacker. IA defense mechanisms include firewalls, intrusion prevention systems, anti-malware, and user validation. User validation may include something the user knows (password), something he has (token or radio frequency identification [RFID] card), something he is (a biometric like a fingerprint), or something he does (signature profile). An IA defense service includes security awareness, training, and education; an aware and educated workforce is a more secure workforce.

To *monitor* is to watch over and look for certain conditions. IA monitoring means watching over the physical environment and information technology environment in search of anomalies or emerging patterns of irregular behavior. IA monitoring includes anomaly detection both in real-time and in batch processing of logs and audit trails. Monitoring is both an automated and manual process. The most effective monitoring resource is the organization's employees. An effective security program raises awareness of what constitutes anomalous behavior and provides a method to report observations of suspicious activity.

To *respond* is to act with forethought as a result of a stimulus. IA² differentiates response from reaction by recognizing that response requires planning, while reaction tends to be instantaneous and reflexive. IA responses include problem reporting, triage, escalation, investigation, isolation, treatment, root cause analysis, and procedural review and modification. IA response services include computer security incident response teams (CSIRTs), subject matter expert (SME) teams (e.g., isolate and treat viruses), and digital forensics specialists.

Figure 2.6 expands on the details of the IA operations cycle.

Producing effective IA operations requires methodical implementation and traceability from operations back to business drivers. Aligning operations with

---

* An audit focuses on more detail than an assessment.

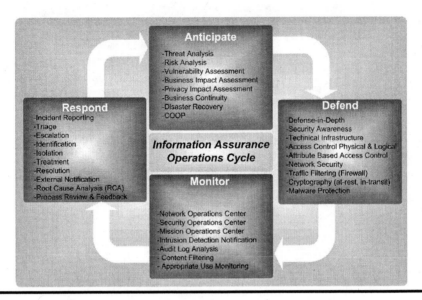

Figure 2.6   IA operations framework overview.

business drivers associates operational costs and benefits with specific business need. This enables the organization to show value in operations, justify further investments, or reduce operations for cost savings. Such alignment proves that operational investments or operational cutbacks are not arbitrary.

2.11   IA² Line of Sight

The best decisions are informed decisions. The IA² line of sight (IA² LoS) is a formal alignment of business drivers with operations and maintenance (O&M). Too often, such alignment between the abstractness of architecture and the specific requirements of operations is a cloud with details left to imagination and intuitive leaps. The IA² LoS (Figure 2.7) provides distinct links from business drivers through to architecture, implementation, and operations.

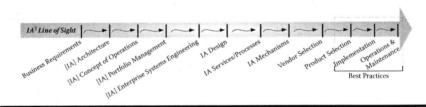

Figure 2.7   IA² LoS.

The IA² line of sight consists of the following links:

- Business requirements
- [IA] Architecture
- [IA] Concept of operations (CONOPS)
- [IA] Portfolio management (PfM)
- [IA] Enterprise systems engineering (ESE)
- [IA] Design
- IA services/processes
- IA mechanisms
- Vendor selection
- Product SELECTION
- Implementation
- Operations and maintenance (O&M)

Many steps from architecture to operations contain "[IA]" as a prefix. This implies that IA is distinct but must be integrated into the business aspect of that step. Business requirements drive enterprise architecture, and while there is also an IA architecture, that IA architecture integrates with the enterprise architecture. Likewise, there is a business CONOPS. The IA architect integrates IA with the business CONOPS using IA². Moreover, there may be an IA CONOPS that also integrates with the business CONOPS. The following sections elaborate on each link in the IA² LoS.

2.11.1   Business Requirements

Business need drives the use of technology. Business risk drives the need for IA. Identifying the risks first requires an understanding of the business requirements. Technical requirements also drive IA; however, those technical requirements find root in business requirements. Moreover, a technical restriction should not redefine the business requirement. If the business requires X, but there is no technology to provide X, then do not redefine the business requirement. The business requirement remains the same and the technology is put forth as a partial solution that is the best available at the time.

Business requirements are articulated in mission statements, organizational strategic objectives, and strategic plans. A request for proposal (RFP) is a formal articulation of business requirements. Contracts, service level agreements, and business plans also contain business requirements. The objective of the enterprise architect is be holistic in terms of the organization. The enterprise architect looks at the current requirements in context of the existing enterprise as well as the future of the enterprise. The IA architect looks at the current business requirements to discern the risks in context of the existing enterprise and the future enterprise.

2.11.2   *[IA] Architecture*

There are several kinds of architectures, including *enterprise, solution, systems,* and *information assurance* architectures. Enterprise architecture (EA) takes on a view of the entire organization. Solution architecture takes on a view of providing a business function or support to a business process; this may take the form of one or more business services. Systems architecture looks at a particular system or application. IA architecture addresses the risks within any of these other architectures.

The IA architect may generate an IA architecture as a stand-alone product. More effective is to integrate the appropriate IA services and IA mechanisms with the enterprise architecture, solutions architecture, or systems architecture. This integration from inception inserts IA as part of the enterprise, solution, or system.

2.11.3   *[IA] Concept of Operations (CONOPS)*

A CONOPS takes an architecture and applies it conceptually to the organization. A CONOPS is a paper-based model of how the architecture will work in context of the enterprise business environment, technical environment, business processes, and overall culture. From an IA^2 perspective, CONOPS gives a better business context to risks and assists to identify additional risks. Circumstances will provide guidance on whether to integrate IA with the CONOPS or to generate a distinct IA CONOPS.

2.11.4   *[IA] Portfolio Management (PfM)*

PfM attempts to manage the architecture from an investment perspective. This includes evaluating the proposed business and technical capabilities in light of existing business and technical capabilities and other proposed capabilities. Relevant PfM questions include the following:

- Business capability
  - Does the proposed business capability exist elsewhere endo-organizationally?
    - If so, why create another one?
    - Can the initial capability be reused in whole? In part? Why or why not?
    - Note: *How to reuse* is an enterprise systems engineering question.
  - Does the proposed business capability exist elsewhere exo-organizationally?
    - Can we purchase the capability exo-organizationally?
    - What are the trade-offs among build, buy, and lease?
    - What is the total cost of ownership (TCO) among:
      - Build in-house

- Buy and install in-house
- Hire a service to perform capability in-house
- Hire a service to perform capability externally (e.g., managed service provider)

■ Technical capability
  - Does the proposed technical capability exist elsewhere endo-organizationally?
    ■ If so, why create another one?
    ■ Can the initial capability be reused in whole? In part? Why or why not?
  - Does the proposed technical capability exist elsewhere exo-organizationally?
    ■ Can we purchase the capability exo-organizationally?
    ■ What are the trade-offs among build, buy, and lease?
    ■ What is the total cost of ownership (TCO) among:
      - Build in-house
      - Buy and install in-house
      - Hire a service to perform capability in-house
      - Hire a service to perform capability externally (e.g., managed service provider)

PfM is both a capability and investment management process that attempts to avoid redundant expenses for the enterprise. The mantra for PfM is "Invest once, leverage many times." There may be a specific IA PfM, or the enterprise PfM may integrate an IA view in business and technical solutions.

2.11.5 *[IA] Enterprise Systems Engineering*

Enterprise systems engineering (ESE) is the interim step between concept of operations and design. ESE examines the enterprise fit including enterprise interoperability and integration. IA ESE examines the enterprise fit of IA services and IA mechanisms and how they address enterprise technical risks as well as business risks. Systems engineering (SE) focuses on a single system, whereas ESE focuses on the enterprise collection of systems.

2.11.6 *[IA] Design*

The architecture provides the business drivers. The CONOPS provides an enterprise business context. PfM provides an enterprise context for capability and investment management. ESE provides a perspective of enterprise technical fit. Design gets down to the specifics of the solution, business process, or system. Design addresses the specifics of the services and mechanisms that comprise the desired capability. There is a blurred distinction between SE and design. Consider SE to be a formal approach to design; SE is an engineering discipline imposed on the design process. Therefore, design uses the discipline of SE to devise the specifics of the solution.

IA design addresses the risks inherent in the services and mechanisms that comprise the solution. Additionally, IA design attempts to integrate IA design specifics into those services and mechanisms.

2.11.7 IA Services

IA services include business processes, functions, workflow, and tasks that provide IA to the organization. IA services include compliance management; IA policy, standards, and procedures development, dissemination, and management; IA education, training, and awareness; security management; privacy management; computer security incident response; vulnerability assessments and other assessments surrounding compliance, risk, business impact, as well as audits; business continuity; and digital forensics. IA services may use IA mechanisms.

2.11.8 IA Mechanisms

IA mechanisms are the technologies of IA. IA policy provides insight to strategic objectives for IA. IA standards specify what to use to implement and enforce policy. IA procedures specify how to implement and enforce policy. Therefore, standards may specify IA mechanisms. Standards complement enterprise systems engineering that looks at the enterprise implications of technology standards, services, and mechanisms, including those for IA. IA mechanisms include anti-malware, firewalls, intrusion detection systems (IDSs), honeypots, content filters, identity and privilege management (e.g., public key infrastructure [PKI]), and secure operating systems and configurations.

2.11.9 Vendor Selection

When systems engineering and design specify capabilities in terms of IA services and IA mechanisms, there are no vendors or products selected. Architecture, enterprise systems engineering, and design are vendor and product agnostic. The point is to architect, engineer, and design to capabilities and business objectives—*not to products*.

With a clear idea of the desired capabilities, the IA architect reviews vendor and product options and proceeds to select the most qualified. There may be constraints on the selection process. The IA standards may specify a particular vendor and multiple products to choose from that vendor. The IA standards may specify a capability and the vendor selection is open as long as the vendors provide the capabilities specified in the standards. IA standards may provide a list of vendors and the project team may choose from that list. IA standards may provide a specific vendor and a specific product and the project team must use that product and no other.

Vendor details like number of employees, financial backing, support capabilities, willingness to place source code in escrow, etc., are all as important as product features, performance, and integration into the enterprise technical environment. The most wonderful technology is no good if the support structure behind it goes out of business.

2.11.10   Product Selection

Product selection is complementary to vendor selection, and the results of both a vendor analysis and a product analysis govern the best choice. Vendor selection criteria look at the business behind the product. Product selection criteria look at the technical capabilities of the product and the ability to integrate that product into enterprise operations.

2.11.11   Implementation

Upon product selection, there remains the challenge of actually getting it to work in the enterprise operating environment. The vendor and product user groups will offer assistance for effective implementation. Implementation guidance includes configuration, administration, establishing a test environment and staging environment, pilot testing, and enterprise deployment.

2.11.12   Operations and Maintenance

Seek out industry best practices for operations and maintenance. User groups often offer far more valuable insight into effective operations than the vendor does. The actual users face the challenges of integrated operations where multiple applications from multiple vendors have to work effectively on the same network and same systems. The vendors themselves do not have the resources to test every possible permutation of integrated environments. Nor, for that matter, does any single user. However, a user group that contains dozens or hundreds of separate users provides valuable insights.

The total cost of ownership includes administration, maintenance, patching, upgrades, and fixing problems. The architectural team provides some insights on the total ownership experience. Seeking out best practices for operations and maintenance adds to this knowledge. One objective for the architectural team is to *manage expectations* of executives, management, and operations personnel. Expectations of adequacy are happy with slightly better than adequate. Expectations of excellence are not happy at all with results slightly better than adequate.

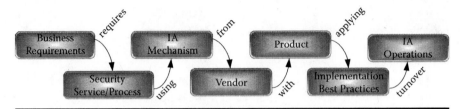

Figure 2.8   IA² implementation taxonomy.

The use of the IA² LoS from an enterprise perspective provides decision support in the review of operational constructs to see if they remain aligned with valid business drivers. If senior management demands O&M budget cuts, the IA² LoS enterprise perspective provides insight into which solutions support which business functions. The blanket cut of *15 percent across the board* is an expedient method of cost cutting, but inefficient at best and fatally damaging at worst. Blanket cuts without thought to what is being cut may affect operations of high business value. A better method is to find those overhead or low-priority business functions that can live without certain services. Effective use of the IA² LoS provides this insight. Cutting 100 percent of a single redundant or unnecessary service may meet budget objectives and leave key business functions untouched. Might does not make right, nor does majority make right, and certainly blind budget cuts for the sake of expediency or simplicity does not make right either.

2.11.13   IA² Implementation Taxonomy

The IA² implementation taxonomy is *<business requirements>* require *<IA services>* using *<IA mechanisms>* from *<vendor>* with *<product>* applying *<best practices>* to turn over to *<IA operations>* (Figure 2.8). The IA² implementation taxonomy is not separate and distinct from the IA² LoS; rather, the IA² implementation taxonomy is an abbreviation of the IA² LoS to reference IA in more operational terms than in architectural terms. The reason for speaking in more operational terms is to convey a concise message to management and operations personnel without the distraction of architectural detail.

2.11.13.1   IA² Implementation Taxonomy Examples

Consider the examples in Table 2.3; e.g., a business requirement for the protection of intellectual property leads to the need for a session encryption security service. There are competing session encryption security mechanisms, including SSL and IPSec. These mechanisms must be evaluated with respect to business requirements, operating environment, mechanism maturity, and the IA². Upon selecting an appropriate security mechanism, there are vendors that offer a variety

Table 2.3   IA² Implementation Taxonomy Examples

Business Requirement	Security Service/Process	Security Mechanism	Vendor X	Product Y	Implementation Best Practice	IA Operations
Protect intellectual property	Secure communications	SSL v. IPSec	Vendor X	Product Y	Standard XYZ	Internal policy X, standard Y, and procedure Z
Protect intellectual property	Secure servers	Host-based intrusion detection system (HIDS)	Vendor X	Product Y	Standard ABC	Internal policy X, standard Y, and procedure Z
Protection between publicly accessible servers and internal network	Firewall	Proxy v. filter v. stateful	Vendor X	Product Y	Standard XYZ	Internal policy X, standard Y, and procedure Z
Test cyber-security defenses	Vulnerability scanning/ penetration testing	Automated tools	Vendor X v. Internet security systems	Scanner X v. ISS	Best practice guide XYZ	Internal policy X, standard Y, and procedure Z
Determine organizational risk exposure	Vulnerability assessment	Interviews and validation tests	Vendor Y	TBD	Standard XYZ	Internal policy X, standard Y, and procedure Z
Secure operations	Computer security incident response team (CSIRT)	TBD	In-house v. outsource	TBD	NIST 800-3: Establishing a Computer Security Incident Response Capability (CSIRC)	Internal policy X, standard Y, and procedure Z

of product implementations. Vendor and product evaluations lead to the appropriate product selection.

The IA² implementation taxonomy provides an abbreviated line of sight from business requirements to operations. The IA² LoS provides the IA architect with a tool to capture more granular detail and rationale for the same line of sight from IA business drivers through to IA operations.

2.12   Conclusion and Commentary

One of the claims that may be made with 100 percent certainty is that the information assurance industry will continue to evolve. Traditional views of security were in terms of standard business costs like door locks, or a *nice to have if there is enough budget*, like video cameras. Only recently has security become a legislative mandate. With the increase in attention to security, there is need to insert security planning, budgets, operations, and justifications into the business processes in terms understood by management and executives. Discussing IA operations in business terms goes a long way in reaching common understanding that includes the knowledge that while security cannot be ignored as a nice-to-have, security budgets are limited and require justification and priorities. A security business case with its foundation in return on investment (ROI) has more chance of success than one built on fear, uncertainty, and doubt (FUD).

Aligning the IA² concepts to business drivers conveys IA to management and executives in terms of business need, business fit, business justification, and business risk. The more the IA material resonates with management, the greater the likelihood of obtaining a sufficient IA budget and ultimately the greater likelihood of producing an appropriately secure operating environment.

There is much to consider in achieving an assured enterprise architecture that ultimately leads to assured operations. The structure of the IA² Framework lends itself to large and small projects. The modularity of IA² provides the ability to use it as a whole or to draw upon the parts as applicable to the IA situation at hand. The next chapter presents a process for the application of the IA² Framework.

Chapter 3

The IA² Process

3.1 Introduction

A process is a prescribed set of actions or activities that must be undertaken to perform a task. The use of a process promotes consistency, completeness, and replication. People following the same process in the same manner for the same situation should end up with reasonably similar results. The IA² Process presents a disciplined, consistent, repeatable manner in which to identify, enumerate, articulate, and address business risk. The IA² Process is a prescribed manner that, when applied upward to the architectural level, will help to develop an IA architecture or integrate IA into an enterprise architecture. When applied downward to the project level, the IA² Process assists with defining IA requirements and IA assessment tasks like gap analysis and remediation analysis. The IA architecture may address all aspects of the IA² Framework, or it may address parts of the IA² Framework. As the IA architect, you decide what is important to the problem at hand.

A general architectural process includes a *to-be* definition, an *as-is* discovery, a gap analysis, and a *transition plan* to move from as-is to to-be. The to-be is the target state and may be a technical system, business function, business service, or any other organizational desire or goal. The IA² Process calls this the intent.

Discovery of the as-is provides a starting point by defining the current business environment, state of operations, security posture, and other relevant aspects to the project. Comparing the as-is to the to-be provides a gap analysis between where the organization is and where it wants to be. The transition plan provides for gap closure. Rarely is there an existing formal document that represents the as-is; therefore, a discovery phase is a large part of the project effort. All these are included in the IA² Process.

3.2 Objectives

The objective of this chapter is to present details of the IA² Process (IA² P). The material in this chapter will enable you to apply a disciplined method for using the IA² Framework to identify, enumerate, articulate, and address risks to your organization overall or the current project you are working on.

3.3 The IA² Process

The IA architect uses the IA² Framework as a conceptual structure that brings order to information assurance. The IA architect then uses the IA² Process to apply that conceptual structure to the business situation at hand. The IA² P may be a single process with a beginning and an end, or IA² P may be a series of processes for the IA architect to apply as circumstances dictate.

The IA² Process consists of eight steps:

1. Articulate the intent of the IA architecture (IA²).
2. Define the environment of the IA².
3. Define the scope of the IA².
4. Identify inputs to the IA² (influences and constraints).
5. Discover and document the current organizational posture.
6. Analyze the discovery findings.
7. Identify outputs from the IA² including documents, products, services, and actions.
8. Produce outputs.

Steps 1 through 4 are preparation and provide the ability to define the to be state for the IA². Step 5 discovers the as-is artifacts, practices, people, and organizational attributes within the scope and environment. Step 6 analyzes the as-is information to understand the current organizational posture with respect to IA within scope. Steps 7 and 8 identify and produce the IA² artifacts and actions necessary to transition from the as-is to the to be state of IA within the scope and environment. Figure 3.1 shows the IA² Process steps.

The IA² Process uses the IA² Framework to decompose complex problems into views and perspectives. Part of the IA² Process is to determine what IA² F views are applicable, then to determine what aspects of those views are relevant. The IA² framework views are: people, business process, policy, systems and applications, information/data, and infrastructure. The perspectives are the drivers (business, technical); intra-, inter-, endo-, or exo-organizational; the compliance require-

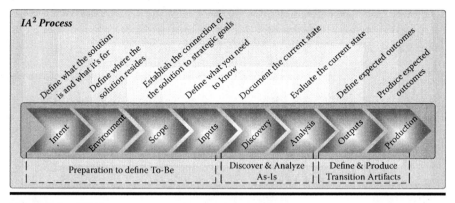

Figure 3.1 IA² Process.

ments, and enterprise life cycle management (ELCM) phases (see Figure 2.1). Each view presents a different operational perspective.

The IA² Process identifies business and technical risks by applying all relevant aspects for each IA² F view against the IA core principles, as well as any applicable compliance requirements (which may need to be identified). The following sections elaborate on each IA² Process phase and provide additional details on the use of IA² Framework during the IA² Process.

3.3.1 Articulate the Intent

3.3.1.1 Define What the Solution Is and What It Is for

There are two parts to the IA² P statement of intent. The first part should articulate whether the IA² P is to generate stand-alone IA documents or to augment a business function, process, workflow, system, or another set of documents. The second part relates to the project at hand, specifically the IA portion of that project. In terms of the project, the statement of intent specifies what the project is for and what the project is; and what the IA is for and what the IA is in relation to the project.

While the project may be to enhance a particular business function, to develop a product, to develop a system or an application, or to create a business service, the IA intent will always address a business risk. State the IA intent in terms of what business risk that IA addresses. In terms of what the solution is, state the intent of IA as an IA service, an IA mechanism, and the specifics of either or both. Perhaps the intent is to develop a hardware device or a software application, or to create a new business function that uses existing people and technology, or a new service that may be a manual service or a Web service. The intent of IA is not separate from the intent of the project. The project may create or enhance a product or service. There are inherent risks of a new product or service. There are inherent risks to modifying an existing product or service. There are enterprise risks when integrating new or modifying existing products' services. The project may not even involve IA services or IA mechanisms; introducing IA products is not the only means of addressing risk. Table 3.1 provides example statements of intent.

The remainder of the IA² P phases determines the letter of the IA architecture; the intent specifies the spirit. The intent of the IA² P may be focused exclusively on IA, or the intent may be to integrate IA with an enterprise architecture, systems engineering plan, product design, service design, implementation, testing, deployment, operations, requirements engineering, product selection, service selection, or compliance management. The intent may be to use IA² as a tool to address business risk by means other than a technical [IA] solution. Clarifying these nuances provides guidance to the remainder of the IA² P phases.

The statement of intent for IA relates to the purpose for the overall project. Example project purposes include enterprise expansion (domestic, international), merger/acquisition, new technical solution, new business function, or developing an E-commerce presence on the Internet. Each presents opportunities and risks, both business risks and technical risks. The IA architect anticipates potential risks, identifies probable risks, and recommends priorities on how to address those risks.

For the example details in Table 3.1, *potential risks* are employee objections to change, media reports on privacy issues, civil liberties objections with regard to personal privacy violations (taking and using of fingerprints), and the remote detection and theft of radio frequency identification (RFID) signals for spoofing or otherwise stealing employee biometric information. *Probable risks* are employee objections to change, media stories, and civil liberties objections. The remote theft of RFID signals and biometrics is possible, but not probable. *Priority risks* are employee change, civil liberties, media, and signal theft. For a more detailed presentation of identifying and evaluating risk, see the chapter, Organizational Views of IA Section, 5.4.1 "The Scope of Risk Governance, Management, and Assessment."

The statement of intent may also reference a formal problem statement and how the IA² will resolve the problem. Appendix I provides guidance on the creation of a formal problem definition. The problem assertion document is a separate tool from the IA² Process, but may be a useful supplement for it.

As you define the intent, consider the IA² F flow and ask:

■ What is the focus of the project from a business perspective? A technical perspective?
■ What are the business drivers behind the intent?
■ What are the technical drivers behind the intent?
■ What are the business risks that emerge from the intent? The technical risks?

Walk through each of the IA² F views and ask questions relevant to intent. For the IA² people view, ask how the end result of the project will be used. Who will

Table 3.1 IA² F Views: Intent Examples

IA² F Views	Statement of Intent
People	The intent of the project is to provide expedient access to the main building for thousands of people (approximately 7,000) within a matter of minutes. Entry detection will be automated, processing time per person will be <1 second, and multiple people will be processed simultaneously. Each person will be assigned an ID card with an embedded radio frequency identification (RFID) chip. Each RFID will be uniquely associated per person. The security requirements of the facility are such that each RFID card will be biometrically activated by the owner of the card placing her right thumb (or alternatively registered finger) on a reading device on the RFID card itself. The RFID card will only activate for the registered owner, not another bearing the same card. The intent of IA is to secure the entry/exit process by preventing signal detection and theft to spoof the RFID system, and to protect the privacy of individuals bearing the card (e.g., secure the transmission of biometric information to the card reader system).
Policy	Existing policies must be modified to include a requirement that all employees register fingerprints and use a biometrically activated RFID card to access company facilities. Security policy should read something to the effect of entry to organizational facilities requires expedient validation of a highly secure claim of identity, multifactor identification. This is accomplished through each person presenting something she has (the RFID card) and validating her identity by something she is (a biometric).
Business process	The current entry/exit process of checking picture identification will remain as a backup process, but be replaced as the primary means of tracking entry/exit.
Systems and applications	The intent is to introduce a new entry/exit system that includes RFID card generation, issuance, revocation, card reader, entry/exit logs, and log analyis.
Data/information	The intent is to introduce new data into individual personnel files that includes a digital representation of an appropriate biometric. The intent is for a right thumb print (primary means), left thumb print (secondary means), or alternative given the absence of the former.

Continued

Table 3.1 IA² F Views: Intent Examples (Continued)

IA² F Views	Statement of Intent
Infrastructure	New physical infrastructure is necessary to channel people through the card reader system while maintaining an image of professionalism rather than surveillance. The intent is to use portable barriers and retractable ropes similar to those used at theme parks and airports.
Internal to the organization	The intent is to manage expectations of employees by preparing details of the new system, holding an awareness campaign, and gathering and responding to any preliminary objections, questions, and concerns.
External to the organization	The intent is to prepare a press release to preempt sensationalistic stories regarding personal privacy. Legal will prepare guidance for dealing with civil liberties organizations.

use it? For what purpose? How will they know they need to use it? How will they know how to use it? How will they know they are using it effectively? Securely? For IA² view on policy, ask what policies are necessary? Do they exist? What content will address what the project is for?

For IA² business process view, ask if part of the intent is to affect workflow. Procedures? Tasks? Manual tasks? Cognitive tasks? What technology supports or will support these tasks? For systems and applications, ask if new systems or applications are to be developed or acquired. What data or information is affected? In what states are the data affected (at rest, in transit, in use)? What infrastructure components are affected? Is the intent of the project to focus exclusively internal to the organization? Are there external considerations as well? External dependencies? Partners? Customers? Suppliers? Service providers?

As you ask these and other questions, use the IA core principles as a basis for identifying each risk and its specific nature. At each intersection of the IA² Process intent phase and IA² view, question what risks there are to *confidentiality, integrity, availability, possession, authenticity, utility, nonrepudiation, authorized use,* and *privacy.* For each risk, ask what the business implications are.

Tables 3.2 and 3.3 provide examples using IA core principles to describe/define risks from the perspective of the IA² views. Analyzing the results obtained from these perspectives may capture insights with regard to governance, management, building, operations, users, and leadership (see the OCF in chapter 11). One view may capture governance insights with regard to compliance requirements and strategic objectives. Another view may capture management insights that convert strategic objectives to strategic plans, tactical objectives, and tactical plans. The details from these tables provide input to the IA² Process for defining intent for IA (e.g.,

Table 3.2   First Three IA² Views by IA Core Principles: Examples

IA² View → */IA Core Principle*	*People*	*Policy*	*Process*
Confidentiality	NA	To protect storage of RFID card details that contain biometric information	NA
Integrity	NA	Ensure the integrity of biometric information to guard against substitutions and fraud	NA
Availability	NA	Ensure availability of biometric information to ensure expedient processing of entry/exit	NA
Possession	Retaining possession of RFID card	Card issuance, use, and revocation policy; lost card policy	
Authenticity	Fingerprint of individual actually belongs to that individual; identity credential validation prior to RFID card issuance	NA	NA
Utility	NA	NA	NA
Nonrepudiation	NA	Transaction log policy to ensure any modifications to entry/ exit details may not later be denied	
Authorized use	NA	NA	NA
Privacy	NA	To protect transmission of RFID card details that contain biometric information	NA

Table 3.3 Second Three IA² Views by IA Core Principles: Examples

IA² View → /IA Core Principle	Systems and Applications	Data/Information	Infrastructure
Confidentiality	NA	Safeguard access, retrieval, use, modification, and deletion of biometric data	NA
Integrity	Ensure integrity of systems and applications containing biometric data	Ensure integrity of database containing biometric data	NA
Availability	Determine required uptime and performance criteria for RFID card system and engineer the solution to those requirements[a]	NA	NA
Possession	NA; nothing in addition to physical protections already given to IT assets	NA	NA
Authenticity	NA	NA	NA
Utility	NA	NA	NA
Nonrepudiation	NA	NA	NA
Authorized use	NA	NA	NA
Privacy	Validate applicable legislation governing IT that contains personally identifiable information (PII)	Validate applicable legislation governing IT that contains PII	NA

[a] This is a good example of risks and requirements crossing ELCM phases. The example is for design; the same performance criteria carry over as operational SLAs.

governance, strategic objectives); defining the environment for the IA application (e.g., physical infrastructure, safety and comfort of people); and defining the scope (e.g., business processes and the systems and applications that support them).

Appendix B presents a template that offers a single table for capturing risks by the IA² view. The same template applies to each phase of the IA² Process.

Once again, review the IA² Framework in chapter 2. Having documented risks, consider if there are compliance requirements imposing qualifications on business or technical operations. Moreover, the current ELCM phase affects what questions to ask, how to ask them, and who to ask them of. The same process of walking through the IA² F applies to each phase of the IA² Process. The questions may change slightly according to the intent of the IA² P phase.

3.3.1.2   Commentary

Wow! This seems like a lot! Well, yes it is. IA architecture can be quite involved. The traditional approach to IA lacks the discipline of the IA² approach. The shortcomings of the bolt-on approach will become evident as you use the IA² Framework and the IA² Process. So, while it seems like a lot, you now have a discipline to follow to know what IA aspects you have covered and what you have not. The phases of the IA² Process and the IA² views in the IA² Framework provide inherent checklists that provide a consistent, repeatable, and dare we say comprehensive manner to address IA.

3.3.2   Define the Environment

3.3.2.1   Define Where the Solution Resides

The IA² P environment phase identifies the business or technical environment, and then identifies the risks associated with that environment. The IA² P environment includes geography, organization, business, and technical. *Geography* includes location and physical infrastructure. Location addresses demography (country, region, province, state, county, city, municipality) as well as political, legal, social, religious, and environmental (e.g., earthquake, hurricane, flooding) aspects of the location that affect the project and introduce risks. Physical infrastructure addresses campus, building, floor, room, workstation, and device. IA² addresses risks of the physical infrastructure with appropriate safeguards, including lighting, video, guards, access controls, etc.

The *organizational environment* is the type of organization (small business, large business, commercial, government, private, public, or nonprofit) as well as organizational structure and culture. The structure of the organization may be a single business in a single location, a single business with hundreds of locations nation- or worldwide, or a holding company with many separate businesses.

The *business environment* is the business type, business services, and workflow. The business may be a service organization, manufacturing, retail, etc. Business services include activities that fulfill expectations for service requestors. The workflow is how those business services are fulfilled.

The *technical environment* includes data/information, systems and applications, and technical infrastructure.

3.3.2.2   Environment as Seen from the IA²F Views

The IA²F people view of environment includes culture, laws, government, customs, norms, relationships, labor force availability, personnel safety, and comfort. The IA²F policy view addresses compliance requirements for the environment (e.g., Occupational Safety and Hazard Agency [OSHA] requirements) as well as enterprise guidance for other environment characteristics. The IA²F business process view includes workflow with respect to environment, that is, assists to discover risks associated with environment that may affect business processes (i.e., interrupt operations). The IA²F systems and applications view includes software application, databases, and system processes, and new systems versus effect on existing common work environment. The IA²F data/information view addresses new data and effects on old data in transit, at rest, and in use. The IA²F infrastructure view of environment looks at the data center, power requirements, existing power capacity, uninterrupted power supply (UPS) requirements, operating systems, network bandwidth, and capacity planning. Table 3.4 continues the RFID example.

3.3.3   Define the Scope

3.3.3.1   Establish the Connection of the Solution to Strategic Goals

With a good understanding of the environment, the next step is to determine what characteristics about the environment are in scope. Define scope in terms of breadth and depth. Breadth of scope covers things like the number of people, the number of business processes, and the remainder of the IA² views with respect to variety and quantity. Depth of scope covers the attributes of people or business processes, systems and applications, etc. For example, attributes of people may include identification, privilege, role, education level, training, expertise, and experience. Part of the IA² Process is to discern how much depth is necessary to achieve the IA² intent. The fact that people are included in the IA² Process at all is part of the question in determining scope breadth. The attributes or characteristics about the people are a question of scope depth. The same considerations apply to the other IA² views. The IA² views assist in defining the scope. Table 3.5 provides guidance for determining scope breadth and depth; Table 3.6 provides examples of scope.

Table 3.4 IA² F Views: Environment Examples

IA² F Views	*Details*
People	The organizational culture includes both white-collar and blue-collar workers. Most blue-collar workers are members of a union. There is acute awareness of personal privacy within all employees. Moreover, existing legislation governs what information we may gather, how we can use it, what we must protect, and minimal protection requirements. Employees are also aware of the need for shorter processing times for entry/exit to the facilities.
Policy	Policy modifications must reflect appropriate guidelines within TBD legislation. Policy may also address the increase in safety by accounting for all employees in the event of emergency.
Business process	The business process environment is the workflow of getting employees in/out of facilities. Additional processes that may be affected are HR (time accounting for entry/exit) and security operations monitoring for false-positives (grant entry when should not) and false-negatives (deny entry when should).
Systems and applications	The systems and applications environment includes a new RFID system and log analysis software. This system will integrate to the existing network operations center (NOC) and security operations center (SOC).
Data/information	New data at rest includes digital representation of biometric and RFID no. on the RFID card; additionally, new data at rest includes database fields for the same. Data in transit includes transmission of RFID card information to card reader and card reader to database for authentication and authorization.
Infrastructure	Infrastructure environment includes physical entry/exit areas to channel people for effective card reading. The environment also includes a secondary reader system for failures and manual backup (visual validation by guard) for secondary failure.
Internal to the organization	Environment is internal only.
External to the organization	N/A

Table 3.5 IA² F Views: Scope Guidance

IA² F Views	Breadth	Depth
People	Determine if people are part of the scope; number of people affected by the results of the project.	Identification, privilege, role, education level, training, expertise, and experience; training requirements for people that will use the results of the new project
Policy	Existence of security policies that address the project risks	Quality of security policies that address the project risk
Business process	The number of business processes that use or will benefit from the project; identify the workflows that will use the results of the project.	The attributes of the workflow that will change as a result of the project
Systems and applications	Enumerate the systems and applications that will be affected by the results of the new project.	Articulate the attributes of the systems and applications that will be affected.
Data/information	Identify the data that will be touched by the results of the new projects; specify in terms of input (dependencies) and output.	Specify the attributes of the data necessary for the new project; may include data structure, classification, and metadata.
Infrastructure	Identify the infrastructure affected by the results of the new project.	Identify the attributes of the infrastructure, e.g., configuration change to all routers for traffic priority.
Internal to the organization	What business functions are in scope; what workflows that fulfill the business functions are in scope	Determine the attributes of the business functions and workflows that are in scope.
External to the organization	Determine the external dependencies.	Determine the attributes of the external dependencies.

Table 3.6 IA² F Views: Scope Examples

IA² F Views	Breadth	Depth
People	People are part of the RFID card scope; all 7,000+ employees need to be aware; administrators and operators need training.	Resolve potential individual, cultural, and union issues on the capturing and use of biometric information.
Policy	Policies do exist that may accommodate the additional details for the RFID card project.	The existing policies do not cover all the details necessary for the RFID card.
Business process	The main business process is employee entry/exit to the facilities. Additional processes for reconciling employee presence (verification of entry) are necessary at least until the RFID process proves accurate within acceptable ranges.	Redirecting employee entrance/exit paths appropriately to effectively process entry/exit
Systems and applications	HR system (additional details for biometric information and RFID card registration, issuance, and revocation). There will be X fingerprint readers added to HR for processing biometric registration.	Server XYZ in data center ABC; system owner is manager, HR.
Data/information	Employee table in database XYZ	Additional fields to accommodate
Infrastructure	Identify the infrastructure affected by the results of the new project.	Identify the attributes of the infrastructure, e.g., configuration change to all routers for traffic priority.
Internal to the organization	All scope is internal.	
External to the organization	N/A	

Table 3.7 IA² F Views: Input Guidance

IA² F Views	Details
People	Roles (governance, management, operations, users)
Policy	Internal policy that reflects compliance requirements and enterprise mission
Business process	Documents, owners, practitioners, users; see ECF
Systems and applications	Location, function, owner, custodian, O&M, documentation, vendor, product, version, release, patch
Data/information	Location, producer, consumer, owner, classification
Infrastructure	Physical, technical, mechanisms, services
Internal to the organization	Mission, policy, standards, procedures
External to the organization	Compliance requirements, industry standards

3.3.4 Identify Inputs to the IA² (Influences and Dependencies)

3.3.4.1 Define What You Need to Know

This phase in the IA² Process identifies the inputs necessary to generate an IA architecture. Inputs may include formal documentation, interviews with personnel, or other artifacts and actions from outside the organization. Some artifacts and actions may not be direct input with direct relevance to the IA²; however, they may have *influence* on how to proceed with the IA². *Dependencies* are those inputs that the IA² must have to produce quality results. Table 3.7 presents input guidance; Table 3.8 continues the example IA² Process.

3.3.5 Discovery of As-Is (Current Organizational Posture)

3.3.5.1 Document the Current State

The articulation of intent, the definition of environment and scope, and the enumeration of required inputs, influences, and dependencies are all scope parameters for the as-is discovery process. *Discovery* is the process of gathering documents, interviewing personnel, and other activity with respect to obtaining details about the current state of the organization within scope. Expect the discovery process to produce additional insight and modifications to environment, scope, and inputs.

Table 3.8 IA² F Views: Input Examples

IA² F Views	Details
People	Input from executives, business management, legal, and technical management provides governance for determining the business need, business fit, and business justification for the RFID system.
Policy	The governance process will validate policy changes and forward to XYZ, chief operating officer, for final signature.
Business process	There are no documents regarding the current business processes in which the RFID card will fit.
Systems and applications	System and application documentation is necessary for the in-scope systems and applications. Vendor input is necessary to verify that application XYZ may accommodate additional biometric details and interface to biometric registration and processing systems.
Data/information	Location, producer, consumer, owner, classification
Infrastructure	The network operations team will provide input regarding bandwidth capacity as well as server capacity and performance to ensure necessary simultaneous entries/exits are technically possible.
Internal to the organization	N/A
External to the organization	N/A

The IA² Process phases are often iterative, with details from one phase providing additional insight for other phases.

The manner of discovery and the level of detail to record are situational dependent. The templates and guides in the appendices are tools that may assist in the discovery process.

3.3.6   Analysis

3.3.6.1   Evaluate the Current State

The results of the discovery effort require analysis to determine applicability and fit with an IA² that identifies, enumerates, articulates, and addresses the business risks. Such analysis may address people, business drivers, policy, business process, workflow, operations, culture, motivation, business environment, technical environment, mechanisms, and services. The analysis process compares the as-is to the desired outcome, or the intent. This comparison identifies what exists, if what exists is adequate to support the desired outcome, and documents the gaps between the current state and the desired outcome.

Good analysis also questions convention. Current practices may be the best, but they are never the best simply because "that's the way we've always done it." Strike a balance between chronological snobbery* and the anchor of tradition. Analysis determines what is best for the situation. If the tried-and-true fits the bill, great; if not, innovate to find a better solution (see the innovation framework in chapter 12). Table 3.9 provides analysis examples.

3.3.7 Identify Outputs

3.3.7.1 Define Expected Outcomes

Analysis provides insight on how to proceed with closing the gaps between as-is and to be. In this phase, identify the necessary outputs to convey the current state of the organization and the transition from the current state to the desired state. Outputs exist in three categories of artifacts, actions, and influences. **Artifacts** include documents, schedules, diagrams, etc., produced by the IA² P. **Actions** include actions on the part of the IA² architect or other persons. **Influences** include those policies, standards, procedures, guidelines, and other documents or actions that the IA² may influence. The result of an IA² P may not be a series of new policies, but a series of modifications to existing policies. These influences are distinct from IA² artifacts. Potential IA² influences also include integration of IA features to the following processes and documents:

- Enterprise architecture (EA)
- Systems engineering (SE)
- Enterprise life cycle management (ELCM)
- Governance—determining strategic objectives and organizational policy
- Management—determining tactical objectives and tactical plans; standards
- Operations—running and maintaining services and mechanisms; procedures
- Users—user performance of tasks; guidelines

Table 3.10 provides output examples.

---

* Term used by C. S. Lewis to describe a penchant toward the new simply because it is new. Chronological snobbery perceives newer as better by virtue of being newer; it perceives tradition as bad just because it is tradition.

Table 3.9   IA² F Views: Analysis Examples

IA² F Views	Details
People	Employees are used to carrying an identification badge. This badge is not currently RFID enabled, nor have employees been asked to register a biometric reading for use by the organization.
Policy	Currently policy does not require biometric registration. Policy should reflect this as a requirement for employment with notable exceptions for a minority who may not have fingers with which to register. The need for policy is also to ensure the biometric requirement applies to all employees capable of providing such.
Business process	The current business process of manually checking identifications is inaccurate and causes lines to build up during peak entry/exit times.
Systems and applications	The current systems and applications may accommodate the RFID technical requirements. The new RFID systems and fingerprint readers are compatible with existing networks, servers, databases, and applications.
Data/information	The data requirements may be met by existing databases and applications.
Infrastructure	The additional bandwidth utilization, data center space, and processing times are all within the capacity of existing infrastructure.
Internal to the organization	TBD
External to the organization	The organization must prepare to deal with external entities who may question or object to the use of biometrics and the requirement for biometric registration as a condition of employment. The external entities who may raise a question include the union and civil liberties organizations. This point should not be hit too hard, but reasonable preparation with legal guidance will provide management and media spokespeople with a consistent message.

Table 3.10 IA² F Views: Identify Output Examples

IA² F Views	Details
People	N/A
Policy	Policy modifications to accommodate the RFID card system will occur for the following policies: Employee handbook XYZ security policy
Business process	No outputs for business process
Systems and applications	Outputs for systems and applications include new systems and modifications to existing systems. New systems and applications include: Biometric registration system, RFID card creation, RFID card reader. Modifications to existing system and applications include: Change EMPLOYEE table in XYZ database on server ABC, Add RFID no., and digital representation of biometric
Data/information	See systems and applications modifications for database changes.
Infrastructure	No new technical infrastructure is necessary. New physical infrastructure includes entry/exit pathway management (see diagram XYZ).
Internal to the organization	Prepare internal awareness, training, and education program.
External to the organization	Prepare press releases, media communications guidelines, and communication guidance for unions and civil liberties organizations.

3.3.8 Produce Outputs

3.3.8.1 Produce Expected Outcomes

Produce the outputs enumerated in the previous phase. If there are no templates for the outputs, be sure to produce templates as aids to the next IA² Process. The production of outputs can be a very large effort. The presence of tools, templates, and methodologies that facilitate the production process permits multiple efforts to occur in parallel, and may provide an opportunity to capture best practices. Tools may include a standard glossary, an interpretation guide (e.g., SOX legislation interpretation), and spreadsheets to capture IA² P input details (i.e., who has action items and who has delivered). Templates include an IA² P template (see appendix A). Methodologies explain the tools and templates to ensure their appropriate use.

3.3.9 Summary of IA² Process Phases

To define what it is, you need to know what it is for (**intent**).

To build it, you have to know where it will reside (**environment**).

To modify it, you have to know what to change (**scope**).

To plan it, you have to know what you have to work with (**inputs**).

To analyze it, you have to obtain it (**discovery**).

To know what to do with it, you have to evaluate it (**analyze**).

To know where you need it, you have to define expectations (**outcomes**).

To finish, you have to produce results (**outcomes**).

3.4 Conclusion and Commentary

The IA² P uses the IA² F to identify, enumerate, articulate, and address business risk. The IA² P provides a repeatable and consistent methodology that produces consistent results from project to project, architect to architect, and team to team. A capability maturity model (CMM) defines maturity levels roughly equivalent to those in Table 3.11.

The IA² Framework and IA² Process provide the ability to reach CMM level 3; all in all, this is a worthy goal and a great accomplishment to take into your next performance appraisal. In keeping with level 4, there is an increasing demand by executives for *quantification—Show ROI! Show hard results in business terms!* With respect to security, forget the FUD (fear, uncertainty, and doubt) factor; *show the business value of security!* But how? The next chapter presents an IA² quantification process (IAQP) and an IA² quantification framework (IAQF). These are methods to use when thinking about IA quantification. They are not

Table 3.11 CMM Overview

Level	Name	Description
1	Ad hoc	The processes are usually ad hoc, and while they produce results, the results are inconsistent and often over budget or over schedule.
2	Repeatable	The organization possesses a disciplined approach, a repeatable process.
3	Defined	Formal definition, retention, and management of processes
4	Quantified	Insert performance and quality management (e.g., SLAs) into process.
5	Optimized	Continual review and improvement to optimize performance of process

formulas or models for exact answers. They are not a return on security investment (ROSI) model. Rather, they present how to think about quantifying IA, and the IA quantification at various organizational levels, including executive, governance, management, and operations.

Chapter 4

IA Quantification

4.1 Introduction

There is an increasing need to show the business value of information assurance with hard, objective measurements that directly align to performance, revenue, and cost management. The act of measurement requires something to measure. The IA quantification framework (IAQF) provides guidance on where to look for opportunities to quantify IA or to find parameters to measure that represent IA, and a way to look at IA quantification from different perspectives. The IA quantification process (IAQP) provides a method to determine metrics and measures for IA that provide an objective view of the enterprise security posture and can establish an objective quantified baseline from which to trend the performance of IA services and IA mechanisms.

A *metric* is a standard of measure; a *measure* is an amount. An American football field is 100 yards long; the measure is 100, the metric is yards. There are 100 centimeters in 1 meter; 1 and 100 are measures, and meter and centimeter are metrics. What are the metrics and measures of information assurance? What do they mean?

Good metrics are measurable, collectible, usable, and meaningful. A metric is no good if it is not measurable, there must be a value. A metric is no good if it is not collectible, you must be able to obtain the measure. A metric is no good if it is not usable. The measure must fit into calculations in a manner that provides useful results. A metric is no good if it does not have meaning to the organization. A good metric must relate to business drivers, strategic objectives, or otherwise to the mission.

Security does not have an inherent or intrinsic value. There is no way to look at an IA service or an IA mechanism and say we can measure that to be 42 *risk*ometers. We may count the number of IA mechanisms (e.g., quantity of firewalls). We may impose service levels on the security operations center (e.g., respond to incidents within X minutes). Absent inherent value, we can impose an artificial measure that represents reality and has meaning to the enterprise. For artificial measures to have meaning, they must be consistently applied from person to person and operation to operation using a uniform, repeatable process.

The relevance of metrics and measures is defined by the group that uses them. Operations is more interested in performance metrics such as service level agreements (SLAs) (e.g., uptime of a mechanism, successful blocks of spam). Executives are more interested in the monetary terms of ROI. Management is more interested in terms of delivery schedules and annual budgets. Legal is more interested in legislative compliance levels. All of these offer opportunity for IA quantification. The following sections present an IAQF as a framework of what to look for, and an IAQP as a process that will help you identify IA quantification opportunities and actually quantify IA.

4.2   Objectives

The objectives of this chapter are to introduce the following:

- IA² quantification framework
- IA² quantification process

At the end of this chapter, you should be able to use a disciplined approach to identify potential manners to quantify IA.

4.3   IA Quantification Framework (IAQF)

Quantifying information assurance is a nontrivial endeavor. There are no intrinsic values to IA; any values associated with IA are representative of operational conditions, performance levels, and threat space, or represent stakeholder terms (dollars, public safety, etc.). Many IA aspects are measurable. The challenge is to find them, impose a measurement process, and report them in manner that has meaning to the organization. Each of the following four perspectives provides opportunities for IA quantification:

- Stakeholder
- Asset/target
- Vulnerability
- Threat

The following IA Quantification Framework (IAQF) provides guidance for each of the four perspectives:

- People (actors)
  - Learning phases of awareness, understanding, use, effective use, and secure use
- Process (actions), Technology (entities), Policy, or other non-person thing
  - Operational descriptions of existence, characteristics, quality

The learning phases were introduced in the section Goals for the Reader. Learning phases apply to people and their awareness, understanding, and use of processes and technology. The operational descriptions apply the same to processes and technology. A technology exists or it doesn't. There a characteristics of a process that define what it is supposed to be and what it is supposed to accomplish. For example, a computer security response triage process is supposed to review events to determine if they are security incidents, who should handle the security incident, and the priority in which to address the incidents. These characteristics of what defines a working triage process are potential parameters for measurement. Assuming that a technology or process exists and it works at all, the next consideration is to the quality of how they are working. Quality includes timely operation, accuracy, and efficiency.

A series of standard questions outlines the beginning of quantification. Assume that X in the following list can represent a technology or a process.

- Do the right people exist within the organization?
- Are they aware of X?
- Do they understand the operation of X?
- Do they understand the enterprise role and relationship of X?
- Do they use X?
- Do they use X effectively (timely, accurately, efficiently)?
- Do they use X securely?
- Does X exist at all?
- Does X exist within the organization?
- Does X work at all?
- Does X work effectively (timely, accurately, efficiently)?
- Does X work securely?

The benchmark of using or working securely is relative to the security standards the organization adopts.

4.3.1 IA Quantification: Stakeholder Perspective

Stakeholder interests drive the form, flow, and content of quantification results. At the highest level, stakeholder interests are strategic or tactical. Stakeholder terms determine how to present the content. Stakeholder terms become the IA quantification terms.

4.3.1.1   Audience Dependent

The stakeholder perspective is audience dependent, that is, who the stakeholders are. There is little hope for universally understandable or universally relevant IA quantification. Even financial terms only have meaning to those interested in money, and money may not be the primary stakeholder concern. The point is to develop an audience framework that provides insight into expressing IA quantification in terms readily understood and accepted by the stakeholder. Chapter 12 presents an Organizational Context Framework (OCF) that includes governance, management, operations, and users. Each of these audiences has different interests in IA quantification. Users may have no interest at all in IA performance other than it should not interfere with their job performance.

4.3.1.2   Spam Blocking Example

Assume a working environment of 52 weeks per year, 5 workdays per week, which yields 260 potential workdays per year. Subtract 10 holidays, 10 vacation days, and 5 sick days to get 235 actual workdays per year per employee. The department employs 25 people. E-mail records show that on average each employee receives 10 spam messages per actual workday and takes on average 15 seconds to process each spam message (or .25 minutes).

Lost productivity due to spam processing is ((235 * 25 * 10 * .25)/60), or approximately 245 hours per year or over 30 eight-hour workdays in annual lost productivity. The productivity return for spam blocking is a function of how many spam messages are actually blocked. If spam blocking achieves 100 percent blocking, this is an annual 30-day productivity return for a department of 25 people. Even 80 percent spam blocking success yields a productivity return of over 24 days annually.

In monetary terms, assume an average employee cost (including benefits) of $60,000 per year. This is a daily expense of about $255 per employee. The 80 percent success in spam blocking provides a $6,000+ annual return to this one department of 25 people. Given all the same assumptions, this is a return of $60,000 for an organization of 250 people and $600,000 for an organization of 2,500 people.

4.3.1.3   Strategic Interests

Consider the strategic implications of IA quantification. If the audience is a CxO (i.e., CEO, CFO, COO, CIO, CSO, etc.), the stakeholder currency is likely to be literally currency (e.g., dollars, euros, pounds) and the IA message should be in financial terms. At the strategic level, the financials should show the effect of IA on the balance sheet, income statement, financial ratios, return on investment (ROI), internal rate of return (IRR), and hurdle rates. A CEO's primary motivation is to make a profit; moreover, the goal is to *optimize* profit for investors. If investing the $1 million in T-bills is going to have a higher return than investing in the deployment of the latest security wonder widgets, T-bills it is.

As an IA architect, you are the liaison between business, technology, and IA. Your job includes awareness of stakeholder motivations, business drivers, technical drivers, and inherent and implied risks. Moreover, your job is to explain the risks and how to address those risks in terms that resonate with the audience.

4.3.1.4 Tactical Interests

Line managers are likely to see the value of IA quantification in terms of operations, procedures, workflow, effect on infrastructure (e.g., increase mean time between failures [MTBF]), and financials in terms of cash flow, revenue stream generation, or revenue stream preservation. These tactical concerns ultimately roll up into the balance sheet and income statement. However, line managers relate more to annual budgets and productivity levels than to line items on the balance sheet and income statement.

From a tactical perspective, consider what you should do (business drivers) in terms of compliance requirements and good business practice. Use the articulation of what you should do as a comparison for what you've done. Discover the actual and compare against the objectives. A comparison of actual to target provides a percentage completion. This can be in terms of existence, characteristics, and quality of each business driver. For example, given an investment in 100 firewalls for the organization, there is business value in knowing how many are deployed (how many exist), how many are working at any given time (do they work at all), how many pass a standard penetration test to verify minimal security configuration (do they work well).

4.3.1.5 IA Quantification Terms

The terms used to express IA value will vary among organizations. The IA architect should express IA quantification (e.g., risk quantification, operational parameters) in the appropriate stakeholder terms, or the appropriate stakeholder currency. The same IA results may be expressed differently to a commercial company's CEO (e.g., balance sheet dollars) than an operations manager (e.g., SLA parameters). If the audience is military, the appropriate stakeholder currency is lives. Political currency is votes. Law enforcement currency is public safety. Nonprofit currency is optimizing the number of people who benefit from the free or low-cost service they offer.

While terms of how to express IA value will vary among organizations, arguably, all organizations are concerned about money. And indeed even the most altruistic of nonprofit organization needs money to provide its benefits. The point is to be aware that IA quantification has many potential expressions. Moreover, expressing IA value in terms that resonate with the audience provides for a better understanding of IA and increases the tolerance for IA if not outright acceptance.

4.3.2 IA Quantification: Asset/Target Perspective

Assets are the targets of threats. Even if a threat has no volition (e.g., hurricane), there are still assets that may be the target of a hurricane, albeit unwittingly. An outline of the IAQF asset/target perspective includes:

- Financial (currency measurement)
- Development (quality measurement)
- Operational (functional parameter measurement)
  - Risk management (standard risk assessment quantification)
  - Mission integrity boundary model
  - Attack modeling

4.3.2.1 Financial (Currency Measurement)

The ROI framework in chapter 12 provides a basis for financial quantification. The ROI framework is:

- Revenue
  - Revenue increase
  - Revenue sustainment
- Cost
  - Cost reduction
  - Cost avoidance

For example, revenue increases in terms of customer satisfaction that translates past performance reference for new sales, and revenue sustainment in terms of realizing the organizational mission and maintaining mission integrity that translates into meeting SLAs and results in customer satisfaction and contract renewal. Cost reduction may be in terms of reduced time spent chasing malware issues and more time now spent on core services to customers; cost avoidance is in terms of legislative compliance or avoidance of SLA penalties.

With the above as a guide, implementing IA may provide return on security investment (ROSI) from the perspectives of revenue generation, revenue protection, cost reduction, and cost avoidance. For example:

- Revenue increase may come from a managed security service (MSS) where the security organization offers subscriptions to other organizations. A safe and thus highly available solution may generate additional sales to customers with high service level expectations.
- Safeguarding a retail E-commerce system protects and sustains the revenue stream generated by that system.
- As E-risk insurance becomes more prevalent, appropriate IA safeguards may reduce insurance premiums (cost reduction); likewise, the appropriate safeguard technology may reduce labor costs (e.g., personnel manually isolating and treating malware).
- Cost avoidance comes in the form of legislative compliance and avoiding the fines associated with noncompliance.

4.3.2.2 Development (Quality Measurement)

The software development industry has a long history of bugs, tracking bugs, and adding design and development features to find and fix bugs as early in the development cycle as possible, the premise being that it is cheaper to fix a bug earlier than later. This process is software quality assurance (SQA). Treating security flaws as one form of software bug uses SQA techniques as an IA tool in the development process. All the quantified benefits of SQA also apply to IA.

4.3.2.3 Operational (Functional Parameter Measurement)

Operational quantification may consist of risk management and attack modeling; these are models that may provide insight into what-if scenarios that will illuminate the results of implementing or not implementing IA safeguards, or maintaining, lowering, or raising certain levels of security.

4.3.2.4 Risk Management (Standard Risk Assessment Quantification)

The risk assessment quantification includes the standard asset value, exposure factor (EF), annualized rate of occurrence (ARO), single loss expectancy (SLE), annual loss expectancy (ALE), etc. There are many books dedicated to risk assessments. An effective risk assessment approach remains a challenge for the IA industry.

4.3.2.5 Attack Modeling

A system supports the fulfillment of a business function. Vulnerabilities reside within systems. A threat exploiting a vulnerability will have an effect on that sys-

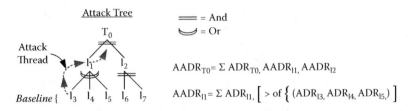

Figure 4.1 Attack defense rating (ADR) metric. (Attack tree nomenclature inspired by Bruce Schnier's attack modeling.)

tem and the business function which that system supports. Attack modeling provides a method to examine the potential effect of a threat on a system and on the business function.

4.3.3 Attack Modeling: An Example

Defense-in-depth involves many safeguards between a threat and a potential asset of value. Each physical safeguard (e.g., firewall) may be an interim target on the way to the asset of value. Each physical device will be a target (T) or intermediate target (I): T_0, T_1, T_i; I_0, I_1, I_j. Develop an *artificial quantification* for attack difficulty, a relative scale deriving value from intramodel consistency and consistent application across the organization. Each entity and entity component is assigned an attack defense rating (ADR). Additionally, each entity has physical components and logical components that may be assigned ADR values. Attack modeling separates the primary service (e.g., firewall) from support services and processes, and separates primary service vulnerabilities from secondary vulnerabilities (e.g., *support process* buffer overflow vulnerability).

Lowest-level entities are baseline entities, and all levels above the baseline have an *aggregate ADR* (AADR) (Figure 4.1). Establish target AADR tolerance parameters to evaluate existing defense-in-depth architecture or to model prospective changes to defense-in-depth architecture. You may also add ADR *weighting* to further define relative importance or to reflect risk mitigation.

The ADR model may also represent what-if scenarios, thus providing a predictive model for new threats and modifications to the defense-in-depth environment.

4.3.4 IA Quantification: Vulnerability

Vulnerabilities are weaknesses open to exploitation that may damage the organization. Vulnerability management is a process identifying vulnerabilities and resolving or otherwise working around them to minimize the risk of their exploitation by a threat. Anything in the enterprise may be vulnerable. A vulnerability framework must cover all aspects of the organization. The Enterprise Context Framework (ECF) (chapter 12) and enterprise dynamics provide a framework within which to consider vulnerabilities. The macro level categories are:

- Entities—technology
- Actors—people
- Actions—process

There are many contexts in which to consider enterprise dynamics. These contexts include:

- Business
  - People
  - Process
    - Management
    - Production
    - Operations
- Organization
  - Hierarchical structure
  - Command and control
- Physical
  - Location
  - Site details of campus, building, floor, room, and workspace

Vendors release patches to fix vulnerabilities. Part of vulnerability management is *patch management*. A formal patch management process monitors industry and vendor announcements of known vulnerabilities and a manner in which to address those vulnerabilities. However, installing the patches introduces risk to operations, because a patch may interfere with existing software and affect performance levels. This is another example of the need to maintain mission integrity. Introducing a patch for a security hole as quickly as possible is good, but not at the expense of negatively affecting the business purpose of the patched system.

4.3.5   IA Quantification: Threat Perspective

The threat perspective of IA quantification includes deductive and predictive approaches.

4.3.5.1   Threat Probability Assessment (TPA)

Traditional focus of a risk assessment starts with the organizational asset space. This approach to risk management first attempts to identify assets with high dollar

Table 4.1   TPA Rating Template

TPA Parameter	Rate	Confidence Level	Description	Comments
Means	<Rate>	<Level>	Budget, expertise, equipment	<Insert comments>
Method			Tactical preferences, previous actions, patterns	
Motivation			A reason to act	
Mission			A target to act upon	

value or assets of high business value. Risk mitigation decisions are then made on the results of this internally focused risk assessment.

The TPA approach operates under the premise that a vulnerability with no threat is less of a risk than a vulnerability under threat. TPA focuses on the threat space first and asset space second. TPA discerns higher probability threats, then looks to the asset space and asset vulnerabilities that the threat space may exploit. The objective is to guide intelligent resource allocation to mitigate risks in the asset space targeted by high probability threats.

A framework for adversary TPA includes evaluating adversary capability (means); tactical preferences (method); leadership, individual psychology, group and social dynamics, and political psychology (motivations, operations, and interests); and potential adversary objectives (mission). Evaluating potential threats using TPA identifies the probable threat space within the possible threat space. A simple TPA quantification method is a 0 through 4 capability scale, where 0 implies no capability, 4 implies fully capable, and 1, 2, and 3 imply low, medium, and high capability, respectively. Table 4.1 provides a template to record TPA ratings. Rating determination is subjective and largely depends on what you know and what you think you know. A confidence level serves as a separate data point to consider in the overall TPA profile. Again, use a 0 through 4 scale to represent no confidence, low, medium, high, and 100 percent certain, respectively.

TPA is an artificial system of metrics and measures. For consistent application of TPA, there is need for a rating guide and a confidence level guide. Table 4.2 provides a sample TPA rating guide, and Table 4.3 provides a sample TPA confidence-level guide. The guides will convey the rationale behind TPA to various audiences within the organization.

As an example, consider a TPA rating interpretation of an organization known for industrial espionage. It is fully funded, possesses full knowledge, and possesses appropriate equipment for many exploitive activities. Its methods are predictable and known to be effective. Therefore, both means and method are rated as 4s.

Table 4.2 TPA Rating Guide

TPA Parameter	0	1	2	3	4
Means	No means, no budget, no knowledge, no equipment	Known to have a low degree of funding, knowledge, and access to equipment; may have a little of each of these, but not enough to be a serious threat	Known to have some degree of funding, knowledge, and access to equipment; may have one of two	Known to have a high degree of funding, knowledge, and access to equipment; may have two of three	Fully funded, full knowledge, possession, or easy access to equipment
Method	No methods, no prior activity	Known for some probing; use of some scripts; no sophistication	Known for some attack sophistication; some manual, mostly canned scripts	Known for high attack sophistication	Fully capable of performing attack; there are known methods and history of performance
Motivation	No known reasons to attack	Attacker motivation is more one of casual opportunity	Attacker is somewhat motivated to attack your country and entities like yours; not specifically motivated to launch an attack now or in the near future	Attacker is highly motivated to attack your type of organization and has been known to do so; no specific knowledge of your organization as a specific target	Fully motivated to carry out an attack; attacker is known to hate or otherwise desire to attack your organization; history of prior attacks
Mission	No known targets	General knowledge of adversary interest in your organization; no specific knowledge of adversary desires and no rational guesses	Adversary objectives are not easily guessed and may include Web site, R&D, financial information, strategic planning, databases, etc.; mission may be denial of service, stealing information, or violating any of the IA core principles	Adversary objectives toward your organization may be guessed with a high level of confidence, e.g., you are a bank, they want the money	Full knowledge of adversary desired targets and desired effect on those targets; this requires specific knowledge of adversary intent

Table 4.3 TPA Confidence Level Guide

TPA Parameter	0	1	2	3	4
Means, method, motivation, mission	No direct knowledge; no rationale assumptions or guesses	Gut feeling, but no rational reason, history, or specific knowledge	Reasonable, good, rational guess, but no history and no specific knowledge	No specific knowledge, but guesses are highly rational and align with history of adversary	Direct knowledge; specific intelligence of adversary

However, with respect to your assets, this organization may have a 0 motivation to exercise its means and method. A 0 motivation means there is no specific target. The TPA rating points to a low probability from this potential threat. The business implication is no IA resources are necessary to specifically address state-sponsored threats. Even though espionage is possible, it is not probable, and therefore is not a priority for the IA budget.

Applying the TPA guidance is not a rote methodology; it does not support a simple 3 in this box, 4 in that box, add them up, and multiply. *The numbers are a clue, not a conclusion.* Considerable subjective evaluation is necessary. If the means of adversary depend upon money, knowledge, and equipment, the presence of two out of three may not be enough to make that adversary a high priority, that is, enough of a priority to redirect budget from another priority. However, subjective judgment enters when trying to determine how close an organization is to obtaining the missing piece; e.g., an export embargo on a specialized piece of equipment is only as effective as a smuggler's ability to bypass customs and border patrol. These subjective judgments are important and require a confidence level to assist in objectively evaluating threats as potential, probable, or priority.

Confidence levels are determined the same way for means, method, motivation, and mission; however, each TPA parameter must be assigned its own confidence level. To continue the above example, the confidence level in means and method are 4s even without specific, direct knowledge. A reasonable assumption is that the espionage organization has funding and methodologies to draw upon. Determining confidence level for motivation comes from examining your business environment and your knowledge of competitive interests. Moreover, what you perceive as a target for the mission may not be of interest to a prospective adversary. Assigning a confidence level forces you to think about your situation a bit more critically and question your own knowledge. If you are confident, great! If you are not, also great—because now you know it, acknowledge it, and can act upon your conclusions accordingly.

Colin Powell provides good guidance on the point of confidence levels with, "Tell me what you know. Tell me what you don't know. And then, based on what you really know and what you really don't know, tell me what you think is most likely to happen."*

Chapter 5 contains additional details on TPA. This chapter introduces TPA as an option to quantify the IA threat space where threat space is one attribute of the IA quantification framework.

4.3.5.2 Deductive Approach

Deductive reasoning produces a conclusion that is found in the premises. The acceptance of the premises ensures the conclusion. The deductive approach attempts to

---

* http://www.fas.org/irp/congress/2004_hr/091304powell.html (accessed October 2007).

answer the question, *does the activity, event, incident we see now fall into a pattern that we've seen before?* The question can be answered by entering details of all security events into a database to create a historical record; these include those from direct organizational experience and vicarious experience (from articles, surveys, studies, etc.). Additional information to the database includes speculation on what may happen. The deductive approach evaluates actual and vicarious experience (empirical history) and specific cases of *what may be* derived from expert opinion (enumerated speculative future), and compares details from this event repository to current emerging circumstances. The deductive model draws conclusions from what is known or what is specifically guessed—a powerful model, but with limits.* There remains the need to look beyond known facts and attempt to draw conclusions beyond the known.

4.3.5.3 Inductive Approach

Inductive reasoning is the complement to deductive reasoning. While the premises support the conclusion, they do not ensure it because the inductive conclusion extends beyond the known facts. The inductive model assigns probabilities to anticipated future events focusing on permutations of speculative, what-if circumstances. The inductive model attempts to infer security events outside of actual, vicarious experience.†

These two approaches to threat analysis offer a balanced approach that considers the tried and true as well as the innovative. The discussion of risk must include a discussion of probabilities. Because something is possible, that does not make it probable: a meteorite falling through the data center roof and taking out a key server is possible; however, the likelihood of this happening is so small as to be negligible. The point is to determine the real threats (probable threats) and focus limited resources on the highly probable threats that if realized will have significant impact on the organization.

4.4 IA Quantification Process (IAQP)

The *IA quantification process* (IAQP) describes how to build a quantitative model. Neither IAQF nor IAQP is an actual model to plug in numbers and generate an answer. Expectations for a universally applicable IA quantification model are not realistic. Rather, both the IAQP and IAQF provide a thought process behind model generation with the expectation that useful models will be customized to the organization and to the situation at hand.

---

* Paraphrased from Willett, Keith D., and Gardner, Robert K., *Risk Analysis and Assessments: Focus on Intelligent, Coordinated, Non-State Adversary*, Computer Sciences Corporation, p. 16.
† Ibid., p. 16.

The IAQP (Figure 4.2) starts with a narrative of the business scenario that includes desired state of operation, capability, or behavior. The narrative also includes potential and probable risks in business terms, and the IA services and IA mechanisms that will address the risks. Analysis of the narrative attempts to identify parameters that represent relevant points with respect to business objectives, risk, and risk mitigation. With that set of parameters, consider what about them is measurable and in what terms (in what metrics). The IAQP then prompts you to articulate how to obtain the measures, analyze the measures, and report the measures within the organization.

Figure 4.2   IA quantification process.

The following sections describe each step in the IAQP to determine the appropriate metrics and measures for your organization.

4.4.1   Narrative

The IA quantification process provides guidance for determining how to quantify a particular scenario. The first step is to provide a narrative describing that scenario. Define the problem, define the intent (see IA^2 Process), and define the objective in business, technical, and IA terms. Articulate the scenario to capture the business objectives, the risks, and the intent of IA. Do not initially attempt to state what you may quantify. Later IAQP steps will identify what you may quantify, how to obtain the measures, and how to use them.

4.4.2   Parameters

Review the narrative using the Reality Check Framework (who, what, why, when, where, and how). Identify the entities, actors, and actions. Question each of these in terms of what may be quantified. Find and note any inherent metrics or measures, a way to count them, or a way to superimpose artificial metrics. Potential parameters include a quantity (the number of), e.g., the number of firewalls, the number of security incidents. Another parameter may be a dollar figure such as cost of IA or ROI for IA. Another parameter may be a compliance level, i.e., current security posture contains X features as compared to a baseline standard of Y features, therefore, $X/Y = \%$ compliance level.

4.4.3 Quantification

The objective of the quantification step is to determine the metrics and measures for each parameter. Inherent metrics and measures should have been identified by the narrative. If not inherent, look for established metrics and measures (e.g., SLAs, uptime objective, or MTBF). If a parameter is important and there are no intrinsic or established parameters, find something about it to measure or impose an artificial system.

Consider whether the parameters provide metrics and measures that correlate to recognized industry benchmarks. If there is no comparison to industry benchmarks, are the parameters quantifiable in such a manner that the results may show internal consistency and provide business value through relative comparisons? Compliance levels fall into this latter category. Compliance has no intrinsic value; however, determining a measure of compliance is possible by superimposing an artificial measure using the features of the compliance requirements that exist within the organization.

When applying the IAQP, consider the following list of questions with respect to the IA parameters and measuring these parameters. The list is exemplary of the types of questions to think of during brainstorming and development of a quantification model.

- Is the value something it has intrinsically, or is the value an artificial metric and measure?
- Is the appropriate value to measure something it does not have?
  - Measure the absence of X to prove security, and conversely, the presence of X points to insecurity.
- Is the value to measure something it gains (growth)/does not gain (stasis)?
  - Maintain secure operations through a predictable gain of X within Y, where Y ∈ [system | log | network | other].
  - Maintain secure operations through a steady state of X within Y, where Y ∈ [system | log | network | other]; a gain of X implies tendency toward mission entropy.
- Is the value to measure something it loses (loss)/does not lose (stasis)?
  - Secure operations is compromised through loss of X.
  - Does not lose (conservancy principle)
- Are metrics static or dynamic?
  - Not the value of the parameter, but those parameters measured; do they change under certain circumstances?
    - For example, parameters measured are relative to DHS* alert level; higher alert level implies an increase in the number of parameters to measure.

---

* Department of Homeland Security.

■ Are there thresholds and what do they mean?
  - Consider ceiling thresholds that if exceeded result in an alert.
  - Consider floor thresholds that if fallen below result in an alert.
    ■ Define alert parameter levels/layers.
■ Direct measurements versus correlating or coincidental events
  - If an IA aspect does not possess an intrinsic value or cannot be assigned a meaningful arbitrary value, is there a correlating or coincidental [event | condition | parameter] that can be measured?
■ Discrete events versus aggregate events
  - Any individual parameter that falls outside desired operational thresholds may not indicate a severe problem; however, several of these conditions may point to a severe problem—there is need to consider event aggregation in the IAQF.
■ What activity adds/detracts from risk/risk measurement?
  - Acts of commission
    ■ The fact that X occurred may indicate a problem.
  - Acts of omission
    ■ The fact that X did not occur may indicate a problem.

4.4.4 Discovery

The IAQP discovery step describes how to obtain the measures for analysis. The discovery step describes what to do to accomplish discovery; it is not the discovery itself. Discovery methods may include assessments, audits, interviews, log reviews, or usage tracking (e.g., Web site hits or file downloads). Other methods may include surveys or quizzes to test understanding of an ethics program, security policy, or legislative requirement. Points to include in the discovery description are who can provide inputs, what to ask them for, how to obtain the information, and how to record discovery data.

The discovery step may articulate the need for tools, templates, guidance, and methodology for a formal discovery process. Preparing for and executing an effective discovery process may be a project in itself. For example, preparing to discover the organization's current compliance posture with Sarbanes–Oxley or other legislation is quite an effort.

Thoughts with regard to what you will do with the discovery data (analysis) provide clues for determining what to collect. That is, the IAQP is not necessarily a linear process, but an emerging process where latter steps provide insight to previous steps. An important note: The IAQP is a process for invention, it is not a model to plug in numbers and get a result. You must invent a quantification process for your organization or for your situation. The IAQP provides a discipline to guide your thoughts.

4.4.5 Analysis

The IAQP analysis step describes how to analyze parameters in terms that have meaning to the intended audience, i.e., executives, management, operations, and users. The result of analyzing the IA quantification data provides input to the reports. Therefore, consider who will read the report, who will benefit from the analysis, what key points they are looking for, and what decisions they will make with the analysis.

If the measure is artificial, the objective is to apply the quantification with consistency to ensure results are comparable from person to person, team to team, and time to time. Analysis may show levels of awareness and understanding, number of installations, uptime of mechanisms, mean time between failures (MTBF), or SLAs. Analysis may compare the security posture of one system to another system, or compare the security posture of one location to another location.

The results of the analysis can distinguish who is performing well and who is not, and who has the best compliance levels. An aggregation of multiple discovery efforts may show the enterprise security posture. Performing the same discovery process 12 months later now provides the ability to compare results. Doing the same discovery process year after year provides the ability to trend the security posture.

4.4.6 Report

The IAQP report process determines the target audience that will benefit from the analysis, how will they benefit, and the report form, flow, and content for the audience to derive the most benefit. The target audience may be an executive desiring charts with a bottom-line financial flavor or an operations line manager who desires to modify workflow. The report process may describe report templates for various audiences. You, the IA architect, use the IAQP to invent a quantification process. Conveying the results of IA discovery and analysis is a challenge. An important note: The IA reports are what the organization sees of IA. Your job as an IA architect is to develop a line of sight from business drivers to IA services and IA mechanisms in operations. This is the opportunity to convey IA's business value in a professional tone.

4.4.7 Feedback

Finally, consider how the quantification model will accept feedback from the target entity for subsequent modification of the model.

The IAQP maps out how to quantify IA. The end result of the IAQP is the articulation of what aspects of IA need to be measured, which may be measured, what the metrics and measures are, how to obtain them, how to analyze and report them, and what they mean to the organization.

There are two levels of outcome for organizational feedback, IA in *balance* and IA in *harmony* with the business. Balance implies a give-and-take to reach equilibrium, an equilibrium that may result in less-than-optimal security in balance with less-than-optimal business operations. IA in harmony with operations implies an *integration* of both. The result is optimal business operations that are also optimally secure. A goal of IA quantification is to represent IA in harmony with the organizational mission and operations; neither stands alone and each contains a bit of the other. Harmonious IA mitigates risk and minimizes operational impact.

4.5 Conclusion and Commentary

Two themes in IA^2 are business need drives technology and business risk drives IA. The IAQF provides a discipline to discern various ways to represent risk and IA. The IAQP provides a discipline on *how* to find the metrics and measures for the business scenario at hand. The IAQF offers a discipline of *what* to consider for metrics. The IAQF and IAQP are not themselves IA quantification models, but provide guidance on finding the raw material from which to develop IA quantification models. To assist with understanding the IAQP, appendix C provides both a template and an example of how to apply the IA quantification process.

APPLIED IA^2

Chapter 5

Organizational Views of IA

5.1 Introduction

The Organizational Context Framework (OCF) presents an organizational hierarchy of *governance*, *management*, *builders*, *operations*, *users*, and *leaders*. The OCF also provides a framework for *organizational views* of IA (Figure 5.1). Organizational views of IA can be seen from two perspectives: the message of IA to the organization in terms it can understand and relate to, and the use of organizational views on IA for the effective planning, implementation, and operation of IA services and mechanisms. Discussing IA in terms relevant to these organizational views will help raise awareness, understanding, and use of IA throughout the enterprise. Moreover, applying these perspectives to IA will help make IA more effective in the greater enterprise context.

5.2 Objectives

The objectives of this chapter include:

- Elaborate on the OCF organizational views.
- Use OCF to present a variety of organizational views of IA.

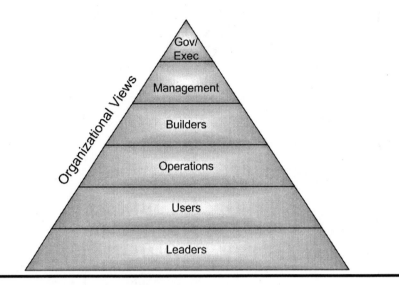

Figure 5.1 OCF—organizational views of IA.

At the end of this chapter, you should be able to articulate a better IA message at various organizational layers and better understand how to use the perspectives of different organizational layers in architecting IA solutions.

5.3 The Message of IA to the Organization

Business professionals too often view information assurance as a stand-alone concern with no real business value. The attitude toward IA is one of vague necessity and grudging tolerance rather than acceptance. The responsibility of IA professionals is to convey IA in terms meaningful to the audience. You must see IA through many organizational views, understand their perspectives, and present IA business value accordingly.

When you apply the IA² Process and IA² Framework, consider IA from these organizational views (Figure 5.1). Discern what is significant from each perspective. This will help you to discover, plan, and convey the IA message throughout the organization in terms that will resonate with a variety of audiences.

Governance defines business drivers in terms directly related to the core reasons for the existence of the organization. Executives are the highest level of governance in the organizational hierarchy. They establish strategic objectives and policy to meet those objectives. Complementary to governance is adjudication. Adjudication is a formal process to resolve conflict or disputes. Adjudication settles differences in interpretation and application of legislation, policies, standards, procedures, mission, strategy, etc.

Governance looks for the IA contribution to the fulfillment of strategic objectives. Executives look for IA contribution to revenue and cost management in terms of the balance sheet and income statement. To speak of IA services or IA mechanisms at the governance level is inappropriate. Rather, speak in strategic terms and financial terms, and how IA contributes, supports, enables, or furthers stakeholder interests.

Management establishes strategies that meet strategic objectives. These strategies take form in strategic plans to implement strategies, tactical objectives (high level), and tactical plans (high level). Management defines the first steps to *operationalize* a strategic idea.

Management regards IA services and IA mechanisms as strategic tools that align with strategic plans in support of strategic objectives. For example, compliance management addresses risks of legal action being taken against the organization. Also, compliance management addresses litigation management to minimize the effects of legal action against the organization. IA contribution to compliance management directly relates to the fulfillment of a strategic objective of cost management, specifically cost avoidance through fines and court costs.

Builders execute to the tactical objectives and tactical plans to meet those objectives for the initial setup of operations. There is a significant difference between builders and operations. Builders set up and hand off to ongoing operations. Both must work together to ensure smooth transition from setup activities to ongoing activities.

Builders need to understand how IA will impact project budget and schedules, and how to integrate IA into the project. Builders need to understand and resolve trade-offs among cost, performance, risk, and schedule. The introduction of IA may reduce risk, but increase cost, lengthen schedule, and reduce performance levels. You need to help builders understand how and why, as well as the benefits of risk reduction and if they are actually worth the trade-offs.

Operations establishes tactical objectives (details) and tactical plans to meet these objectives for ongoing operations. Operations includes activities that support end-user functions. Operations roles may include operations manager, system administrator, engineer, etc. Operations support workflow for the fulfillment of a business function.

Operations need to understand the effects of IA on operations personnel (training, task performance) and on the successful execution of business processes. Operations need to understand how IA affects performance levels of existing systems and applications, format and structure of data and information, and IA's effects on technical and physical infrastructure requirements.

Users is a relative term referring to the consumers of a particular system, capability, product, or service. Users focus on the execution of tasks. Users want to understand what they need to accomplish their tasks effectively. Users do not necessarily look to be aware of or understand IA. They need a certain minimal level of awareness to know what constitutes anomalous behavior or results, and how to report the anomaly to operations via help desk or security operations center. For the most part, users expect IA to be transparent.

A **leader** does not fit neatly into the OCF hierarchy with respect to superior subordinate relationships. There are leaders at every level of governance, management, builders, operations, and users. Leaders are the action-oriented champions that drive progress. The point of this distinction is twofold. First, no framework within this book is or claims to be exhaustive. There are always exceptions, modifications, additions, and detractions to fit your particular circumstance. Second, the distinction of leader is an important one to make in context of the OCF; these are the people to engage to get things done at whatever organizational level they reside.

Leaders look to IA for potential contributions to innovate, to initiate and manage organizational change, and empowerment for organizational action. More importantly to you, if leaders understand IA, they will be more likely to champion IA as part of innovation and organizational change.

5.3.1 OCF Layer Relationships

Understanding the OCF layer relationships helps you to discern what each is looking for in IA solutions and IA contributions to enterprise solutions. Tables 5.1 and 5.2 present OCF in relation to the simple system framework of input, process, and output to show the OCF layer relationships in planning and implementation. The outputs of each layer provide direction or value to the other organizational layers. The inputs illustrate how information flows between the layers, and creates dependencies upon which each layer's process in planning and implementation must rely.

Table 5.1 presents OCF layer relationships in terms of planning and implementation, which is more a top-down flow.

Table 5.2 provides an OCF layer view of tracking and reporting relationships (more a bottom-up flow). The planning and implementation view starts with governance and flows down to operations and users. Users perform tasks that ultimately fulfill the organization's mission. In contrast, tracking and reporting starts with user and operations and flows up to governance to convey the level of success in mission fulfillment from the lowest level of detail through to executive summaries.

The remainder of the sections present the use of the organizational views for the governance of IA, management of IA, and operations of IA.

5.4 Governance and IA

Business drives technology. Business risk drives IA. IA² provides a method to identify, enumerate, articulate, and address risk. Risk governance includes decisions for risk mitigation, risk sharing, risk transference, and risk acceptance. Risk governance is the authoritative direction or control of risk management. Risk management is the execution of the organizational directives. The risk governance process

Table 5.1 OCF Layer Relationships (Planning and Implementation)

Systemic → /OCF Layer	Input to OCF Layer	OCF Layer Process	Output from OCF Layer
Governance	Business drivers, organizational mission, compliance requirements	Review business drivers with respect to the core reasons that the organization exists.	Strategic objectives, policy
Management	Outputs from governance	Convert strategic objectives into strategic plans and tactical objectives.	Strategic plans, high-level tactical objectives, high-level tactical plans, budgets, timelines, target capabilities/functions
Builders	Outputs from management	Convert tactical objectives into tactical plans to create.	Tactical plans (to create local or enterprise solutions)
Operations	Transition from builders	Convert tactical objectives into tactical plans to operate and maintain.	Tactical plans (to operate and maintain solutions)
Users	Business needs in terms of executing tasks to fulfill the organizational mission	Business functions, workflow	Mission fulfillment; generate products and services that are the core reasons the organization exists
Leaders	From any OCF layer	Innovate, support, question, facilitate, find answers, challenge status quo	Anywhere and everywhere

Table 5.2   OCF Layer Relationships (Tracking and Reporting)

Systemic → /OCF Layer	Input to OCF Layer	OCF Layer Process	Output from OCF Layer
Users	The user experience in using products and services to fulfill the organizational mission	Users execute tasks using operations, services, and mechanisms as built to the direction of management.	Users provide feedback (report) to operations on the effectiveness of operations, services, and mechanisms.
Operations	Operations take user feedback in the form of surveys, trouble tickets, or unsolicited input. Operations also track performance levels like availability, uptime, mean time between failures (MTBF), SLA parameters, SLAs met and unmet.	Operations gather the input from various sources and compile operational performance reports to management.	Performance reports to management; feedback to builders
Builders	Feedback from operations; lessons learned from project experience	Compile lessons learned; generate options and recommendations to improve the building process.	Report to management as input to subsequent strategic planning.
Management	Reports from operations and builders	Evaluate performance reports in terms of satisfying strategic plans and relationship to strategic objectives.	Performance reports in terms of strategic plans and status of fulfilling strategic objectives
Governance	Accept reports from management throughout the enterprise.	Evaluate performance in terms of business drivers, mission, and strategic objectives.	Compile management reports into enterprise performance reports with meaning to stakeholders (shareholders, voters/ constituents, owners).

produces strategic objectives for risk management. Therefore, executives in governance roles need to be aware of and understand risks to the organization to deal with them effectively. A key question is which assets are the highest priority for risk mitigation. The answer comes from a combination of a threat assessment, risk assessment, vulnerability assessment, and a business impact assessment.

A **risk assessment** determines the rate or amount of possible loss or injury to the organization. A **vulnerability assessment** identifies vulnerabilities within people, policy, process, systems/applications, data/information, and infrastructure and determines the degree of harm those vulnerabilities present to the organization. A **threat probability assessment** determines the highest probable threats. (Vulnerabilities may exist with no threat to exploit them.) A target probability assessment determines the highest probable targets. A **business impact assessment** (BIA) determines the organizational impact of a threat successfully exploiting asset vulnerability.

The combination of assessing risk, vulnerability, threat, and target probabilities along with business impact should lead to intelligent resource allocation decisions for addressing risk (see section 3.4.2.2).

5.4.1   The Scope of Risk Governance, Management, and Assessment

Traditionally, a risk assessment is asset centric. A comprehensive risk assessment also looks at the threat side. An exhaustive analysis of threats is not practical, if even possible. Therefore, you need to separate threats into classifications (Table 5.3), determine threat status (Table 5.4), and then provide rules to handle threat classes and specific threats according to threat status.

The threat classes provide guidance to determine the potential risks to your organization. Physical location provides insight into natural risk exposure, e.g., earthquake, tornado, hurricane, ice storms, or brush fires. The physical location of the data center also provides insight into potential accidents, for instance, at the end of an airport runway, under a freeway exit ramp, or next to a chemical manufacturing plant.

The *contrived* threat class, especially the *contrived—specific* class, includes adversaries. An adversary knows your organization, specifically targets your organization, and operates with intelligence and intent against it. Moreover, threats appearing natural, accidental, or technical may be the result of an intentional act; e.g., the ISP* connection outage may be the result of an adversary-operated fiber-seeking backhoe. Hence, any assessments of threats must be aware that the visible threat may be a symptom and not the threat itself. *Threat status* represents the sense of immediacy to the organization. Table 5.4 presents threat status categories.

---

* Internet service provider.

Table 5.3 Threat Classes

Threat Class	Definition/Examples
Natural	Occurring without the benefit of human intervention; acts of God: hurricane
Accidental	Occurring without specific intent; acts of Clod: open laptops do not make good coasters and are by nature not absorbent; travel accident seriously injures entire C-level team
Contrived—general	Threat to the organization without specific intent to harm the organization: virus, worm infection, laptop stolen during auto theft
Contrived—specific	Attack specifically targeting a business or site: bank robbery, live cyber-attack on network or servers
Technical	Loss of power, power surge; application failure (undocumented feature); hardware failure

Table 5.4 Threat Status

Threat Status	Definition/Examples
No threat	X is a threat so unlikely as to be essentially no threat: magnitude 7 East Coast earthquake
Potential threat	An identified threat with no signs of being a problem: hurricane forming in the Caribbean, failure of northeast power grid
Probable threat	Though not visible, good authority confirms its presence: announcement that terrorists have an interest in exploiting an organization like yours
Imminent threat (priority threat)	A threat that's on the radar: ice storm on the way; new virus disseminating via e-mail technology used by your organization
Active threat or kinetic threat (priority threat)	The threat in action: hurricane rages, real-time cyber-attack

Figure 5.2   P³ approach.

A threat status of *no threat* acknowledges the existence of the threat, but the likelihood of the threat acting against a vulnerability is so low as to be essentially nonexistent. For example, the data center roof is not likely to be meteor-proof. However, the probability of a meteor striking the data center is so low as to not warrant the expense of reinforcing the roof.

Potential threats abound in our everyday lives. There is risk in driving to work with threats from other drivers (fatigued, careless, or distracted). There is risk in using the Internet with threats from spam, viruses, and spyware. Many, many threats are possible; far fewer threats are probable. Figure 5.2 shows the P³ (P-three) approach to identifying the potential, differentiating the potential from the probable, and establishing priorities to deal with the probable. The P³ approach applies to risks, threats, and vulnerabilities.

The collection of potential threats will be quite large. Assessing the probability of their occurrence yields a list of highest probable threats (high priority) to lowest (low/no priority). A threat may affect one or more vulnerabilities within the organizational asset space. Those assets containing vulnerabilities that may be exploited by high-priority threats become high-priority assets for risk mitigation; those assets with the highest business value become top priorities. The following sections elaborate on this concept. The IA² threat probability assessment enables you to distinguish potential threats from probable threats and to establish priorities from the collection of probable threats.

5.4.2   Guiding Risk Analysis with Threat Assessments

5.4.2.1   Threat Probability Assessment

A model for adversary threat probability assessment (TPA) must evaluate adversary capability (*means*); tactical preferences and operations (*method*); leadership, individual psychology, group and social dynamics, and political psychology (*motivations*); and interests and potential objectives (*mission*). These evaluations provide insight into a potential threat versus a probable threat, and a probable threat versus a priority threat.

A known adversary may desire your company's secrets, but if it lacks the knowledge to carry out the espionage activities and lacks the funding to hire the expertise, this known adversary remains a potential threat status and a low probability on the TPA scale. If, however, the adversary has the means (i.e., knowledge or funding) and information on the adversary shows activity toward your company, then known targets of interest or speculative targets of interest in your asset space must move high on your priority list for receiving risk mitigation resources.

Subsequent details regarding threat *durability* (how long the threat may last) provide parameters for calculating the duration of the security safeguards. For example, if a known thief desires a museum's rare diamond, then the threat remains as long as the thief is free and the museum remains in possession of the diamond. If the museum transfers possession of the diamond, the threat refocuses interest on another target, thus freeing up some of the museum's security resources. While the diamond remains at the museum, however, ongoing security resources are necessary and become part of the total cost of the diamond's ownership.

The threat class and threat status assist in determining the appropriate risk management stance, that is, to accept, ignore, share, transfer, or mitigate the risk. To continue with the example, the museum's board may choose to accept the risk of theft. They may choose to share the risk by purchasing an insurance policy. They may transfer the risk by sending the diamond to a security service that guards such valuables and completely accepts liability for its safekeeping. The museum may mitigate the risks by installing a secure display and an alarm system. All expenses to safeguard the diamond become part of the cost of ownership. The price of the diamond may be X; the cost of owning the diamond is X + Y, where Y includes safeguards, storage, and insurance. Indeed, there is a significant difference between *price* and *cost*, where cost is much more than just the purchase price.

Figure 5.3 presents attributes to calculate threat probability. A threat from incidental effects of malware in e-mail is still a risk; however, malware targeted specifically at the organization is a greater risk. Motivation determines if there is a person or group with reason to target your organization specifically. Status determines if the threat is a potential threat (e.g., it is hurricane season, so hurricanes are a potential threat) versus a kinetic threat, which is a threat currently in action (e.g., Hurricane Terri is 12 hours from landfall within 20 miles of the data center).

The likelihood of identifying all these factors with a high degree of certainty is low. However, such a threat probability assessment decomposes threat and permits focus on its specific attributes. The macro perspective of identifying viable threats, their prospective intention, and the organization's vulnerabilities provides guidance to risk assessments to look for the highest business value assets with the vulnerabilities subject to the highest probable threats. This results in intelligent resource allocation for risk mitigation.

Figure 5.4 presents attributes that reflect asset value. An asset may have *intrinsic value*, e.g., money, gold, or jewel; it may have a business value,

Figure 5.3 Threat probability attributes.

based on the business function it provides or the results it produces. The
intrinsic value of the asset may be seven
or eight thousand dollars. However, the
business value of the asset is in terms
of the amount of revenue generation it
supports, which could easily be in the
hundreds of thousands of dollars per
day. *Key assets* have an immediate and
significant effect on revenue or costs. *Support assets*, although still important, do not
have an immediate and significant effect on revenue or costs.

Figure 5.4   Asset value attributes.

Assign risk mitigation resources to risks with the highest combined probabilities
of immediacy and asset value according to the risk priority matrix (Figure 5.5).

Figure 5.5 contains assets A, B, C, and D, each with a degree of vulnerability. The placement of these assets represents the combination of asset value, asset
vulnerability, and threat probability against that asset. For example, asset C is the
main headquarters building. The value of the asset is high in both structure and
land value. The threat probability is relatively low given its location in the suburban
United States. A similar location in an urban Middle East city may have a higher
threat probability because of civil disturbance and civil infrastructure (roads, fire
protection, police protection, water access, etc.). Asset B represents the E-commerce service that generates 40 percent of revenue. The asset's intrinsic value is
moderate but its business value is very high. The organization is well known, there
is public disaffection toward it, and a high probability threat level. Moreover, the

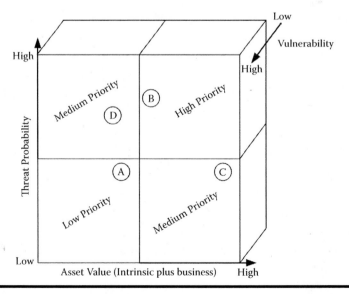

Figure 5.5   Risk priority matrix.

Table 5.5   Cost of Asset Loss and Recovery

Loss	Loss $	Recovery	Recovery $
Asset	Asset book value	Recover cost of recovering stolen asset, e.g., private investigation	
Business loss	Loss revenue, goodwill, customers, trust, stock value	Restore	Cost to restore business function/ operations; cost to restore equipment
Asset	Cost to replace	Replace	Cost to replace equipment

organization competes against companies that may benefit from stealing its intellectual property. These competitors have both private and state-sponsored backing with relatively high means, method, and motivation, again contributing to a high threat probability level.

Table 5.5 provides a framework to calculate cost of asset loss and recovery. Total business impact of loss equals the (asset book value + business loss + cost of recovery + cost of restoration + cost of replacement). When a particular total business loss is zero, good business practice is to record the fact that it is zero and why. This maintains a record of conscious omission of mitigation and avoids any claims to omission by oversight.

5.4.2.2   Intelligent Resource Allocation

Intelligent resource allocation for risk management is the allocation of limited resources (people, equipment, budget, and time) so as to mitigate high-loss risks associated with vulnerabilities in high-probability targets subject to high-probability threats.

The threat probability assessment is a methodology for intelligent resource allocation. The defender against risk cannot equally protect all assets all the time from all threats; therefore, the organization makes informed decisions to protect high-value assets subject to the highest probable threat. Predicting a specific attack on a specific target at a specific time requires explicit intelligence. It is highly improbable to calculate such accuracy from an aggregate assessment of discrete facts. An imminent threat or active threat with known interest in a particular target, or that is highly skilled at exploiting a certain vulnerability, narrows the potential target space considerably.

The risk management process provides a framework to assess threat and target probability; probable targets include personnel, physical, and cyber assets. The process is flexible enough to accommodate corporate espionage, terrorists, kidnappers, and other threats of intelligence and intent. Chapter 13 elaborates on a threat schema and threat taxonomy.

5.4.3 Scope of Control

No amount of planning or investment will provide the organization with complete control over all operational aspects. Therefore, the organization must prepare to deal with aspects over which it has:

- ■ Direct control
- ■ Indirect control
- ■ No control
- ■ Influence
- ■ Control response

When the organization has **direct control** of an asset or process, a risk can be identified, mitigation options examined, risk management measures implemented, and operational adjustments made. Now consider that your organization provides 95 percent of Company Y's revenue, and a risk in Company Y has been identified. Your organization has **indirect control** over Company Y's mitigation efforts. Your organization has **no control** over electrical power supply interruptions due to natural events.

However, your organization may be able to **influence** its place on the power company's power restoration priority list, thus limiting operational losses and reducing expensive investments in power generators. Similarly, the importance of your revenue to Company Y may give you a level of influence in that company's approach to mitigating risk that may affect your organization.

This also exemplifies an organization's ability to **control its response** to situations over which it has no control. Perhaps it cannot control loss of power, but it can control its response; choices include risk acceptance (*we're out of power so send everyone home*) or risk mitigation through installing UPS (*we can control our response to a loss of power by supplying our own power for a time*).

The point is to be aware of scope of control during the architectural process and address risk governance and risk management from the proper perspective. Assign accountability for risk mitigation appropriately and set expectations that although not all risk management is under direct control, the organization does control its response to risks.

5.4.4 E-Insurance

Chief executive officers (CEOs) make investments in risk management, not security. Risk management options include risk acceptance, mitigate risk, share risk, or

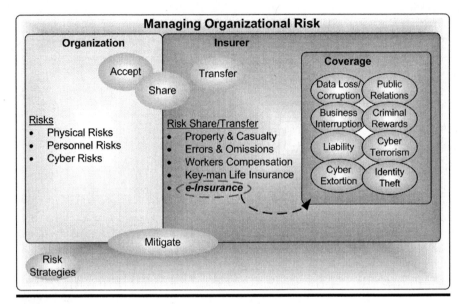

Figure 5.6   E-insurance as an organizational risk management tool.

transfer risk. Insurance provides one avenue of risk sharing or risk transference; E-insurance is one insurance option. E-insurance coverage is a specialized insurance policy that the insurer tailors to the specific needs of a company. The underwriting process considers the technology in use and the level of risk involved.

Figure 5.6 provides a perspective of E-insurance both with respect to managing organizational risk and in context of other insurance coverage. Given any significant investment or dependency on E-business or technical infrastructure, consideration of E-insurance falls squarely under the responsibilities of managerial due diligence. Table 5.6 presents some E-insurance coverage options.*

The business case for E-insurance boils down to money; how much of the risk management budget goes to risk mitigation versus risk sharing. Consider the following example:

Assume a hypothetical total risk of $500 million and a premium cost of $5 million for risk *transference* to an insurance company. As an alternative to risk transference, consider that an annual risk mitigation investment of $3 million results in residual risk of $100 million. The risk transference of $100 million may cost $1 million in annual premium; there is already an annual savings of $1 million for a blended solution of risk mitigation and risk transference. Further, consider that risk *sharing* of $50 million may cost $500K in annual premium. If the organization is willing to accept or self-insure the other $50 million, there is a potential annual savings of $1.5 million over pure risk transference. Although these numbers

---

* Excerpts from *Most Companies Have Cyber-Risk Gaps in Their Insurance Cover Coverage* and description of Zurich's E-RiskEdge™ product.

Table 5.6   E-Insurance Coverage Options

Coverage	Description
Loss/corruption of data	Covers damage to or destruction of information assets resulting from viruses, malware, and Trojan horses
Business interruption	Covers loss of business income resulting from an attack on a company's information technology that limits the ability to conduct business
Dependent business interruption	Extends business income loss coverage to vendors of goods and services that are critical to the performance of the insured's E-business activities
Liability	Covers defense costs, settlements, judgments, and sometimes punitive damages incurred by a company as a result of: Breach of privacy due to theft of data (e.g., credit cards, financial, or health-related data); transmission of a computer virus or other liabilities resulting from a computer attack that causes financial loss to third parties (i.e., downstream liability); failure of security that causes network systems to be unavailable to third parties (i.e., loss of use); rendering of Internet professional services; allegations of copyright or trademark infringement, libel, slander, defamation or other "media" activities in the company's Web site
Cyber-extortion	Covers the settlement of an extortion threat against a company's network, as well as the cost of hiring a security firm to track down and negotiate with blackmailers
Public relations	Covers those public relations costs associated with a cyber-attack and restoring of public confidence
Criminal rewards	Covers the cost of posting a criminal reward fund for information leading to the arrest and conviction of the cyber-criminal who attacked the company's computer systems
Cyber-terrorism	Covers those terrorist acts covered by the Terrorism Risk Insurance Act of 2002 and, in some cases, may be further extended to terrorist acts beyond those contemplated in the act

Continued

Table 5.6   E-Insurance Coverage Options (Continued)

Coverage	Description
Identity theft	Provides access to an identity theft call center in the event of stolen customer or employee personal information. Depending on the policy, coverage can apply to both internally and externally launched attacks as well as viruses that are specifically targeted against the insured or widely distributed across the Internet. Premiums can range from a few thousand dollars for base coverage for small businesses (less than $10 million in revenue) to several hundred thousand dollars for major corporations desiring comprehensive coverage.
Intellectual property development costs	Pays the actual cost incurred to restore electronic data or software that has been destroyed or damaged by a loss event

are hypothetical, the options are sound considerations. The bottom line is to use E-insurance as a part of the organizational risk management program, not as an apparent quick fix.

E-insurance plays a role in organization risk management. Appendix K elaborates on the E-insurance concept.

5.5   Management and IA

Managers and executives are constantly challenged to juggle often-conflicting requirements (Figure 5.7) for cost management, revenue generation, profitability, legal requirements, and personal and corporate ethics. All must be balanced to optimize shareholder value, and now the risk of personal liability and the ever-growing uncertainties of a highly competitive world market add to the difficulty of keeping many objects in the air successfully. And in the midst of all this there enters additional uncertainty and risk.

Manager liabilities reside under:

■ Law
  – Legally defined liabilities with sanctions including fines and jail time
■ Economics
  – Due diligence and due care to stakeholders, e.g., shareholders; failure of such obligation may result in personal suits over negligence or fraud.
  – Attaining financial objectives

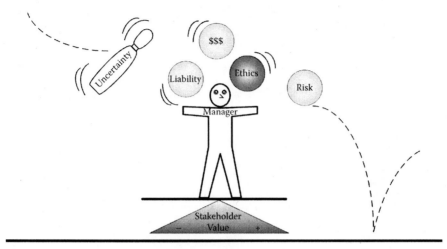

Figure 5.7 Manager responsibility juggling.

- Ethical codes
  - Professional organizations where membership requires adherence to proper behavior
  - Personal integrity and values; personal morality based on faith or religious practice
- Risk
  - Identifying, prioritizing, and determining the best way to address risk, and budgeting

The process of getting to business drivers is a lot like root cause analysis; after weeding through a lot of things that sort of look like what you are after, an educated guess is often as good as it gets. The bottom line for most commercial businesses is money, be it shareholder value, CEO bonus, balance sheet ratios, revenue, or cost management. Information assurance (IA) may align with revenue generation, cost reduction, cost avoidance, or risk management. *Managing business risk* is a key business driver for managers and executives.

A comprehensive business risk management program addresses stakeholder value in terms of risk acceptance, risk mitigation, risk sharing, and risk transference all in context of:

- People (IA² people view)
  - Safety of personnel
  - Security education, training, and awareness (SETA) for personnel for effective management, administration, and use of IA
- Mission (IA² policy view)
  - Define the mission and boundaries for mission integrity.

- Define what constitutes effective operations.
- With respect to each IA² view and the IA core principles
  - Define what constitutes secure operations.
- Process (IA² Process view)
  - Business process.
  - Align information security with business processes.
    - Policies
    - Standards
    - Procedures
  - Reflect external compliance requirements including legislation (e.g., HIPAA) and regulation (e.g., SEC).
  - Support mission integrity.
  - Disseminate policies, standards, and procedures to employees.
  - Track breadth and effectiveness of dissemination.
    - Ensure the message reaches the appropriate audience.
    - Ensure the audience understands the message and complies.
- Assets (IA² views for systems and applications, data and information, and infrastructure)
  - Physical assets
  - Virtual assets
  - Intellectual property
    - Patents, trademarks, copyrights, proprietary

The following sections provide examples of employment practices as part of the IA² people view and compliance management as part of the IA² policy view.

5.5.1 Employment Practices and Policies

The IA² Process evaluates the existence and adequacy of employment practices and policies from the following perspectives:

- Due diligence requirements
  - Perform background checks.
  - Special care in hiring workers dealing with the public.
  - Identify and isolate/terminate problem employees immediately.
- Corporate liability
  - *Respondeat superior*; an employer is legally liable for employee actions if the employee is acting under the course and scope of employment.*
  - Careless hiring and retention.

---

* *Employer Liability for an Employee's Bad Acts*, Nolo (www.nolo.com; last accessed July 2007).

- Cost management
  - Hiring people of probable high ethics (or at least an absence of a felonious background) results in less theft, internal threats, higher customer satisfaction, and an all-around good atmosphere that promotes fewer turnovers.

IA architecture consideration of employment practices and policies includes:

- Pre-employment
- Post-employment
- Employee monitoring
- Employee evaluation criteria
- Employee termination
- Employee references

5.5.1.1 Pre-Employment

Considerations for pre-employment practices include background checks (e.g., criminal, credit, references). The extent of such checks depends on position responsibility and exposure to corporate secrets and intellectual property. Also, include resume evaluation and verification of experience, education, certification, or other professional claims. Hold phone and in-person interviews and judge the person's fit with respect to position requirements, corporate culture, and social dynamics. Provide for a trial period of mutual evaluation. Discuss potential post-employment activities and determine the applicant's sensitivity to further investigation into his or her background and personal life.

In-house background checks may include verification of U.S. citizenry and credit check; however, these are not in all cases. Any incidents of fraud, false identity claims, or not possessing the academic or professional credentials and experience claimed should result in immediate termination.

5.5.1.2 Post-Employment

Post-employment practices include revocation of user identifications, identification cards, and all privileges that include physical access and access to information and information technology.

5.5.1.3 Employee Monitoring

IA architecture plans include the possibility of employee monitoring in security policies. Employee monitoring policy, services, and mechanics are organization and job dependent and extend from keystroke capture and security cameras to monitoring personal activity like international travel and contact with foreign nationals.

5.5.1.4 Employee Evaluation

IA policy compliance, ethical behavior, and other IA-related activities should be included in employee evaluations and contribute to determining promotions and raises. This is a strong message to employees, promotes compliance with corporate policy, and drives appropriate behavior.

5.5.1.5 Employee Termination

The IA architecture addresses employee termination: how, when, situations of notice versus escorts out the door, account termination, repossession of identification badges, access keys, and organizational property.

5.5.1.6 Employee References

Although not an IA issue, corporate policy should address how future references are given (or not) for former employees.

5.5.1.7 Commentary

Short of a world consisting of angels of the first order, there is need to provide for pre-employment, post-employment, monitoring, and evaluation of employees to protect organizational interests such as intellectual property, customer relations and satisfaction, and general employee safety.

5.5.2 Compliance Management Program

One management responsibility is to identify relevant compliance requirements (e.g., legislation) for the organization. Subsequent to identification is the need to reflect these compliance requirements in organizational policy, disseminate the policies, and ensure these policies are read and understood and that employees adhere to them—hence the need for a *compliance management program*. The IA architect may assist greatly with this endeavor through a formal methodology and formal documentation. Like any other aspect of security, compliance management is a process, not a destination; therefore, initial implementation of a compliance management program precedes an operations and maintenance phase.

Business drivers behind compliance management include legislative drivers; thou shall comply to stay in business, out of jail, and avoid fines. Other drivers include management responsibilities and liabilities, due diligence, litigation management, and responsibility to stakeholders (e.g., shareholders). A compliance management program consists of:

- Compliance assessment process
    - E.g., Health Insurance Portability and Accountability Act (HIPAA)
- Security policies
- Dissemination
- Awareness and understanding tracking
- Compliance monitoring
- Results reporting

This section provides details for one aspect of business risk management—legislative drivers; note that legislation is only one driver behind a compliance management program. The compliance management program establishes policy to guide business operations and provides for policy dissemination, managing awareness and understanding, tracking, monitoring, and reporting. The next challenge is to select, implement, and maintain the appropriate services and mechanisms to execute and enforce policy.

Legislation like Sarbanes–Oxley and the Health Insurance Portability and Accountability Act (HIPAA) drive a lot of information assurance activity in public companies and the health care industry, respectively. Additionally, there is a greater and increasing need today to justify IA spending as a valid and valuable business investment. Such a need requires formal alignment of IA with business operations and business drivers, one aspect of the latter being external compliance requirements (e.g., legislation)—hence the need for a compliance management program, an overview of which Figure 5.8 provides.

Drivers behind a compliance management program (CMP) include management responsibilities and liabilities. The CMP includes a compliance assessment process (CAP); a specific instance of a CAP may be for the Health Insurance Portability and Accountability Act (HIPAA). The CAP addresses a current snapshot of policy versus compliance requirement. Remediation efforts to close gaps in policy include the generation or enhancement of security policies. The remainder of this section provides further details on management responsibilities and liabilities, the compliance assessment process, and security policies.

5.5.2.1 Compliance Assessment Process

The compliance assessment process provides a formal and quantified method to discern organizational compliance levels. The assessment is a security service that aligns with the business driver of managing business risk. The results of the compliance assessment produce results useful for operations managers, system admin-

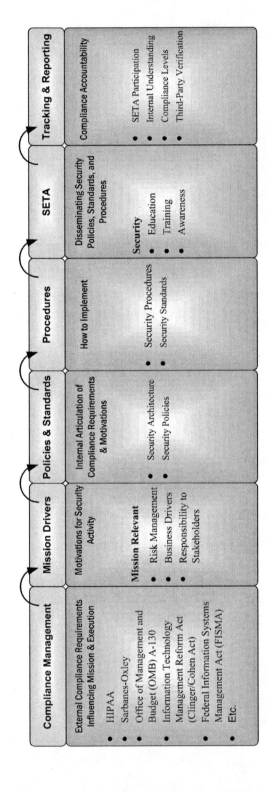

Figure 5.8 Compliance management program overview.

istrators, and network administrators. The gap analysis and remediation analysis provide insight into weak areas. Moreover, the compliance assessment results may provide insight into intelligent resource allocations to produce the highest return on investment (ROI) for remediation investments. This phrase addresses management and executives who are not interested in the specifics of firewall updates or patch management; they are interested in how much remediation is going to cost and what the effect is on business risk. Compliance quantification goes a long way in providing this answer at the enterprise level.

5.5.2.2 Security Policies

The Organization for Economic Co-operation and Development's (OECD) *OECD Guidelines for the Security of Information Systems and Networks* provides nine principles for participants at all levels in the use of information systems (Table 5.7).*

As a complement to compliance managements, consider the concept of litigation management. The intent of compliance management is to *avoid* litigation. Compliance management identifies applicable legislation and works through increasing compliance with that legislation. Even the best preparations still result in incidents that end up in court. Litigation management attempts to minimize the risks of the organization being found guilty as well as minimizing their culpability in the event they are found guilty. The lower the culpability, the lower the potential fines and potential jail time for officers. Chapter 8 of the Federal Sentencing Guidelines, "Sentencing of Organizations," contains guidelines on culpability calculations. Two major factors in calculating culpability are the presence and quality of an ethics program and the presence and quality of a security program. The *Norwich University Journal of Information Assurance* (NUJIA) contains a paper "Litigation Management as Part of a Comprehensive Compliance Management Program" (http://nujia.norwich.edu/2_1/2_1_art02.html†) with more details on this subject.

5.6 Builders and IA

Builders create. IA² provides many tools for builders and provides insight on how to create tools for organization-specific solutions. Chapters 8 and 9 offer many insights and tools for builders of IA solutions.

---

* *OECD Guidelines for the Security of Information Systems and Networks*, pp.10–12.
† Last accessed July 2007.

Table 5.7 OECD Policy Development Principles

Principle	Description
Awareness	Participants should be aware of the need for security of information systems and networks and what they can do to enhance security.
Responsibility	All participants are responsible for the security of information systems and networks.
Response	Participants should act in a timely and cooperative manner to prevent, detect, and respond to security incidents.
Ethics	Participants should respect the legitimate interests of others.
Democracy	The security of information systems and networks should be compatible with essential values of a democratic society.
Risk assessment	Participants should conduct risk assessment.
Security design and implementation	Participants should incorporate security as an essential element of information systems and networks.
Security management	Participants should adopt a comprehensive approach to security management.
Reassessment	Participants should review and reassess the security of information systems and networks, and make appropriate modifications to security policies, practices, measures, and procedures.

5.7 Operations and IA

IA builders turn over solutions to operations via a *transition* process. There is a vast difference between *dump-and-run* and *transition*. Dump-and-run (a more typical handover tactic between builders and operators) often leaves operations wondering: *What is this? What's it for? What's the business intent? This is not what we expected.* Generally, the development budget has run out and the builders are long gone, with operations left to figure everything out for themselves—or not. Many times a good solution (or what could be a good solution) is left unused or underused because the operations group is unsure of where and how to use it most effectively.

In contrast, transition engages operations early in the building process. At best, the operations group provides some insight to how the application should work. At the least, operations is informed during the development process as to the intent, function, business fit, and nuances of the application. Moreover, operations takes part in implementation, pilot, and deployment so when it comes time for a full turnover, operations understands the application, the benefit to the organization, and how to administer it effectively. Chapters 8 and 9 offer many insights and tools for IA operations, including insights into what questions to ask of builders to ensure a smooth transition. Moreover, some of the leadership IA tools in section 5.9 apply to operations, including professional development, vendor relations, and problem solving.

5.8   Users and IA

Users are the first line of defense and monitoring. The user base has the most eyes and ears and is more acutely in tune with how operations are going. User awareness of security, the ability to detect anomalies and escalate them to a help desk or security operations center, is essential. However, users should be aware of only what they need to know. This is not due to secrecy, political territoriality, or technical snobbery. This is so that IA will not become a distraction. The technical aspects of IA should be transparent to the user.

5.9   Leadership and IA

The true IA professional transcends the über-geek persona and provides holistic thought to add business value; these are the *leaders* in IA. Leadership skills apply to intrateam relations, interteam relations, as well as representing ideas to management, executives, and customers. The IA architect may provide leadership guidance to employees in strategic values that include integrity, respect, accountability, passion for excellence, customer centric, and innovation. Skill in each is critical to championing organizational information assurance. The IA champion's position is often solitary, and the enemy the IA architect sees clearly is often invisible to others. While industry tolerance for the quixotic is low, sometimes the IA professional must point out that the windmill everyone else sees is indeed a well-disguised dragon.

IA leadership tools assist the IA architect in considering the holistic IA^2 view. Traditionally, deference to technology first and business concerns second minimized or ignored consideration of the people factor. The mantra of the IA^2 professional is: *Executives and managers do not buy security; they buy business risk management solutions.* The tighter the alignment with IA services and mechanisms to business operations, the higher the ROI. Further, the tighter the alignment between IA solutions and people, the more effective are the IA solutions. The IA leadership tools include:

- Personal development

- Championing IA outside the IA arena
- Perception management
- Ethical decision making
- Vendor relations
- Problem solving

5.9.1 Personal Development

Addressing how to maintain a qualified IA workforce is part of the IA architecture. The IA[2] Framework provides six IA[2] views, one of which is *people*. The IA[2] people view addresses individual psychology, ethics, group dynamics, politics, and professional development, including the continual development of IA professionals within the organization. Security is dynamic. Successful IA programs require continually improving IA professionals under the guidance of an IA professional development program.

Business drivers behind an IA professional development program include enticing quality people to join the organization. One way to hire and keep quality IA people is to keep them engaged in enterprise activities, exposed to current industry trends and practices, and to train them. Strategic business objectives drive technology; both business and technical risk drive IA. An IA professional development program includes business, services, and technical mechanisms all in the name of identifying and resolving organizational risk. The organization puts forth the expense of hiring the best available; they should invest in keeping them the best to keep them at all.

A good story of IA professional development may carry the title "The Never-Ending Story." Take personal responsibility for your own education and encourage other IA professionals to do the same. Supplement core knowledge with readings in classical thought, philosophy, psychology, business, finance, your industry, etc. Such readings provoke new perspectives, increase personal knowledge, and spark ideas to contribute to industry knowledge. Adopt learning maxims like the following:

- "I am still learning." —Michelangelo
- "Always work hard. Always improve. If your current employer isn't willing to pay you what you're worth, your next one will." —Zig Ziglar
- "Even when walking in the company of two other men, I am bound to be able to learn from them. The good points of the one I copy; the bad points of the other I correct in myself." —Confucius
- "It's what you learn after you know it all that really counts." —Harry Truman (advice to college students who seem to think they know it all)
- "If you think education is expensive, try ignorance." —Derek Bok

5.9.2 Championing IA Outside the IA Environment

To be an IA champion takes broad shoulders, diplomacy, tenacity, and a bit of ornery heel digging. Many practitioners like enterprise architects, system architects, project managers, business line managers, and executives do not see the need for information assurance; these people need a lot of selling and education.

The FUD factor* is not appropriate in IA leadership, nor is "the sky is falling" approach. Successful IA marketing delivers IA in small, digestible chunks all positioned in terms of business benefit. For example, the enterprise architect will relate well to the abstract visions of as-is, to-be, and transition states. Approaching the EA with technical details about a wonderful new IDS product or firewall is not appropriate. These are solutions to a would-be problem yet to be discerned or defined. Going to the EA with an IA architectural plan showing an IA² Framework and how to develop hooks into their to-be architecture presents useful information in terms they are looking for.

5.9.3 Perception Management

Information assurance is a relatively unknown term. When IA is rephrased as *computer security*, a knowing nod still gives way to a glazed stare of misunderstanding. When faced with difficult business questions of IA justification, IA professionals often turn to ever-deeper technical explanations, configurations, and reports. That approach often widens the gaps of communication, understanding, and credibility. The IA architect must communicate the IA story in terms readily understandable and embraced by the audience, the project manager, customer, management, and executives whose interests lie in investment, return on that investment, and shareholder value, not the technical nuances of the latest IA wonder-widget.

5.9.3.1 Accommodate the People Factor in IA Perception

Perception management is the reason for distinguishing among governance, management, operations, and users; the architect must create the right message delivery for the right audience. Communicate with people in terms they understand and want to hear. For example, the CxO interests in IA are project investment, ROI, internal rate of return (IRR) to hurdle rate comparison, market share, effect on revenue per employee, cost of doing business, and aligning IA with a larger effort and justification as part of overall cost of doing business. The bottom-line justification is shareholder value in the private sector and constituent value in the public sector.

---

* Fear, uncertainty, and doubt.

5.9.4   Ethical Decision Making

The IA[2] Process identifies the existence and adequacy of organizational ethics programs. *Compliance management* attempts to avoid litigation by formally identifying legislative requirements and managing organizational adherence to legislation. *Litigation management* attempts to minimize organizational impact of an incident where the organization is found guilty of a legislative violation. For example, the U.S. Federal Sentencing Guidelines Chapter 8 Sentencing of Organizations looks for the presence and quality of an ethics program as part of calculating the degree of organizational culpability. The presence of a quality ethics program reduces culpability which in turn equates to a lesser fine and lesser opportunity for officer jail time.

One driver behind an organizational ethics program is legislative compliance. For example, the Sarbanes–Oxley (SOX) Act of 2002 addresses the need for ethics rules and standards of conduct for board members and executives. Another justification is *litigation management*, where the presence of an ethics program reduces organizational culpability in the event of an incident going before a judge. Similar to the approach for SETA, the IA professional may work with other parts of the organization (e.g., HR and legal) to determine a baseline requirement for organizational ethics, derive the appropriate ethics messages, and devise an ethics dissemination program that includes acknowledgment of reading, understanding, and compliance.

5.9.4.1   The Ethics Message

Driving behavior toward highly ethical actions requires an environment that communicates and fosters ethics. Proper behavior from the top down and strong messages of intolerance for inappropriate behavior go a long way in promoting ethical behavior. Establishing an ethical standard, writing and disseminating ethics policies, is one thing; enforcing ethics policies is another. Higher education has little tolerance for plagiarism, and an enforcement policy includes suspension or even expulsion. Peer pressure from hardworking students also plays a factor in social acceptance and dealing with others as academic peers. Similarly, organization culture should promote ethical behavior as a criterion for acceptance into the organization and maintaining the individual as a contributing member.

Without a solid foundation of personal as well as corporate ethics, ethical appeals in any context roll off individuals like waves off a jetty. The diminishing focus of public education on ethics and the constant bombardment of the media on antiethical behavior (e.g., reality show du jour) have provided the workforce with many individuals who lack exposure to ethical behavior. Therefore, do not rely exclusively on altruistic motivation to ensure security policy enforcement—*trust, but verify.*

Ethics in technology is an instantiation of this broader ethical framework. Professional societies need to establish and enforce ethical compliance for their members; a good example is (ISC)²®. The goal is to present the existence of ethical models and their implications to professional conduct. Raising awareness is certainly an excellent step toward broader acceptance of and compliance with ethical precepts.

Is all this the responsibility of the IA architect? It is, in the sense that IA^2 does provide insight into ethical considerations and challenges of policy adherence and compliance management. Too often IA and security measures are viewed as invasive, snooping, and big brother incarnate. IA can, however, be presented as an ethical approach to conducting business. Ethics creates a standard for behavior. If a person believes he has a right to do as he wishes, steal what he wants, and generally use others to get ahead, this creates a difficult environment for the organization to operate securely and poses extreme challenges for the IA professional. Insider threats are real threats; they can be far more insidious than a direct outside attack. An ethics program is part of preempting the insider threat.

5.9.5 Vendor Relations

5.9.5.1 Vendor Roles in the IA

One of the first questions in implementing IA is buy versus build and in-house versus outsource. Is the right talent available? Can that talent be hired? Is that talent affordable? Is it worth diverting focus from core competencies to run IA in-house? These are just a few of the pertinent questions in the buy versus build scenario. There are many excellent IA COTS* products, a far less expensive and complex option than building.

When decomposing the IA implementation process, consider the following needs: IA architecture, design, installation, configuration, compliance verification, training, and operations and maintenance (O&M). Further, consider the in-house talent and tolerance to handle any or all these tasks. Outsourcing to a managed security service provider (MSSP) may produce a better IA outcome.

5.9.5.2 Vendor and Product Selection

Vendor and product selection evaluates both the technology (the product as a viable solution) and the organization (the vendor as a viable company). Organization considerations include sales and service; local, regional, national, and international presence; number of people; years in business; long-term viability that includes appropriate financing; and more. Evaluating the organization determines if it is able to provide the level of service necessary for implementation, maintenance, patches, upgrades, and new releases. Technical considerations include product features, both breadth and depth. Looking at product feature breadth (horizontal features) examines the number of features and the relative importance of those features to

---

* Common-off-the-shelf solutions (COTS).

your organization. Feature depth examines the characteristics of each horizontal feature and if there is an adequate level of customization by way of parameters or other configuration settings.

Business requirements drive vendor and product selections. The IA^2 LoS (chapter 2) presents a series of links from architectural drivers through product and vendor selection to operations and maintenance. Business drivers describe a desired capability and performance level in terms of user productivity. Technical drivers also play a role in vendor and product selection. An enterprise systems engineering plan may provide technical standards with the intent of providing overall enterprise interoperability. These technical standards may describe functionality and leave the product selection up to the project team so long as the product meets minimal functionality standards. The technical standards may list a series of products to select from; this limits project team's options. The technical standards may specify a particular product with the intent of technical interoperability as well as a central purchase agreement that leverages enterprisewide licensing. All of these are perfectly valid approaches that satisfy varying business objectives.

5.9.6 Problem Solving

When things go right and when things go awry, understanding *why* in both cases is good business practice. A forward-looking organization must capture success and failure and use the lessons from both in a continual optimization scheme for business, technical, and IA performance.

5.9.6.1 When Things Go Right

The IA organization monitors activities, log files, audit reports, detected probes, and vulnerability analyses, and captures the results in effectiveness metrics. It then compiles and formats concise operational reports and presents them to management and executives on a regular basis. The IA organization sells, markets, trumpets, heralds, or otherwise informs the rest of the organization when they are doing things right because it will surely be evident when things go awry.

Successful IA operations does not imply absence of attacks; rather, successful IA operations implies user transparency in the event of attacks, and minimal operational interruption. Understanding *out of sight, out of mind* and referring back to organizational psychology, there is an opportunity in reporting IA problem solving; hence, when things go awry, find out why.

5.9.6.2 When Things Go Awry

IA complexities require a formal problem-solving structure that includes problem-solving services, a toolkit, philosophies, and processes. Easier, more common problems may warrant resolution within the standard IA operating process; that is, attention to capturing details, but no extra effort beyond good operational practice already in place. Problems that are more complex may warrant setting up a problem resolution team. The goals of the team are to discover the root cause of the problem via a formal root cause analysis (RCA), identify potential solutions, choose a solution with the best systemic fit, participate in solution implementation, verify improvement and enterprise effect, and identify and disseminate lessons learned. An RCA repository provides quick reference for problem recurrence and promotes organizational learning. If one team has identified and proven a solution, other teams should first seek solutions from the RCA repository.

5.9.6.3 Problem-Solving Influence on IA² F

Problem-solving teams and the RCA process are part of the IA operations cycle: anticipate, defend, monitor, and respond. Responses include problem identification, isolation, treatment, and resolution. Formalizing the process provides feedback into anticipatory, defense, and monitor phases. The objective of an RCA is to stop the problem from recurring or at least minimize operational effects of recurrence.

IA problems can be quite complex, with multiple symptoms leading to causes from many different directions; when the whole is too daunting, divide and conquer. When faced with a daunting IA problem, use a formal decomposition to divide the environment into manageable parts. Appendix H provides a guideline and template for a root cause analysis that assists in this decomposition.

5.10   Commentary and Conclusion

Life offers no ultimate safety except in the ultimate end (Figure 5.9). The best risk minimization approach is to identify highly probable threats, targets, assets, and asset vulnerabilities supporting critical business functions; the results drive appropriate business continuity actions and security resources to satisfy recovery time objectives (RTOs), downtime tolerances, and loss tolerances.

Information assurance is traditionally a technology bolt-on and business process afterthought; IA is far more effective when *integrated from inception*, not a post-implementation forced fit. IA needs to be an integral part of the enterprise architecture, systems architecture, business process, technical development, administrative policies, and operations. Deliver the IA message to the

Rest in Peace
Risk is Past

Figure 5.9   Risk is past (RIP).

organization in terms they understand using the OCF as organizational views on expectations from IA. Also, use the OCF organizational views as guidance to perform IA integration, governance, management, development, and operations.

Chapter 6

IA Business Drivers

6.1 Introduction

No book may tell you what the business drivers are for your organization. Only you can determine that. However, *Information Assurance Architecture* can help you determine what your business drivers are. *IA requirements engineering* is a formal, repeatable approach to record and track what is necessary to address risks associated with a project or with the enterprise depending on the scope of the effort. IA requirements engineering applies the IA² Process and draws upon the IA² Framework and other frameworks to decompose the larger problem into manageable pieces.

Business need drives the need for technology. Business risk drives the need for IA. IA requirements engineering looks at the business need and the technology to satisfy that need, identifies the risks, and aligns IA solutions to address those risks. We will look at IA requirements engineering from the perspectives of compliance management and systems engineering.

Compliance management deals with sources of business drivers and decomposes those sources into requirement statements that are actionable, traceable, and provable. **Systems engineering** focuses more on the solution requirements and providing traceability to business drivers. Compliance management is more broadly focused on the enterprise, whereas systems engineering is more deeply focused on the solution.

Formally defining requirements is an iterative process. You may receive business requirements in words that express a high-level desire; e.g., *to better manage production, inventory, and shipping schedules, we want the ability to obtain customer purchase information in real-time.* To begin to understand the organizational implications to business functions, workflow, tasks, systems, subsystems, and components, there is need to decompose this high-level requirement into manageable and understandable pieces—pieces that have meaning to day-to-day operations. The stated requirement in the example above is at least in business terms. At times, you will receive requirements from the business side in technical terms; e.g., *to better manage production, inventory, and shipping schedules, we want a database of customer purchases.* In this case, the iterative process for decomposing the requirement starts with asking the requestor to restate their requirement in business terms. Perhaps a database is the right solution and perhaps not, and there may be much more needed than just a database. That determination follows understanding the business need.

You may receive business requirements in terms of "we need to comply with Sarbanes–Oxley." Approaching this requires decomposition of the legislation into requirement statements. Subsequent requirements for modifying the organizational operating environment, workflow, and systems will all trace to one or more of these legislative requirement statements.

6.2 Objectives

The objective of this chapter is to present IA requirements engineering as another tool in the IA² toolkit. The material in this chapter will enable you to determine, align, record, and track business drivers behind IA solutions.

6.3 IA Requirements Engineering and Compliance Management

Every business driver may be articulated as a compliance requirement. A comprehensive compliance management program addresses all organizational requirements, including legislation, regulation, directives, instructions, codes, mission, stakeholder objectives, policies, standards, procedures, etc. *IA compliance management identifies all compliance requirements that dictate the organization's IA posture.* Compliance requirements include those external and internal to the organization. External requirements are those imposed upon the organization by sources outside the organization, like regulatory bodies, national laws, and local codes. Internal requirements are self-generated or self-imposed to guide organizational behavior and include a mission statement, policies expressing organizational behavior, standards to express what to use to implement and enforce policies, and procedures to express how to use the standards. All of these compliance requirements are candidates for business drivers.

Although all are candidates for business drivers, you need to discern which apply to the problem at hand. Moreover, any given compliance source may apply in its entirety, or only part of any single compliance source may apply. Requirements engineering identifies all relevant sources, decomposes the relevant sources into compliance requirement statements, then uses these as justification for technical specifications and IA specifications.

A Compliance Management Framework consists of the following:

- External
  - Explicit
    - Legislation, regulation, codes of conduct
  - Implicit
    - Derived from explicit requirement statements
- Internal
  - Explicit
    - Self-generated
      - Internal policies, standards, and procedures
    - Self-imposed
      - Industry standards like ISO 27001 and ISO 27002
  - Implicit
    - Derived from internal requirements

The **compliance management process** includes *discovery*, *decomposition*, *analysis*, *tracking*, and *reporting* of compliance requirements. The compliance management process discovers the requirements, decomposes them into requirement statements meaningful to the organization, analyzes them for intent and implications, tracks dissemination of requirements to appropriate areas throughout the enterprise, and reports awareness, understanding, and actual compliance levels. The *IA compliance management process* is the integration of IA into the discovery, decomposition, analysis, tracking, and reporting of compliance requirements.

A **compliance assessment process** evaluates the current posture of the organization against the compliance requirements. The assessment process discovers the current posture of the organization, compares the current posture against the compliance requirements, analyzes the gaps and how to address the gaps, and produces reports of the findings and recommendations for gap closure. The *IA compliance assessment process* is the integration of IA into discovery, comparison, analysis, findings, and recommendations as part of an overall compliance assessment.

IA compliance management thus far means the *integration of IA* into the broader compliance management program. That is, IA integrates into the business solution not as IA itself, but as modifications to the business solution to address the risks. For example, moving a fax machine that receives medical supply orders from a public area to a closed office addresses one aspect of privacy with respect to the health industry. This simple modification does not introduce an IA solution, but rather modifies the existing work environment to address an IA issue.

Another completely appropriate approach is to isolate IA and treat IA compliance management as a separate set of requirements from the broader compliance management program. When to integrate and when to treat separately is up to you and the business situation at hand. For example, the building of an IA service (e.g., computer security incident response center [CSIRC]) is an IA-centric effort. The CSIRC service integrates into the larger enterprise. However, the requirements for a CSIRC are largely IA requirements.

6.3.1 IA Compliance Requirements Engineering

There are similarities in the form and flow of compliance requirements engineering and SE requirements engineering. Both deal with motivations from outside the organization and inside the organization. Both capture business drivers in the form of requirements, but compliance requirements are produced at a broader enterprise perspective (e.g., legislation), while SE requirements are produced at a deeper project-focus perspective (e.g., capability, product, or service). Both document the following:

- Requirements hierarchy
- Requirements traceability
- To-be vision
- As-is snapshot
- Gap analysis
- Remediation analysis
- Transition plan

A formal IA requirements hierarchy documents the alignment of business and technical drivers with IA requirements. It records and tracks both initial and ongoing business justification for IA. It also documents the traceability of the IA services and IA mechanisms to the business requirements and business risks that motivated them.

As presented in chapter 3, the IA^2 Process consists of eight steps: intent, environment, scope, inputs, discover, analyze, outputs, and production. In terms of IA compliance requirements, *intent* means identifying what compliance requirements are applicable, differentiating external and internal IA requirements, and differentiating explicit and implicit IA requirements. The nature of the requirements will provide guidance on how IA is further influenced by the *environment*. For instance, geographical and climate differences may require different IA responses; nations and states may impose legislative mandates that call for different IA responses. The *scope* may be enterprisewide; it may be a set of related systems or a single system storing a particular kind of data (e.g., personally identifiable information [PII]). The *outputs* include a requirements hierarchy, requirements traceability matrix, to-be vision of compliance management, an as-is snapshot of compliance management, a gap analysis, a remediation analysis, and a transition plan. Figure 6.1 provides example IA considerations with respect to IA compliance management in context of the IA^2 views.

Recording the requirements in a series of traceability matrices is essential to tracking *what needs to be done* and *why it is being done*. If business drivers change, there needs to be the ability to isolate that part of the solution that is affected by the change. A traceability matrix is also a useful reference as memories fade and initial motivations behind particular business functions are lost. Too often, the justification for a business operation is "well, that's just the way it's always been," which is the most unforgivable excuse for continuing a business practice. The traceability matrix provides a living document that aligns business practices to the business motivations behind them, including IA practices and their respective business risk motivations.

6.4 IA Requirements Engineering and SE

The SE process begins with a *request* for a capability, product, or service. The request may be a business need (business driver) or a technical need (technical driver). The first step to fulfilling the request is a *system design*, which includes requirements engineering and a solution definition. Requirements engineering is the process of identifying, enumerating, articulating, and addressing the specifications for the capability, product, or service. The solution definition uses a work breakdown structure (WBS) to define the component parts of the solution and how the component parts fit together. The solution definition maps to the requirements in a formally constructed set of tables known as a requirements matrix. The SE process continues with the production and delivery of the system (the realization of the capability, product, or service). Moreover, SE provides for *technical management* that includes project planning, scheduling, and general oversight for the SE process.

IA requirements engineering is the process of identifying *risks to* the capability, product, or service and *risks caused by* the capability, product, or service. IA requirements engineering also identifies risks to the success of the SE process itself; for example, a lack of input from representatives of the business side is a risk to fully capturing and understanding the business requirements.

In a hypothetical example, market research shows that an E-commerce site will increase profits by 25 percent; therefore, the business objective is to establish an E-commerce presence that includes business-to-business transactions via private communications and business-to-consumer transactions via the Internet. This business objective prompts many activities to design an enterprise solution. Part of the architectural process is to use the IA^2 P and IA^2 F to identify, enumerate, articulate, and address the risks. One manner of addressing risk is to mitigate risk,

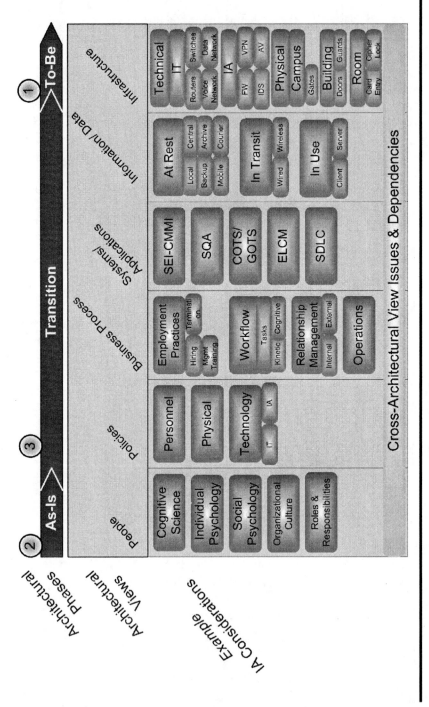

Figure 6.1 Expansion of IA² views for example IA considerations.

that is, build in safeguards to reduce the effect of various threats. The details to mitigate risk throughout across the solution are the IA requirements.

Requirements may be directly received from the customer and be very clearly stated. Other requirements may be derived indirectly. Decomposing customer RFP/RFQ/SOW* will produce requirements. The inherent nature of the solution architecture or solution design will produce more requirements. Overall, engineering requirements fall into categories similar to compliance requirements:

- Explicit
  - Direct
    - Requirements specified in a project request
  - Indirect
    - External documents referenced by project request
      - Legislation, policy, procedure, guideline, etc.
  - Principles, constraints, and assumptions (PCAs)
    - Architectural, design, or other enterprise life cycle management (ELCM) PCAs directly stated in the project request
- Implicit
  - Emerge from
    - Project requirements
      - Business process
      - Technical
      - Security and privacy
  - Principles, constraints, and assumptions
    - Architectural, design, or other ELCM PCAs derived from explicit requirements, operating environments, etc.

Explicit requirements are stated outright. The IA architect derives implicit requirements from explicit requirements as well as from the emerging architecture, design, CONOPS, and functional considerations. Implicit requirements need a formal recognition/review process so that as complete a list of requirements as possible is created. Enumerating both explicit and implicit requirements will benefit from a formal requirements engineering approach.

IA^2 uses two macro approaches to requirements engineering: *decomposition* and *domain functional isolation*. The decomposition approach may use *process decomposition* or *systemic decomposition*. The domain functional-isolation approach identifies entities and their interactions. The goal of all decomposition methods is to divide and conquer through defining discrete views that promote looking at the business requests from multiple perspectives.

The IA architect states explicit requirements in business and technical terms, and always starts with business objectives (business drivers). Determining the

---

* Request for proposal, request for quote, statement of work, respectively.

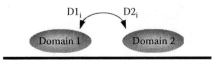

Figure 6.2 Domains and domain interfaces.

full depth of requirements requires a decomposition of explicit requirements to yield the implicit ones. Following the principle of divide and conquer, the IA architect examines requirements in terms of process (business), system (technical), and compliance (business and technical), and decomposes each requirement to finer granularity to the point of having business meaning in an enterprise context. Following are descriptions of business process decomposition, systemic decomposition, and compliance requirement decomposition.

6.4.1 Business Process Decomposition

Business process decomposition begins with identifying the workflows (see the Enterprise Context Framework in chapter 11). Workflows consist of procedures (formal statements of processes), which in turn consist of tasks. People (actors) or technologies (entities) perform tasks (actions). Collections of actors, entities, and actions comprise a domain. The interaction of actors, entities, and actions (domains) is the enterprise dynamics.

Many people in the organization will think they know what the business drivers are and often look askance at the person who seeks clarification. Much time and money have been spent developing solutions to the wrong problem because everyone understood what the business drivers were (or rather everyone understood what the business drivers were supposed to be). Business process decomposition will often illuminate what the internal business drivers really are and help to articulate the real problem and how to address that problem (see appendix I for more on problem definition).

Figure 6.2 shows two domains (domain 1 and domain 2) and interaction by way of their respective interfaces ($D1_i$ and $D2_i$). The IA architect identifies each domain, domain interactions, domain interfaces through which they interact, domain activities (tasks), and domain products (the end result of the domain activity) with respect to each of the IA core principles. The IA architect asks the following questions at each step:

- What are the business risks? Technical risks? People risks? Mission integrity risks? What are the possibilities of loss or injury to the organization?
  - Identify, enumerate (list), and articulate (describe) each risk.
- How should the organization address these risks?
  - Accept
  - Ignore
  - Share

- Transfer
- Mitigate
■ What are the requirements to address the risk?

There are five methods to address risk. The organization may **accept** or **ignore** risk (ignoring risk is implicit acceptance). Risk acceptance increases the exposure of the organization to additional costs or revenue interruptions. The organization may **share** risk by outsourcing noncore operations or engaging a service manager. The organization may **transfer** risk to an insurance provider. The vulnerability still exists, and probability of incident still exists; however, the financial burden resides with the insurance carrier. Risk **mitigation** implies the introduction of security services and mechanisms to reduce vulnerabilities, reduce the number of security incidents affecting the organization, and lessen the impact of security incidents. The right approach for any given organization is a balance among all these. The correct balance considers budget, schedule, expertise, and available resources.

The domains and domain interface representation above are abstract. A more focused example of domain interaction is service-oriented architecture (SOA). SOA is a design philosophy. This design philosophy advocates the use of technology to build a technical infrastructure or technical environment to support the creation and interaction of services. SOA services are software solutions that find each other and initiate relationships without the necessity of manual intervention. Consider that service A fulfills some need on the part of a service requestor, depending on context. The nature of a service (including service A) is to find other services to assist in the fulfillment of its purpose. Therefore, service A may be a service provider or service requestor. Other services used by service A may come in and out of existence. Service A is indifferent to whom or what fulfills a service request so long as the result is delivered within acceptable parameters of time, accuracy, and completeness.

Figure 6.3 shows SOA *foundational attributes*, where foundational attributes are characteristics fundamental to SOA. Fundamentally, SOA consists of a service requestor (SR) and a service provider (SP). An SP provides a service, e.g., proactive notification of new product releases/upgrades. An SR seeks a result without specific concern to where that result comes from; that is, the specific service that provides the result is irrelevant and perhaps even unknown to the SR. SRs and SPs interact with each other via interfaces (SR_i, SP_i). Data (d) flows (f) occur between the SR and SP through the interfaces, and metadata (md) contains information about the data. Their desire and ability to communicate defines their relationship (R).

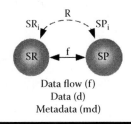

Data flow (f)
Data (d)
Metadata (md)

Figure 6.3 SOA foundational attributes.

The foundational attributes are an abstract representation of SOA. Moreover, the same abstract representation applies to all technical services and web services, not only SOA. This abstract representation of services and service relationships facilitates the discovery of IA requirements. The IA architect may ask questions regarding risks to services, risks of introducing services, and risks of service relationships, interfaces, data flows, data, and metadata. How can SP advertise itself to ensure it is discoverable by would-be service requestors? How can the SP be sure the SR is allowed to request SP's service (trust relationship)? How can the SR be sure the results it receives from the SP are valid (actually sent by SP)? How can the SR be sure the results sent by SP arrive unchanged (integrity)? How can SR ensure the metadata actually belongs to the data it arrives with? Table 6.1 presents examples of SOA security considerations in context of the nine IA core principles.

Process decomposition requirements engineering is a way to identify security requirements by identifying and understanding the business components and their interactions. The business components may include technical aspects, but the focus in this method is on the process more than the technical mechanisms. The following requirements engineering process, systemic decomposition, provides a method to delve deeper into the technology.

6.4.2 Systemic Decomposition

Systemic decomposition uses the hierarchical categories of the WBS framework—*system, subsystem, components, subcomponents, assemblies,* and *subassemblies*—to the degree of granularity that befits the situation. Albert Einstein said, "Make things as simple as possible, but not simpler." Likewise, decompose systems to a manageable point, but not further. Too granular a decomposition adds complexity, which is the very thing you are trying to reduce through decomposition. Figure 6.4 shows an example of intrasystemic relations where the system (S_0) consists of subsystems (S_1 and S_2) that in turn consist of components (C_x).

Systemic decomposition decomposes each system into various layers of constituent parts. Upon completing the decomposition, consider the discrete requirements for each component. Additionally, consider the requirements for the aggregation of the component parts into subsystems and systems. The IA architect uses iterations of the IA^2P to define system (S_0) IA requirements, subsystem (S_n) contribution to systemic IA requirements (they in turn become subsystem IA requirements), component contribution (C_n) to subsystem IA requirements, etc. The IA architect asks questions regarding the security needs of components as individual artifacts, e.g., clearing memory after each use in a software application. The IA architect also asks questions regarding the aggregate effect of the safeguards in context of overall IA objectives for the system.

The IA architect may use systemic decomposition requirements engineering alone or in conjunction with business process decomposition. The requirements

Table 6.1   IA Core Principles and Relevance to SOA Foundational Attributes

Security Element	Safeguard Purpose	Example SOA Relevance
Confidentiality	Nondisclosure	SR is valid and authorized to request/receive material from SP; this requires robust identity and privilege management solution to authenticate and authorize use. Secure communication paths to protect confidentiality of data flows.
Integrity	Accuracy	Ensure information the SR receives is the same as sent by the SP; this requires encryption, key management, and VPNs.
Availability	Usable on demand	Begs consideration of service redundancy for load balancing and provision of service at request
Possession	Owner/custodian maintains custody	Physical security protects information infrastructure assets.
Authenticity	Conforms to reality	Validation mechanisms to ensure information conforms to reality; external PKI certificate is indeed authentic and valid.
Utility	Accessible for use	Ensure information is accessible for use; encryption key management to ensure encrypted data may be decrypted.
Privacy	Individual rights	Enumeration and assessment against privacy compliance requirements; requires a compliance management facet to SOA development and operations
Nonrepudiation	Nondeniability	Ensure SRs cannot deny requesting a service and that SPs cannot deny providing a service; requires unique identity for each person/entity and robust log management to capture activity
Authorized use	Appropriate access to services	Ensure that only authorized people may invoke cost-generating services; e.g., long distance and toll-fraud protection in a new environment of a voice server on the network versus the traditional closed system of a PBX

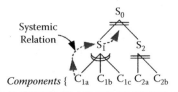

Figure 6.4   System relations. (This representation of systemic relations is inspired by Bruce Schneier's work on attack trees.)

engineering process can be quite involved and take quite a bit of time. Using the discipline of the IA^2 Process will provide a consistent, repeatable process that applies at every level of decomposition.

6.4.3   Domain Functional-Isolation Requirements Engineering

Domain functional isolation identifies the entities or collection of entities and decomposes their interactions through their respective interfaces. The methods above decompose the larger process (a relative perspective) into its constituent parts. The domain functional-isolation requirements engineering method starts with the domain concept, but rather than decompose the domain into its constituent parts, the focus here is on domain functionality. Domain functionality includes intradomain and interdomain operations. Interdomain functionality is how the domain gets inputs and provides outputs. Intradomain functionality is how a domain processes the inputs and produces the outputs.

A domain may be a single entity or a collection of entities. Domain interfaces facilitate *domain interactions*. Domain environments define the scope of domain operations; domain environments may be physical or cyber. Domain environments bounded by physical proximity are *regions*, while those bounded by logical relationships are communities of interest (COIs). When addressing a single entity, the phrases "entity functional isolation" and "domain functional isolation" are interchangeable. Domain interfaces are the visible parts of the domain to other domains.

Requirements describe the desired behavior. Security requirements describe qualifications or restrictions on the desired behavior. The intent of these security requirements is to mitigate business risk. *Domain behavioral constraints that mitigate risk are the security requirements.*

For example, Figure 6.5 shows five domains and a variety of interactions. The domains are person X, person Y, laptop, wireless access point (WAP), and server. Person X interacts with person Y via their respective interfaces. Both people interact with the laptop; e.g., person X may be a security guard and uses the laptop to validate person Y's identity by having person Y swipe an identity card and use

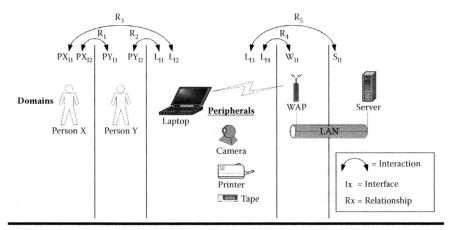

Figure 6.5 Domain functional-isolation requirements engineering.

Table 6.2 Domain Attributes Template

Domain	Interfaces	Relationships	Data Flows
Person X			
Person Y			
Laptop			
WAP			
Server			

the fingerprint reader for biometric validation. The laptop interacts with the WAP domain via wireless network. The WAP domain interacts with the server domain via the wired network. The labels R_x denote the domain relationships.

The IA architect determines IA requirements by examining each domain, each domain interface, each domain interaction (relationship), and data flows with respect to each IA core principle. Table 6.2* provides a template to list the domains and capture details of their respective interfaces, relationships, and data flows. Table 6.3† provides a template to capture the risks and how to address the risks with respect to the IA core principles.

IA requirements obtained using system decomposition or domain functional isolation must eventually trace to business drivers in the form of high-level business requirements. There is a need for requirements traceability from the lowest-level technical and IA requirements to the highest-level business drivers behind them.

---

* Table purposely left blank.
† Table purposely left blank.

Table 6.3 Domain Risks Template

Domain	Confidentiality	Integrity	Availability
Person X			
Person Y			
Laptop			
WAP			
Server			
Domain	Possession	Authenticity	Utility
Person X			
Person Y			
Laptop			
WAP			
Server			
Domain	Nonrepudiation	Authorized Use	Privacy
Person X			
Person Y			
Laptop			
WAP			
Server			

6.5 Requirements Traceability

Whichever method provides the IA requirements, there is need to provide formal and comprehensive requirements traceability. Table 6.4 provides a template for a requirements traceability matrix. Most projects will have a series of traceability tables that together make up one large traceability matrix. Depending on the granularity of the WBS, a single traceability table may represent a component. Multiple component tables may trace to a single subsystem table. Multiple subsystem tables may trace to a single system table. All traceability tables should ultimately trace to a business requirement table that contains the root business drivers, e.g., RFP, legislative compliance, mission, or strategic objective. An effective requirements matrix provides many benefits, including:

■ Ensures meeting of the minds between architect and sponsor

Table 6.4   Requirements Traceability Table Template

Requirement ID	Requirement Source	Requirement Description	Degree	Trace to	V&V	Comments
xx.1	Legislation XYZ	<Description>	Must	Legislation XYZ section	Assess	
xx.2		<Description>	Must		Audit	
xx.3		<Description>	Should		Test	
xx.4		<Description>	May		Review	
xx.n		<Description>	May		Review	

- Ensures meeting of the minds among architect, engineer, builder, tester, and operator
- Ensures project activity traces directly to a contractual requirement
- Assists in tracking project progress
- Aligns operational constructs with business drivers/requirements

The requirement ID uniquely identifies the requirement within this table and also within the entire traceability matrix, which may be multiple tables. The prefix "xx" in the requirement ID denotes a table reference where xx uniquely identifies the table. Requirement source is for the specific name of the legislation, regulation, instruction, directive, RFP, CONOPS, contract, or SOW. The requirement description is the verbiage from the source or otherwise a derived statement from verbiage in the requirement source. The degree denotes the importance of the requirement. The degree is must, should, or may (or other appropriate terms to the same intent). A *must* requirement is a nonnegotiable imperative. A *should* requirement is a negotiable imperative. A *may* requirement is no obligation, but a good idea if time and budget permit.

The "Trace to" column aligns the current requirement with the source motivating the requirement. A good heuristic is to always trace upward unless using an automated tool that provides bidirectional traceability. To trace upward means that more detailed requirements trace up to more general ones. For example, business requirements trace to legislative drivers. System requirements trace to business requirements. Subsystem requirements trace to system requirements, etc. Verification and validation (V&V) denotes the type of test to ensure the requirement is in the final solution. V&V options include audit, review, inspection, test, simulation, and other situational-dependent methods. Verification implies a less rigorous test, e.g., visual inspection. Validation implies a more rigorous test, e.g., hands-on testing with formal test cases. The URL http://vva.dmso.mil/Ref_Docs/VVTechniques/VVtechniques.htm* offers a formal V&V taxonomy.

There are two kinds of requirement matrices, one for the project and one for the enterprise. The project requirement matrix is a tool for the duration of the project. The usefulness of the project matrix ends upon successful delivery, testing, and sign-off of the solution. The enterprise matrix is a living document to maintain a formal enterprise IA² LoS. The latter refers to the IA² Framework, where the IA² LoS traces business drivers through to operational constructs. This provides ongoing insight into the effects of operations on business requirements, and the business drivers behind operations. If the business drivers change, the enterprise traceability matrix provides a way to evaluate the effects on operations and to evaluate the effect of operational changes on the business.

For example, if the operations require a 20 percent budget cut, the too often traditional solution is to cut 20 percent across the board. This is not by default the

---

* Accessed July 2007.

ideal method. The first question should be: *Do we have operations that no longer fulfill a valid business need?* The enterprise traceability matrix that aligns business drivers with O&M provides insight to the answer. If an operational service no longer fulfills a valid business need or fulfills a business need of relatively low priority, that operational service may be either scaled back or eliminated. To continue the example, if the elimination of that service reduces budget expenditure by 10 percent, you are halfway to the 20 percent reduction objective. Now there is need to reduce the remaining operational budget by 10 percent. The business benefit of creating and maintaining an enterprise traceability matrix is smarter, faster business decisions that have a higher degree of confidence.

6.6   Conclusion and Commentary

To add business value, you have to know what value the business is looking for. Formally capturing business drivers as requirement statements provides traceable motivation for the development of capabilities, products, and services, and traceable motivation behind IA. Capturing the root drivers provides you with the capability to discern and convey the business value of IA at various organizational levels. The next chapter looks at IA technical drivers.

Chapter 7

IA Technical Drivers

7.1 Introduction

Business need drives technology. Business risk drives IA. Technology may also introduce risk to the business. The operational benefits from technology often override concerns about risk and security. The responsibility of the IA professional is to identify, enumerate, articulate, and address all business risk, including those business risks introduced by technology.

7.2 Objectives

The objectives of this chapter include:

- Introduce technology as sources of business risk.
- Present how to use IA² to identify and address these risks.

At the end of this chapter, you should be aware of the potential for technology to introduce risks and the need to use the IA² Framework, IA² Process, and other tools to specifically identify technical risks, align and explain technical risks with business risks, and address technical risks as part of the IA architecture.

7.3   IA² Technology Drivers

Business need drives technology and technology may introduce risk. Wireless technology is an example. Business need for a mobile or a nontethered workforce drove the introduction of wireless communication. Wireless communication provides business benefits as well as introducing new risks. Hence, the need for secure wireless networks provides motivation behind IA activities. The following are additional examples of technology drivers:

- Voice and data convergence (V over X, where $X \in$ [IP, ATM, FR])
- Laptops
- PDAs
- Cell phones
- Universal serial bus (USB) devices, e.g., memory sticks
- Service-oriented architecture (SOA)

Laptops provide the ability to carry applications and data outside organizational facilities. Good for productivity, but high exposure for theft of the laptop and, worse, theft of the data. Personal digital assistants (PDAs) offer similar mobile productivity, but with risk exposure to organizational information (reports, finances, customer data, employee personal data). A cell phone offers a great opportunity to finalize terms of the deal while on the golf course or at lunch, and anyone in range gets to hear the details as well. USB memory sticks are great for sneaker-netting large amounts of data and documents from one PC to the next. They are also small and can transport large amounts of organizational information out the door inadvertently or otherwise. The following sections elaborate on wireless networks and voice and data convergence as two examples of IA technical drivers.

The following sections present principles behind technology as a driver for IA. Specific technology drivers are dynamic by nature and even fleeting; today's technology drivers are tomorrow's techno-reliquary dust collectors. Specific technologies become outdated quickly; principles, however, survive the test of time.

You can use the IA² Framework views to consider technology drivers. The people view examines who will use the technology. The policy view determines directives for when the organization will use the technology. The business process view examines where the organization will use the technology, as well as captures what business functions will use the technology. The systems and applications view examines the technology itself and its overall fit in the technical environment. The information/data view examines what the technology will accept as inputs, what it will to the inputs, and what outputs it will produce. The IA² LoS captures business need for the technology and the alignment from business need through to operations. The line of sight details captures alignment of the technology with the mission.

Table 7.1 Wireless Terms

Term	Definition
Wireless	Wireless describes telecommunications in which electromagnetic waves carry the signal over the communication path. The communication occurs without the use of wires.
RF wireless	Radio frequency (RF) is a rate of oscillation that corresponds to alternating current electrical signals. An alternating current input to an antenna generates an electromagnetic field that emanates from that antenna.
IR wireless	Infrared radiation (IR) wireless is the use of wireless technology in devices or systems that convey data through infrared radiation. Infrared is "below red," or below visible light.
Bluetooth	Bluetooth is a short-range radio-frequency-based communications technology intended for personal area networks (PANs). Bluetooth supports intercommunications among portable devices such as laptops, PDAs, mobile phones, and headsets.
Wireless local area network (WLAN)	A WLAN is based on radio waves and provides the ability for wireless computer networking. The standard IEEE 802.11 specifies the technologies for wireless LANs. The standard includes the wired equivalent privacy (WEP) encryption method.
Wired equivalent privacy (WEP)	The IEEE wireless fidelity (Wi-Fi) standard, 802.11b, specifies WEP as a security protocol for WLANs; WEP security encrypts WLAN data in transit.

7.4 Wireless Networks: An Example

Wireless technology offers an economical alternative to replace or extend a wired LAN; however, a number of security risks accompany the economic advantages. Managing these risks includes the use of proximity access controls, transmission encryption, and continuous real-time scanning to monitor, detect, and notify of malicious or unauthorized activity. Wireless LAN configurations include the implementation of layers of security, including virtual private network (VPN), firewalls, and encryption.

7.4.1 Definitions

Table 7.1 provides some useful definitions with respect to wireless technology.

7.4.2   Security Concerns

Wireless LAN security is a combination of three perspectives: securing data transmitted over a wireless link, securing the wireless network from unauthorized access, and securing the wired network from unauthorized access from the wireless side. Securing the wireless network from unauthorized access includes protection against unauthorized users as well as protection from rogue access points that may be authorized users over an unauthorized link.

7.4.3   Policy

The IA architect should view wireless (security) policy from an organizational perspective and from an employee perspective. The corporate perspective addresses network configuration and is more relevant to network designers and system administrators. The employee perspective includes desktop, laptop, cell phone, and other wireless devices with which an employee directly interacts.

7.4.3.1   Corporate Perspective

Wireless technology is inherently insecure. Physical/facility compromise is not necessary to intercept wireless transmissions or to gain access to wireless devices. Wireless security policy considerations include:

- Defense-in-depth
  - All items below are part of a layered security approach; none are standalone solutions.
- Wireless LAN traffic to wired LAN
  - Use of a VPN or firewall
- Minimum encryption strength standards
- Routing rules
  - Restrict routing to multiple networks.
- Modify equipment default settings and standard settings for configurable parameters.
  - Set WAP to not broadcast service set identities (SSIDs).
  - Modify all WAP default SSIDs to a unique identifier.
- Implement OSI layer 2 access control lists; Media Access Control (MAC) filtering.
- Monitoring and alerting
  - Monitor WLAN use via wireless sniffers and intrusion detection systems (IDSs).
  - Provide alerting to network or security operations center.

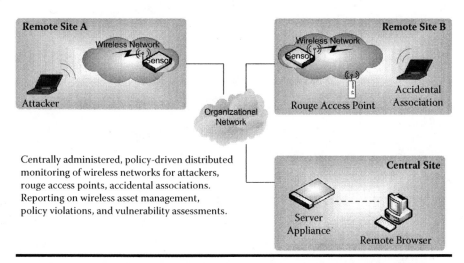

Figure 7.1 Wireless security configuration overview. (The configuration is based on AirDefense technology [www.airdefense.net], accessed July 2007.)

- Signal emanation
  - Strength of signal and direction of signal within building or campus boundaries
  - War driving assessments

7.4.3.2 Employee Perspective

Provide policy that governs use of wireless technology on PCs and laptops, including laptops brought by employees into the work environment. Moreover, provide security recommendations for home networks that are used to perform work from home. The additional benefit is to protect any corporate information that may find itself, intentionally or otherwise, on a home PC. Employee-focused wireless security policy considerations include modifying default names and accesses to wireless routers and wireless LANs, and use WEP or other encryption methods to safeguard transmissions. Note that using WEP to secure wireless transmissions is like using a lock on your front door. Both keep out the casually curious, but not a motivated and prepared adversary.

7.4.4 Practice

For wireless security, practice includes the definition of configuration standards and procedures; policy drives both of these. One potential wireless security configuration is seen in Figure 7.1; the configuration is based on AirDefense technology.

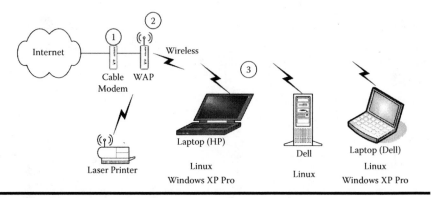

Figure 7.2   Generic home configuration.

Figure 7.2 presents a generic home wireless networking and wireless security configuration.

Key security features based on the numbered items in the figure include:

1. No specific security feature; wired Ethernet connection to wireless access point (WAP).
2. On WAP, modify factory default service set identification (SSID); this is the name of the wireless network. Set up wireless equivalent privacy (WEP)—128 bit key is stronger; however, results (i.e., wireless link remains up) are more consistent using 64 bit key. Add filtering of Media Access Control (MAC) addresses.
3. Set up devices accessing WAP with consistent SSID and WEP key.

7.4.5   IA² Perspective

When developing wireless security, the IA architect should seek out guidance on industry best practices like NIST SP 800-48: *Wireless Network Security—802.11, Bluetooth and Handheld Devices*. Moreover, consider that wireless is more than just data. Wireless includes voice, still picture, and video. Wireless technology ranks high in the high-security risk category. Some risks are subtle, as with camera phones, and some more obvious, like wireless laptops, including IR links. Corporate policy needs to address internal use of wireless as well as use of wireless devices on customer sites.

IA requirements for wireless and mobile technology are far more than securing the technology. The IA² views provide guidance for determining risks to information as an organizational asset as well as decisions that depend on information. People need to be aware of the risks and prepared to mitigate risks. Policies provide for risk mitigation, e.g., using hard drive encryption on laptops so the loss of the asset does not include disclosure of the data, and backup policies so that same laptop theft does not include loss of data.

7.5 Communications (Voice and Data): An Example

Communications includes person to person, person to groups (e.g., presentation), group (e.g., meetings), person to technology (e.g., desktop PC), and technology to technology (e.g., client/server). The communications infrastructure includes voice and data in traditional and emerging configurations. Voice communications include public switched telephone network (PSTN) and private branch exchanges (PBXs); data communications include networking.

Communications is the core of operations. Without communications, there are no operations, or at most, there are *flying-blind* operations, based on the last communication. Continuity of operation plans (COOP), business continuity, and disaster recovery planning for communications are essential in today's information-critical environment, and even more critical when considering the time sensitivity of information is measured more in terms of (micro-)seconds than hours or days.

7.5.1 Traditional Communications

Traditional communications consist of disparate infrastructure and functionality separating voice and data. Voice communications essentially separates into private and public; only rarely do private voice communications not interface with the public voice infrastructure. The public switched telephone network (PSTN) provides central office service for local residential or commercial connectivity. Central offices connect regionally, often under one operating entity, the regional Bell operating companies (RBOCs). RBOCs in turn interconnect via interexchange carriers (IXCs). RBOCs typically provide local service and IXCs provide long-distance service; this distinction is recently blurring with RBOCs' ability to offer long distance and vice versa for the IXCs.

Private branch exchanges (PBXs) offer organizations the ability to set up private voice services where station-to-station calls occur exclusively within the PBX and do not involve the PSTN for phone calls. PBXs may support voice service within a building, campus, metropolitan, regional, national, or global scope. Long physical PBX connections (e.g., Washington, D.C., to San Francisco) are typically via leased line (e.g., T1) and may be via wired or wireless (e.g., satellite) medium.

These options provide a complex array of choices for voice-related emergency preparedness with respect to PSTN connectivity and intra-PBX connectivity. Further emergency preparedness concerns include redundant processor choices, redundant intercabinet connections, redundant inbound/outbound voice services and paths, and much more.

7.5.2 Emerging Communications

Emerging communications are converging communications. More robust data communications are available over voice infrastructure (e.g., Digital Subscriber

Line [DSL]), and more options exist to run voice service over data networks. Following is an overview of voice-over-data with a bit more detail on IP telephony.

Voice-over-data extends the telephony (telecommunications) transport fabric beyond the PSTN and private links to include Ethernet, Frame Relay, and ATM. Internet Protocol (IP) telephony is the extension of traditional telecommunications/telephony services, capabilities, and applications across TCP/IP.* Any topology that supports TCP/IP or encapsulates TCP/IP may facilitate VoIP† traffic. IP telephony is the broader term encompassing applications, topology, and transport; VoIP is merely one of many voice-over-data transport methods.

Telephony operations include bearer traffic (voice) and data traffic (signaling). Signaling enables the voice system to operate. Signals are sent from PBX to station, PBX to central office, PBX to PBX, PBX to voice mail, and much more. These signals traditionally traverse dedicated voice links like house wire, PSTN T1s, and tie lines. Convergence enables the bearer and data traffic to traverse the data network. Bearer traffic on a data network is generally referred to as voice-over-data; signaling over the data network is generally thought of as just another data application—in this case the application resides on a voice server (e.g., old term: PBX) and voice clients (e.g., station). Transmitting telephony bearer channels and signaling over a data network has special meaning and exciting implications to voice experts, but is generally unknown and unappreciated by most others, including those proficient in the data world.

As an example of the complexities involved with IP telephony, consider Figure 7.3, which depicts various IP telephony endpoints and connectivity of the voice server and the PSTN. These connectivity options present a variety of operating conditions using network convergence.

Points 1 and 3 show voice server connectivity to the local (LAN) data network. Point 2 shows private tie lines (IP trunks) between voice servers. Points 4 to 6 show various IP station connectivity options, including IP softphone (phone software on a PC) or IP phone (voice hardware connecting directly to the LAN). An extension call between a traditional analog phone and IP phone happens exactly as a traditional extension call would; the same goes for ten-digit external calls from an IP phone, long-distance calls, etc. There is complete user transparency.

Rules may be set up within the voice server to direct calls over the IP trunks or over traditional PBX tie lines. This latter presents many options to build in redundant trunk paths and provide user transparency if either the data service or PSTN service goes down. All of these together offer many options for IA planning with respect to voice services.

---

* Applied IP Telephony course by Keith D. Willett, July 2000.
† Voice-over-IP.

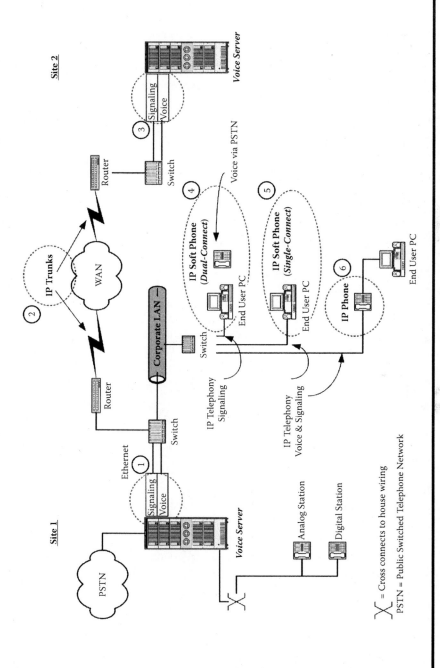

Figure 7.3 IP telephony endpoints overview. (*IP Telephony—The Business Case*, Keith D. Willett, April 2002.)

7.5.3 Communications Influence on the IA² F

The complexities of voice and data communication to information assurance extend to business process, technical infrastructure, policies, and people. Continuity of operation plans (COOP) requires the identification of mission-critical operations. The IA architect subsequently considers the infrastructure supporting those critical operations. The first point of recovery is invariably voice—get people talking. The second point of recovery is data infrastructure supporting mission-critical operations and applications. Business continuity requires redundancy for key components (e.g., processor), intrasystem links (e.g., WAN links), outside services (e.g., PSTN T1s and Internet), and configurations that minimize operational interruption due to single points of failure. Emergency preparedness in voice and data is a must in today's E-commerce environment, where a competitor is merely a mouse-click away.

7.5.3.1 Voice Communications

Threats to voice communications include denial of service, confidentiality violations via eavesdropping on live conversations or compromising voice mail, and authenticity compromised by stealing enough recorded messages to piece together a false message in a recognizable voice. A common threat to voice communications is toll fraud; this theft of service costs companies many billions of dollars annually.

Voice systems are computer systems running on proprietary hardware, operating systems, and applications. Although users typically do not have access to the operating system functions, they do have access to configuration parameters and a responsibility to configure those parameters to create a safe operating environment. Part of this configuration is class of service and class of restriction, where groups of users and stations receive common privileges. This promotes only authorized use of sensitive features like long-distance or international dialing access.

7.5.3.2 Data Communications

Data communications support many business operations and have become so intertwined with the business process that loss of data communications often implies cessation of business. Every aspect of IA contributes to keeping this critical infrastructure up and running. IA policies link business requirements to IA services and define how IA services support the business. IA policies also contribute to data communications infrastructure installation, configuration, and administration to establish and maintain secure operations.

7.5.3.3 Convergence

As the business fit and cost savings possible with IP telephony become more visible, the voice infrastructure will grow increasingly dependent on the data network.

Anyone who has experience with voice knows that user tolerance for downtime is measured in nanoseconds. The implications for IA are to use creative combinations of voice and data networks to create redundancy and self-healing link-loss configurations. Further, loss of PSTN voice service to site A may not affect IP software-based phones with the ability to simply sign on to another site. The business benefit is to keep mission-critical operations going (e.g., revenue-generating call center agents) even though other phone users on traditional stations are out of commission.

7.6 Conclusion and Commentary

Business need drives technology; however, technology introduces both business benefit and business risk. The complexities of some technology are sufficient to warrant a deep exploration of the risks inherent in the technology and how those risks affect technical operations and mission integrity.

Chapter 8

IA²: Context of
IA Services

8.1   Introduction

This chapter presents details of IA services, including how to think about them and how to apply them in context of the enterprise and IA². The IA services described here are not comprehensive; however, you may use these examples as a starting point to identify other IA services to place in the appropriate context and flow of an IA architecture that uses the IA² F, IA² P, and IA² line of sight (LoS).

8.2   Objectives

The objectives of this chapter include:

- Distinguish IA services from IA mechanisms
- Place IA services in context of the enterprise and IA²
- Provide architectural insight to IA services

By the end of this chapter, you should be able to identify the difference between an IA service and an IA mechanism, have some insight into the fit of IA services in the architecture process, and some insight into architectural considerations for IA services.

8.3   IA Services

A service is the act of satisfying some demand (*service* as a verb) or the entity that satisfies some demand (*service* as a noun). IA services are akin to business functions. These IA business functions provide information assurance services to the organization. As shown in Figure 8.1, business requirements drive security services. Security services in turn may use security mechanisms. Personnel and technology may provide security services.

This chapter and the next place IA services and IA mechanisms in an enterprise context as well as introduce how IA^2 assists in aligning IA services and IA mechanisms with business drivers.

When a risk is identified, there is a short list of options: *accept* risk, *ignore* risk (implicit acceptance), *share* risk, *transfer* risk, and *mitigate* risk. Risk mitigation requires investments in security controls. Effective implementation of security controls creates defense-in-depth, where layers of security increase the difficulty and cost of a successful attack. Generally speaking, if someone wants something you have badly enough, they may be willing to take extraordinary steps get it. The objective of security is to make the cost of getting it more than the adversary is willing to spend. One goal of defense-in-depth is to make a breach so difficult as to be cost prohibitive in terms of both means (money and knowledge) and method (effort).

IA service examples include:

- Compliance Management
- Assessment and Audit
- Policy Management
- Security Education, Training, and Awareness
- Privacy Management
- Computer Security Incident Response
- Vulnerability Management
- Digital Forensics
- Business Impact Assessment
- Business Continuity Management

Consider IA services as part of an overall defense in depth strategy.

8.3.1   Defense-in-Depth Perspective

There are key business functions that both define and fulfill the reasons for the existence of the organization. Key personnel are those people that perform key business functions or have key business knowledge. Key technology is that technology used by key personnel to perform key business functions. All other business functions,

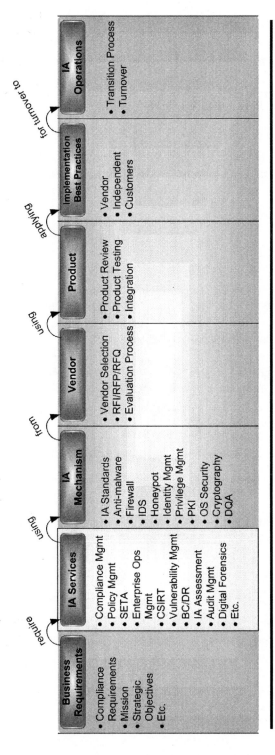

Figure 8.1   IA services in context of IA² implementation taxonomy.

personnel, and technology are support and overhead. This is not to say nonkey areas are not important—indeed they are. However, in context of fulfilling the organizational mission, there are key areas and there are support and overhead areas. The distinction becomes particularly important in context of business continuity and disaster recovery; key areas are of higher priority.

Core aspects of the technology reside at the center of organizational operations, figuratively if not literally. The core in most organizations houses data centers, servers, databases, data, and information. Much of core technology is also key technology, but not all. Moreover, not all key technology resides at the core. Neither do all key business functions and personnel reside in the core. Layers of security controls (defense-in-depth) are necessary for both core and key business functions, personnel, information, and information technology. The principle of defense-in-depth introduces layers of protection that surround core and key aspects of the organization.

The introduction of firewalls in the mid-1990s produced somewhat hardened network perimeters; however, if an attacker made it through the firewall, he had free reign over the interior network. This is the proverbial "crunchy on the outside, soft on the inside" network. Subsequent safeguards began to address the inside of the network at various layers (e.g., intrusion detection systems). Moreover, the use of firewalls within the perimeter to segregate sections of the internal organization also provides an additional layer of defense-in-depth.

Defense-in-depth takes on two macro views, *exogenous* and *endogenous*. Exogenous is activity occurring outside the organization. Endogenous is activity within the organization. An elaboration of these two views is as follows:

- Exogenous
  - Scope of control
    - Control
    - Influence
    - Controlled response
- Endogenous
  - Physical
    - Perimeter
    - Core
  - Data state
    - In transit
    - In use
    - At rest
  - Principle or IA operations cycle
    - Anticipate
      - Prevent
    - Defend
    - Monitor
      - Detect

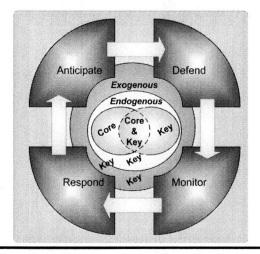

Figure 8.2 Exogenous and endogenous defense-in-depth: core and key perspective.

- Respond
    - Notify
    - Triage
    - Escalate
    - Isolate
    - Treat/fix
    - Restore
    - Root cause analysis (RCA)
    - Organizational feedback

Figure 8.2 presents core and key aspects of the organization in context of exogenous and endogenous defense-in-depth. Endogenous defense-in-depth priorities are core and key; however, a purely endogenous view is limited. The exogenous perspective looks at the threat space external to the organization and considers defense-in-depth from the perspective of preemption.

8.3.2 Exogenous View of Defense-in-Depth

When dealing with environments outside the organization, the IA architect examines organizational scope of control. The organization may indeed control the external environment, for instance, when considering IA services for a wholly owned subsidiary. When dealing with partners, vendors, and customers, the organization will likely not exert much control, but it may exert influence; it is unable to control or influence the outside environment, but it may control its own response to external events. For example, the organization may depend on a utility company to provide electricity.

The organization likely has little to no control or influence on the ability of the utility company to provide quality electricity on a continuous basis. There will be power fluctuations (spikes and valleys), brownouts, and blackouts. The organization does have control over its response to these events. It may introduce power-smoothing devices that eliminate negative effects of power fluctuations. It may employ uninterrupted power supply (UPS) systems that continue operations during brownouts and blackouts.

Your organization may not be able to control other's use of security controls; however, your organization may influence by choosing to do business with companies that practice and prove effective use of security controls.

Other organizations that desire connectivity to your network must comply and prove compliance with minimal security standards. This extends the defense-in-depth concept to other networks that may introduce malware or otherwise act as conduits for inadvertent or adversarial activity. Another exogenous defense-in-depth activity is to implement inbound traffic filtering services by way of a managed security service (MSS) or Internet service provider (ISP). This reduces the opportunity for malware to enter the perimeter of the organization and reduces the demand on organizational computing resources to find and filter malware. Moreover, exogenous defense-in-depth extends to off-site activity with respect to backups, archives, business continuity, continuity of operations, and disaster recovery.

You may also discover additional exogenous defense-in-depth options by using risk management options of accept, ignore, share, transfer, and mitigate. Extending IA outside the organization typically involves sharing and transferring risk. Mitigation is more often employed as endogenous safeguards. Awareness, understanding, and consideration of both exogenous and endogenous options for defense-in-depth provide details for rational decisions on risk acceptance.

8.3.3   Endogenous View of Defense-in-Depth

Endogenous defense-in-depth is safeguarding your own organization. There are many views of the same safeguards. These views provide different perspectives on organizational investments in risk mitigation solutions. The views are physical, data state, and the IA operations cycle.

8.3.3.1   Physical

The physical view of endogenous defense-in-depth begins with the perimeter and connectivity between the organization and outside entities, which may be customers, partners, vendors, or the Internet. Once inside the organization, you may wish to distinguish subsets of the organization in some logical or physical grouping. Each enclave may have its own additional defense-in-depth safeguards. For example, the data center may be an enclave. The organization as a whole may have a firewall between the organization and the Internet to enforce policy on public network access. However, the data center may have its own firewall to enforce policy on internal organizational access to the firewall. This is one example of layering safeguards. If there is a breach in the Internet facing firewall, the firewall protecting the data center remains.

8.3.3.2 Data State

Data states are *at rest*, *in transit*, and *in use*. Data at rest is on a permanent storage medium, e.g., hard drive, tape, CD, or DVD. Data at rest may be on a server (e.g., database) or a document on a PC (e.g., organizational strategic plan); data at rest may be a backup or archive; data at rest may be a hard copy. Safeguards for data at rest may include hard drive encryption or otherwise encrypting the data prior to writing to permanent storage. In terms of defense-in-depth, additional safeguards may include physical protections of locked cabinets, safes, fire-retardant safes, off-site storage, underground vaults, or 24/7 security guards. Safeguards that restrict access to the computer housing the medium also add a protection layer, e.g., requirements for user IDs and passwords.

Data in transit refers to data traversing a network. Defense-in-depth safeguards for data in transit include restricting access to the medium (wired network or wireless network), monitoring for unauthorized access to the medium (intrusion detection), or encrypting the transmission.

Data in use is in virtual storage (e.g., RAM). Such data resides in RAM due to its current use by an application. Ineffective safeguards on memory access or failure to clear memory effectively after application termination places data in use at risk. Defense-in-depth safeguards for data in use include computer access controls, monitoring for unauthorized access or use of the computer system (e.g., host-based intrusion detection), or software development rules (e.g., clear memory after use and other software quality assurance measures).

8.3.3.3 IA Operations Cycle

The IA operations cycle is a continuous flow through anticipate, defend, monitor, and respond. The cycle begins with *anticipating threats* and the necessary safeguards to mitigate the risks from those threats. The organization *defends against those threats* by implementing the safeguards. The organization then *monitors* the effectiveness of the safeguards and for additional threats that require additional defenses. Upon detection of an anomaly, the organization then *responds* appropriately. An appropriate response may be to ignore the anomaly if it is a false positive. The section below on computer security incident response team (CSIRT) provides additional details of other potential responses.

Figure 8.2 shows the IA operations cycle surrounding core and key aspects of the organization. Core aspects reside at the center of the organization either figuratively or literally. Core includes data center operations. Core aspects may include key business functions, people, information, or information technology. Key aspects of the organization are those that have a direct and significant impact on fulfilling the primary mission of the organization. Key aspects may reside at the core and other places within the organization.

Key aspects may also reside outside the organization, for instance, in a managed service provider (MSP). An MSP arrangement does not mean the organization can transfer all IA issues to the MSP. At the very least, the organization must provide IA requirements to the MSP and provide for SLAs that ensure appropriate risk management. Even if the MSP is contractually obligated for monetary recompense in the event of a security incident, there may still be a risk of both the MSP and your organization going out of business if the appropriate safeguards are not in place. The point is that although an MSP—or any outside service provider—may take on operational responsibility and a large part of the risk, it does not take on all risk. There is still a responsibility on the part of IA professionals to ensure that risks to their organization's interests are appropriately addressed.

8.4 IA Compliance Management Program

A comprehensive compliance management program addresses all relevant compliance requirements. Relevant compliance requirements include contractual obligations, legislation, standards, regulation, policy, strategic objectives, mission statements, and more. An IA compliance management program identifies, enumerates, and articulates compliance posture for all security-related compliance requirements. The first challenge is to identify all relevant compliance requirements—not an easy task. Having identified the compliance requirements, the next challenge is to decompose them into manageable categories and elements that serve as high-level requirements—an even more difficult task. This set of compliance requirements then becomes the baseline for organizational IA policy, standards, procedures, and practice, or the baseline for the to-be state of IA compliance.

A compliance assessment compares existing policy, standards, procedures, and practice (as-is) against the to-be. Differences between the as-is and to-be are IA compliance gaps. The IA architect and other appropriate business representatives must review these gaps, identify risks with less-than-full compliance, and recommend steps or methods to address these gaps. Addressing gaps includes explaining why that particular to-be requirement is not applicable to the organization. Addressing gaps also includes investing in remediation, e.g., IA services and IA mechanisms to increase security posture, thus increasing compliance levels.

A reasonable question is: *Why even have a to-be requirement if the organization is not going to fully comply with it?* Many organizations are subject to legislative compliance requirements, e.g., HIPAA, Sarbanes–Oxley, etc. Many legislative compliance documents want the requirements to be *addressed*; the legislation does not necessarily require the organization to introduce safeguards. Now let us be very clear here: there are many legislative requirements that the organization must address with the introduction of safeguards, but not all. This implies that for some compliance requirements, the organization must acknowledge the requirement, but not necessarily act upon that requirement. For final judgment on which requirements may be addressed versus which must be acted upon, seek legal advice from a qualified attorney. The best approach is to record an organizational response to all compliance requirements, whether acted upon or not. This supports the principle of conscious omission with good rationale versus omission by oversight.

8.4.1 Compliance Assessment

The activity of comparing as-is current compliance posture with to-be target compliance posture is a *compliance assessment*, which consists of four phases:

- Discovery
- Analysis
- Reporting
- Follow-up

The discovery phase identifies existing policy, standards, procedures, and practices. The analysis phase compares the details of each of these to the compliance requirements. The reporting phase produces gap analysis and remediation analysis reports. The follow-up phase produces remediation plans and progress tracking. The policy, standards, and procedures are paper or electronic documents. Practice is actual actions taken by personnel or agents of the organization, and implementations of various safeguards. Compliance assessments performance may take on two general flavors. The first is an interview assessment. This entails many interviews to discuss policy, standards, procedures, and practice. The second is a validation assessment. This entails hands-on or eyes-on validation of the details in policy, standards, procedures, and practice.

Compliance assessments reporting may take two formats: a *subjective* narrative (the traditional manner) or an *objective* quantification of compliance analysis results.

8.4.1.1 Compliance Assessment: Subjective

The traditional approach to compliance assessment includes devising a questionnaire and using it during a series of interviews to gather information regarding the organization's current situation. Subsequent analysis of the information helps produce a gap analysis report and remediation report. This is a reasonable method and reasonably useful for smaller efforts. A major challenge is consolidating many separate findings in a single, aggregate enterprise report. Any given gap analysis may be many tens of pages. The accompanying remediation analysis may be the same. If there are many tens of sites, a purely subjective aggregate report becomes confusing. The need to consolidate the findings from 20 different sites, each with a 20-page gap report and 20-page remediation report, can result in as many as 8,000 pages of raw reports, or more. Consolidating these findings in a single, comprehensible, useful report is extremely difficult. A better approach is to add objective quantification to assist in making sense of the consolidated findings.

8.4.1.2   Compliance Assessment: Objective (Quantification)

One solution to produce an aggregate enterprise report is via assessment *quantification*. Objectively quantifying subjective observations means that compliance levels can be represented numerically. Although such numeric compliance scores find no basis in legislation, consistent quantification provides useful, internally relevant comparisons. The benefits to such quantification include:

- The initial score provides a baseline to compare future assessments against to objectively measure progress, stasis, or regression.
- Executive summaries may include an easily understood X% compliance level summary, including graphic depictions of:
  - Top and bottom sites/divisions in compliance
  - Compliance elements with largest gaps across the enterprise
- Consistent results can be obtained from concurrent multiteam, multisite efforts.
- Assessors may make recommendations for intelligent resource allocations in remediation efforts all based on measurable results versus gut feel.

The compliance score reflects the level of compliance. Whatever scale is used, it will be an artificial scale with no basis in inherent value or really have any meaning outside the organization itself. A suggestion for the compliance level scale is 0 for nothing, 4 for full compliance, and partial compliance scores of 1 through 3, representing low, medium, and high, respectively. This low-granular quantification is more likely to find consistency across multiple assessors. A scale of higher granularity (0 through 20), which attempts to quantify nuances of high compliance, often results in inconsistent results. A simple guide as to what constitutes low, medium, and high will assist multiple assessors to interpret findings in a consistent manner. Consistency is important among the various sites or divisions for any given assessment, as well as from one assessment to the next. Consistent results promote the ability to generate statistics, and track and trend over a series of assessments.

8.4.2 IA² Perspective

Compliance requirements are part of what defines business drivers. The IA² perspective considers compliance management an integral part of managing business risk. Specifics under compliance management include identifying and articulating management responsibilities and liabilities, performing compliance assessments, and generating appropriate policies. Identifying legal obligations and establishing policy through tracking mechanisms to ensure organizational compliance with these legal obligations goes a long way in minimizing organizational culpability, officer culpability, and the potential for fines and jail time.

8.5 IA Assessment and Audit

The assessment process starts with examining the existence and adequacy of X, where X is policy, procedures, operations, technical infrastructure, controls, security infrastructure, etc. This is an assessment of X, including what X is, what it does, how many there are, where they are, plus the security controls or security information relevant to X; this is the as-is state of X. Determining or defining the compliance requirements for X provides the to-be state of X. A gap analysis highlights the differences between as-is and to-be. A remediation plan provides direction on how to close the gap between as-is and to-be. Following execution of the remediation plan, an audit of X should verify the controls work as intended; this is a form of compliance verification.

The relevant compliance requirements and security standards drive the details of audits and assessments. A general security assessment may use ISO 27002* to define the to-be state; a specific security assessment may address a particular compliance requirement. Variations of standards like ISO 27002, NIST, IEEE, and others attempt to provide compliance guidelines to specific legislation; in many cases, an aggregation of pieces of multiple standards is the solution. With respect to standards, a one-size-fits-all typically, doesn't. There are many compliance requirements that are subject to audit:

- Sarbanes–Oxley Act of 2002
- Health Insurance Portability and Accountability Act (HIPAA) of 1996
- The Gramm–Leach–Bliley Act of 1999
- Federal Information Security Management Act (FISMA) requirement for civilian federal government use of NIST standards that imply the need for certification and accreditation (C&A)

---

* Formerly called ISO 17799.

Other compliance requirements may include project requirements, application design requirements, internal policies, and more. All compliance requirements are potentially subject to audits to ensure compliance verification.* The audit process provides the steps to perform this compliance verification.

A comprehensive architectural approach to auditing examines the existence and adequacy of assessment and audit policy, standards, and procedures; various audit perspectives; and the audit process and details of each phase.

8.5.1 Audit Perspective

Audit perspectives include:

- Audit performance
  - Internal audits
  - External audits
- Operations
  - Automated audit logs via operating system (OS), network operating system (NOS), application, centralized log management, support for forensic analysis of activity (reconstruct actions and timeline)
- Subjects of an audit
  - People [activity | relationship audits]
    - For example, conflict of interest, separation of duties
  - Process
    - For example, financial accounting practices, technical operations procedures
  - Technology
    - For example, system logs
- Audit purpose
  - Compliance verification of:
    - External legislation and regulation
    - Internal policy
      - Technical, e.g., password, authentication
      - Process, e.g., accounting with regard to Sarbanes–Oxley
    - Stakeholder policy
      - Customer policy
      - Managed services
      - On-site management
      - On-site contracting
    - Operational SLAs
      - Internal operations
      - Customer operations

---

* Compliance verification is part of the IA^2F.

8.5.2   Audit Process

A generic audit process consists of:

- Audit trigger event; something that kicks off an audit task
  - Calendar-driven (e.g., quarterly, annually, coincides with fiscal year)
  - Event-driven (e.g., security incident)
- Audit notification
- Determining responsibilities
- Audit performance
- Analysis of discovery data
- Reporting results
- Organizational review and internal feedback

The following sections elaborate on the audit process.

8.5.2.1   Audit Trigger Events

An audit policy includes statements regarding potential audit trigger events, for example:

- Calendar-driven
  - An audit specifically related to system vulnerabilities shall be performed on each segment of the Company X network, at least annually.
  - Company X reserves the right to audit all or any part of the Company X network as often as deemed necessary.
- Following security breach or incident investigation
- Following significant IT or IA infrastructure modifications
- Following any indication that the information security or business threat environment has changed or is about to change significantly

8.5.2.2   Audit Notification

The audit policy provides parameters for notification of audit and may include statements such as the following:

- Under normal operations, department/team X notifies the CTO and affected business unit prior to the initiation of any audit.
- Prior to the initiation of any audit under this policy, the prospective auditors shall notify the Company X CTO and the affected business unit CIO(s).
- A formal approval by the CSO shall direct the scheduling of corporatewide audits for vulnerabilities.

■ Formal approval is required under normal operating circumstances; no formal approval for audit is necessary under the following conditions:
  - Following a security breach or incident investigation
  - Following a significant IT or IA infrastructure configuration changes (e.g., hardware upgrades, application changes or upgrades)
  - Immediately following any indication that the information security or business threat environment has changed or is about to change significantly

The focus above is vulnerability management-centric. Similar audit notifications are appropriate for HIPAA, Sarbanes–Oxley, or other compliance management processes that require audits. A more efficient approach is to abstract all the above into a general audit policy and call out specifics only when necessary.

8.5.2.3 Audit Responsibilities and Performance

IA² identifies audit responsibilities including the use of both internal and external auditors. Internal audits are both *means to an end* (a preliminary task prior to a formal external audit) and *an end unto itself.* An internal audit as preliminary activity to an external audit provides internal operations the insight and opportunity to correct any obvious noncompliance issues. The internal audit process also prepares personnel to deal with external audits more effectively.

The audit policy should state that all personnel, subcontractors, consultants, business partners, vendors, and personnel affiliated with third parties who have access to organizational and client data shall ensure compliance with the audit policy. Audit policy specifies the primary group responsible for conducting network security audits, who implements audit policy, who coordinates audits, and who approves audit and assessment tools.

8.5.2.4 Reporting Results

The IA² Process identifies who and how audit results are owned, secured, and maintained. The storage and disclosure of audit data is to be fully compliant with privacy laws, regulations, and policies applicable in the area where the data resides.

8.5.2.5 Organizational Feedback

The purpose of the assessment or audit is to provide verification that existing X functions as intended, or identify gaps and a gap closure plan. The final step is to provide the insights garnered from the assessment or audit back into organizational structure, policy, standards, procedures, operations, relationships, etc.

8.5.3 Sarbanes–Oxley: An Audit and Assessment Example

In deference to space considerations, the following example is very brief and is in essence a reflection of the above assessment and audit details. The Sarbanes–Oxley Act of 2002 (SOX) is intended to protect investors by improving the accuracy and reliability of corporate disclosure with respect to finances; IA audits cover security controls of financial systems. One approach, by no means the only approach, is to perform an initial internal audit prior to an external audit. The preceding assessment to the internal audit identifies the scope of the target systems. The internal audit prepares employees for the audit process, flushes out the obvious noncompliance issues, and provides feedback and opportunity to remediate noncompliance.

The SOX compliance assessment process (CAP) includes:

- Obtain executive backing.
- Define scope.
- Assemble SOX CAP team.
- Assign tasks to team member.
- Execute SOX CAP.
  - Current controls
    - Identify and document.
    - Verify.
  - Gap analysis
- Produce and publish results.
  - Findings
  - Remediation plan (gap closure)
- Assess roadblocks and resolutions.
- Lessons learned

8.5.4 Commentary

A preliminary internal audit is expensive but has many positive effects, including *discretely* identifying and fixing obvious noncompliance issues, and preparing internal personnel to participate in an audit. Expect the unexpected, do not be surprised if the audit sets out to discover X and issues Y, Z, A, B, and three or four variations of C crop up. For example, one organization had such a diverse collection of financial applications that some data center managers were completely unaware that financial applications resided on servers under their care. This was a critical finding of the internal audit to rectify immediately… awareness before understanding.

Sarbanes–Oxley compliance and compliance management are likely to affect many aspects of the financial accounting support infrastructure. For example, consolidation of accounting applications will both reduce the number of applications and reduce the number of data centers housing financial applications; the benefit is to narrow the SOX technical and operational scope, thus reducing the complexity of compliance management.

8.6   Policy Management

Policy management includes:

- Establishing corporate policy
- Communicating policy to employees
- Implementing and enforcing policy

The purpose of policies is to state appropriate behavior or actions for the organization. Policies manage expectations of the organization for employee behavior, and expectations on the part of the employee on how the organization will treat him; this warrants a considerable effort for policy generation and policy content. The goal of security policies is to convey appropriate actions with respect to addressing business risk and maintaining mission integrity.

The scope of security policies addresses physical infrastructure, technical infrastructure, intra- and intercompany relationships, and interactions that use or support information and information technologies relevant to the organizational mission. A bit of careful planning and writing produces policies that are extensible to accommodate various compliance requirements (e.g., HIPAA, SOX). Writing a complete set of separate policies for each individual compliance requirement creates redundant work and may result in inconsistency or, worse, conflicting policies. Rather than generate a set of HIPAA-specific policies or SOX-specific policies, generate a set of security policies and add qualifications to accommodate the legislation. Policies focused on IA rather than today's legislation will be extensible to accommodate the legislation of tomorrow.

IA policies should address the full spectrum of organizational concerns: personnel, physical, cyber, technology, infrastructure, servers, applications, and more. Each policy should be concise and follow a consistent format to promote ease of generation, maintenance, and readability. Many online and print resources offer suggestions for policy subjects and language.

8.6.1   Security Policies

Policies bound and qualify organizational behavior and are in essence corporate law. Policies are a subset of the internal compliance requirements that also include standards, procedures, mission statement, and SLAs. The act of creating policies is a subset of compliance management.

Security policy categories include *administrative*, *personnel*, *physical*, and *cyber*; specific security policy examples are password, encryption, access, firewall, intrusion detection, and anti-malware. The development process for any specific security policy includes:

- Identify compliance requirements.
  - Legislative and regulatory: Sarbanes–Oxley, Clinger–Cohen, and HIPAA
- Identify governing body.
  - Judicial system, Securities and Exchange Commission (SEC), Federal Trade Commission (FTC), Food and Drug Administration (FDA), Office of Management and Budget (OMB)
- Identify governing body audit process and audit guidance.
  - OMB Circular A-130
- Choose industry standards and best practices.
  - Organization decides to hold itself accountable to an industry standard or industry best practices
    - ISO 27002, NIST Special Publications (SP), COBIT
- Assess current situation.
  - As-is state of policy
    - Determine if policy exists, if it is viable, and if it is comprehensive with respect to compliance requirements.
  - As-is state of practice (i.e., policy implementation, how operations aligns with policy)

Organizational policy should include security controls. A generic security controls policy statement may read:

> Organization Y requires appropriate security controls to protect information and information technology from threats. These security controls include a combination of policies, standards, procedures, guidelines, employee awareness, and physical, hardware, and software safeguards.

A comprehensive policy includes physical access, intellectual property protection, and system and network access controls. Policies reflect compliance requirements and convey details of appropriate organizational behavior. Figure 8.3 presents the relationship among policies, standards, procedures, and guidelines.

8.6.1.1 Roles and Responsibilities

Roles and responsibilities specific to security policy development include:

- Sponsors—Those providing the financial backing and corporate clout
- Initiators—The point of accountability who starts the process

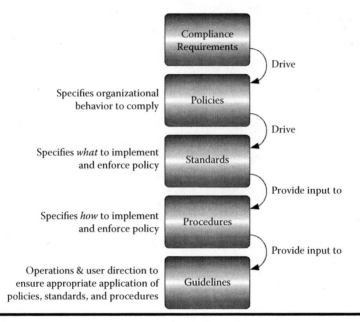

Figure 8.3 Policy, standard, and procedure relationships with compliance requirements.

- Developers—The researchers and writers
- Submitters—The formal provider to reviewers; may be the same as initiator
- Reviewers—Peer or management team to validate content
- Approvers—Formal set of approvers; often take recommendation of reviewers
- Implementers—Apply policy to business operations, technical infrastructure, and solutions

Policy sponsors are more often technology and security managers; less often, executive sponsors dictate the need for policy (e.g., policy to guide organizational behavior in support of Sarbanes–Oxley). Steps to policy design and implementation include:

- Write policies in support of external compliance requirements, industry standards and best practices, and business drivers.
- Peers and various line managers review and comment on policy from their particular perspectives.
- Place review emphasis on the practicality of policy and balancing operational effectiveness with security.
- Reviewers provide recommendations to approvers, who ultimately sign off on the policy prior to its internal publication and dissemination.

■ Business managers, system administrators, and security administrators reflect published policy in operations.

8.6.1.2   Policy Drivers

Drivers behind security policy development include both business and technical. Business drivers precede the need for the technology that supports it. The introduction of new technology requires policies to guide its appropriate and secure use. The policy development process applies to both initial development and ongoing maintenance.

8.6.1.3   Commentary

Policies may represent corporate law but should not be caught up in the semantics of actual law, where entirely too much emphasis is put on the letter of the law and not its spirit. Corporate policy should state the intent of the policy, provide examples, and provide guidance on appropriate action and on consequences for noncompliance. The bottom-line message should be, *when in doubt, act in keeping with the spirit of the policy; keep the best interests of your fellow employees and the organization in mind.*

Policy should be a driving force behind individual action; unfortunately, many employees remain unaware that policies exist and the details of the contents. Policy creation must go hand-in-hand with policy dissemination, often in the form of an awareness program.

8.6.1.4   Policy Examples: E-Mail and Internet Appropriate Use

The business drivers include optimizing productivity by minimizing time-wasting activity such as searching the Internet for personal reasons. Another goal of appropriate use is to avoid liability claims and litigation costs because of offensive material disseminating through organizational equipment. The IA architect must balance this big brother perspective against employee empowerment and against creating an oppressive workplace atmosphere.

Appropriate use policies for e-mail and the Internet are two instances of a broader concern: appropriate use of electronic communication media. Although e-mail and Internet figure prominently as the two most widely used electronic media, an IA architecture requires a more comprehensive approach. An effective IA architecture provides for appropriate use of at least:

■ E-mail
■ Internet/WWW
■ Intranet

- Electronic portals (e.g., virtual private network [VPN] access)
- Facsimile
- Telephone
- Cell phones
- Voice mail
- Laptops
- Wireless networks
- PDAs
- Intellectual property
- Customer information/data

The IA^2 Process evaluates existence and adequacy of appropriate use policies (AUPs) from the perspective of the organization. Policy provisions should not only include employees at work, but also partners, subcontractors, vendors, and even customers using organizational information and information technology. The IA^2 Process determines what exists, defines what AUPs are necessary, defines the desired details of AUPs, and provides a transition plan to generate or modify AUPs. The IA architect derives AUP details from external compliance requirements, internal legal requirements, operational requirements, and empirical history of the organization (e.g., burned once on X, now X is included in policy).

8.6.1.5 Policy Details

Appropriate use of electronic media policies covers at least the following areas:

- Duty not to waste electronic resources
  - Consumable resources (e.g., electricity, long-distance calls) and contending resources (e.g., bandwidth for critical applications versus streaming audio of personal interest)
- Prohibitions
  - Blocking of inappropriate content
  - Games and entertainment software
  - Illegal copying
- Accessing the Internet and usage
  - Time restrictions, site restrictions, downloading legal and illegal files
- Disclaimer of liability for use of the Internet
  - Employee violates corporate policy and the law at his or her own risk.
- Monitoring of computer usage, including e-mail and Internet
  - Organization reserves the right to monitor, but not duty to monitor, usage activity.
  - Reserving the right provides fair warning; excluding the duty provides for not having to catch everyone (anti-discrimination claim/waiver).

- Virus detection
  - Installation
  - Signature file updates
- Enforcement
  - Clearly state the consequences of inappropriate behavior.
- Enforcement stages: Manager meeting, manager meeting with HR representative, letter of reprimand, suspension with/without pay, and termination

8.6.1.6   Policy Enforcement

How strict can the organization be? How strict does it want to be? Too strict a policy will push people to circumvent safeguards. Accessing inappropriate Web sites may be purely accidental. Creating a situation where the employee must justify activity may be embarrassing all around. A suggested method is to promote self-policing. Publish the most frequently visited Internet sites on the corporate policy intranet site. When the top ten sites fall into categories of sports, finance, travel, and online auctions, most employees will get the message that management is aware of what's going on. If this gentle nudge toward appropriate use does not work, the elbow-in-the-ribs method still remains an option.

8.6.2   Using Social Psychology to Enforce Policies

The Enterprise Context Framework (ECF) presents a business process hierarchy that includes *workflow*, *process*, and *tasks*. Task types include kinetic (manual) tasks, automated (service) tasks, and cognitive tasks. Cognition (mental processes) segues into psychology. Psychology includes individual psychology, organizational psychology, group dynamics, and relationships. The point is that psychology plays a role within any organization. The intent of using psychology is not to be manipulative; rather, the intent is to be more effective. To that end and intent, the psychology of persuasion increases the effectiveness of awareness and training programs, especially when disseminating policy and attempting to instill awareness, understanding, and compliance.

The IA² Framework provides an IA² people view. The IA² Process addresses the existence and adequacy of policy dissemination programs as a potential business risk. Many policy dissemination and security awareness programs attempt to be a one-size-fits-all. Given that a one-size-fits-all solution rarely fits any particular situation well, various tailored approaches will increase effectiveness. Architecting a framework for driving behavior toward IA policy awareness, understanding, and compliance is organizational specific. For example, passive IA policy dissemination (e.g., posting policy on an intranet Web site) may be appropriate in some cases, but active IA policy dissemination (e.g., live training) may be more appropriate in others.

8.6.2.1 Audience Framing and Message Delivery

Interviews and surveys are useful to discern the audience current state of awareness and learning method to which they will be most receptive. The results of the survey provide insight to categorizing employee current state of awareness, knowledge, and needs with respect to organizational policies. The following categories provide guidance for what to look for in level of awareness and knowledge:

- Introduce IA awareness: Initiate the unaware that IA exists and establish a knowledge foundation on which to build.
- Increase IA awareness: Present why IA is important.
- Practicalize IA: Move from the abstract to the pragmatic—how IA applies to the organization, business process, and technology.
- Personalize IA: Present how IA is important to the individual and individual role in IA.
- Habitualize IA: How to make IA part of everyday operations, awareness.

The means to achieve these goals depend on the audience, how they think, and what mental state they are in; thought modes and mental state present clues to what tools to use to provoke change. The content of the message (the depth and breadth of IA policy information) depends on the audience's current stage of learning, that is, where the individuals are in the audience framework.

People generally lean toward one of two thinking modes: systematic and heuristic. Systematic thinkers actively seek facts to evaluate logically. Heuristic thinkers are "aware of the situation, but they are not thinking carefully enough to catch flaws, errors, and inconsistencies."[*]

The two general categories of influence tools are arguments and cues. Arguments appeal to systemic thinkers and include "facts, evidence, examples, reasoning, and logic."[†] Cues appeal to heuristic thinkers who are receptive to "easy to process information like the attractiveness, friendliness, or expertise of the source."[‡] Most people are heuristic thinkers. As evidence, look at the average TV commercial and its references to vague promises from attractive actors in fun situations versus a chart and real statistics on what the user of the product may actually expect. Despite TV commercials not addressing the realities of the product, they are effective in selling them.

The situation is similar for IA policy dissemination and enforcement. The objective is to raise awareness and achieve compliance. The question is how to achieve a high level of effectiveness for IA policies. Using heuristic tools that provide cute, clever, easily remembered messages is more effective.

---

[*] Booth-Butterfield, S., *Steve's Primer of Practical Persuasion and Influence*, p. 8.
[†] Ibid., p. 9.
[‡] Ibid., p. 9.

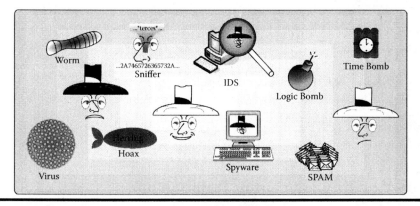

Figure 8.4 Heuristic icon and character samples.

Cartoon icons and characters make the message more memorable to the heuristic thinker. Figure 8.4 contains examples to use in a heuristic-focused policy dissemination campaign. Cartoons or similar iconic figures representing viruses, logic bombs, stereotypical good guys (white hats), and bad guys (black hats) help the message stick. For example, *spyware* as a word has less impact to the average employee than a picture of a spy-like figure peeking out from the computer screen.

8.6.2.2 Commentary

The difference between a builder and an architect is when the builder is given the blueprints, he goes off and builds the house. When the architect receives the blueprints, he asks questions about your lifestyle, likes, and dislikes. The architect addresses who you are, what you want, why you want it, and how you live, including an assessment of social psychology and social dynamics to the objective of providing a better solution.

Chapter 9 provides details with respect to security standards. Security standards describe what to use to implement and enforce policy. Policy implementation is the practical, effective fulfillment of the policy. IA policy implementation may include the acquisition or development of IA services and mechanisms. Policy enforcement is the ability to detect policy violations and to act upon those violations with corrective measures or sanctions. IA policy enforcement includes monitoring and responding to violations of policy. As an analogy, consider legislation. There are many laws on the books and a well-defined process to propose, debate, refine, and ratify laws. These laws are implemented in so far as they have been ratified and now exist. Moreover, there exists a judicial system to enforce laws. However, the existence of a law does not guarantee its enforcement. Law enforcement officers may not be aware of the law, or they may not understand its application in day-to-day activities. Moreover, the judicial system may not have precedent to base decisions on, and therefore is hesitant to enforce the law. Likewise for policies; they may exist and there may be mechanisms to enforce them, but they may not actually be enforced.

Security procedures describe how to implement and enforce policy. Security procedures incorporate best practices for configuration and operations (see the IA² LoS in chapter 2). Details of security procedures are organizational and situational specific. Risk assessments, threat space assessments, vulnerability assessments, and business impact assessments all provide considerations for the degree of security. Security procedures reflect how to implement and maintain that degree.

8.7 Security Education, Training, and Awareness Management

In the beginning of the this book, in the section Goals for the Reader, Figure 8.5 presents learning phases to progress from unaware through to fluency and specialized skills. The same principles apply to a security education, training, and awareness (SETA) program.

SETA is a comprehensive program for introducing and expounding on security issues within the organization in a series of iterative and ongoing steps, as shown in Figure 8.6. External compliance requirements and internal policy drive the need for one or more aspects of SETA. Security awareness targets the broader employee base to communicate:

■ That there are security issues
■ What those issues are
■ How to recognize anomalies as security issues

Architecting a security awareness program determines what issues to communicate, how to communicate them, and how to measure the effectiveness of

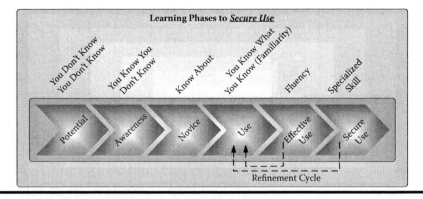

Figure 8.5   Learning phases to secure use.

	Security		
	Education	Training	Awareness
Attribute	Why	How	What
Level	Insight	Knowledge	Information
Objective	Understanding	Skill	Recognition
Teaching Method	Theoretical Instruction - Seminar, discussion, background reading	Practical Instruction - Lecture, case study, hands-on	Media - Videos, newsletters, posters, etc.
Test Measure	Essay	Problem Solving	Objective True/False
Impact Timeframe	Long-Term	Intermediate	Short-Term
Potential Audience	Architects, designers, managers, strategists	Administrators, developers, tacticians	Broad employee base

Figure 8.6   SETA comparative framework. (Derived from NIST SP800-12. *An Introduction to Computer Security,* **p. 147.)**

the program. Many of these answers lie within determining and evaluating the potential audience.

8.7.1   Security Education, Training, and Awareness (SETA) Policy

The IA architecture addresses the need for a *SETA policy*. This policy is not so much concerned with means and method of delivery as it is with specifying a minimum SETA requirement and providing traceability to business drivers. A SETA policy specifies new employee induction, including what to cover, a timeframe for delivery, how to deliver, and various acknowledgments (e.g., sign-off on understanding and compliance). SETA policy covers similar specifications for ongoing security awareness and tracking participation and acknowledgment. The policy may also address the need for visible reminders, such as posters, periodic e-mail, newsletters, and a permanent intranet site dedicated to security awareness.

Once the SETA policy is developed, the challenge is to create an effective delivery that promotes understanding and compliance. Architecting a security awareness program requires identifying and evaluating each potential audience to determine what issues to communicate, how to communicate them, and how to measure the effectiveness of the program.

8.7.2 SETA Architecture

The SETA architecture foundation lies with the organizational compliance requirements, internal policy, and results of the security awareness evaluation. An outline of SETA architecture includes:

- Evaluate current SETA environment.
  - Programs, delivery media
  - New hires, existing employees
  - Alignment with security policies and other business drivers or external compliance influences
- Define SETA principles.
  - Align with corporate goals and policy.
  - Define core competencies; minimal knowledge base for an effective <position title> within <company name>.
- Minimal knowledge base
  - Enumerate list of minimal knowledge.
  - Create a list or table of skills and training to develop skills.
- Specialized knowledge base
  - Similar to above, only in specialized areas (e.g., IT, security, finance, sales, etc.); the focus in IA architecture is security.
- Evaluate skill base
  - Survey employees to determine current skill level.
  - Compare against minimal knowledge base.
  - Generate training plan to achieve minimal knowledge base and increase specialized knowledge base.
- Define development plans.
  - Prioritize according to:
    - Imminent need
    - Gap closure for policy compliance
- Determine best delivery method.
  - Active
    - Live/in person, broadcast video, Web cast
  - Passive
    - CBT, Web based, document download

To avoid being arbitrary, devise the SETA architecture in consideration of best practices and industry standards, best practices for general security issues (horizontal issues across all industries), and security issues specific to industry verticals such as HIPAA for health care and FISMA for federal civilian agencies. Industry standards include:

- NIST SP 800-12 and SP 800-50 to develop a SETA program
- ISO 27002 to determine best practices
- SSE-CMM to develop quality, repeatable results

8.7.3 SETA Deployment

Security awareness deployment is part of a larger SETA deployment effort. Security education provides insight into the whys of security; security training provides the how-to skills of security; security awareness is information about security.* Security awareness is critical for all personnel that lack a basic understanding of security. For the initiated, it may take their awareness to a new level; it will at least reinforce an awareness that turns "recognition of events that could indicate a security incident into reflex."†

8.7.4 Commentary

Although the Employee Security Awareness Evaluation is an excellent part of the overall vulnerability assessment process, it will fall short without an in-depth assessment of the social and individual psychology that results in a focused IA policy dissemination campaign. Section 8.6.2 offers insight into a more in-depth, focused approach to achieve security understanding and compliance.

Now that employees are aware of the policies and know where to get them, do they understand them? How do you promote understanding? *Understanding* is the goal of the training program, that is, conveying the message so that the employee gets it. Given that the employee is now aware, possesses a copy, and understands the policy, there remains the need to ensure he actually complies with it. Conveying compliance expectations is part of policy, including very clear sanction policies for noncompliance. Monitoring and tracking addresses the occurrence and effectiveness of the IA solutions with respect to the business and technology drivers behind them.

8.7.5 Effectiveness Metrics (Tracking)

Compliance verification ensures the IA solutions work as intended and as prescribed in the compliance requirements documents. The IA² Framework includes filtering

---

* Paraphrased from Trygstad, Ray, *Security Policy*, Illinois Institute of Technology, p. 50.
† Randolph, K., Warshawsky, Gale, and Numkin, Louis, *Security Awareness*, p. 2.

architectural drivers through compliance requirements during each phase of the system development life cycle:

- Technical infrastructure IA^2 verification
  - C&A procedures (e.g., NIST SP 800-37, NIACAP, DITSCAP)
  - SSE-CMM
- Development IA^2 verification
  - Common Criteria
  - SEI-CMM/SEI-CMMI
- Administrative IA^2 verification
  - COOP tabletop exercises
- Business process IA^2 verification
  - Is X [consistent | extensible | scalable | auditable | agile | process oriented | as simple as it can be | as complex as it needs to be, but no more | etc.], where X ∈ (policy, process, procedure, plan, tool, intelligence gathering, intelligence processing, end-user interface, end-user data collection, etc.)?
- Training and education and training and awareness
  - NIST training standards in SP 800-50 and SP 800-16

SETA effectiveness metrics measure the success of dissemination, awareness, understanding, and compliance.

Dissemination metrics may track number of communications sent (number of e-mails, snail-mails, Web pop-ups, voice mail reminders, and live training sessions via conference call or online chat). **Awareness** metrics may track number of communications read (number of e-mails opened via return receipt, pop-up acknowledgments, voice mail retrievals, and live session attendees). Consider providing a survey; consider using statistical sampling to avoid involving the entire employee population. **Understanding** metrics are derived from a quiz or survey with required participation. Finishing the quiz sends a unique employee identifier plus a score. **Compliance** metrics track number of calls to help desk or security desk since training/awareness program, or track number of violations since training/awareness program compared to pretraining/awareness.

8.8 Privacy

Webster defines *privacy* as "the quality or state of being apart from company or observation; freedom from unauthorized intrusion."* The Privacy Act 1974 mentions "privacy" five times and does not provide a definition. The Health Insurance Portability and Accountability Act (HIPAA) Final Privacy Rule (FSR) mentions

---

* http://www.webster.com/cgi-bin/dictionary?book=Dictionary&va=privacy (accessed December 2004).

"privacy" over 1,600 times, and although it does not directly define privacy, it alludes to definitions through third-party references, including:

- "Alan Westin, *Privacy and Freedom* (1967) and Janna Malamud Smith, *Private Matters: In Defense of the Personal Life* (1997). These writings emphasize the link between privacy and freedom and privacy and the 'personal life,' or the ability to develop one's own personality and self-expression."[*]
- "In 1890, Louis D. Brandeis and Samuel D. Warren defined the right to privacy as 'the right to be let alone.'"[†]
- "Or, as Cavoukian and Tapscott observed the right of privacy is: 'the claim of individuals, groups, or institutions to determine for themselves when, how, and to what extent information about them is communicated.'"[‡]

8.8.1 Privacy Qualifiers

The concept of privacy is one consideration, but what privacy applies to is quite another. The focus for online privacy is personal information or personally identifiable information. Consider the examples in Table 8.1.

8.8.2 Compliance Requirements

There are external and internal compliance requirements. Internal requirements include organizational mission and other convictions concerning the protection of privacy of client, vendor, partner, and employee information.

Various legislative compliance requirements (external), including the HIPAA Privacy Rule, the Privacy Act 1974, and the Freedom of Information Act, provide privacy qualifiers. The PATRIOT Act encroaches on personal privacy in the name of national security; both are foundations of American way of life and the two must work in harmony, each containing a bit of the other.

8.8.2.1 External Privacy Qualifiers

Organization type and industry will dictate which external compliance requirements come into play with respect to privacy. Organizational types include commercial, nonprofit, and both civilian and defense government. Industry-specific concerns include health care, financial, and those that qualify as part of United State's critical infrastructure.

---

[*] HIPAA Final Security Rule, p. 15.
[†] Ibid., p. 16.
[‡] Ibid., p. 16.

Table 8.1   Privacy Qualifier Examples

Qualifier	Description
Personally identifiable information (PII)	"Any information that identifies or can be used to identify, contact, or locate the person to whom such information pertains."
Personal health information (PHI)	"The Privacy Rule defines PHI as individually identifiable health information, held or maintained by a covered entity or its business associates acting for the covered entity, that is transmitted or maintained in any form or medium (including the individually identifiable health information of non-U.S. citizens)."
Electronic personal health information (EPHI)	The HIPAA Final Security Rule (FSR) goes to some length to carefully define electronic media.
Personally identifiable transactional data	Information that describes your online activities such as the Web sites that you have visited, addresses to which you have sent e-mail, files that you have downloaded, and other information revealed in the normal course of using the Internet.

8.8.2.2   Internal Privacy Qualifiers

Organizational policies and standards that address privacy include privacy statement, security policy, privacy policy, and HR policies. Motivations behind these policies and procedures include legislative and regulatory compliance, liability management, proactive litigation management, customer trust, and reflections of such trust in the balance sheet line item *goodwill*.

Note that litigation management includes a review of the potential laws and guidelines that govern litigation should circumstances come to that end. For example, chapter 8 of the Federal Sentencing Guidelines, "Sentencing of Organizations," provides for the calculation of culpability. The guidelines provide insight on how a judge may determine guilt as well as the extent of guilt, the latter having a direct correlation with the extent of fine or jail time. Proactively managing for the potential of litigation is good business practice and should be part of a comprehensive IA^2 approach.

8.8.3   Privacy IA² Perspective

Privacy should not be a hidden attribute under confidentiality; this is why the IA core principles separate out privacy as a distinct principle. Many organizations formulate and implement a security management program. Privacy deserves the

Table 8.2   Censorship Guidelines

Potential Result	Action	Comments
Litigation	Block at all times.	These include hate groups, porn sites, or sites facilitating illegal activity (e.g., child porn).
Time wasters	Block during working hours.	These include dating services, chat groups, etc.

same attention. The business benefits for addressing privacy in detail include legislative compliance (e.g., HIPAA Privacy Rule), new business, customer retention, and increase to goodwill on the balance sheet. Appendix J provides an outline of a privacy management program.

8.8.4   Censorship

Do employers have a duty to protect their employees from offensive material? Do they have a right? One person's offensive material is another's art. Can a balance be struck? In the case of censoring online material in the workplace, the balance is between providing a positive work environment (i.e., neither oppressive micro-management nor big brother) and maintaining acceptable levels of productivity. A simple yet effective censorship framework is to implement appropriate Internet use software to filter Internet material using the guidelines in Table 8.2.

Establishing stringent guidelines and restricting access to other potential distractions such as financial sites, travel information, and sports information is problematic. Many employees may need access to travel sites for business travel. Most at the executive level access financial sites and sports information; if the CEO says unblock, unblock.

Enforcing complex filtering of Internet information may be very costly, only partially effective, or even totally ineffective. Establishing and communicating policy and implementing a self-policing system may produce higher compliance rates than automated blocking. For example, on the organization's intranet, publish a list of the top ten sites visited. There is no need to associate personal information with access, just the fact that www.<top 10>.com were accessed. Employee awareness often prompts self-restraint, especially if the top ten are non-business-related.

8.8.5   Censorship IA² Perspective

With respect to IA², censorship, or appropriate use enforcement, is a service within the IA² LoS. Supporting mechanisms may include firewalls, appropriate use software, and audit logs.

8.9 Enterprise Operations Management: IA Context

The IA² Process approaches operations security from the perspective of enterprise operations management (EOM). The IA architect derives operational security needs from external compliance requirements as well as internal strategic and tactical (operational) requirements and goals. A careful assessment will determine what exists (as-is), help define what EOM aspects are necessary to maintain expected performance levels (to-be), and provide a transition plan to modify operations (transition plan). The EOM approach considers:

- Enterprise network operations center (ENOC)
    - Covers the IT infrastructure, including routers, switches
- Enterprise systems operations center (ESyOC)
    - Covers key applications, servers (e.g., voice server)
- Enterprise security operations center (ESOC)
    - Covers the IA infrastructure, including firewall (FW), VPN, anti-virus (AV), IDS
- Enterprise management operations center (EMOC)
    - Provides intelligence gathering and intelligence analysis of internal operations plus external factors that may influence internal operations decisions
    - Provides evaluation of event/incident aggregation

EOM also monitors personnel, including identity management, privilege management, exercise of claim of privilege, employee location (in/out building/room/ data center), plus physical aspects, including campus, building, room access control, and monitoring of environmentals (i.e., temperature, humidity, fire, flood) and more. The expense of a comprehensive EOM may be prohibitive for many organizations; however, the IA² Process should examine the need for EOM attributes (Figure 8.7).

The information assurance architecture development process considers the need to integrate security operations into other technical and business operations as well as security operations as a separate but integrated part of overall operations. The following sections elaborate on the EOM attributes in Figure 8.7.

8.9.1 Network Management

Network management includes management models, services, mechanics, products/vendors, operations, compliance requirements, and technical infrastructure. Starting with architecture and design and going through implementation, network management is in the operations stage.

Traditional client/server applications provide a 1:1 session link between server applications or data and client applications. The mainframe delivery model pro-

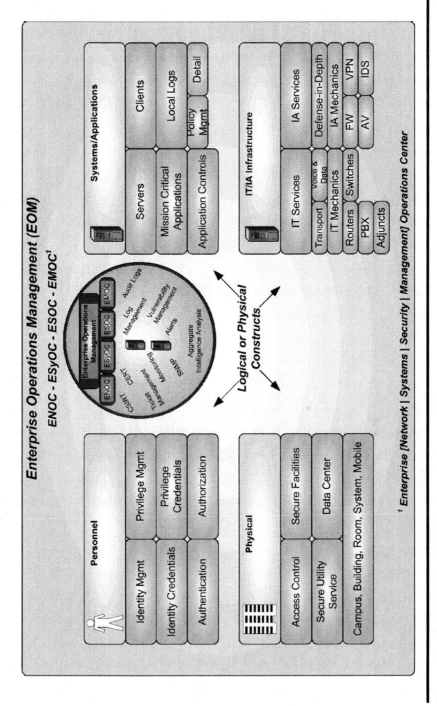

Figure 8.7 Enterprise operations management overview.

vides a very thin client, often a terminal with no independent intelligence from the central processor. The distributed server model provides like services on a regional, campus, or departmental level; servers provide specialized functionality (e.g., order entry) and multiple servers provide applications and data to a thick client, the desktop PC (the latter provides a 1:1 session link). Application service delivery (ASD) is an emerging model where the service provider abstracts applications from the infrastructure. Clients request a service and a software agent picks up the request and finds the most efficient way to deliver the results to the client. Clients no longer have dedicated servers, and the 1:1 session link gives way to server and service transparency.

The ASD is a new technical model, a new way to deliver technical capabilities, and a new method of managing resources on a network. This is an example of a technical driver for IA². Accompanying the business benefits of ASD are new risks—risks that are discernible by examining network operations and technical service delivery using the IA² Process. Implications to network design and network management include designing multiple paths between clients and agent services as well as between agent services and servers. Such designs promote load balancing and redundancy to keep operations going in the event of individual agent, server, or link failures.

8.9.1.1   Network Management Services

The network operations center (NOC) watches over the technical infrastructure of voice and data communications to ensure functionality and steer alignment with business goals. Extensions of the NOC are security operations center (SOC) and management operations center (MOC) services. Whereas NOC focuses on the communications infrastructure, SOC focuses on the information assurance issues of communications and other areas of the business.

MOC is a service that may compile intelligence from the NOC, SOC, and other areas, and perform and report on intelligence analysis. MOC concerns include a meta-view of the mechanics of operations (e.g., network performance) as well as in context of the business process; the latter is the value-add for the MOC. Each service is logically separate, though there is likely overlap in personnel and equipment.

8.9.1.2   Network Management Mechanics

The NOC watches over the technical infrastructure using automated tools and industry standard protocols like the Simple Network Management Protocol (SNMP). Infrastructure devices alert a central server of potential problems, for example, via SNMP traps. The server displays a picture of the device in error and may alert via audio, page, cell phone call, or e-mail, or initiate a trouble ticket with a local help desk.

The mechanics of network management also include voice and data traffic management. Careful planning of voice networking may vastly reduce long-distance and local per-call access charges. Although worth a bit of planning, overcomplicating voice management has diminishing returns in an environment of $.02 per minute long-distance charges. Data traffic management includes ensuring quality of service (QoS) for streaming traffic (e.g., voice and video) and traffic shaping to handle traffic between disparate bandwidth links (e.g., T1 pipe encountering a 256K bottleneck).

SOC mechanics include the IA infrastructure (firewalls, etc.) and application of IA philosophies like defense-in-depth. Additionally, SOC mechanics include a watch-the-watcher configuration to monitor IA infrastructure operations. The firewall may watch Internet traffic; the meta-view of the firewall watches the firewall to ensure proper functionality.

8.9.1.3   Network Management and IA²

IA must be integrated with existing business and technical operations, including network management. IA training prepares NOC personnel to be aware that operational anomalies may be infrastructure problems or may be symptoms of an attack. For instance, NOC must be able to determine whether 100 percent CPU utilization on a server is a runaway application or an attack signature. From a denial-of-service perspective, the end is the same. However, the response activity is significantly different. An extension of the NOC is the security operating center (SOC). Whereas NOC personnel keep an eye on network infrastructure, the SOC personnel keep an eye on the IA infrastructure, ensuring proper operations of firewall, VPN, IDS, and AV. They are accountable for patch management and IA updates like the latest AV virus signature files.

8.9.2   Operations Security Management

Operations are the support, control, monitoring, and maintenance of information, information technology, physical infrastructure, and personnel that support the organizational mission. Operations security is the assurance these aspects function in compliance with organizational policy and within defined safety parameters. Operational concerns include cyber, physical, and personnel.

To achieve a good baseline of operational security, consider the following:

■ Continuity management
  – Continuity of operations
  – Disaster recovery
  – Backup and recovery, backup media rotation and off-site storage

- ■ Identity and privilege management
  - – Authentication and authorization management
  - – Access control; cyber, physical, badging, identity management; privilege management; visitor management, including monitoring, logging, forensic data analysis, enforcement, and interdiction
  - – Access to production data, applications, operations center
- ■ Operational impact managment
  - – Scheduling off-hours activity; principle of least-impact or no-impact changes
- ■ Configuration management
  - – New COTS/GOTS (government off-the-shelf software); staging development to production
  - – Risk management, back-out/recovery plans
- ■ Production management
  - – Monitoring resources, systems, infrastructure; service level agreements (SLAs)
  - – Logging, log management, log review, activity reconstruction
  - – Patch management

An IA architectural principle is: *security is an intrinsic element of service delivery and is everyone's business.* Approaching security throughout the SDLC and ELCM ensures the IA architect considers security at every step. The budget may not allow for all security measures, but conscious risk acceptance is better than a big, expensive, after-the-fact surprise. The rules in Table 8.3 provide good security guidelines and may provide key elements of a security awareness program.

8.10 Computer Security Incident Response Team (CSIRT)

An incident response team (IRT) responds to organizational security events; a computer security incident response team (CSIRT) responds to organizational computer security events. The CSIRT resides within the operations group, likely as a subset of security operations. Figure 8.8 shows CSIRT as an elaboration of the IA operations cycle *respond* phase, an operational construct under the security operations aspect of enterprise operations management (EOM). EOM includes network operations, security operations, system operations, and management operations. A comprehensive EOM monitors cyber, physical, and personnel security and includes consolidated log management, aggregate log analysis, and aggregate intelligence analysis.

An effective CSIRT infrastructure includes security incident management: technology, process, and personnel (Figure 8.9). Moreover, effective CSIRT also requires a meta-view of CSIRT activities that provides analysis of effectiveness,

Table 8.3   Operations Security Guidelines

Rule	Description
Enforce security policies.	The security policies establish rules for organizational activity and use of information and information technology. Create awareness of policy, enforce policy with IA mechanisms, and sanction violators appropriately.
Be malware aware.	Every electronic file is a potential carrier of malware, and every network connection a potential pathway for malware. Check files upon entry to the organizational information technology environment.
Be generally aware.	Protect confidential information and information technology. Understand what constitutes suspicious or anomalous behavior. Learn how to report it within the organization.
Knowledge work products are organizational assets.	Knowledge workers produce organizational assets in the form of documents. Store these documents on accessible servers that are part of the backup process. Do not only store documents on an individual PC.
A core IA principle is possession.	Theft of information or an information technology asset results in loss of the value of the asset, but more importantly, loss of what that asset does or contains may be many factors greater than the value of the asset. Protect IT assets against theft.
Passwords	Do not underestimate the power of using passwords. Follow standards for strong passwords as befits the environment. Treat passwords like a toothbrush—do not share them and change them every three months.
Authorized software only	Do not introduce unauthorized software into the IT environment. Free downloads may not have a price, but they have a high potential cost in loss of productivity (games) and loss of proprietary information (spyware).

Continued

Table 8.3 Operations Security Guidelines (Continued)

Rule	Description
Laws protect livelihoods.	Pirate is a romanticized term for thief. Do not copy licensed and copyrighted software, documents, music, books, pictures, videos, etc. Someone making a living from these documents likely worked hard for the revenue they will produce.
Enforce access controls.	Protect access to buildings, floors, rooms, offices, and technology. Activate password-protected screen savers when leaving systems unattended. Enforce a policy of automatic logoff for inactivity.
Business use only	Use information technology for business use only. This includes not using PCs for personal activities (e.g., games, balancing checkbooks, running a side business). Check the news like you check your hair in the mirror—usually a quick fix will do—but then back to work.

identifies lessons learned, and provides feedback for CSIRT as well as organizational operations improvement.

8.10.1 Compliance Requirements

Legislative requirements for a CSIRT include the Federal Information Security Act 2002 (FISMA), which addresses the need for a federal information security incident center (§ 3546), and the need for procedures for detecting, reporting, and responding to security incidents. Although FISMA addresses the U.S. civilian government, it does highlight an IA service of interest to commercial organizations as well.

Commercial compliance requirements (primarily legislative) are likely not to have explicit requirements for CSIRT; however, deriving implicit CSIRT requirements in support of explicit HIPAA, Sarbanes–Oxley, and other legislative requirements is highly probable.

8.10.2 CSIR Policy

A computer security incident response policy (CSIRP) should be part of a comprehensive set of enterprise security policies. The CSIRP addresses CSIRT responsibilities in so far as preparing and planning for incident management, preestablishing priorities (e.g., preserving existing revenue streams), incident notification, incident identification, incident response, and recording incident details and lessons learned.

Tasks	Services	Mechanisms	Comments (People, Skills, Knowledge, Equipment, Access, Authority)
Prerequisites	Awareness Training • CSIRT	• Ticket Mngmt	Provide awareness to discern and mechanisms to report security incidents.
Incident Reporting	• CSIRT - Contact Center Agents	• E-mail • Phone • IM • Automated Alerts	Predefined Rules with respect to: Mission Integrity, Operational Priorities (revenue v. security v. safety), etc.
Triage	• CSIRT - Analysts	• Priority Lists	CSIRC may escalate to specialized teams; e.g., trained anti-virus personnel
Escalation	• CSIRT	• Contact Lists	Identify systems, servers, applications, malware, and other incident specifics
Identification	• CSIRT – Subject Matter Expert (SME)	• Discovery Tools (e.g. AV)	Eliminate spreading of problem; minimize organizational impact
Isolation	• On-Site Contacts • CSIRT Dispatch	• TBD (situational dependent)	Treat the issues; may be symptoms, not problems
Treatment	• IA infrastructure: AV, IDS, etc.	• E.g. Inoculation Tools, Install Disks Ad hoc tools	Resolve issues to restore operations; may or may not be problem resolution at this point
Resolution	• CSIRT – SME • Vendor	• Testing tools	
Root Cause Analysis	• CSIRT – Analysts • RCA SME • RCA Methodology	• RCA Tools	Perform RCA to identify and treat problem v. previous treatment of active symptom
Process Review & Feedback	• Tracking methodology • Organizational feedback methodology	• Knowledge repository of empirical encounters and lessons learned	Eliminate recurrence or minimize organizational impact of recurrence

Pre-Incident
Active Incident
Post-Incident

Figure 8.8 IA operations cycle: *respond* details.

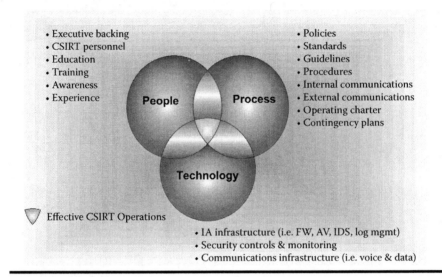

Figure 8.9 Effective CSIRT operations.

8.10.3 Practice

CSIRT procedures fall within the *respond* quartile of the IA operations cycle of anticipate, defend, monitor, and respond. Figure 8.10 provides details of an incident response taxonomy.

8.10.4 Best Practices

Best practices for CSIRT can be found in Carnegie Mellon University's *Handbook for Computer Security Incident Response Teams (CSIRTs)*, NIST SP 800-18: *Guide for Developing Security Plans for Information Technology*, and Forum of Incident Response and Security Teams (FIRST) *Best Practice Library*.

8.10.5 IA² Perspective

The CSIRT is an IA service in the IA² LoS; CSIRT operations include:

- Threat monitoring and analysis
- Validation and risk assessment
- Vulnerability management
  - Alert receipt, remediation accountability, and reporting
  - Patch management
- Security information internal dissemination

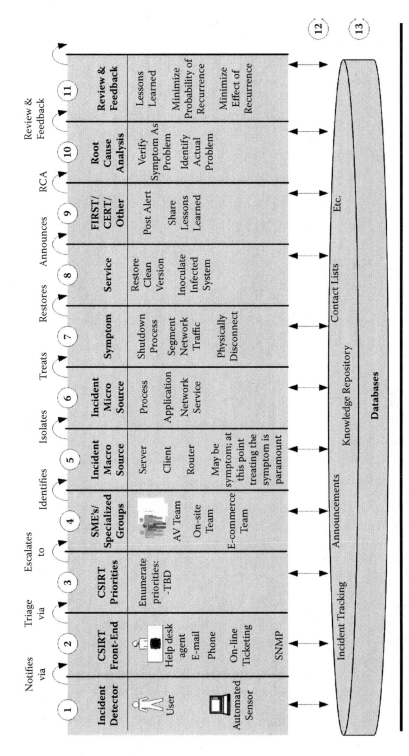

Figure 8.10 Incident response taxonomy.

- Web based
  - CSIRT Web site
  - CSIRT Web services
  - Is there any other acceptable/useful means besides the Web?
- Incident response and remediation coordination and assistance
  - Service restoration teams
  - Root cause analysis (RCA)
  - Organization feedback
    - Lessons Learned
- External liaisons
- Dealing with incident reports from other CSIRTs
  - For example, FIRST

8.11 Vulnerability Management

Vulnerability management includes vulnerability assessments that consist of vulnerability scanning, penetration testing, war driving, and war dialing. Vulnerability management also includes patch management that receives alerts from vendors regarding newly discovered vulnerabilities and how to remediate those vulnerabilities. Remediation activity includes installing patches.

8.11.1 Vulnerability Assessments

A vulnerability assessment is the act of determining the degree to which an organization's information and information technology are open to attack or damage. An abstract assessment process consists of identifying compliance requirements, comparing policy against compliance requirements, generating a gap analysis, and defining a remediation plan; plus comparing practice against policy, generating a gap analysis, and defining another remediation plan.

This framework applies to many assessment variations and is a useful tool throughout the IA² Process. For example, a compliance assessment process (CAP) is one assessment variation. CAP variations include HIPAA, Sarbanes–Oxley, and many others. A vulnerability assessment (VA) is one instance of a broader, more abstract assessment process.

A technical vulnerability assessment focuses on information and information technology internal parameter settings, configuration, and safeguards. A nontechnical vulnerability assessment focuses on non-cyber-aspects, including people (e.g., security awareness levels), physical (e.g., building security), and process (e.g., guard enforcement of entry procedures or property management procedures). These are the steps in the vulnerability assessment process:

- Determine existing infrastructure.

- Determine compliance requirements (to-be).
  - Industry best practices and vendor recommendations assist in determining ideal operating state of existing infrastructure.
    - Hardware settings
      - Application
      - Servers
      - Clients
      - IT infrastructure
      - Routers, switches
      - IA infrastructure
      - FW, VPN, AV, IDS
    - Operating system
      - Servers, clients, routers, switches, FWs, etc.
      - Parameter settings
      - Background processes
      - Patch levels
    - Applications
      - COTS
      - In-house
- Scan existing infrastructure (as-is).
  - Perform technical scan of existing infrastructure.
- Perform a gap analysis between as-is and to-be.
  - Compare scan results against ideal operating state.
- Remediation plan (a.k.a. transition plan)
  - Develop a plan to get from as-is to to-be.
- A valid part of the plan is a waiver process; this is an acknowledgment that the to-be state may be ideal, but for some reason (typically cost), the remediation plan is not feasible.

8.11.1.1   Deliverables

Vulnerability assessment deliverables include the following documents:

- Current operating state (as-is)
  - Nontechnical assessment questionnaire (if applicable)
    - Assessment questionnaire determines policy and procedure as-is.
    - Include traceability to compliance requirements; this is the basis for the assessment, the to-be comparison.
  - Technical assessment
    - Vulnerability scan
      - Assessment determines part of practice as-is.
    - Eyes-on and hands-on validation
      - Assessment determines other part of practice as-is.

- Ideal operating state (to-be)
  - Assessment questionnaire determines as-is.
  - This is the basis for the assessment, the to-be comparison; include traceability to business drivers.
- Gap analysis report
  - Align with questionnaire and provide value-added insight regarding as-is.
- Remediation plan
  - Transition plan between as-is and to-be.
  - Provide options as well as recommendations.
- Proposal

The assessment found X as-is, the to-be goal is Y, and the remediation plan is Z; the proposal is a formal document of cost and schedule to perform gap closure activity.

8.11.1.2 Deliverable Format and Content

Consider the goal of the assessment is to identify the current state of affairs and compare it to some desired end, the compliance requirement. Compliance requirements may find form in legislation (e.g., HIPAA or Sarbanes–Oxley); these are very broad and at times very vague, and defining the exact goal is matter of interpretation. Compliance requirements may also be a standard (e.g., ISO 27002 or NIST). For defense organizations, DoD instructions or directives plus other sources define compliance requirements. There are many sources for compliance requirements, and their applicability is entirely situational.

The discovery process determines the current state of policy, standards, procedure, and practice. The discovery questionnaire reflects the compliance requirements and aligns with the organization type (e.g., commercial versus government) and the organization-specific requirements. The vulnerability assessment will be a subset of the topics in the discovery questionnaire. The specifics of the vulnerability analysis are a result of customer requirements and their current situation. At the least, the results of the discovery questionnaire provide insight into existing IT and IA infrastructure on which to perform a technical scan. Additional deliverable templates are necessary for gap analysis, remediation plan, and proposal for gap closure.

8.11.2 Patch Management

Operating system vendors and application vendors constantly release patches as awareness of new vulnerabilities arises. The organization cannot just simply install patches as they arrive because many patches affect key aspects of the operating system (OS) and may render currently running applications unusable. Out of necessity, many software vendors program around a shortfall in an operating system. When the OS vendor fixes that shortfall, the software application may not work at all or not work with the same integrity as it did under the prepatched OS. The organization must set up test environments for key software applications to validate patch compatibility prior to installing patches in production environments.

8.11.3   *IA² Perspective*

A large part of the architectural process is discovery—discovery of what exists, what the organization desires, motivations, and constraints (technical, business, cultural, geographical). An effective assessment process facilitates the IA² Process. An assessment process is a construct that provides a framework for various assessment services. Assessment services include vulnerability assessment, risk assessment, and compliance assessment.

The assessment process is very similar to the architectural process of determining the as-is enterprise architecture or the as-is IA architecture, subsequently defining the to-be architecture, gap analysis, and transition plan.

The assessment process framework provides an abstract model to apply to any compliance assessment, risk assessment, or vulnerability assessment situation. The most effective assessment process finds foundation in industry best practices, including discovery questions directly traceable to applicable industry standards (e.g., ISO, NIST, and DoD instructions). The ultimate goal is to automate the assessment process to promote cost-effective execution and consistent repeatability.

8.12   Digital Forensics

Digital forensics is the application of scientific knowledge to legal issues surrounding information and information technology. Many organizations have a need for digital forensics. For most it is a post-incident afterthought that quickly turns to regret when the necessary logs are found wanting for detail, if they exist at all. As with other successful IA constructs, IA architects need to integrate digital forensics with operations, not bolt-on after the fact.

Digital forensics includes the "preservation, identification, extraction, documentation, and interpretation of computer media for evidentiary and/or root cause analysis."* "Digital Evidence is any information of probative value that is either stored or transmitted in a binary form" (SWGDE,† July 1998). Later "binary" was changed to "digital." "Digital evidence includes computer evidence, digital audio, digital video,

---

* *Computer Forensics: Incident Response Essentials.*
† Scientific Working Group on Digital Evidence.

cell phones, digital fax machines, etc."* Digital forensics also involves audit log analysis, and reconstructing or verifying event and transaction details and chronology.

8.12.1 Business Drivers

A business driver may be nonrepudiation for communication (i.e., e-mail) and transactions (e.g., customer bank withdrawal request or bank teller processing). This business driver may be the result of legislative requirements. The introduction of sophisticated cyber-legislation requires sophisticated tools to pursue prosecution, prove due diligence, and protect the innocent. Business drivers behind digital forensics may be subtle. For example, U.S. Customs applications log every border crossing and associate details with the processing Customs agent. The business driver is to provide trend analysis on border crossings, identify anomalous activity, and reconstruct chronology and details of historical crossings to identify activity patterns, including potential collaborative activity at multiple crossing points. To accurately reconstruct border-crossing activity requires transactional nonrepudiation where agents may not deny an activity in the log.

8.12.2 Compliance Requirements

Compliance requirements include legislation, RFP, CONOPS, and corporate policy.

8.12.2.1 Legislation

Although no legislation directly requires the application of digital forensics, the complexity of cyber-crime and cyber-legislation requires the right tools for the right job; there is an implicit legislative driver behind digital forensics.

8.12.2.2 RFP

Many RFPs build in the need for digital forensics by requiring transactional nonrepudiation, log management, and ability to identify unauthorized, unusual, or illegal activity; moreover, reconstruct event details and chronology—all forensics activities.

8.12.2.3 CONOPS

■ Business
  - Transactional nonrepudiation; user oriented
  - Event nonrepudiation; process oriented

---

* *An Historical Perspective of Digital Evidence*, p. 4.

- Technical
  - Nonrepudiation requirements imply the need for mechanisms to support unique identification for users and possible servers, applications, and processes.
  - Discrete event tracking/reconstruction; host-based and network-based

Aggregate event tracking/reconstruction; cradle-to-grave tracking of sessions or individual activity, including systems visited, processes and applications executed, threads initiated, files accessed, transmissions initiated, hops to other systems, etc.

8.12.2.4 Policy

Organizational policy directly specifies either the need for digital forensics or the need for a CSIRT that may support digital forensic activities.

8.12.3 Policy

Digital forensics guidelines provide direction on forensics procedures, investigation guidelines, and technical aspects of forensics, including how to approach a particular system and recommendations on forensics tools; example guidelines include:

- U.S. Secret Service *Best Practices for Seizing Electronic Evidence*
- *FBI Search and Seizure Manual*
- NIST SP 800-72: *PDA Forensics Guide*

8.12.4 Practice

Figure 8.11 summarizes the digital forensics workflow. A trigger event prompts contacting CSIRT, who goes through discovery, fact gathering, analysis, reporting, and follow-up with organizational feedback from root cause analysis and determining lessons learned.

8.12.5 Best Practices

Digital forensics best practices include:

- U.S. Secret Service *Best Practices for Seizing Electronic Evidence*
- International Organization on Computer Evidence (IOCE) *Guidelines for Best Practice in the Forensic Examination of Digital Technology*
- U.S. Department of Justice *Forensic Examination of Digital Evidence: A Guide for Law Enforcement*

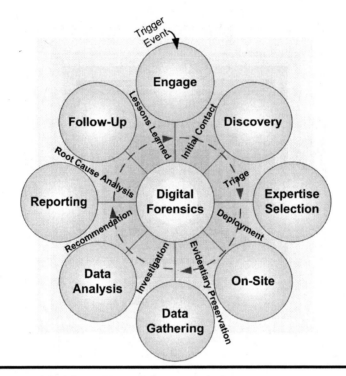

Figure 8.11 Digital forensics workflow overview.

■ Scientific Working Group for Digital Evidence (SWGDE) *Best Practices for Digital Evidence Laboratory Programs*

8.12.6   IA² Perspective

Effective use of digital forensics requires an IA architectural approach that builds in appropriate tracking mechanisms, including cyber, personnel, and physical logs. Cyber-logs include IT infrastructure (e.g., routers, switches), IA infrastructure (e.g., FW/VPN, AV, and IDS), host, client, and application logs as well. An effective digital forensics analysis provides for not only log consolidation but also aggregate log analysis.

Forensic planning and activity take place in each phase of the IA operations cycle. *Anticipatory* actions include planning and preparation from architecture throughout the solution development life cycle. Policies include what to log in COTS, servers, clients, and custom applications. SETA includes awareness for every user to be on the lookout for activity, when and how to report activity, and preserving evidence in questionable situations. *Defense* actions include optional logging from standard business as usual to high-alert logging.

Operational snapshots provide baselines to discern atypical activity. Monitoring includes log management, monitoring, and filtering expected traffic to identify anomalies, filtering anomalies to identify events, and filtering events to identify incidents. Response involves the CSIRT, which may lead to a digital forensic investigation.

Event-driven activities (i.e., trigger events) kick off forensic activity that may include automated real-time log filtering to post-event reconstruction; forensics is an integral part of the IA operations cycle. Forensics analysis may include physical, personnel, and cyber security; addressing such aspects as failed building or room access attempts; presentation of false identity or privilege claim; or unauthorized or questionable network or host activity. Successful forensics requires binding unique identification with an individual, going through a robust authentication process, plus managing the assignment of appropriate privileges and going through a robust authorization process. This series of rigid procedures provides the raw data and accountability necessary for a successful forensic investigation.

8.12.7 Commentary

A seemingly simple request for transactional nonrepudiation implies the need for identity management and authentication that strongly bind activity to individuals. This implies the need for digital signatures and public key infrastructure (PKI) or similar infrastructure. This also implies the need for robust application logging that binds digital signatures with activity, plus log management, filtering, and reporting—all under the requirements of evidentiary preservation. The architectural considerations are extensive. The ability to draw on a formal $IA^2 F$ and $IA^2 P$ to blueprint these complexities is critical to effective implementation and operations.

8.13 Business Impact Assessment

A business impact assessment (BIA) is the radar for organizational viability; it identifies those business functions critical for organizational survivability and the necessary recovery time objective (RTO) for the organization to survive. "A mission impact analysis (also known as business impact analysis [BIA] for some organizations) prioritizes the impact levels associated with the compromise of an organization's information assets based on a qualitative or quantitative assessment of the sensitivity and criticality of those assets."* In brief, the BIA is a methodology to provide guidance to focus limited resources on critical business areas during a continuity or recovery event. The four pillars of BIA are *survivability, criticality, priority,* and *accountability.* Survivability determines the downtime tolerance (DTT) or recovery time objective (RTO) for each business function. Criticality assigns

---

* NIST SP 800-30, revised: *A Risk Management Guide for Information Technology Systems*, p. 24.

relative importance to business functions. Priority determines which business functions to address first in continuity and recovery situation. Accountability identifies key players (decision makers and doers—not to imply decision makers do not do, but rather that most doers are not decision makers).

The BIA methodology applies to disaster recovery (DR), business continuity (BC), or BC variants like contingency planning (CP) or continuity of operations plan (COOP). The need for a BIA varies according to the status of the organization and organizational change. Figure 8.12 provides a decision process for the performance or reperformance of a BIA.

8.13.1   Compliance Requirements

Compliance requirements in so far as legislation or regulation do not specifically address business impact assessments. NIST SP 800-30: *Risk Management Guide for IT Systems* does mention an impact analysis as part of the risk assessment process. However, the impact analysis is in context of how a threat affects confidentiality, integrity, and availability; this is not the same approach as a BIA focus on business functionality. Organizational policy is more likely to define BIA compliance requirement as a precursor to business continuity and disaster recovery planning.

8.13.2   Policy

Security policies address the need for and provide details on disaster recovery and business continuity; these policies address the specific need for BIA. BIA-specific documentation finds form in guidelines and methodologies. The organizational risk management policy should also address BIAs. Risk management policy should primarily maintain a business focus and coincide with the need to present security solutions in business terms.

8.13.3   Practice

The BIA methodology outline includes:

- Define scope
  - Physical (e.g., geographic region)
  - Functional (e.g., finance/accounting or manufacturing)
  - Enterprisewide
- Interviews/questionnaires
  - Interview guidelines
  - Questionnaires
    - Subjective opinion (individual perspective) versus fact (accepted conventional perspective)

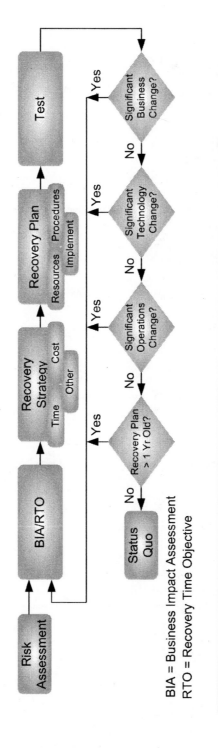

BIA = Business Impact Assessment
RTO = Recovery Time Objective

Figure 8.12   BIA performance decision process.

- Quantifiable opinion (individual perspective) versus fact (accepted conventional perspective)
  - *Caveat*: Do not overestimate the usefulness of a (stand-alone) questionnaire or underestimate the effectiveness of interviews; the bottom line is that eye-to-eye conversation gets more than just pen to paper.
- Determine key business functions.
  - Define
  - Categorize
- Per key business function:
  - Survivability
    - Recovery time objective (RTO)/downtime tolerance (DTT)
  - Criticality
    - Operational impact of loss or performance reduction
  - Priority
    - Define what gets high-availability resources.
    - Define what receives first recovery efforts.
  - Accountability
    - Determine key personnel—who is critical to operations and how.
      - Primary
      - Alternate
      - Direct manager and department head
      - Decision makers; situational adjudicators
  - Determine critical infrastructure—information, information technology directly providing key business function.
  - Determine supporting infrastructure—site, environmental, utilities supporting personnel and critical infrastructure.

The BIA is a critical step to scope and focus efforts for business continuity, disaster recovery, IT operational safeguards, personnel and physical safeguards, and much more.

8.13.4 Best Practices

Disaster recovery and business continuity best practices typically mention the need for a business impact assessment (BIA). BIA best practices include Queensland government's Standard 18: *Information Architecture Information: Best Practice Supplement*, and ISO 27002 includes business continuity and impact analysis.

The foundation of NIST security is asset categorization, where *high* denotes critical systems, *medium* denotes important, and *low* is minimal; all consider the potential organizational impact given the loss of the asset. The NIST model is asset-centric, whereas the BIA model is process-centric or business function-centric. At the least, the NIST model provides best practice guidance when evaluating supporting key infrastructure to key business functions; at the most, align BIA business function identification and evaluation with NIST-like categorizations of high, medium, and low.

8.13.5 BIA Deliverables

The BIA report is a communication of assessment results to management/executives and typically consists of the following sections:

- Executive summary
- Critical processes
- Objectives
- Assumptions
- Findings
  - Organizational impact
- Prioritized critical application list
  - Associated key personnel
  - Associated key infrastructure

The BIA report goes to IT and IA planners as a foundation for business continuity planning, continuity of operations planning, contingency planning, and disaster recovery planning. The BIA provides the business focus and justification for technical actions.

8.13.6 IA² Perspective

The BIA is an IA process within the IA² LoS. Supporting mechanisms include discovery questionnaires, asset valuation models, RTO/DTT models, and BC/DR mechanisms.

8.13.7 Commentary

The business impact analysis (BIA) provides critical operational insight from which to determine the continuity and recovery strategies. The BIA is the foundation on which to consider organizational disaster tolerance and associated complexity of continuity and recovery solutions. High-availability services (e.g., RAID* or replication) are complex but potentially provide immediate failover, with no or little

---

* Redundant Array of Independent Disks (RAID) is a methodology for reliability through redundancy; multiple physical disks create a single logical unit where the failure of any single disk does not jeopardize the data stored on the array.

downtime. The other end of the strategy spectrum contains disaster recovery services (e.g., quick ship). Although it is less complex to ship replacement equipment than maintain duplicates for failover, there are inherent delays in ordering, shipping, and installing. Budget constraints apply as well, with high-availability solutions typically more expensive than recovery solutions.

The results of a BIA include:

- Identify key business functions and their dependencies on information, key personnel, and key infrastructure, where infrastructure includes physical and information technology.
- Identify single points of failure for key business functions and their dependencies.
- Discern and explain the impact of disruption to key business functions.
- Determine organizational risk tolerance and express in terms of downtime tolerance, uptime objectives, and recovery time objectives.
- Document and report on expected organizational outcomes as a result of key business functions, e.g., services, products.
- Determine dependencies on key business functions.
  - Key customers, vendors, or partners
- Document who is accountable for key business functions (management and operations) in terms of decision makers and adjudicators for continuity decisions.

A useful by-product of the BIA is greater awareness of the purpose behind the organization. Such an objective awareness is useful in continuity and recovery, as well as in making everyday business decisions.

8.14   Business Continuity Management

Business continuity planning (BCP) determines cost-effective means to keep operations going in the event of adverse conditions with an initial goal of no or very low interruption to the business workflow (high availability); that failing, BC evolves to disaster recovery options involving perhaps some delay, but still with the same focus of maintaining operations.

Planning a response, not reaction, mitigates risk! The objective of a business continuity program is to minimize organizational loss due to business interruption. A threat probability assessment (see chapter 5) provides insight into potential business interruption causes. For most organizations, the probability of business interruption is low. Therefore, justification for business continuity comes from the level of potential loss in the event of interruption. Business continuity planning provides business value by minimizing uncertainty during the stress of business interruption. Armies may train for years without the threat of war; however, such preparation is essential to protect national interests when necessary. Similarly, the organization may prepare and maintain BCP for years without actually needing it; however, such preparation may be essential to organizational survival. A comprehensive examination of BC includes:

- Determine compliance requirements.
- Focus on risk management in business terms.
  - Business operations impact
  - Key people as facilitators of operations
  - Technology as a support structure for key people and operations
    - Note that technology is important, hence it is on the list, but it is not first because it is not the driving factor.
- Devise a business continuity plan that includes:
  - Prevention
  - High availability
  - Response
  - Resumption
  - Recovery
  - Restoration

8.14.1 Compliance Requirements

Compliance requirements for business continuity and variations (i.e., continuity of operations planning [COOP] and contingency planning [CP]) exist throughout government and the commercial environment. The Department of Homeland Security (DHS) *IT Security Handbook for Sensitive Systems (MD4300A)* includes DHS continuity policy, and roles and responsibilities. DoD Instruction 8500.2: *Information Assurance Implementation* contains 24 controls under continuity. A major goal of NIST FIPS 191: *Guideline for the Analysis of Local Area Network Security* is to ensure LANs have appropriate contingency plans or disaster recovery plans to provide continuity of operation.

8.14.2 Policy

BC policy reflects how the organization manages and controls risk. State the BC policy in quantifiable business terms; sample statements include:

- A business impact assessment (BIA) identifies key business functions, key being:
  - Contribution to the top 80 percent of recurring revenue stream
  - The loss of which will cause imminent and future loss of revenue

- Preventive measures will stop 90 percent of accidental and intentional cyber-attacks in the form of viruses, worms, network attacks (e.g., DoS), Trojan horses, and spyware.
- High-availability safeguards ensure business operation interruption not to exceed 60 minutes per calendar quarter.
- A single downtime occurrence greater than ten minutes results in escalation to CSIRT to initiate response and restoration activity.

A quantifiable policy provides business direction to the development of standards, procedures, controls, and guidelines; it directs the selection of appropriate vendors/products to meet quantified SLAs.

8.14.3 Practice

Following the BIA, the BC planning process (Figure 8.13) begins with preventive measures that attempt to preempt the occurrence of incidents. If those preventive measures fail, the first focus is on the high availability (immediate continuity or very low interruption) of key functions. Subsequent focus is on resumption, recovery, and restoration, depending on the severity and longevity of the adverse circumstances.

Business continuity encompasses disaster recovery—hence the flow from high-availability solutions to more long-term solutions involving resumption, recovery, and restoration. The difference between a continuity incident involving a key

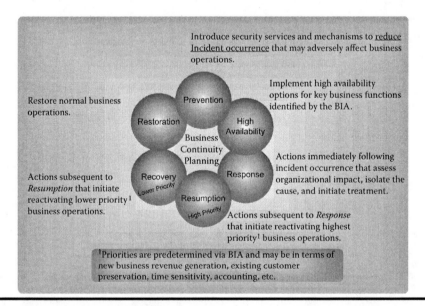

Figure 8.13 BC planning process.

business function and a disaster is merely one of clock time. After X [minutes | hours | days] an annoying interruption to a key revenue stream becomes a threat to survivability.

8.14.4   Best Practices

ISO 27002 provides for business continuity management and addresses BC issues, including BC management process, impact analysis, writing and implementing continuity plans, BC planning framework, and testing, maintaining, and reassessing BC plans. Table 8.4 provides a view of BC best practices.

8.14.5   COOP: Determining Priorities

Those users that carry out the organizational mission include those who generate the revenue, perform the service, produce the widget, fly the airplane, and install the equipment. All other aspects of the organization *support* the execution of the core mission in one manner or another. Support roles include accounting, human resources, information technology, and information assurance. To be in a support role is not less, more, worse, or greater than being in a role that directly fulfills the mission; it is just different. One framework that must consider the distinction between mission and mission support is the continuity of operations plan (COOP) framework:

- Key business functions (mission functions)
- Key personnel
- Key infrastructure
- Support functions
- Support personnel
- Support infrastructure

Organizational survivability is like organism survivability, e.g., a human. A person can survive without an arm or a leg; however, a human cannot survive without a head. All extremities are important; some are critical to survival and some are not. Likewise for an organization, where all aspects are important, but some are critical to survival. For example, a human resources (HR) database is important, but not imminently critical to the survival of the organization, where people, technology, and activities that directly satisfy customer demand (i.e., fulfill the mission) are critical to survival. For purposes of continuity and disaster recovery, mission critical takes priority. The COOP framework assists in identifying these priorities.

The COOP framework provides guidance to defining a business continuity/ disaster recovery (BC/DR) plan where continued operations or recovery of key

Table 8.4   Business Continuity Best Practices

Best Practice	Rationale
Executive buy-in and backing	No clout, no cash, no continuity
Dedicated BC personnel	A business continuity policy is a start. A BC plan is better, and a tested plan even better. Dedicated personnel who are accountable for implementation, testing, review, and modification are the best.
Dedicated BC budget	A plan and personnel cannot happen without the budget. Part of the ROI is determining how much potential loss there is for downtime of key business functions (see Figure 8.14).
The key term in business continuity is business.	Too often, the focus is on technical continuity or technical recovery. The intent of a working technical infrastructure is to support the business functions and personnel that use it. Recovery of business function requires a location, personnel, and the technology to support them.
Recovery strategy	Recovery strategy that includes people, process, technology, physical site, and documents—paper documents that may be key to successful recovery process and recovery of operations
Recovery plan exists	The initial plan exists and policy and procedures for periodic review and modification. The review cycle includes BIA, document review, technical review, review of BC and recovery plans, gap analysis between BIA and BC plan, and remediation plan.
Data storage strategy and policy	Store organizational data on commonly accessible servers that are part of the backup process. Create and enforce policy that no critical data is exclusively stored on local PCs.
Testing	Test that X is prepared to support the recovery effort, where X ((site [hot, warm, or cold]), servers, clients, backup tapes, etc.). Personal experience found an initial recovery test that took three days could be shortened by lessons learned to three hours.

Table 8.4 Business Continuity Best Practices (Continued)

Best Practice	Rationale
Keep it simple and concise.	Disaster implies chaos. Complexity in chaos is ineffective. Continuity and recovery plans should be simple, straightforward direction with clear roles, responsibilities, contacts, and alternative personnel ready to step in.
Involve knowledgeable and capable people.	Personnel require knowledge on how to deal with disaster situations and the capability to apply that knowledge under stress. This implies the need for personnel that have rational knowledge of what to do and the emotional capability to perform.
Identify alternates to key personnel.	Disaster may affect technology, physical location, and personnel. The loss of key personnel requires an alternative to step in and take over.

business functions takes priority over support functions. Communication with and among key personnel in support of key business functions takes precedent over support communications; continuity of key infrastructure takes precedent over support infrastructure. Creating such an alignment during planning assists with providing ROI justification, e.g., an information assurance project that directly supports a key business function that increases uptime of that function by X% is sound justification.

An effective COOP process uses a BIA to identify and scope key operations; these are the primary focus. The next focus is on the key people that support key operations, and then on key infrastructure supporting key personnel and key operations. Together, these are the scope of concern for a COOP-active state of operations (Figure 8.14). Noncritical operations are still important, but not critical to the imminent survival of the organization. In a global economy where the Internet provides instant gratification, customer expectations are high and tolerance levels are low. An alternative to your product or service is but a mouse-click away. The proverbial New York minute is an eternity compared to the Internet second.

8.14.6 IA² Perspective

BC is a security process under the IA² LoS. The BIA and BC policies drive the services and mechanisms that support the BC process. The constructs herein provide guidance and decision tools for use during the IA² Process. Such constructs promote consistent, comprehensive, and repeatable architectural efforts.

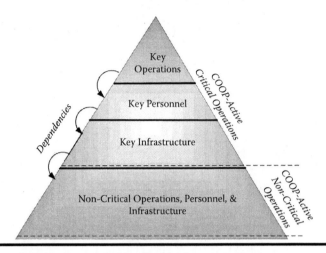

Figure 8.14 COOP operational dependencies.

8.15 Disaster Recovery Planning (DRP) and Disaster Recovery Management (DRM)

Where BC focuses on high availability, DRP focus is on resumption, recovery, and restoration of business operations. The invocation of DR implies circumstances are more adverse than the high-availability options under BC can accommodate. DRP is the process of preparing to minimize the effects of extended interruption to normal business operations. The goal of DR is to restore mission operations to normal operating levels. A comprehensive DRP process includes:

- Determining recovery time objective (RTO) and downtime tolerance (DTT) via BIA
- Off-site preparation
- Contact information
- *Information* information
- Information technology information
- Costs, budget, and other constraints

8.15.1 Compliance Requirements

The IA architect finds compliance requirements for disaster recovery planning throughout government and commercial environments. The Department of Homeland Security (DHS) *IT Security Handbook for Sensitive Systems (MD4300A)* includes DHS disaster recovery policy, and roles and responsibilities. DISA STIG* for *Unix*

---

* *Defense Information Systems Agency Security Technical Implementation Guide.*

Security contains disaster recovery requirements. The HIPAA Final Security Rule requires a contingency plan that specifically calls for the inclusion of a disaster recovery plan. FISMA requires plans and procedures to ensure the continuity of operations; although FISMA does not specifically name disaster recovery, a safe assumption is that it is part of the intent. DoD Instruction 8500.2: *Information Assurance Implementation* contains 24 controls under the Continuity section; the Continuity control numbered "CODP-3" specifically calls for disaster and recovery planning.

8.15.2 Policy

Disaster recovery policies exist throughout government and commercial environments. Examples include the U.S. Customs *Information Systems Security Policy and Procedures Handbook* and Chairman of the Joint Chiefs of Staff Instruction (CJCSI) 6510.01C: *Information Assurance and Computer Network Defense*. Any organization that does not have a disaster recovery policy needs one. This is a general security policy format that also accommodates disaster recovery:

- Purpose and objectives
  - The purpose of the disaster recovery policy is to satisfy legislative requirements pertaining to <TBD>; these include:
    - <Enumerate requirements>
  - The primary objectives of disaster recovery policy are:
    - To establish a plan for the restoration of key business operations following a disaster
    - To communicate responsibilities to key personnel and supporting personnel
- Policy statement
  - Each key [business unit | major location | agency | etc.], as identified in the BIA report, must have a disaster recovery plan that provides <TBD>.
  - The focus of the plan must be on [business | mission] resumption, recovery, and restoration, in that order.

The above is not comprehensive, but presents the start of an outline.

8.15.3 Practice

Disaster recovery strategies fall into the following categories:

- Hot site solution
- Warm site solution
- Cold site solution
- Use of development environment

- Reciprocal
- Reserve
- Commercial

8.15.3.1 Hot Site Solution: Dedicated

A hot site contains all the necessary computing equipment and software within a production-ready infrastructure. Delay between disaster and resumption operations is obtaining backup media and recovering the latest production data.

8.15.3.2 Warm Site Solution: Shared (Warm)

A warm site contains partial computing equipment and software within a production-ready infrastructure. Delay between disaster and resumption operations is obtaining and installing company-specific equipment as well as backup media and recovering the latest production data. Warm site benefits over hot site include the potential to share the site among multiple companies; each brings its own specialized equipment in the event of disaster. Drawbacks include a regional disaster that causes contention for warm site space.

8.15.3.3 Cold Site Solution

The cold site strategy provides a physical infrastructure (building, data center, raised floor) with supporting utilities (e.g., electric, phone lines, HVAC) but with no computing equipment. The site is ready to receive replacement computing equipment in the event of disaster. An implication of cold site is the delay inherent in equipment procurement, shipping, receipt, installation, testing, and data recovery.

8.15.3.4 Development Environment

The development facility is a tempting choice to use for production disaster recovery; after all, this is where the production systems were created. Some organizations may view the development environment investment as a disaster recovery by-product. This is not a good idea for many reasons. Developers become unproductive, and this is an expensive resource held up for an indeterminate amount of time. Moreover, a development environment is typically unstable; full of experimental this and that, it rarely reflects the more static production environment.

8.15.3.5 Reciprocal Agreement

This is where two or more organizations offer spare production capacity to each other as disaster recovery space. Aside from the obvious technical differences

(Company A uses Linux and Company B uses Sun Solaris), the hosting company production environment is exposed and vulnerable to new and unknown people, equipment, network traffic, and applications. The logistics of understanding the implications to hosting an unfamiliar visitor are daunting if not downright scary to any aware security professional.

8.15.3.6   Reserve System

A reserve system provides key functionality at some reduced capacity. For example, if ten Web servers typically provide the full breadth of E-commerce new business generation solutions, three Web servers with carefully chosen key applications may provide 50 percent capacity. Maintaining 50 percent capacity for 24 hours may be enough to buy time for broader resumption efforts. Certainly, 50 percent for 24 hours is better than 0 percent for 24 hours. The appropriate balance is a factor of ROI and a clear *reserve system* business case.

8.15.3.7   Commercial Service

A commercial service is a contractual service that provides cold or warm facilities in the event of disaster. A major drawback to a commercial service is any regional disaster will result in contention for oversubscribed space in the backup facility. Even if physical space exists, the appropriate amount of external bandwidth and phone lines required to support operations varies tremendously with business type.

The compliance assessment process provides an effective approach to defining a DRP modification or creation action plan. Like other assessments, the DRP assessment identifies the as-is state of DRP and the to-be state (i.e., compliance requirements), and provides a gap analysis and a transition plan. An outline of the DRP assessment includes:

- Disaster recovery plan elements
  - Background information
  - DR plan structure, format, outline, and content
  - Disaster recovery organization
    - Roles and responsibilities
    - Accountability
    - Key players
  - Disaster declaration criteria
  - Escalation path
  - Action plans
    - Standard
    - Contingency

- ■ Default
- ■ Key functions, personnel, and infrastructure documentation
  - Hardware configurations
  - Software, including types and versions of OS, COTS, and custom applications
- ■ Recovery time objective (RTO); time between declaration and a recovery-active state (e.g., 24 to 72 hours)
  - An alternative expression of RTO is downtime tolerance (DTT).
- ■ Recovery scope objective
  - Comprehensive enumeration of:
    - ■ Key business functions
    - ■ Key people
    - ■ Supporting key infrastructure
    - ■ Recovery process exercises
    - ■ DRP and DR process documentation
    - ■ Plan
    - ■ Procedures

8.15.4 IA² Perspective

One point of view is to approach disaster recovery tactics by considering individual threats and defining specific steps to deal with each one. Much time and effort is put into devising comprehensive threat lists (e.g., fire, flood, earthquake, malware, spyware, etc.). The endeavor to provide such an exhaustive list is exhausting and not practical. A complementary approach to make DRM and DRP more manageable is to create asset-centric disaster classifications:

- ■ Loss of site
- ■ Loss of site access
  - Bio, chemical, weather, transportation
- ■ Loss of a data center
  - Fire, flood, or any number of causes
- ■ Loss of data center access
- ■ Loss of key server or equipment
- ■ Loss of key service, where service may be a business service or technical service

The categorizations above provide a shorter list of disaster contingency plans and are threat agnostic. The focus remains on the disaster, not the threat. When enumerating specific threats and planning for specific responses to those threats, focus the top most probable threats (see threat probability assessment [TPA] in chapter 5). Use the combination of disaster classifications and highest probable threats as guidance for devising recovery procedures.

Subsequent abstraction of operating states will assist in providing more flexible disaster management plans:

- Business as usual
- Alert states (potential trouble; known virus traversing Internet—has not hit here yet)
- Post-disaster transition
- COOP-active/BC-active
- DR-active
- Resumption
- Recovery

DR planners may define workflows, SLAs, security issues, key personnel, etc., according to operating state categorizations; such categorizations and preplanning remove the panic factor in the heat of adverse operating conditions or when attempting to resume normal operations.

8.15.5 Commentary

Disaster recovery is a subset of business continuity. Address the broader issue of BC first, and then DR as a series of steps beyond the high-availability focus of BC. The first objective of BC is high availability—essentially rendering the disaster to be a nonevent. The next priority is resumption, even if at a reduced capacity. The next priority is restoration of full capacity, even if under chaotic operating conditions, and the next priority is recovery—same operating state as prior to the disaster.

> **Caveat:** Information and information technology security do not become less important during a disaster; quite the contrary, vulnerabilities to sensitive information increase in unfamiliar operating conditions. All DR and related planning should clearly address secure emergency operations.

Internal operations never function in a vacuum. BC and DR are strongly affected by nonlinear cause and effect. The feedback loop among internal processes, the feedback loop to the organization from external relationships, and the effect of random influences can alter operations. Information assurance architecture attempts to put order to this chaotic model by enumerating operational classifications and constructs to allow for a variety of contingencies. Figure 8.15 shows a high-level view of a nonlinear cause–effect model representing the myriad recursive cause–effects on internal operations and, by extension, disaster recovery operations.

Continuity and disaster management is a dynamic, evolving process. It is important to identify what aspects are under the control of the organization. Fur-

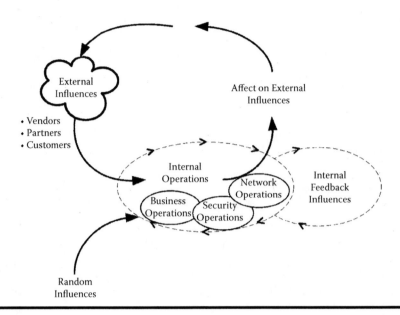

Figure 8.15   Disaster management: a nonlinear cause–effect model.

ther, identify what aspects the organization may influence (e.g., vendor agreements). Finally, identify what aspects the organization has no control over and prepare contingency plans so that at least the organization can control its response.

8.16   Backup and Recovery

With respect to information technology, *backup* is the act or process of making a secondary copy of information in the event adverse circumstances destroy, corrupt, or otherwise render unusable the primary media. *Recovery* is the act or process of restoring the secondary copy to production. Backup and recovery are operational constructs within the IA^2P.

A comprehensive view of data backup and recovery includes:

■ Business/technical drivers
■ Compliance requirements
■ Policy
  – Define backup and recovery strategy
■ Roles and responsibilities
■ Operations
  – Backup and recovery procedures (tactics)
  – Performance metrics (i.e., SLAs)
  – Secure backup process and backup media management
  – Secure recovery process

8.16.1   Business/Technical Drivers

Business and technical drivers behind backup/recovery include:

- Organizational viability and survivability
- Executive due diligence
- Archival mandates (legislative or regulatory)
- Balance between speed of recovery and risk avoidance
  - Speed of recovery drives the type and method of backup
- Support for:
  - Business continuity or BC variation
  - Disaster recovery
  - Downtime tolerance (DTT) or recovery time objective (RTO) as deter-mined by BIA

8.16.2   Compliance Requirements

Backup/recovery compliance requirements include legislation, regulatory require-ments, concept of operations, and organizational policy. These compliance require-ments should coincide with business drivers. Resulting services and mechanisms support the execution of backup/recovery, the specifics of which exist in organiza-tional standards, procedures, and guidelines.

8.16.3   Policy

Policies covering contingency planning and disaster recovery will address backup and recovery. The business impact assessment (BIA) provides focus for policy parameters (e.g., recovery time objective, downtime tolerance). These objectives provide guidance for the appropriate selection of backup/recovery services and mechanisms. Key policy attributes include roles and responsibilities, training requirements, training, exercises, testing, BC/DR plan maintenance, etc.

8.16.4   Practice

Principles for managing data as business assets are in short: *do it, do it well,* and *do it securely*:

- Governance—Establish ownership or sponsorship for establishing data requirements.
  - Includes adjudication when faced with contention over data access or use

Table 8.5 SLAs for Backup/Recovery

Data Type	Backup Type	Backup Frequency	Retention	Media TTL[a]
Normal	Incremental	Daily	1 week	360 cycles or 1 year
Normal	Full-W	Weekly	1 Month	156 cycles or 3 years
Normal	Full-M	Monthly	6 months	60 cycles or 5 years
Normal	Full archive	Quarterly	X years	20 cycles or 5 years
App-X log files	Full	Daily	1 month	360 cycles or 1 year

[a] TTL is *time to live* and begins with first media use; destroy and replace media after TTL expiration.

■ Quality metrics—Verify integrity and performance against compliance requirements where compliance requirements define ideal operations.
■ Security—Provide security services and mechanisms to create, capture, transport, store, recover, and dispose of data.

Testing may occur pre-backup and post-backup. Pre-backup tests verify the media is capable of accepting the backup. Such tests may include a successful format step; format failure results in notification to replace media. Post-backup tests include verification of backup process (i.e., no software errors) and verification of data via subsequent read from backup media. Testing is typically automatic. Error detection results in operator notification and manual intervention. Table 8.5 presents sample SLAs for backup and recovery.

The intent of the SLA parameters is to provide the highest assurance of quality, accuracy, dependability, and recovery according to organizational downtime tolerance. SLAs should address frequency of backups, time of day to avoid contention with production activity, restrictions on system effects (e.g., availability), and backup storage, transport, retention, and cycling of media. SLAs should also address the need and frequency for off-site storage and obtaining backups from off-site storage for recovery; e.g., an off-site storage facility that closes Christmas Eve through January 2 is not much use to a data center having trouble processing retail receipts and inventory during the holidays.

8.16.4.1 Strategy

Figure 8.16 presents a backup strategy decision tool. The axes focus on business drivers of *recovery speed* and *risk tolerance*. The decision tool may expand to include a variety of backup services and mechanisms that support each of the categories: file copy, co-resident media, independent image, and off site.

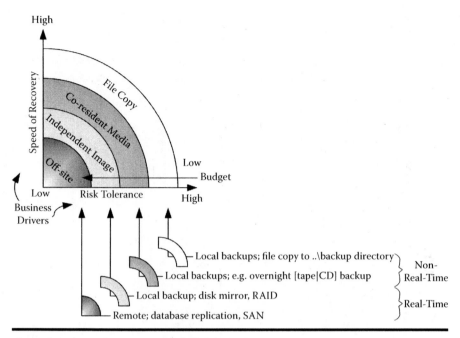

Figure 8.16 Backup strategic decision tool.

8.16.4.2 Tactics

Figure 8.17 is a tactical complement to Figure 8.16. Backup tactics include media selection, on-site backup, off-site backup, backup to hot swap media, fast recovery media, media transport, storage, and access for restoration.

8.16.5 Best Practices

Best practices for backup and recovery include ISO 27002: *Information Technology—Code of Practice for Information Security Management*, COBIT *Control Objectives*, DISA* *Field Security Operations*, and NIST SP 800-34: *Contingency Planning Guide*. Best practices for backup and recovery include:

- Stagger full backups throughout the week.
  - Schedule a percentage of full backups every night to maximize resource utilization.
    - For example, X_M full backups and Y_M incremental backups on Monday, X_T full backups and Y_T incremental backups on Tuesday, etc.

---

* Defense Information System Agency.

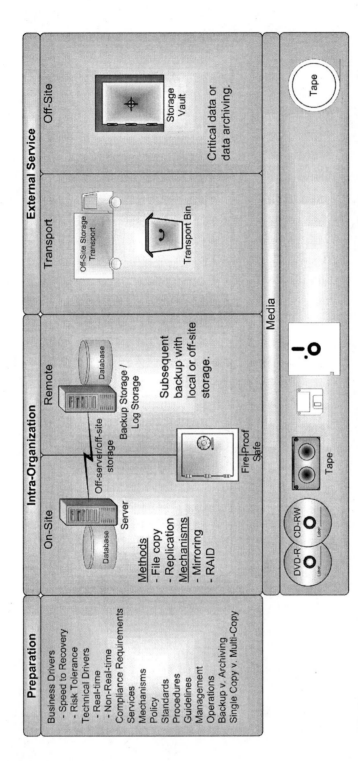

Figure 8.17   Backup tactical decision tool.

- Full/cumulative backup policy
  - For servers with low data volatility, reduce full backup schedule (once per month for example) and execute cumulative (differential) nightly backups.
  - Server restoration requires applying full backup and then last cumulative only.
- Operating system backup policy
  - Treat the application server as an appliance and implement operating system functions such as <platform-specific software>.
  - Implement the backup and recovery of operating system executables and configuration data outside the backup process.
  - Implement a policy of backing up data, not servers.

8.16.6   *IA² Perspective*

From an IA architectural perspective, focus on the end game, that is, what are the potential scenarios and requirements for data recovery. Recovery needs may include corrupt data, wrong data, hard drive or other system failure, system destruction, site destruction, or site/system inaccessibility. All these cases require the restoration of the latest data available. The business impact assessment determines recovery time objectives (RTOs), which may be seconds, minutes, hours, or days. Business continuity plan and disaster recovery plan specify high-availability requirements through to resumption, recovery, and restoration. All of these factors drive the services and mechanisms for backup and recovery.

Information assurance architecture (IA²) addresses the need for secure backup creation, transport, storage, access, and disposal, as well as secure recovery procedures that maintain confidentiality and integrity of the data.

8.16.7   *Commentary*

The IA architect focus is on business drivers first, and services and mechanisms in support of business drivers. Begin with an eye on the recovery end game to determine front-end backup services and mechanisms that will satisfy organizational requirements for continuity and recovery.

8.17   Security Controls

There are many industry standards that provide insight into security controls. Appendix D provides a security management program framework based on NIST SP 800-53: *Recommended Security Controls for Federal Information Systems*. The SMP framework provides an outline within which to define organizational-specific security controls. The SMP framework itself provides guidance for determin-

Table 8.6 Security Controls Overview

IA² LoS	Preventive	Detective	Reactive	Corrective
Business requirements				
IA services				
IA mechanisms				
IA vendor/product				
IA operations				

ing what security controls are necessary. Also, use the IA² LoS that begins with business requirements and provides links through to security control services and mechanisms. Supplemental to these, consider security controls in terms of defense-in-depth preventive, detective, reactive, and corrective controls. Table 8.6* provides a template to consider cross sections of IA² LoS and defense-in-depth.

Each subsequent row in Table 8.6 refines the business requirements into control services (e.g., identity management), control mechanisms (e.g., card reader for presenting claim of identity, biometric for identity validation), vendor products in support of the security control mechanisms, and operational procedures and guidelines. This process of aligning operational constructs with business drivers is a common theme throughout IA² P. Such alignment assists in ROI and ongoing justification for operational processes. Moreover, if the business requirement goes away, so should the operational constructs; such alignment quickly identifies useless overhead from core operational support.

8.18   Conclusion and Commentary

IA services are organizationally focused with respect to services provided by IA professionals to and throughout the organization. Many IA services require trained, experienced professionals. Most IA services involve the use of tools, or IA mechanisms. Some of these mechanisms run continuously without manual intervention, while other mechanisms are applied as necessary by IA professionals using a combination of science and art, e.g., digital forensics. A selection of IA mechanisms is presented in the next chapter.

---

* Table purposely left blank.

Chapter 9

IA²: Context of IA Mechanisms

9.1 Introduction

Addressing risk includes risk mitigation. Some risk mitigation uses IA mechanisms. This chapter presents IA mechanisms, including how to think about them and apply them in context of the enterprise and IA². The mechanisms presented are not comprehensive; however, the IA architect may use these examples as a starting point to determine further IA mechanisms to place in the appropriate context and flow of an IA architecture that uses the IA²F, IA²P, and IA²LoS.

An IA mechanism is a piece of equipment, a tool, or component to mitigate business risk. Examples of IA mechanisms include firewalls and intrusion detection systems. Many devices contain security features that may be activated to address risk. These devices are not themselves IA mechanisms; however, there are mechanistic IA configurations that may address risk. While each IA mechanism performs an IA task, that IA task is part of a broader IA function; that is, IA mechanisms and mechanistic IA configurations are parts of a broader IA capability. Therefore, this chapter presents the following IA mechanism examples in context of three categories:

- **IA devices**
  - Anti-malware
  - Firewall
  - IDS

- Honeypots
- PKI
■ **IA configuration settings**
- Operating system security
■ **IA capabilities (aggregation of IA mechanisms)**
- Identity and privilege management
- Protecting the information infrastructure
- Local area networks
- Cryptography
- E-commerce safeguards
- Development quality assurance

Mechanistic IA configurations are settings on or within devices that activate or restrict certain capabilities of that device. For example, an operating system configuration may activate the enforcement of strong passwords at system logon. IA devices are dedicated to and perform a specific IA function; e.g., filter traffic between the internal network and the Internet. Combinations of IA devices and IA configurations support a variety of IA capabilities. These IA capabilities are not IA services, but aggregations of IA functionality that satisfy a broader business objective. For the sake of brevity, the use of the term IA mechanism in the remainder of this chapter may refer to all three of categories. The context of usage will clarify which categories are relevant.

9.2   Objectives

The objectives of this chapter include:

■ Distinguish IA mechanisms from IA services.
■ Relate IA mechanisms to the enterprise and IA².

By the end of this chapter, you should be able to identify the difference between an IA service and an IA mechanism, have some insight into the fit of IA mechanisms in the architecture process, and have some insight into architectural considerations for IA mechanisms. Moreover, you should have a better idea of the organizational context of IA mechanisms.

9.3   IA² Context of IA Mechanisms

Figure 9.1 provides a context of IA mechanisms as part of the IA implementation taxonomy. For simplicity, the alignment between business requirements and IA services and mechanisms in Figure 9.1 occurs in a single step. The IA² LoS interim

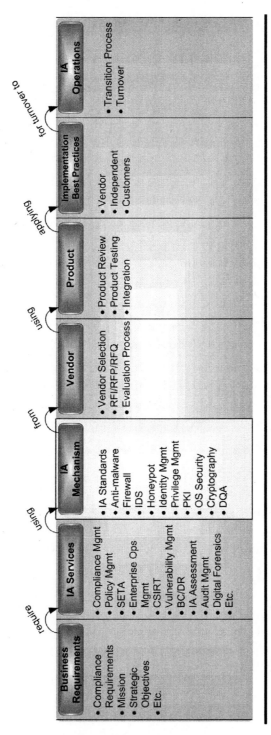

Figure 9.1 IA mechanisms in context of IA implementation taxonomy.

Table 9.1 Aligning IA Mechanisms with IA Core Principles

IA Core Principles	Risk	IA Mechanisms
Confidentiality	Disclosure	Cryptography, PKI, access controls, identity management, privilege management
Integrity	Corruption	Backups, integrity checks (e.g., cyclical redundancy check [CRC]), hashing, PKI
Availability	Denial of service	OS security, host configuration, IDS, anti-malware
Possession	Theft	Physical security
Authenticity	Fraud, counterfeit, deceit	PKI, verification and validation, reliability check (source and content)
Usability	Unusable	PKI, key management
Nonrepudiation	Deniable, false attribution	Digital signatures
Authorized use	Theft of service	Identity and privilege management
Privacy	Public disclosure, misuse of personal information	Cryptography, physical controls, firewall, IDS variations

steps of architecture, systems engineering, concept of operations, and IA design add more details in the alignment of the more abstract architecture with the solution-specific services and mechanisms.

IA mechanisms can be aligned with the business risks they address by using the IA core principles (Table 9.1). This alternative to the IA implementation taxonomy demonstrates to the IA architect that different perspectives provide a variety of ways to decompose and view the problem. Is a different way necessary? In the sense of necessary to reach a good solution, no; the IA implementation taxonomy may provide a good solution. The taxonomy approach provides *a way*, not *the only way*. Multiple paths to the same objective prompt different thought processes that complement each other to produce a better result. The many frameworks in *Information Assurance Architecture* are for just that, mutual complements to guide you in producing a better result than using a nondisciplined approach or any single framework. Moreover, the many perspectives prompt you to articulate the problem for a wide variety of audiences within the organization.

What is the appropriate perspective? The appropriate perspective is relative to the scenario and the prospective audience. The IA implementation taxonomy provides alignment from business requirements through to IA operations and is perhaps more detail than executives or management would like. Aligning IA mechanisms with IA core principles provides a more abstract perspective for IA planning. Subsequent alignment of IA core principles with business drivers provides an indirect link between business drivers and IA mechanisms.

The IA² Framework uses the IA core principles as a filter to decompose larger risk management problems into more manageable chunks. For each identified risk, Table 9.1 above provides an alignment to the appropriate IA mechanism that addresses that risk. Like the other tools in this book, Table 9.1 is not exhaustive. Rather, it offers a framework in which to define details relevant to your organization and for your problem.

Table 9.2 further decomposes Table 9.1 to create a matrix of IA core principles and IA operations cycle phases. The detail in Table 9.2 includes both IA services and IA mechanisms, and presents an alternative view of IA mechanisms' fit within the organization.

9.3.1 Applied IA²

The applied IA² details in the examples in this chapter describe how to apply IA² and provide examples by using a snapshot of a particular IA² perspective. The snapshots are not an exhaustive portrayal of how to apply IA². The snapshots are just one way to look at the problem, provide an IA solution, and explain that IA solution. The intent of the snapshot is to show the relationship between IA² and IA mechanisms. Table 9.3 provides an Applied IA² framework in the form of an applied IA² template and a description of the contents of the table fields. The IA mechanism examples in this chapter use this table format to present an IA² context of that mechanism.

The applied IA² examples provide a bottom-up view from mechanism to architectural alignment. Most organizations have existing IA services and IA mechanisms. Capturing these IA capabilities in context of the IA architecture provides the ability to track IA capabilities and to provide insight into what may be missing from an optimal enterprise security posture.

9.4 Organizational Context of IA Mechanisms

The organizational application of IA mechanisms follows a distinct pattern for planning, assessing, tracking, and reporting on IA mechanisms. This pattern includes determining:

Table 9.2 IA Services and IA Mechanisms in Context of IA Operations Cycle

IA Core Principles	Risk	Anticipate[a]	Defend	Monitor	Respond
Confidentiality	Disclosure	Security policy, risk assessment, threat assessment, vulnerability assessment, BIA, IA^2 Process, IA^2 Framework, security management program (SMP), SETA, compliance management program (CMP)	Cryptography, PKI, access controls, identity management, privilege management, security operations center (SOC)	Audit log creation, log management, content filtering, SOC	SOC, CSIRT, digital forensics
Integrity	Corruption	Ditto	Backups, hashing, PKI	IDS, integrity checks (e.g., cyclical redundancy check [CRC])	Self-corrective (e.g., retransmit), CSIRT, BC/DR, backup recovery
Availability	Denial of service	Ditto	OS security, host configuration, IDS, anti-malware	NOC, SOC, automated "heartbeat" monitoring	Redundant service activation, CSIRT

Possession	Theft	Ditto	Physical security, asset management	Asset tag scanning, RFIDs	CSIRT, notifying legal authorities
Authenticity	Fraud, counterfeit	Ditto	PKI, employee awareness	Verification and validation, reliability check (source and content)	CSIRT, notify source
Usability	Unusable	Ditto	Cryptographic key management, e.g., key escrow	User awareness	Key recovery
Nonrepudiation	Deniable, False attribution	Ditto	Digital signatures	User awareness	SOC, CSIRT, legal investigation
Authorized use	Theft of service	Ditto	Identity and privilege management policy (e.g., time of day, day of week restrictions)	Service use/abuse monitoring	SOC, CSIRT, service access review, policy review, review enforcement mechanisms for policy compliance
Privacy	Public disclosure, misuse of personal information	Ditto	Cryptography, physical controls, firewall, IDS variations	Log review, anomaly awareness	SOC, CSIRT, legal investigation

[a] The purpose of anticipatory actions is to identify potential threats, vulnerabilities, and risks. The same general activities for developing, performing, or using security policies, risk assessments, vulnerability assessments, BIAs, the IA² Process, the IA² Framework, SMP, SETA, and a compliance management program are relevant to all IA core principles.

Table 9.3 Applied IA² Template

IA² Topic	Description
<Section header>	E.g., "Applied IA² Summary"
Drivers	Describe drivers behind IA mechanism.
IA² views	Describe applicable IA² views: People, policy, business process, systems and applications, information/data, infrastructure (technical, physical)
IA core principles	Describe applicable IA core principles: Confidentiality-integrity-availability (CIA), Possession-authenticity-utility (PAU), Privacy–authorized use–nonrepudiation (PAN)
Compliance requirements	Legislative, policy, guidelines, executive order, presidential directive, or other requirements specifically calling out or implying the use of specific standards
ELCM application	Describe applicable ELCM elements: Concept, architect, engineer, develop/acquire, implement, test, deploy, train, O&M, retire
Verification	Describe applicable verification methods, e.g., system test and evaluation (ST&E), certification and accreditation (C&A), and others
Operations	List applicable IA operations cycle phases: Anticipate, defend, monitor, respond

- IA mechanism function
- Business need
- Business fit
- Rationale
- Policy
- Standard
- Procedure
- Practice

Determine what the IA mechanism function is in terms of and determine what it can do for the organization. Then determine if the IA mechanism function fulfills a business need; that is, determine if there is a risk that the IA mechanism will mitigate. If so, proceed to discover the business fit of the IA mechanism. Business fit for IA mechanisms mostly focuses on operations, and specifically security operations. Articulate the details of the business need and fit in a rationale that aligns the IA mechanism with the business need. The applied IA² examples throughout this chapter introduce methods to determine the details of determining business need and business fit.

Articulation of the rationale for an IA mechanism in terms of business need will provide insight on how the IA mechanism will align under existing policy or if there is a need for a new policy. Policies, standards, and procedures are prospective guidance to the organization. Prospective in the sense of providing guidance on what the organization *should do*. (Section 9.5 provides additional details on the relationships of policies, standards, and procedures.) Additional to policies, standards and procedures are practices. Practice is what the organization is *actually doing*.

Policies state the bounds and qualifications for organizational behavior. **Standards** provide guidance on *what* to use to implement and enforce policy. **Procedures** describe *how* to apply standards to implement and enforce policy. Security policies convey appropriate behavior to maintain mission integrity in terms of the IA core principles. Security standards convey the appropriate IA tools and settings to implement and enforce IA policy.

9.5   Security Standards

Security standards specify *IA mechanisms* and *mechanistic IA configurations* necessary to mitigate business risk. Security standards specify what to use or what capability to provide. As long as the capability is delivered, the specific mechanism, vendor, and product are left up to the discretion of those implementing the capability. At other times, there may be business need for specific products. For example, a business driver for centralized security support (e.g., help desk, NOC/SOC, CSIRT, installation, deployment, etc.) may require a homogeneous IA environment. To leverage central resources effectively, the organization will benefit from standards that specify acceptable products by manufacturer, product name, version, and patch level.

9.5.1   *Homogeneous versus Heterogeneous IA Environments*

An IA environment that uses a specific product from a particular vendor everywhere is a *homogeneous* environment. An IA environment that uses multiple products (e.g., firewalls from vendor A and firewalls from vendor B) is a *heterogeneous* environment. Like most decisions, there are benefits and drawbacks to both choices (Table 9.4).

Deciding on a homogeneous versus a heterogeneous environment is not straightforward. The first question resides in business need. Is your organization a popular and known target for adversaries? If your organization is a bank, other financial institution, or a military institution, then probably yes. Is the core mission of your organization so critical that it must always be available? The answers to these questions help determine whether the cost of a heterogeneous environment provides an adequate ROI. There are trade-offs in cost, efficiency, and secu-

Table 9.4 Homogeneous versus Heterogeneous Environment Benefits and Drawbacks

Type	Benefits	Drawbacks
Homogeneous	Cost: Single purchase agreement Site licensing management: Leverage central expertise (e.g., help desk, administration). Easier vulnerability management (detection and patching) Schedule: Leverage repeated experience with the same mechanisms.	A vulnerability in one is a vulnerability in all. A breach in one is a potential breach in all.
Heterogeneous	Better defense-in-depth: A vulnerability in one does not imply vulnerability in all. A breach in one leaves another obstacle to overcome.	Cost: Multiple purchase agreement Multiple site licensing Multiple maintenance agreements Additional personnel or additional training to accommodate multiple products Management: Multiple varieties of tools add complexity Multiple products for vulnerability and patch management

rity. Determining the answer for the appropriate balance is organizational and situational dependent.

9.5.2 Applied IA² Summary

Table 9.5 provides an IA² context of security standards. The details in the table include the drivers behind the need for security standards as well as list the relevant IA² views, IA core principles, compliance requirements, applicable ELCM phases, method to verify completion, as well as applicable IA operations phases. These details show that there are many paths through the IA² Framework and IA² Process

Table 9.5 Applied IA² Summary: Standards

IA² Topic	*Description*
Section	Security standards
Drivers	Optimal, consistent, quality results of IA efforts; cost management via enterprise purchase agreements and service agreements; standard vulnerability and patch management (if heterogeneous environment)
IA² views	Standards describe what to use to implement and enforce policy. Standards apply to the acquisition and application of IA mechanisms. Standards convey a common manner of doing business or facilitating business; therefore, the applicable IA² views are: Policy, systems and applications, information/data, infrastructure (technical, physical)
IA core principles	Applicable IA core principles include: Confidentiality-integrity-availability (CIA) Possession-authenticity-utility (PAU) Privacy–authorized use–nonrepudiation (PAN)
Compliance requirements	Legislative, regulatory, policy, guidelines, or other documents that specifically call out or imply the use of specific standards; implicit requirements may also call on standards to ensure consistency.
ELCM application	Standards may both drive the ELCM process and evolve from the ELCM process, and therefore apply to all phases: Concept, architect, engineer, develop/acquire, implement, test, deploy, train, O&M, retire
Verification	Formal documentation of applied processes
Operations	Standards affect all phases of IA operations cycle: Anticipate, defend, monitor, respond

that lead to the need for any given IA mechanism. To look at business risk from many perspectives in many contexts assists you to determine the breadth and depth of IA necessary to effectively address those risks.

9.5.3 Standards in the IA² Process: An Example

An example of standards in context of the IA² Process is to align external compliance requirements with the ELCM in the IA² Framework; examples of external compliance include:

Architecture: Federal Enterprise Architecture (FEA)
Design: ISO/IEC 27002
Develop: SEI-CMMI, FIPS 140-2
Test: NIST SP 800-42, ISO 9000, Common Criteria (for product categorization)
Implement: NIST SP 800-53
Train: NIST SP 800-50
O&M: ISO TR 13335, NIST SP 800-18, NIST SP 800-34, Control Objectives for Information and Related Technology (COBIT)
Retire: NIST SP 800-4A, ISO 9001

NIST SP 800-64 directly addresses security within the SDLC, and verification standards exist for each SDLC phase. These include formal methods to assess architecture (e.g., OMB Enterprise Architecture Assessment Framework and Government Accountability Office (GAO) EA Management Maturity Framework). There are also formal methods for certification and accreditation (C&A) applied post-implementation (e.g., NIST SP 800-37). Standards must also apply to retiring technology products and media. Personal privacy mandates (e.g., HIPAA Privacy) and individual awareness of personal privacy exposure (e.g., tax records and other personal data) mean that policies and standards are needed to govern disposition of donated or discarded PCs, floppies, CDs, and hard drives.

The above is a technical focus; additionally, there are business-focused standards that include enterprise life cycle management (ELCM), earned value (EV), risk management, contingency planning, and more. Chapter 8 contains additional details on standards and policy.

The IA^2 Framework permits the use of a variety of security standards depending on the situation at hand: ISO/IEC 27002 and ISO/IEC 27001 for the application of best practices; ISO TR 13335 for managing and planning and mapping safeguards to threats; SEI-CMMI for software quality assurance; SSE-CMM for security engineering; and Common Criteria, an internationally accepted standard for product security. The examples do not advocate any standard over another; the point is that the flexibility of IA^2 accommodates any security standard.

The IA^2 Framework and IA^2 Process are themselves standards for IA architecture and provide a common lexicon, taxonomies, and an IA architecture development methodology. An IA architecture developed using IA^2 implies at least a minimal level of consistency and quality. Applied IA^2 ensures a consistent, security-aware, business-driven approach to the selection and implementation of IA mechanisms and products. The rest of the chapter looks at some of these mechanisms in detail.

Table 9.6   Applied IA² Summary: Anti-Malware

IA² Topic	Description
Mechanism	Anti-malware
Drivers	Protect enterprise information technology from receiving malware. Detect the presence of malware and remove it from information technology. Business drivers include productivity, confidentiality of proprietary information (e.g., keystroke capture spyware), integrity (e.g., malicious modification of data), and availability (e.g., denial of service from virus or worms).
IA² view	Anti-malware is a technical mechanism and aligns with IA² views: Systems and applications, information/data, infrastructure (technical)

IA core principles	Applicable IA core principles include:
	    Confidentiality-integrity-availability (CIA)
	    Authenticity-utility (AU)
	    Privacy–authorized use (PA)

Compliance requirements	Legislation, regulation, policies, and guidelines that reference anti-malware directly or indirectly via liability for initiating or propagating malware
ELCM application	Applicable ELCM elements could be all, though anti-malware is most applicable in O&M.
Verification	Penetration testing; tiger team
Operations	Applicable IA operations cycle phases: Anticipate (potential malware), defend (exogenous and endogenous), monitor (endogenous), respond

9.6   Anti-Malware

The term *malware* is a contraction of the phrase *malicious software*, and is a formal reference to the more colloquial *cyber-nasties*. Anti-malware mechanisms are safeguards against malicious software. These safeguards include anti-virus, anti-spam, and anti-spyware. Table 9.6 presents anti-malware in context of the IA² Framework.

9.6.1   Applied IA²: Anti-Malware

The applied IA² snapshot for anti-malware is very similar to the other technical discussions in this chapter. Anti-malware is an integral part of information assurance.

Consider anti-malware from the perspective of the IA operations cycle: *anticipate, defend, monitor,* and *respond*.

9.6.1.1 Anticipate

- Viruses, worms, spyware, spam, and other malware are present within the Internet and many intranets.
- They will propagate through e-mail, file transfers, file sharing, instant messaging, and other online media and message/file sharing capabilities.
- They have the potential to devastate operations and cost the organization many tens or hundreds of thousands of dollars in lost data, productivity, and revenue.
- Architect, design, and implement an infrastructure to detect and discard malware.

9.6.1.2 Defend

- Maintain (patch and update) an infrastructure to detect and discard malware.
- Data in transit: From Internet to organization; from organization to customers, vendors, partners, etc.
- Data at rest: E-mail server, individual PCs, other servers.
- Data in use: Anomalous memory accesses or network traffic during application use.

9.6.1.3 Monitor

- Monitor for malware presence, detection, and discard status.
- Monitor for updates in malware software.
- Monitor for updates in malware signature files.
- Establish a process that automates each of the above to avoid delays caused by manual intervention.

9.6.1.4 Respond

Establish a response infrastructure that includes:

- Incident reporting (virus detected)
- Triage (relative threat to other current incidents)
- Escalation (who can best resolve the incident)
- Identification (where is the virus)

- Isolation (contain the virus to stop spread)
- Treatment (inoculate affected systems)
- Resolution (root cause analysis)
- Process review (what can be done different to avoid future infection)
- Feedback (direction on process improvement)

9.6.2 Anti-Spam: An Anti-Malware Mechanism

Spam—not father's beloved salted pork and ham, but rather an unfortunate exten-sion of a Monty Python skit involving a restaurant table of horned Vikings singing, "Spam, spam, spam, spam, lovely spam, lovely spam," while a waitress proceeds to explain a menu where every dish contains one, and typically more, helpings of spam (e.g., spam, bacon, sausage and spam; spam, egg, spam, spam, bacon and spam) ad nauseam from a comedic, literary, and gastronomical perspective. Hence, the proliferation of spam in the skit inspired the same term for the proliferation of unwanted, unsolicited e-mail. A more contemporary cyber-version of the skit may include menu options for spam, worms, Red Herring, spam, spam, and phish. Worms and Red Herring are two examples of potential malware riding within spam messages. Phishing is variation of spam with the specific intent to steal per-sonal information to commit fraud and theft.

The organization has no control over being the victim of spam—it is or it is not the victim of receiving spam or spam that uses the organization's name falsely as the sender. And despite the existence of anti-spam laws, enforcing them remains a challenge. Despite lack of control and lack of effective legal recourse, the organiza-tion can absolutely control its response to spam, and hence manage the organiza-tional impact of spam. Internal compliance requirements for anti-spam find root in business risk management, specifically in protecting the organization against loss of productivity, misuse of resources, and liability exposure from having a liti-gious laden spam message pop up offen-sive pictures, symbols, or words. Spam content may include spyware, viruses, worms, Trojans, and other malware. Therefore, anti-spam is also a shield against malware (Figure 9.2).

9.6.2.1 Policy

The IA² architect considers the perspec-tive of the organization and provides IA to protect the organization's busi-ness and technical interests. An effec-tive anti-spam policy is situational

Anti-Spam = Anti-Malware

Figure 9.2 Anti-spam is a shield against anti-malware.

dependent. The following examples provide a variety of perspectives on anti-spam depending on the type and mission of the organization:

- Commercial end user
  - Policy addresses anti-spam as anti-malware
- Software provider
  - Microsoft
    - "Microsoft prohibits the use of the MSN Services in any manner associated with the transmission, distribution, or delivery of any unsolicited bulk or unsolicited commercial e-mail ('Spam')."*
- Service provider
  - Verizon
    - "Verizon specifically does not authorize the use of its proprietary computers, servers, routers and computer network (the 'Verizon Network') to accept, transmit or distribute unsolicited bulk e-mail."†
- E-mail service
  - Xpedite e-mail service
    - Policy "prohibits the use of our email delivery services to send unsolicited communications ('spam'). MediaLinq supports ONLY permission-based, responsible email delivery."‡

9.6.2.2 Practice

Knowing the problem is one thing, developing policy on what to do about the problem is another, and effectively implementing and enforcing policy is yet another. The first decision on implementing anti-spam is in-house versus using a service provider. Figure 9.3 provides a sample anti-spam service provider configuration.

9.6.2.3 IA² Perspective

One of the responsibilities of the IA architect is to think out of the box. In the case of anti-spam, consider potential anti-spam configurations from an abstract perspective and consider whether existing anti-spam configurations are viable. The diagram below provides three alternative perspectives on how to approach an anti-spam solution. None of these may exist in the marketplace; however, the point is for the IA architect to establish multiple approaches to the solution to critically evaluate how available products deal with a particular threat.

---

* http://privacy.msn.com/anti-spam/ (accessed February 2005).
† http://www2.verizon.net/policies/spamming.asp (accessed February 2005)
‡ http://www.medialinq.com/spam_policy.html (accessed February 2005).

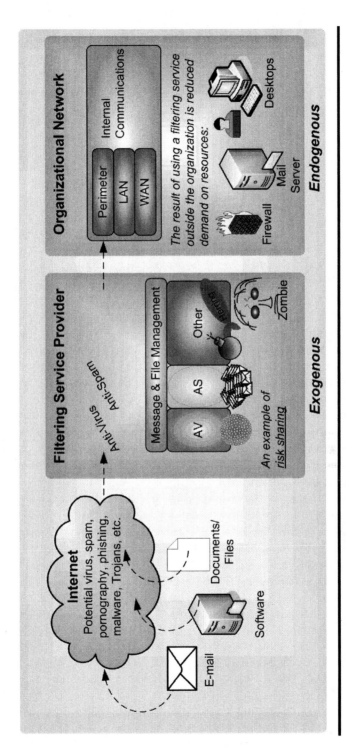

Figure 9.3   Abstract anti-malware (with anti-spam) configuration.

Figure 9.4 shows three anti-spam configurations. Configuration 1 provides an in-band verification of e-mail validity similar to a digital signature; the wrong signature results in bit bucket discard. Configuration 2 provides an out-of-band protocol that independently verifies e-mail validity; timeout with no independent validation results in a bit bucket discard. Configuration 3 provides public key infrastructure (PKI)–like subscription service to provide third-party validation of e-mail; no validation, guess where.

Whatever the method, the goal is for the mail recipient to receive verification of a valid e-mail. By default, any e-mail that is not valid goes to a holding area for review or to the bit bucket. Today's commercial products may or may not follow any of these configurations. Figure 9.4 shows viable abstract configurations and a starting point for commercial product research and evaluation. Architecture starts with the ideal business objective and then searches for products for tactical realization of that business objective. Architecture does not start with product capabilities and then modify business objectives to fit product restrictions.

Spam is a clever marketing campaign that minimizes the cost of reaching a mass audience; however, spam is significantly different from telemarketers or mass USPS campaigns. Traditional marketing costs the marketer where spam costs the recipient. Cost minimization on the part of the advertiser is one thing; however, transferring cost to an unsoliciting audience is criminal. The IA architect's objective is to minimize spam, minimize the organizational cost of handing spam, as well as ensuring protection from the malware that often accompanies spam. The cost of spam to employers is huge in having to process unsolicited e-mail and having this e-mail interfere with business communications and employee productivity. A recent University of Maryland study finds costs to companies at ~$22 billion per year to handle spam. Even if the spam is a relatively innocuous advertisement, there is still lost productivity in employees reading, responding, and discarding the e-mail, and the costs to distinguish the innocuous spam from the harmful are still considerable. Viruses and other malware regularly accompany spam. Restricting spam by extension restricts accompanying malware. Moreover, the savings in productivity time and e-mail technical resources will go a long way in providing hard ROI numbers for anti-spam investments.

Phishing is a particularly intrusive and deceptive form of spam; give a man a phish, he annoys you during dinner, teach a man to phish, and he annoys you for a lifetime. Beyond an annoyance, phishing is a direct criminal act with the fraudulent intent of parting the victim from hard-earned money. Anti-phishing mechanisms protect organizational interests (inadvertent disclosure of private organizational information) as well as employee interests (inadvertent disclosure of personal information).

9.7 Firewalls

Firewalls filter network traffic. A firewall may be a packet filter or a proxy firewall. Packet filters operate on a set of rules that start from the premise that anything not

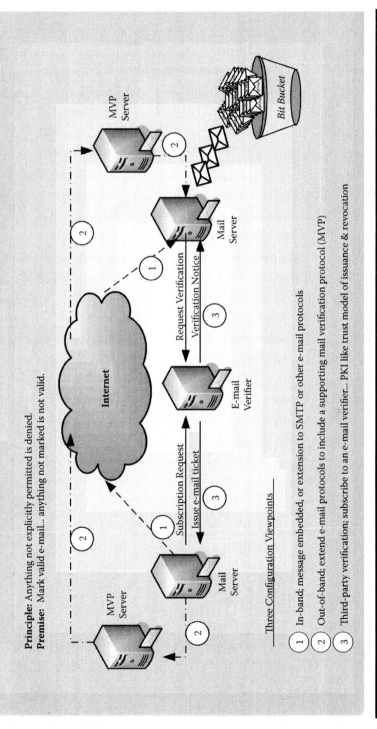

Figure 9.4 Alternative anti-spam methodologies.

Table 9.7 Applied IA² Summary: Firewalls

IA² Topic	Description
Mechanism	Firewall (FW); packet filter or proxy
Drivers	Secure communications; secure Internet access; segregate key business functions (e.g., production) from other parts of the organization
IA² view	Applicable IA² views: Systems and applications, information/data, infrastructure (technical)

IA core principles	Applicable IA core principles:
	    Confidentiality-integrity-availability (CIA)
	    Authenticity (A)
	    Privacy–authorized use (PA)

Compliance requirements	Legislative, policy, guidelines, executive order, presidential directive, or others specifically mentioning the FW or concerns regarding secure traffic management
ELCM application	Describe applicable ELCM elements: O&M
Verification	Applicable verification methods include formal C&A on the FW and integration testing of the FW in enterprise network environment. Penetration testing verifies the FW rules work as intended.
Operations	Applicable IA operations cycle phases: Defend, monitor

explicitly permitted is denied. Subsequent rules specify what Internet Protocol (IP) traffic to permit. A proxy firewall is more complex, but more granular on enforcing filtering rules. A proxy actually simulates the application, for example, SMTP. The proxy firewall launches an SMTP application that performs the same functions as any SMTP program that adheres to the industry standard. The firewall administrator may then tweak the available features to filter on nuances of SMTP traffic. Table 9.7 provides an applied IA² summary for firewalls.

9.7.1 Applied IA²: Firewalls

The appropriate selection of the FW type is dependent on the organization, potential threats, IA budget, and level of knowledge within the organization. Moreover, research must evaluate vendors and products against many criteria, which include Common Criteria rating, third-party performance testing, licensing and pricing arrangements, industry standing, and longevity projections (i.e., will the vendor be in business 12 months from now?). See Figure 9.5 for an example view of FWs in a

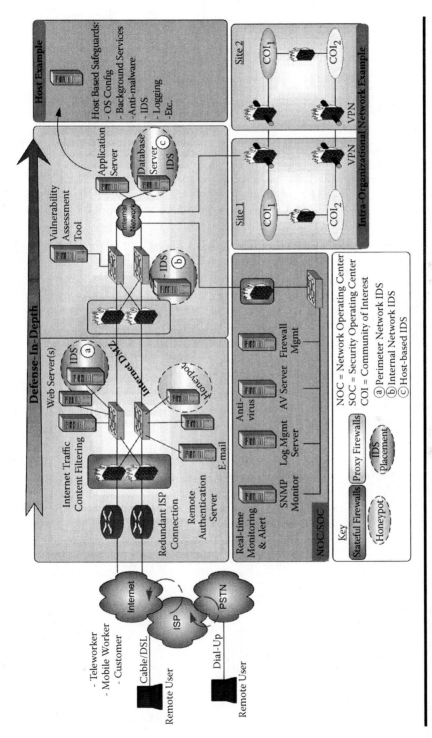

Figure 9.5   IDS and honeypot in context of defense-in-depth.

Table 9.8 FW Benefits with Respect to IA Core Principles

IA Element	FW Role
Confidentiality	Ensuring secrecy of message content is only an FW concern in a virtual private network (VPN), where an encrypted tunnel is established over public network facilities.
Integrity	Ensure that content and transmitted information is unchanged. Such content includes e-mails, session authentication and maintenance, Web site information, and static information (e.g., E-brochure).
Availability	FWs ensure availability of protected resources by blocking undesirable traffic that may introduce denial of service (e.g., SYN flood).
Possession	Provide a level of intellectual property protection by restricting traffic flows used for file transfer (e.g., FTP).
Authenticity	Support authenticity at OSI L3 by prohibiting IP address spoofing; internal network IP addresses attempting to enter from an external network are typically blocked by an FW.
Utility	Ensures the utility of a resource by blocking undesirable traffic that may cause harm
Nonrepudiation	An FW does not provide for nonrepudiation.
Privacy	Protects privacy by ensuring only appropriate traffic enters the protected network; unauthorized traffic is blocked.
Authorized use	An FW does not provide for authorized use directly, but contributes to defense-in-depth protecting against theft of services that incur cost to the organization. For example, an FW defends against unauthorized entry into the corporate network that may result in theft of computing resources, use of specialized applications, access to the public switched telephone network (toll fraud), or access to voice adjuncts (unauthorized use of voice mail or interactive voice response [IVR]).

context of security mechanism aggregation (defense-in-depth). Table 9.8 presents some benefits of firewalls in context of the IA core principles.

The snapshot in Table 9.8 supports product selection. A comprehensively applied IA² includes policies for FW and appropriate use; business processes that address data flow, applications, appropriate use; and people, one example being executive backing.

The result of the applied IA² Process is a firewall blueprint that includes implementation and operations using best practices, verification that the FWs are working as intended, operational policies, justification for vendor and product selection, relevance and applicability to IA core elements, and applicable compliance requirements satisfied via FW. All are directly traceable to business requirements using the IA² LoS. Moreover, FW costs should be clearly identifiable and directly align with the business benefits.

9.8   Intrusion Detection Systems

Intrusion detection systems (IDSs) are technical devices or software that discover wrongful entry or wrongful use of information and information technology. The two IDS types are host-based IDS and network IDS. Host-based IDSs (HIDSs) establish the host's operational baseline for normal usage and then monitor the host for unusual activity such as applications, daemons, processes, utilities, databases, etc. Network IDSs (NIDSs) establish a network's normal usage operational baseline and then monitor the network for unusual activity such as large data transfers, transfers of particular types of data, or data transfers outside of normal business hours. Table 9.9 provides an applied IA² summary for intrusion detection systems.

Table 9.9   Applied IA² Summary: IDS

IA² Topic	Description
Mechanism	HIDS, NIDS
Drivers	Defense-in-depth; detective mechanism; maintain authorized access to enterprise networks and hosts. IDS may assist with real-time intrusion detection efforts and with forensic intrusion detection efforts (after the fact) by maintaining logs of network and host activity.
IA² view	Applicable IA² views: Systems and applications, infrastructure (technical)

IA core principles	Applicable IA core principles:
	    Confidentiality-integrity-availability (CIA)
	    Authenticity-utility (AU)
	    Privacy–authorized use (PA)

Compliance requirements	IDS may assist in satisfying privacy requirements or otherwise protect against and monitor for unauthorized presence in enterprise information systems.
ELCM application	Applicable ELCM elements: O&M
Verification	Penetration testing
Operations	Applicable IA operations cycle phases: Anticipate, defend, monitor, respond

9.8.1 Applied IA²: IDS

Intrusion detection systems (IDSs) are an integral part of the defense-in-depth philosophy. Defense-in-depth uses preventive, detective, and reactive measures to safeguard information and information technology. While a firewall is a preventive security mechanism that filters traffic between network segments, an IDS is a detective/reactive security mechanism. If an intruder makes it past the firewall, the IDS may detect this host or network activity outside normal operating parameters and send a notification to the security operations center (SOC) or invoke an automated reactive procedure (e.g., shut down Internet access).

A business driver behind IDS is to protect mission integrity with respect to confidentiality, integrity, and availability. A technical driver behind IDS is defense-in-depth.

Examples of compliance requirements* and guidelines that cover IDS are:

- NIST SP 800-18: *Security Plan Guide*, p. 34; SP 800-18 includes intrusion detection tools as part of data integrity/validation controls, audit trails (p. 45), and incident response capability (p. 57).
- DISA Network Infrastructure Security Checklist v. 5 r. 2.1 specifies intrusion detection.
- ISO 17799 mentions intrusion detection as part of monitoring system use.
- COBIT mentions intrusion testing and reporting in access control objectives.
- DoD Instruction 8500.2 addresses the need for host-based and network intrusion detection systems.

9.8.2 Policy

NIST SP 800-31: *Intrusion Detection Systems* provides guidance on the need and content of IDS policy:†

- Define the functional goals of the enterprise.
- Consider how formal the system management and operations structure is.
- Organizational security goals and objectives
  - Outside threat focus
  - Inside threat focus
  - Balance
- IDS as a pure security tool or operations management tool
  - For example, IDS may point out performance degradations.

---

* Remember, compliance requirements include externally imposed requirements (legislation) as well as internally imposed requirements (a security standard like ISO 27001 or ISO 27002).

† NIST SP 800-31: *Intrusion Detection Systems*, pp. 28–30.

9.8.3 Practice

Specific parameter settings and operational guidelines are too detailed (too "in the weeds") for architectural consideration. However, consideration of IDS engineering and operations principles and constraints is entirely appropriate; these include:

- IDS monitors data in transit (network) and at rest (host).
- Deploy IDS in every public facing, perimeter network.
- Deploy IDS in every key server farm.
- Define a rule set that governs IDS actions for:
  - One-time anomalies
  - Sustained anomalous activity (e.g., >2 minutes)
  - Specific file types (e.g., CADCAM* files containing engineering drawings)
  - Notification thresholds
  - Reactive measure thresholds (e.g., shutdown network access or traffic flow)
- Operate without impacting essential network bandwidth.
- Integrate within existing network architecture.
- Be able to receive automated updates.
- Pass alerts to security operations center (monitoring).
- Log raw data and detected incidents.
- Detect fraud, waste, and abuse.

In general, security mechanism procedures and guidelines are critical for effective and consistent operations. Although the particulars of procedures and guidelines are beyond architectural consideration, the IA² architect should consider providing format, outline, and content recommendations.

9.8.4 Best Practices

ISO/IEC 18403: *Guidelines for Implementation, Operation, and Management of IDS* provides one example of IDS best practices and addresses both network IDS (NIDS) and host-based IDS (HIDS).

9.8.5 IA² Perspective

In the context of the IA²F LoS, an IDS is an IA mechanism under security monitoring services. In the context of the IA operations framework, IDS is a key defense

---

* Computer-aided design/computer-aided manufacturing.

and monitor tool for data in transit (network IDS) and data at rest (host IDS). The IDS monitors for anomalies that include:

- Real-time monitoring and analyzing of user, system, and network activities
- Analyzing system configurations, files, and audit logs
- Assessing system and file integrity
- Ability to recognize patterns typical of attacks
- Analysis of abnormal activity patterns
- Tracking user policy violations

Real-time input from IDS assists in identifying anomalous events; IA operations engineers are the front line consumer of IDS output. Appropriate training of IA ops engineers rounds out effective real-time response. IDS logs also provide insight into anomaly trends, retroanalysis of incident patterns, and potential areas of performance degradation.

9.8.5.1 Security Service and Mechanism Aggregation

Even the best safeguards have vulnerabilities that provide an adversary with opportunity to bypass those safeguards. Presenting a single obstacle for an adversary to overcome is not effective security; there should be many obstacles. Moreover, these many obstacles should provide coordinated safeguards in well-planned-out defense-in-depth. The aggregation of many IA services and mechanisms where each component fulfills a distinct role in complement to the others is defense-in-depth.

Defense-in-depth involves segmenting the LAN with security boundaries, establishing policy on what technical and business services may reside within those boundaries, establishing policy on interboundary communications, and implementing a combination of the security services and mechanisms to facilitate and enforce the policies. Figure 9.5 provides an overview of defense-in-depth with IDS (and other IA mechanisms) in context.

9.9 Honeypots

A honeypot in the cyber-security sense is an enticement for would-be intruders. The honeypot may look like an important production server, but in reality is in part a distraction and in part a glass slide under a cyber-microscope for system administrators and security personnel to watch intruder activity. The primary honeypot benefits are keeping intruders off real production servers, an early warning system of adversary interest, and a learning tool for security personnel.

Figure 9.5 provides a view of a single honeypot in the perimeter network; its placement is expected to provide an attractive distraction from production Internet-facing servers and to trigger an alarm before the intruder enters the LAN. Security architects may place additional honeypots in various boundaries and particularly in key server farms. Each honeypot will take on a different nature according to its distractive mission.

A honeypot variation is a *stickypot*. The goal of a stickypot is to attract and hold attackers or attack tools in attempt to prevent attacks against other systems and to profile the attacks for potential imminent action and subsequent remediation. In theory, it is more difficult for an intruder to break away from a stickypot than a honeypot. Table 9.10 provides a summary of applied IA² for honeypots.

9.9.1 Policy

A specific honeypot policy is useful guidance to security personnel. The policy should be in business terms and include the goals for honeypot usage (e.g., protect mission integrity with respect to confidentiality, integrity, and availability). Most importantly, the policy should clearly state any legal restrictions on honeypot use, including exposure to downstream liability, and precautions against invasion of privacy.

9.9.2 Best Practices

Honeypot best practices include:

- Distraction
  - Keep intruders from production systems.
- Deception
  - False services, banners, data
- Psychological operations
  - Disinformation; provide intruder with false information (e.g., fake engineering plans).
  - Perception
    - Present false capabilities that give different perception of organizational activity and potential activity.
- Intelligence gathering
  - Hacker tools, method, attack signature
- Sting
  - A bit tricky from a legal perspective, but could provide fake documents with embedded signature or steganography for later tracking and identification

As novel an idea as honeypots are, consider cost and value prior to deployment. Do not overestimate the effectiveness of honeypots; they are only a delaying factor that provide alerts and reaction time. Honeypots are not a power-on and forget it technology.

Table 9.10 Applied IA² Summary: Honeypots

IA² Topic	Description
Mechanism	Honeypots, stickypots, or variation
Drivers	If the organization is an attractive target, present an obvious attractive target as a distraction. May fool many casual observers and provide a clue to the possibility of a more focused effort before that effort reaches the real enterprise information technology.
IA² view	Applicable IA² views: People, systems and applications, information/data, infrastructure (technical) The IA² people view is included here because the effective use of a honeypot includes understanding that part of the threat space that contains intelligence and intent (i.e., people). The honeypot may provide a defensive posture or an offensive posture with disinformation. The offensive posture is a tricky maneuver that requires deeper cognitive analysis of adversaries.

IA core principles	Applicable IA core principles:
	    Confidentiality-integrity-availability (CIA)
	    Authenticity (A)
	    Privacy–authorized use (PA)

Compliance requirements	Honeypots probably find no explicit compliance motivations. Enterprise policy may reflect the need to distract would-be cyber-intruders.
ELCM application	Applicable ELCM elements: O&M
Verification	Tiger team, penetration testing (Where does the use of automated discovery tools take you? To the honeypot [good] or to a production server [not good]?)
Operations	Applicable IA operations cycle elements: Anticipate, defend, monitor, respondHoneypots may provide an early warning and thus enable a preemptive response.

9.9.3 IA² Perspective

In context of the IA² F LoS, security controls are an IA service; deception techniques are a subset of security controls. A honeypot and honeypot variations are IA mechanisms that fall under detection. In the context of the IA operations cycle, honeypots fall within defend and monitor.

Camouflage plays a role in physical security, disguising individuals, vehicles, building, and munitions. Psychological operations include disinformation. Prisoner interrogations discern enemy means and methods; supportive intelligence or supposition provides insight to motive and opportunity. Honeypots and variations perform the same tasks from a digital perspective. They camouflage real production operations by presenting a false target to hackers; they may present false information under the guise of truth. They discern hacker means and methods by recording hacker activity. Bottom line, digital deception is a useful architectural construct in corporate and national security solutions.

9.9.4 Commentary

In addition to the honeypot's distractive and monitoring properties, honeypots may also provide disinformation. As Winston Churchill so eloquently said, "In wartime, truth is so precious that it must be surrounded by a bodyguard of lies." If certain proprietary information, intellectual property, or national secrets are so important that adversaries resort to espionage, then an opportunity exists to give them what they are looking for—or at least what they are led to find—a tricky game to say the least, but an interesting by-product of an already useful tool.

Caveat: As an IA architect, be aware that honeypots set up an attractive target and may draw intruders. Moreover, there is the potential for the claim of entrapment if the organization chooses legal recourse against the intruder. Honeypots can be useful, but are not for every organization.

9.10 Public Key Infrastructure (PKI) and Certificate Authority (CA)

PKI is an infrastructure for the creation, issuance, revocation, and processing of public and private encryption keys. The purpose is to bind a set of public and private keys with a person or device for identity and for privacy purposes when exchanging data. The public key is shared by way of a digital certificate. The private key is given only to the requesting entity and not made publicly available. The function of the private key may be to decrypt a message encrypted by the public key. Another function of the private key is to identify the sender of a message. Because the sender is

Table 9.11 Applied IA² Summary: PKI

IA² Topic	Description
Mechanism	Public key infrastructure (PKI)
Drivers	Implement and enforce a unique, nonrefutable identification with appropriate personnel and information technology components. Business need for nonrepudiation in business transactions, e.g., binding legal agreements via online exchanges of e-mail or other messages.
IA² view	Applicable IA² views: People, policy, business process, systems and applications, information/data, infrastructure (technical, physical)
IA core principles	Applicable IA core principles: Confidentiality-integrity-availability (CIA) Authenticity-utility (AU) Privacy–authorized use–nonrepudiation (PAN)
Compliance requirements	Legislative, policy, guidelines, executive order, presidential directive, or others mentioning PKI
ELCM application	Applicable ELCM elements: Concept, architect, engineer, develop/acquire, implement, test, deploy, train, O&M, retire
Verification	Formal C&A; formal test plans for PKI features
Operations	Applicable IA operations cycle phases: Anticipate, Defend, Monitor

supposed to be the only person in possession of that private key, the private key is a reasonably reliable identity credential, so reasonable that private keys may be used as digital signatures that are as legally binding as physical signatures. Table 9.11 provides an applied IA² summary of PKI.

9.10.1 Applied IA² Summary

Figure 9.6 provides a PKI overview in context of the IA² views, including business drivers, policies, business services, technical services, and mechanics. The Meta View in the diagram provides examples of periphery considerations to PKI that include activities for PKI operations and use. Once the IA architect decides on the appropriate PKI mechanics, he or she follows the IA² LoS through to vendor/product selection and best practices for implementation and O&M.

9.10.1.1 PKI Models (Trust Models)

Business requirements will drive the selection of PKI model. Model choices consist of:

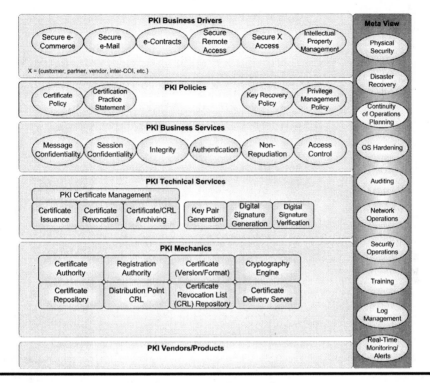

Figure 9.6   PKI overview with respect to the IA² views.

- Self-managed web of trust
  - Each user generates and manages his own keys; no central authority; AKA anarchy model, e.g., PGP*
- Single certificate authority (CA)
- Hierarchical CA
  - CA root with distributed CAs
- Browser trust list
- Policy trust list
- Qualified policy trust list
- Cross-certificate
- Bridge CA

Figure 9.7 illustrates a PKI hierarchical model with a single CA root and regionally distributed CAs and revocation authorities (RAs). A distributed certificate revocation list (CRL) model provides faster certificate revocation checks as well as CRL service redundancy. Such a model supports a geographically dispersed workforce as well as offers time-critical performance for PKI validation or verification of revocation.

---

* Pretty good privacy.

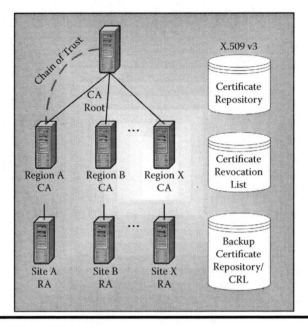

Figure 9.7   Hierarchical model.

PKI is a difficult concept and it is difficult to implement. The IA² Framework provides a divide-and-conquer approach—the ability to decompose PKI into smaller, more easily understood chunks. As shown in the overview diagram (Figure 9.6), there are very clear business motivations behind the PKI technology, clear business and technical services provided by PKI, and a clear delineation and traceability of mechanics to provide those services to meet requirements.

9.11   OS Security

Operating systems (OSs) come with many security features, including the capabilities for IDs, passwords, and login banners. Moreover, an OS has many configuration options: bootup processes, background services, network share points, local and remote port activation and access, etc. Securing an OS includes selecting and configuring the overt security measures, e.g., forcing the use of strong passwords. Securing an OS also includes finding the not so obvious utilities, background processes, and OS configuration parameters that present vulnerabilities. The vulnerabilities may be in software bugs that require patching, or the vulnerabilities may be from the manner in which the software is used or in the way the parameters are set. A secure OS configuration requires removal of unnecessary utilities, turning off auto-start features on unnecessary background processes, and modifying parameters that introduce unnecessary operational risk. The IA architecture should address the need for appropriate OS security policy, standards, and procedures for IA operations.

9.11.1 Applied IA²: OS Mechanistic IA Configurations

The IA² Framework may apply to any OS aspect, including design, development, implementation, and O&M. Depending on business requirements, the IA² Framework assists in OS selection, installation, and configuration to support a defense-in-depth construct, where the host OS is the last line of defense. Table 9.12 provides an applied IA² summary of operating system security.

Business drivers behind OS selection include security, reliability, total cost of ownership, manageability, and vendor support capabilities. Technical drivers behind OS selection include use of open standards, and deployment choices (e.g., multiprocessor support or desktop OS). A critical decision is whether the environment will be homogeneous or heterogeneous (see chapter 8 for details of homogeneity versus heterogeneity).

Table 9.12 Applied IA² Summary: Operating System Security

IA² Topic	Description
Mechanism	OS security
Drivers	Defense-in-depth; protect entry to and use of operating systems and the applications residing on those systems.
IA² view	Applicable IA² views: Systems and applications, infrastructure (technical)
IA core principles	Applicable IA core principles: Confidentiality-integrity-availability (CIA) Authenticity-utility (AU) Privacy–authorized use (PA)
Compliance requirements	Legislative, policy, guidelines, government directives, or other requirements specifically calling out or implying the need to protect information; adding OS security is another layer of information protection.
ELCM application	Applicable ELCM elements: Develop/acquire, implement, test, O&M
Verification	Formal C&A, integration testing, service aggregation testing (defense-in-depth)
Operations	Applicable IA operations cycle phases: Anticipate, defend, monitor, respond

IA² views of OS security provide insight into some IA architectural considerations for selecting an OS:

- Information technology
  - Application support: COTS options vary dramatically between OSs.
- Production
  - The needs of the production environment may drive OS selection.
    - Ultimately driven by business requirements, the technology to support the business may require specialized hardware that drives OS selection.
- Policies
  - Policies will drive OS selection.
  - OS will also drive policies to accommodate for inherent capabilities.
    - Prohibit activity X on OS ABC because of inherent security flaws; however, activity X on OS XYZ is fine due to better implementation.
- Business process
  - The needs of the business process drive the technology.
    - Real-time GPS mapping capabilities for the military, where speed and accuracy preserve lives, are a dramatically different need than an executive looking for the latest daily accounting reports.
- People
  - Technical abilities, technical tolerances (e.g., graphic interface versus command line)
  - User experience levels; training/retraining requirements

OS classifications that may support a variety of architectural drivers include single user, multiuser, multiprocessor, multitasking, multithreading, and real-time. Likewise, OS paradigms lend support to a variety of architectural drivers: centralized—thick server, thin client; distributed—thin server, thick client; or parallel processing—multiple OSs working together on a common task. In addition to OS classifications and paradigms are the OS services supporting secure operations. The most common OS security services include:

- OS structure
  - Kernel construct
    - Static kernel versus configurable kernel
    - Bare bones microkernel with other kernel modules activated/controlled by parameter options
    - Kernel interfaces via abstraction layers and not direct hooks
- Boot-up
  - Pre-OS load options; BIOS configurations to block system hijacking during boot

- Shutdown
  - Clean shutdown versus abrupt (i.e., power off); permissions to shutdown
  - Unexpected; fail-state parameters
- User access/interface
  - Privilege modes
- User management
  - Access
    - Logon permissions
    - Password management: storage/encryption; user modification rules
- File management
  - File system, files, directories, file locking
  - File security hierarchies with read-up and write-down rules
- Process/service management
  - Processes
    - Overhead processes
  - Services
    - Providing services to executing applications, users
    - Buffer management
- Application execution
  - Interprocess communication (IPC)
  - Thread management
- Hardware interface
  - Initial recognition and handshaking
  - I/O: requests, permissions
- Network connectivity
  - Access from network to computer
  - Access to network from computer
- Error handling
  - Faults
  - Traps

9.11.2 Commentary

The IA² Framework does provide a guideline with respect to determining IA architecture; however, the IA architect must still be aware of technology details, in this case the complexities of operating systems and secure operating system configuration. The IA² Framework may provide direction for a novice security architect, but even a novice security architect must have breadth and depth in technology experience. If your knowledge of current operating systems is weak, engage the appropriate expertise to ask the right questions and find the relevant answers to securing the OS.

9.12 Identity and Privilege Management

Identity is the collection of distinguishing attributes that define who a person or device is. An identity credential is an object that contains a set of distinguishing attributes that describe a particular person or device. These distinguishing attributes may be a picture, an employee identity number, a social security number, a Media Access Control (MAC) address, or an IP address. The identity credential may be an identity card, driver's license, or digital certificate. Identity management is the issuance/revocation of identity credentials, processing presentation of credentials, and evaluation of identity credential attributes to verify the bearers of credentials are indeed who they say they are.

The credentialing request may require bearers to present the credential (something they have), enter a pass code or personal identification number (something they know), submit to a biometric reading like a fingerprint or retina scan (something they are), or sign in via electronic signature pad (something they do). The process of validating an identity is *authentication*. The validation of identity is usually in conjunction with processing a privilege request.

A privilege request may be to access a building, room, system, or document. Although a person's identity may be confirmed, there remains a question of permission to have the requested access. The process of validating a privilege is authorization. The attributes of the identity credential may include privilege attributes. A person may have privilege to enter the building, but lack the privileges to enter the data center or the research and development department. The entire process of identity and privilege management can get quite complex. Table 9.13 provides an applied IA^2 summary for identity and privilege management.

9.12.1 Applied IA^2: Identity and Privilege Management Capability

Identities may include associations with encryption keys (public keys and private keys) as well as digital signatures. The introduction of Web services and service-oriented architecture (SOA) adds complexity to identity and privilege management by requiring each Web service to obtain an identity, associate a set of privileges with each service, and then authenticate and authorize each service request. However, automated services may request access to other automated services. The requesting service needs a unique identity. The service provider authenticates the requesting service and makes an authorization decision. Figure 9.8 provides an entity authentication and authorization taxonomy where the service requesting entity can be people or technology.

As shown in Figure 9.8, the entity attempts activity via a request point. The access method is the point of passage to the service provider. This may be physical (guard), video, card reader, computer, etc. The credential is a claim of identity and claim of privilege. The credential details enter a credential system that makes a

Table 9.13   Applied IA² Summary: Identity and Privilege Management

IA² Topic	*Description*
Mechanism	Identity and privilege management
Drivers	Provide a common and consistent capability for people and entity identification as well as a manner to specify their privileges and enforce the restriction of using privileges.
IA² view	Applicable IA² views: People, policy, business process, systems and applications, information/data, infrastructure (technical, physical)
IA core principles	Applicable IA core principles: Confidentiality-integrity-availability (CIA) Authenticity-utility (AU) Privacy–authorized use–nonrepudiation (PAN)
Compliance requirements	Legislative, policy, guidelines, government directives, or other requirements specifically calling out or implying the use of identities and the enforcement of the use of privileges
ELCM application	Applicable ELCM elements: Develop/acquire, implement, test, O&M
Verification	Formal C&A; integration testing; penetration testing using false identities and attempting to use privileges not associated with the identification or not permitted with the identification
Operations	Applicable IA operations cycle phases: Anticipate, defend, monitor, respond

decision of deny request, grant request, or provisionally grant/deny request. A provisional decision may request additional identification, granting a partial answer to the request, or some other variation that is neither an explicit grant or deny.

Business drivers behind identification and authentication include protecting corporate knowledge assets from the following:

- Disclosure (e.g., confidentiality)
- Unauthorized modification (e.g., integrity)
- Destruction (e.g., availability)
- Theft (e.g., possession)
- Restricting use of cost-generating services like unauthorized toll calls (e.g., authorized use)
- Protecting corporate and stakeholder interests in discretion (e.g., privacy)

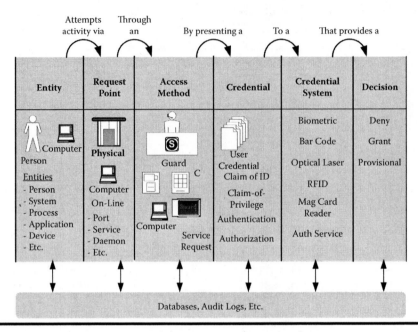

Figure 9.8 Entity authentication and authorization taxonomy.

This is accomplished in part through architecting, designing, and implementing an identity and privilege management infrastructure. Authentication for identification and authorization for privilege are separate functions; the first determines who someone is (or what the process, protocol, or application is), and the second determines what that someone is permitted to do—what privileges he or she has. Identity, once established, is more or less constant; privileges may come and go according to job responsibilities, department, project, etc.

Authentication and authorization services must also manage identification and privilege *revocation*. If someone is a victim of identity theft, new identifying credentials (e.g., a new credit card or driver's license) may need to be issued, and the old credentials must be revoked. Moreover, knowledge of that revocation must be disseminated to those who may use the credentials for authentication. Likewise, when a credential like an ID badge is lost, any privileges associated with that credential must be revoked.

The mechanics of identity and privilege management include security guards, cipher locks, key locks, magnetic card readers, biometric capture devices (e.g., fingerprint, facial recognition, retina scan), and signature capture. Credential and verification reading devices are supported by back-end servers to validate the identification information and verify associated privileges.

The required security levels and budget limitations drive the choice of these IA mechanisms. Depending on requirements, security level may require two-factor or three-factor authentication; that is, providing two or three out of four: what they know (e.g., password or PIN), what they have (e.g., key, badge, magnetic card), what they are (e.g., fingerprint or other biometric), or what they do (e.g., signature mechanics).

9.12.2 Commentary

The process and mechanics of identity management must not violate personal privacy. Personal identification information (e.g., name, SSN, address, etc.) can be isolated or hidden behind a technical construct that uses a user ID and a privilege ID that have no outside meaning. The goal is to provide anonymity as much as possible, whether to the casual observer or the determined intruder. There may be a table or database where the anonymous index is associated with personal information; however, unauthorized access will require multiple depths of penetration or collusion to uncover the personal information.

9.13 Protecting the Information Infrastructure

Infrastructure is the underlying foundation of organizational operations. Infrastructure includes those aspects that on which or in which business activities take place. *Information infrastructure* is the underlying foundation in support of information and information technology. The applied IA² snapshot in Table 9.14 focuses on business and technical requirements behind protecting the information infrastructure.

9.13.1 Applied IA²: Protecting the Information Infrastructure Capability

A comprehensive list of security requirements behind information infrastructure protection includes the following business and technical requirements, where each category considers each IA core principle to form a matrix of requirements that decomposes the larger problem:

- ■ Business
  - – Business process
    - ■ Facilitate secure communications with Company X for customers, vendors, partners, and ad hoc relationships.
    - ■ Secure remote worker connectivity.
    - ■ Minimize administrative intervention during account creation, management, and termination.
    - ■ Ensure messages and transactions are received unaltered and may not later be denied having been sent.

Table 9.14   Applied IA² Summary: Information Infrastructure

IA² Topic	Description
Mechanism	Information infrastructure
Drivers	Protect the information infrastructure environment.
IA² view	Applicable IA² views: Information/data, infrastructure (technical)

IA core principles	Applicable IA core principles:
	    Confidentiality-integrity-availability (CIA)
	    Possession-authenticity-utility (PAU)
	    Privacy–authorized use–nonrepudiation (PAN)
	    Includes the possession of the components (protect against theft), ensuring of appropriate administration (nonrepudiation of modifications to key infrastructure components), and utility of infrastructure

Compliance requirements	Legislative, policy, guidelines, government directives, or other requirements specifically calling out or implying the need to protect the information infrastructure
ELCM application	Applicable ELCM elements: Develop/acquire, implement, test, deploy, train, O&M, retire
Verification	Formal C&A; discrete and aggregate testing of infrastructure safeguards
Operations	Applicable IA operations cycle phases: Anticipate, defend, monitor, respond

- Organization
    - A distributed, multinational organization consisting of 90,000+ associates.
    - Sensitive information communicated across the organization's locations must be protected.
- Physical site
    - Physically distributed within United States and throughout the world with 600+ sites.
    - Many sites are not within Company X's control; they are customer sites or rented offices in publicly accessible buildings.
    - Manage, track, and audit physical access to campuses, buildings, and rooms.
    - Physical proximity to local or regional hazards.
- Technical
    - Data

- Support the transmission, storage, and archiving of data of varying sensitivity levels, including Company X proprietary, customer proprietary, and government (United States and others).
- Assign sensitivity levels to various data elements to assist in managing storage, access, and manipulation.
  - Application
    - Support a variety of desktop applications (e.g., word processing, spreadsheets, etc.), ubiquitous host-based applications (e.g., e-mail), plus specialized applications for internal use and customer use.
  - Technology
    - Provide the infrastructure to support local, wide area, and international voice and data communications.
    - Single sign-on solution.
    - Manage, track, and audit online access to systems, servers, and databases according to respective sensitivity levels.

There is, of course, much more to say about protecting the infrastructure; however, in context of the applied IA² snapshot, the decomposition of business requirements to process, organization, and physical site, and the decomposition of technical requirements to data, application, and technology isolate focus and provide a multidimensional approach to identifying requirements. The traceability between root business requirements and implementation is invaluable in providing justification for IA, cost–benefit analysis between IA efforts and business value, and justification for IA priorities through their link with business priorities.

9.14   Local Area Networks

A local area network (LAN) is relatively small in terms of physical distribution. A LAN may be in a building or in a campus environment. A metropolitan area network (MAN) extends the physical proximity of LAN components from a building or campus to a citywide perspective. A wide area network (WAN) may extend across a nation or across the world. Each has its design, implementation, operational, and security challenges.

One perspective of LAN security is by way of the Open Systems Interconnection (OSI) model (Table 9.15). The contents of the table are not comprehensive; rather, they are an overview and a point in the right direction for further research by the IA architect. Table 9.16 presents an applied IA² summary for LAN security.

9.14.1   *Applied IA²: LAN Protection Capability*

Comprehensive LAN security is security aggregation (e.g., defense-in-depth; Figure 9.5) where the holistic LAN security service is greater than the sum of the

Table 9.15 OSI Model Perspective of LAN Security

Layer No.	Layer Name	Description	Security Considerations
7	Application	Application processing IP data packet; the end user (person) typically invokes a software application that in turn communicates to layer 7.	Malware like viruses, Trojan Horses, worms, etc., may enter the system via the application layer.
6	Presentation	Present data to the application; provides a standard interface to the application layer to present data	Attackers may use unicodes at the presentation layer that drop out of the current session and convey commands to the operating system.
5	Session	Communication session establishment, management, and breakdown between computers/devices	The intent of session management is to go from point A to point B. A man-in-the-middle attack inserts itself between points A and B to see the data flow, copy the data flow, or to modify data in the flow (integrity).
4	Transport	Controls the reliability of the link, e.g., TCP (reliable), UDP (unreliable)	The original intent of TCP, UDP, and other transport protocols was to get data there at all; then there was a concern to get data there effectively, and then to get data there securely. TCP and UDP may be used by attackers to discover systems and map networks. Firewall filtering will resist much of this, e.g., ping is a UDP level tool, NMAP works at layer 4.
3	Network	Routing, routers, IP	Intercepting IP traffic; router access to modify routing rules and route management; keeping router OS patched and up to date
2	Data link	MAC addresses, Ethernet, switches	Intercepting Ethernet traffic; protection of Address Resolution Protocol (ARP) tables that convert physical addresses to IP addresses

Table 9.15   OSI Model Perspective of LAN Security (Continued)

Layer No.	Layer Name	Description	Security Considerations
1	Physical	Cables, network interface cards (NICs), electrical signals, hubs, repeaters, wireless signals	Physical access to cables, wiring closets, demark points from external services; wiretapping (confidentiality), destruction (availability), man in the middle (integrity)

Table 9.16   Applied IA² Summary: LANs

IA² Topic	Description
Mechanism	LAN security mechanisms; a variety applied as defense-in-depth, including firewalls, anti-malware, access control lists (ACLs) to components, traffic routing rules, IDS, OS security, etc.
Drivers	Business and technical drivers span the range of process, organization, location, data, application, and technology.
IA² view	Applicable IA² views: People, policy, business process, systems and applications, information/data, infrastructure (technical, physical)
IA core principles	Applicable IA core principles: Confidentiality-integrity-availability (CIA) Possession-authenticity-utility (PAU) Privacy–authorized use–nonrepudiation (PAN)
Compliance requirements	Legislative, policy, guidelines, government directives, or other requirements specifically calling out or implying the need to protect information and information technology
ELCM application	Applicable ELCM elements: Concept, architect, engineer, develop/acquire, implement, test, deploy, train, O&M, retire
Verification	Formal C&A; integration testing; service aggregation testing (defense-in-depth)
Operations	Applicable IA operations cycle phases: Anticipate, defend, monitor, respond

individual security mechanisms. LAN security services with their associated mechanisms include:

- Traffic filtering
  - Firewalls
- Protect against inadvertent and purposeful penetration by cyber-nasties
  - Anti-virus/anti-malware
- Appropriate use of LAN resources
  - Content filtering
- Secure LAN traffic
  - Encryption (at the application layer, not network)
- Authorize access
  - Authentication
    - Identity
    - Privilege
- Audit trails and forensic analysis
  - Logging/log management
- Real-time awareness of LAN activity
  - Intrusion detection system
  - Real-time monitoring/alerting

Service aggregation involves segmenting the LAN with security boundaries, establishing policy on what technical and business services may reside in each boundary, establishing policy on interboundary communications, and implementing a combination of the above security services and mechanisms to facilitate and enforce the policies.

Evaluating IA² against LAN security highlights the need for a meta-view of the IA infrastructure and the need to provide for logging, log management, forensic analysis, real-time monitoring, and real-time alerts.

9.15 Cryptography

Plain text is text conveyed in its native language and a form that is understandable to a literate reader with a degree of fluency in that language. Cryptography modifies plain text such that the original message is now hidden and not readily understandable by the reader. The process of encrypting a plaintext message into cipher text may use a simple mathematical formula or a simple letter substitution. These basic cryptographic variations are easily broken and the hidden message easily decrypted. Cryptography as used by national governments to transmit national secrets employs quite complex mathematical formulae. PKI uses a very complex mathematical process to generate public/private keys whose relationships are mathematically based. Drivers behind the use of cryptography include business requirements surrounding

Table 9.17 Applied IA² Summary: Cryptography

IA² Topic	*Description*
Mechanism	Cryptography
Drivers	Confidentiality of data in transit over a network or data at rest on a hard drive or other storage device. Business need for cryptography includes protection of customer data (customer trust) and organizational proprietary information. Privacy requirements may also drive the need for cryptography.
IA² view	Applicable IA² views: Systems and applications, information/data, infrastructure (technical)
IA core principles	Applicable IA core principles: Confidentiality-integrity-availability (CIA) Authenticity-utility (AU) Privacy–authorized use–nonrepudiation (PAN)
Compliance requirements	Legislative, policy, guidelines, government directives, or other requirements specifically calling out or implying the use of encryption or cryptography
ELCM application	Applicable ELCM elements: Develop/acquire, implement, test, O&M
Verification	Applicable verification methods include system test and evaluation, penetration testing, encryption-cracking tools.
Operations	Applicable IA operations cycle phases: Defend

confidentiality, integrity, authenticity, authorized use, privacy, and nonrepudiation. Table 9.17 provides an applied IA² summary of cryptography.

9.15.1 Applied IA²: Cryptography Capability

9.15.1.1 Business Requirements

Consider the business drivers behind cryptography from an operational perspective. The IA architect may decompose business operations into a generic framework of front office, back office, and the flows between the two. Structures within this framework include business, technical, and an operational meta-view. The IA architect may then view these structures from the perspective of each IA core principle (Table 9.18), thus providing a granular decomposition of business requirements driving discrete IA functions.

Table 9.18 Cryptographic Business Drivers Linked to IA Core Principles: Overview

IA Element	Cryptographic Business Driver
Confidentiality	Ensure X is kept secret; X × (message contenty, stored datay); Y × (end user, vendor).
Integrity	Ensure X remains unaltered; X (message sent versus messaged received). Included in integrity is nonrepudiation; ensure X cannot deny action taken; X × (message sent, order placed).
Availability	Note: Encryption does not ensure availability.
Possession	Ensure X is protected in event of theft; X × (information on portable devices, data on hard drive or tape).
Authenticity	Ensure X generator is who/what it claims to be; X (message sender, data provider, identified user).
Utility	Ensure usability of X; X × (encrypted hard drive). Solutions include key escrows (e.g., lost/forgotten keys).
Authorized use	Encrypt identity, privileges, and validation information. Identity includes user name, privileges include application or data access, and validation includes password, challenge response, or biometric.
Privacy	Adherence with privacy policy or legal requirements (e.g., Privacy Act 1974 or HIPAA)

The front office includes customer-facing people, processes, and technologies such as call center agents, cashiers, Web sites, retail outlets, etc. The back office activities include customer fulfillment and supporting administration, including product packaging and shipping, accounting, and customer databases. The flows between the two include the communications infrastructure, voice, and data.

Data concerns include customer data collection, what data traverses the communications infrastructure, what data is stored, where it is stored, data sharing policies, and privacy issues. Applications and technology (networking) support the data collection, processing, dissemination, and storage.

The operational meta-view includes infrastructure data, data about what keeps things going (e.g., routing protocol information, SNMP traps). Additional metadata includes activity logs, e.g., <customer X> used <interface Y> on <date> at <time> and was assisted by <agent>. Evaluation of the metadata may provide clues to optimize profitability and provide trends in customer interaction preferences. The metadata also includes IA activity data collected by the NOC/SOC; the challenge is to present it in useful business terms.

9.15.1.2 Cryptographic Services and Mechanisms: A Brief Example

Assume the business at hand is an Internet-based E-commerce site that provides consumer product ordering. The front office interface device is the consumer's PC. The type of PC is unpredictable; however, the consumer's Web browser is an industry standard. Further, communication between the consumer PC and the E-commerce site is nonpermanent, meaning the consumer will likely log on, perform whatever transaction is desired, and log off; this is contrary to establishing a permanent link into the E-commerce site, which may be of more interest to a business partner than a consumer.

Further, assume the cryptographic service of choice is session encryption, which narrows to two types:

■ Symmetric
  – DES, IDEA, AES
■ Asymmetric
  – RSA, Diffie–Hellman

Cryptographic mechanics supporting session encryption include Secure Sockets Layer (SSL) and IPSec. In this example, SSL is selected based on the benefits and drawbacks of the two alternatives. Note the clear mapping between the business requirement of secure E-commerce and the IA mechanism of IPSec supporting that requirement.

9.15.1.3 Cryptographic Influence on the IA² F

Customer interface subsystems in this example include E-commerce Web site, retail assistant, cashier, and the call center agent. Consider an abstract transaction. Customers will encounter an interface subsystem either to request assistance or to make a purchase. This subsystem collects customer data, which is processed locally, within the subsystem, or sent to a regional or central location for processing. If all goes well, the customers exit the subsystem with their expectations satisfied.

IA concerns in the scenario above include security and privacy in subsystem data collection, transmission, back office processing, transmission of results, data storage, data sharing, and later data analysis outside of the literal transaction context. Overall, this is quite an IA task that includes technology infrastructure, policies, business process, and people. There is need for identity management, privilege management, and nonrepudiation.

The complexities of cryptography clearly exemplify the need for a logical mapping of business requirements to the choice of cryptographic services, mechanics, and the application of cryptography in the business flow. Abstracting from the particulars of cryptographic influence, the IA² F must map business requirements to IA operations. This mapping is useful in both the appropriate application of cryptography and the evaluation of cryptography effectiveness with respect to ROI. This mapping will align IA operations with business goals and provide the correlation of operating costs to business benefit.

9.16 E-Commerce Safeguards

E-commerce is the term for the emerging business presence on the Internet. E-commerce presents the organization to a worldwide market as well as a world of cyber-vandals, thieves, hackers, and perhaps less than ethical treatment of your site by competitors, if not exactly illegal. The IA architect needs to protect the E-commerce presence and organizational interests while also facilitating ease of use for customer access; this is a difficult balance. Table 9.19 provides an IA^2 summary of E-commerce safeguards.

Table 9.19 Applied IA^2 Summary: E-Commerce Safeguards

IA^2 Topic	Description
Mechanism	E-commerce safeguards
Drivers	Specific application of IA to E-commerce business process
IA^2 view	Applicable IA^2 views: People, policy, business process, systems and applications, information/data, infrastructure (technical, physical)
IA core principles	Applicable IA core principles: Confidentiality–integrity–availability (CIA) Authenticity–utility (AU) Privacy–authorized use–nonrepudiation (PAN)
compliance requirements	Legislative, policy, guidelines, government directives, or other requirement specifically calling out or implying the need to protect E -commerce. The more likely relationship of E-commerce safeguards to compliance requirements is via due diligence and fiduciary responsibilities of executives to stakeholders.
ELCM application	Applicable ELCM elements: Concept, architect, engineer, develop/acquire, implement, test, deploy, train, O&M, retire
Verification	Applicable verification methods include formal component testing and systems testing (aggregate E -commerce system) that include vulnerability scanning and penetration testing.
Operations	Applicable IA operations cycle phases: Anticipate, defend, monitor, respond

9.16.1 Applied IA²: E-Commerce Safeguard Capability

Business drivers behind E-commerce include expanding current revenue streams or introducing new revenue streams through Internet Web access. These may include B2B, B2C, or C2C* transactions or communications. E-commerce may be examined through every IA architectural view: people, business process, policies, development, and information technology. Moreover, unless all views are working in harmony, E-commerce is a short-lived venture if not the catalyst for bankruptcy.

Every aspect of the SDLC comes into play, including integrating E-commerce into legacy infrastructure and systems, creating a secure operating environment that includes defense-in-depth (firewalls, IDS, AV, internal secure network segments), and more.

The fundamental architecture questions for E-commerce are: What is E-commerce? How is it different from traditional commerce? How is it different from retail, wholesale, bricks and mortar? How is it different from call center and phone orders? These are significant E-commerce issues:

- Presence or infrastructure to support the transaction
  - These are the largest differences among Web site, call center, bricks-and-mortar retail outlet, etc.
- Presence awareness
  - Consumer knowledge of Web site; business knowledge of extra-net capability—boils down to marketing
- Service
  - Initial and ongoing satisfaction of expectations
- Trust
  - Receive what paid for
  - Secure execution of transaction
    - Protect proprietary or personal privacy interests

IA plays a role in each of these areas. All four have some internally imposed requirements, the specifics of which boil down to economics—what will most positively affect the bottom line, optimize revenue, and minimize costs. The last, *trust*, also has some externally imposed legislative compliance requirements (e.g., HIPAA, Sarbanes–Oxley, etc.). When considering compliance, the bottom-line motivation still holds true, but from the more one-sided perspective of cost avoidance, that is, compliance to avoid fines. IA can achieve real protection and show due diligence by setting up protections recognized under the reasonable man legal assessment.

---

* Business to business, business to consumer, and consumer to consumer, respectively.

9.16.2 Health Care E-Commerce Example

These excerpts are taken from an outline architecting information assurance for a health care E-commerce solution:

- ◼ Architectural drivers
  - – Business: Cost reduction, employee productivity increase.
  - – Technical: Take advantage of private, virtually private, and public communications infrastructure to minimize costs, optimize revenues, and provide redundancy for business continuity.
- ◼ IA² views
  - – People
  - – Business process
  - – Policies
  - – Development
  - – Information technology
- ◼ IA core principles
- ◼ Compliance requirements
  - – HIPAA: Compliance required to:
    - ◼ Avoid fines and other unbudgeted penalties
    - ◼ Accomplish patient privacy protection
- ◼ Compliance verification
  - – Although compliance assessment is costly, verifying HIPAA compliance is appropriate. Budget justification comes in the form of one poorly designed/implemented Web site that discloses hundreds of patient records.

Identifying E-commerce IA concerns is easiest by first abstracting the E-commerce process into front office, data flows, and back office processes. Figure 9.9 shows these categories and subsequent decomposition in more detail; a brief list of IA issues is included in context.

The simple framework of front office, back office, and data flows categorizes operations, supporting personnel, and supporting constructs; further consideration is given to the interfaces and relationships between all. Although the example focuses on health care E-commerce, much is repeatable to other E-commerce circumstances.

Figure 9.9 depicts the first steps in decomposing E-commerce into manageable chunks. For example, subsequent decomposition of PDAs as *security domains* with *security domain interfaces* and *security domain interactions* will isolate specific security and privacy concerns. Subsequent decomposition of the various transport media into component parts that become security domains likewise leads to isolation of specific security and privacy concerns.

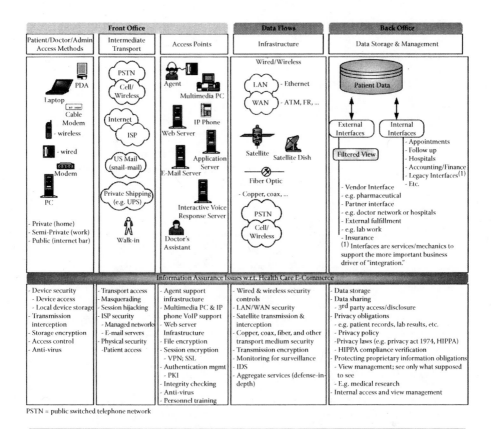

Figure 9.9   Health care E-commerce and IA issues overview.

Considering the decomposition of the intermediate transport clouds, there are some things over which the health care organization will have direct control, others over which it will have influence, and some over which it will have no control at all (e.g., weather, economic cycles). However, the organization can still manage its reaction or response to unexpected events over which it has no control. This same taxonomy of decomposition as in Figure 9.9 is useful for many aspects of E-commerce.

9.17   Development Quality Assurance

Development quality assurance (DQA) is a superset of software quality assurance (SQA). DQA addresses the entire development process and environment. SQA focuses on software development specifically. Table 9.20 presents an IA² summary of DQA.

Table 9.20 Applied IA² Summary: DQA

IA² Topic	Description
Mechanism	Development quality assurance (e.g., SQA)
Drivers	Business risk management; liability and operations; protection against sloppy development practices as well as the purposeful introduction of backdoors and malware; global economy, including global competitive posture and the use of non-domestic-manufactured information technology
IA² view	Applicable IA² views: Systems and applications, infrastructure (technical)
IA core principles	Applicable IA core principles: Confidentiality-integrity-availability (CIA) Possession-authenticity-utility (PAU) Privacy–authorized use–nonrepudiation (PAN)
Compliance requirements	Legislative, policy, guidelines, government directives, or other requirement implying the need for a secure information technology environment
ELCM application	Applicable ELCM elements: Concept, architect, engineer, develop/acquire, implement, test, deploy, train, O&M, retire
Verification	Quality testing; the challenge lies with test thread design and execution; regression testing on upgrades or introduction of a new component; preemptive checks vendor pedigree (not a guarantee, but a clue)
Operations	Applicable IA operations cycle phases: Anticipate, defend, monitor, respond

9.17.1   Applied IA²: DQA Capability

The IA architect promotes integration of quality assurance (QA) with every information assurance concept. The purpose and process of developing an IA² Framework is to increase the consistent quality of IA architectures. A significant part of IA² is aligning IA with the SDLC; the IA² Framework includes calling out specific IA concerns for each SDLC phase. The DQA example focuses on the SDLC development phase and specifically addresses software quality assurance (SQA); note that SQA may also apply to software selection during the design phase in circumstances where COTS applications are preferable to building.

External guidelines to SQA include the Systems Engineering Institute Capability Maturity Model Integration (SEI-CMMI), Systems Security Engineering

Capability Maturity Model (SSE-CMM), Six Sigma, and ROSI (return on security investment) as quality assurance ROI.

SQA in the development phase may include a formal software engineering approach (e.g., SEI-CMMI*). CMMI models provide many benefits to organizational management of processes, including the following as paraphrased from the SEI CMMI Web site:†

- Align business objectives to management activities.
- Better manage products and services to meet customer expectations.
- Capture and leverage lessons learned.
- View organizational functions from an enterprise perspective.

SSE-CMM is similar to SEI-CMMI, but SSE-CMM addresses security issues in general, not software development. Six Sigma provides a statistical quantification approach to QA where the successful application of Six Sigma in software development provides for less than 3.4 defects per million opportunities, or 99.9997 percent error-free—not quite Nirvana, but at least a balcony view.

The ever-elusive quest for hard ROSI figures is partially satisfied through QA quantification from a ROI perspective. Finding and fixing software bugs early in the development process is far less expensive than finding and fixing after delivery or sitting on the shelf as COTS: "Researchers concluded that fixing [one set of] four defects during the testing phase cost $24,000. Fixing the same defects after deployment cost $160,000, nearly seven times as much."‡ With executive attention on risk management and the bottom line, the example presents a hard ROI for addressing security flaws as software bugs.

Another foundation of IA² is the IA quantification framework (IAQF). Development QA contributes to the IAQF by quantifying security flaws as software bugs and providing the monetary justification to fix those bugs early in the development process. SQA provides direct input to the IA² development view.

9.18 Commentary and Conclusion

The intent of this chapter is to provide insight into the definition and fit of IA mechanisms in context of IA services and IA². All too often, despite good intentions, the focus of security professionals is exclusively on the mechanisms, on the technology. Managers and executives are interested in the business benefits of IA mechanisms, not the technical details. The business benefits are seen in terms of

---

* http://www.sei.cmu.edu/cmmi/ (accessed May 2004).

† http://www.sei.cmu.edu/cmmi/general/general.html (accessed April 2004).

‡ Berinato, Scott, Finally, a Real Return on Security Spending, *CIO Magazine*, February 15, 2002.

risk management, risk mitigation, effect on the bottom line, and ROI. To get to these answers, there must be an alignment of IA mechanisms with the business drivers behind them. IA^2 provides a methodology to discern, record, track, and report this alignment. Easy? No. Quick? No. Necessary? Yes, to prove the initial and ongoing business value of IA.

On the other hand, the devil is in the details. Someone, somewhere, somehow must deal with the intricacies of the IA mechanisms to get them to work. This chapter barely touches on the immense quantity of details involved in securing a technical environment. No one individual can know it all. It takes a team of technology, security, and business professionals to identify potential risks, prioritize relevant risks, and address those risks with available time, resources, knowledge, and budget.

Chapter 10

Aligning IA² and EA Standards

10.1 Introduction

Architecture is the art of consciously forming a coherent structure. This definition applies to physical architecture (the Frank Lloyd Wright kind), to enterprise architecture, and to security architecture. Architecture is not engineering, not design, not a network, and not a system. So many times, people speak of architecture while looking at a network diagram—that is not architecture, that is engineering (maybe), and more often just a network design.

Enterprise architecture is a holistic practice that considers business drivers, and then aligns technology to them. Any business endeavor includes risk. IA² architecture is a business risk focus on people, policy, business process, systems and applications, information, and infrastructure. IA² provides a discipline to find the risks (*identify*), list the risks (*enumerate*), describe the business implications of risks (*articulate*), and manage the risks in an appropriate manner (*address*), which accepts, ignores, shares, transfers, or mitigates risks. Then IA is aligned with business drivers and integrated to the enterprise architecture. This chapter provides an overview of how IA² works with EA to integrate an understanding of risk and risk management.

10.2 Objectives

Enterprise architecture and the standards that provide an EA discipline are broad and deep subjects with many books and manuals dedicated to them. The details this book offers are very high level and certainly not comprehensive. A full description of any single EA standard and a comprehensive description of how to integrate IA using IA^2 are subjects for another book. The objectives of this chapter are to provide awareness of the following:

- Enterprise architecture (EA) standards
- The Federal Enterprise Architecture (FEA) standard
- *FEA Security and Privacy Profile* as one methodology to align IA with EA
- Relationship of IA^2 to EA standards using FEA reference models and Department of Defense Architecture Framework (DoDAF) products

By the end of this chapter, you should be able to research EA standards that may apply to your organization and have a general idea of how IA^2 can integrate IA into enterprise architecture.

10.3 Federal Enterprise Architecture (FEA): An Introduction

There are many EA standards, and Table 10.2 provides a list of some of the more popular ones. IA^2 is distinct from a specific EA standard and is able to support the integration of IA into any EA standard. The Federal Enterprise Architecture (FEA) is an enterprise architecture model created by and for the U.S. federal government. The Office of Management and Budget (OMB) and the Office of E-Government (E-Gov) and Information Technology (IT) established FEA to build a comprehensive business-driven blueprint of the entire federal government.* FEA core principles include† EA being business driven, proactive and collaborative across the federal government, and that architecture improves the effectiveness and efficiency of government information resources.

FEA is a business-centric tool that gives direction and context to information technology and information assurance. Similarly, EA in the commercial marketplace is business driven, proactive, and collaborative across the enterprise (disparate business units, partners, joint ventures, and customers). Architecture improves the effectiveness and efficiency of organizational resources. Although the intent and specifics of FEA are directed toward the U.S. federal government, the same principles apply to any commercial endeavor. Likewise, the principles of integrating IA

---

* Paraphrase from the *FEA Consolidated Reference Model*, May 2005, p. 4
† Ibid., p. 4.

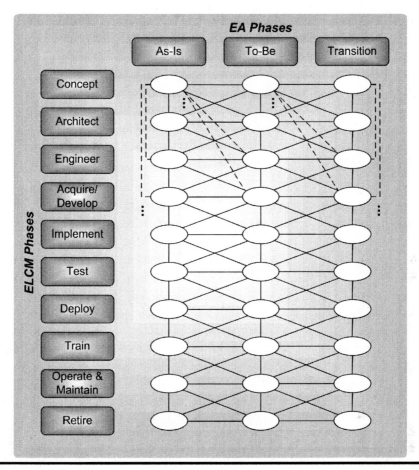

Figure 10.1 Phase cross sections among ELCM and EA phases.

using IA² with FEA apply to commercial EA standards and other government EA standards as well.

As the IA architect, you will apply IA² F and IA² P in an iterative process as the FEA reference models go through their respective enterprise life cycles. Use the perspectives of as-is, to-be, and transition to discern reference model objectives, current state, and how to achieve the objectives starting from the current state. Each phase intersection (Figure 10.1) is a unique perspective that influences other phase cross sections in a large variety of permutations. At each visit to each cross section, use the IA² P, IA² F, and other frameworks herein to identify, enumerate, articulate, and address risks. *But this is a lot of work!* Yes, it is. *This is expensive!* Yes, it can be. *This will take a lot of time!* Yes, it can. But that is the benefit of IA². IA² provides a discipline with a variety of embedded checklists to be direct, comprehensive, and consistent to eliminate guesswork. By virtue of being a process, IA² is more efficient than an arbitrary approach. With effective application, IA² provides excellent results in less time and money than an arbitrary approach. However, it takes effort and practice to develop fluency in the application of IA².

10.3.1 FEA Reference Models

The FEA consists of five reference models:

- Performance reference model (PRM)
- Business reference model (BRM)
- Service component reference model (SRM)
- Technical reference model (TRM)
- Data reference model (DRM)

10.3.1.1 Performance Reference Model

The PRM is a framework to measure the performance of IT and its contribution to the business functions it supports and the overall enterprise. The purpose of the PRM is to measure business value, that is, to articulate the contribution of IT to business results. Performance criteria and performance measurements objectively track and report performance improvement of IT and the improvement of the business results to which IT contributes.

The PRM specifies metrics and indicators (SLAs) that define successful mission fulfillment. The FEA PRM distinguishes among the following:

- Measurement area
- Measurement category
- Measurement grouping
- Measurement indicator

A measurement area addresses performance aspects at the output level for agencies or programs. There are four measurement areas: mission results, customer results, processes and activities, and technology. A measurement category is a collection within each measurement area describing the characteristics to be measured. There are three measurement categories: citizen services, service delivery support, and government resource management. A measurement grouping is a refinement of a measurement category into specific types of measurement indicators. A measurement indicator is the specific measures. Working through each area and relevant categories, groupings, and indicators produces a list of IA questions (*What are the risks?*) and answers (*Address the risks by _____*).

SLAs become increasingly significant as the federal government moves towards performance-based contracts where the government bases contract award and payment in terms of *performance* versus *deliverables*. Understanding PRM and the business drivers behind PRM is equally important for government and those wishing to do business with the U.S. government.

10.3.1.2 Business Reference Model

The BRM is a framework within which to articulate the business structure and its intent. The FEA BRM includes 4 business areas, 39 lines of business, and 153 subfunctions. The business areas convey the purpose for government, how to achieve the purpose, support functions, and resource management functions. The lines of business convey the purpose of government in functional terms. The subfunctions are a further decomposition of the lines of business.

The BRM provides context and conditions to relate business processes to mission; this is a functional view. The BRM provides four business areas:

- Services for citizens—purpose of government
- Mode of delivery—mechanisms to achieve purpose
- Support of service delivery—operational support
- Government resource management

Lines of business (LOBs) are the products of granular decomposition of BRM business areas. FEA distinguishes between internal LOBs and external LOBs, but refers to them collectively as just LOBs. Of the 39 LOBs, 19 are for service to citizens; these are also considered external LOBs. The 20 internal LOBs describe functions necessary to provide service to citizens. Each LOB is in turn a collection of subfunctions.

10.3.1.3 Service Component Reference Model

The SRM is a framework to capture details of business components, applications, application capabilities, services, and mechanisms to evaluate the potential for reuse of any of these elsewhere throughout the enterprise. A business component may be an environment that can accept the addition of a new software application. The implication is that the cost of generating the new software application does not have to include the environment to make it available to the enterprise as that environment already exists. An application may be a software application or a solution that uses multiple software applications. The details of the SRM are separate from the business functions.

The SRM is a business-driven framework to classify service components that support business (BRM) and performance (PRM) components. There are 7 service domains and 30 service types. The service domains are:

- Customer services domain
- Process automation services domain
- Business management services domain
- Digital asset services domain
- Business analytical services domain
- Back office services domain
- Support services domain

Service domains consist of service types, and service types consist of components. The component is the smallest granular size in the SRM. SRM defines a component as "a self contained business process or service with predetermined functionality that may be exposed through a business or technology interface."*

10.3.1.4 Technical Reference Model

The TRM is a framework to capture standards and technologies that promote the delivery of service components and capabilities. The purpose of the TRM is to promote the reuse of technology and service components across the enterprise. The TRM consists of four core service areas. Each service area consists of "multiple Service Categories, Service Standards, and Service Specifications that provide the foundation to group standards, specifications, and technologies that directly support the Service Area."†

TRM service areas include service access and delivery, service platform and infrastructure, component framework, and service interface and integration. Service categories by service area include:

- Service access and delivery
  - Access channels (Web browser, wireless/PDA); delivery channels (Internet, intranet)
- Service platform and infrastructure
  - Delivery servers (Web servers, application servers); database; hardware/infrastructure (LAN, videoconferencing)
- Component framework
  - Security (security services, infrastructure); data interchange (data exchange)
- Service interface and integration
- Integration, interoperability, interface

---

* *FEA Service Component Reference Model (SRM)*, version 1.0, p. 5.
† *FEA Technical Reference Model (TRM)*, version 1.1, p. 7.

10.3.1.5   Data Reference Model

The DRM is a framework to promote the common identification, sharing, and use of data across the enterprise. DRM provides for the standardization of data structure, categorization, and exchange. *Structure* promotes a common format to data from its basic representation (e.g., ASCII) to the bundling of data elements. A common data structure is necessary if some parts of the enterprise are to find, receive, and use the data from other parts of the enterprise. Data *categorization* describes the general business purpose for the data, or the business context. Data *exchange* describes the bundling or packaging of data for transfer between business units or business nodes. Effective data exchange depends on structure and categorization.

10.3.2   IA² Alignment with FEA RMs

Effective alignment of IA² with FEA integrates risk management into the FEA artifacts. The use of IA² will provide you with raw data for a risk management narrative. In brief, IA² provides a framework that includes six IA² views and nine IA core principles; this alone provides a matrix of 54 distinct perspectives from which to identify and manage risk. The Organizational Context Framework (OCF) provides six organizational layers, each with a distinct interest in IA. The ELCM has ten phases, each with distinct activity to support the life cycle of the capability, service, or product. The IA² LoS provides 12 steps from business requirements to O&M. A matrix of IA² views and OCF offers 36 distinct content perspectives. A matrix of IA² views and ELCM offers 60 granular perspectives on IA throughout the life cycle. Appendix B provides templates for these and other matrices that will support the integration of IA into enterprise architecture.

Which matrices apply? That is up to you. Ask yourself what the problem at hand requires. Because this is a chapter on enterprise architecture, the applicable ELCM phase is likely to be *architect*. The IA² views and IA core principle matrix apply throughout IA integration to EA. The IA² LoS steps are likely business requirements, IA architecture, and CONOPS. Use the appropriate matrices to prompt questions and record answers regarding risk and how to address that risk for each element in the FEA reference models.

10.3.2.1   IA² Alignment with PRM

PRM attempts to measure business value; integration of IA captures how to measure the business value of IA in terms of business risk management.

The process of developing a PRM includes decomposing the [enterprise | business unit | program | project | solution | system] into FEA measurement areas, categories, groupings, and measurement indicators. These are the *success measures* that indicate the solution is performing to expectations. With regard to IA, ask the following questions:

- How can IA support the attainment of these success measures?
- Does IA enable success? How specifically?
- Does a lack of IA jeopardize success? How?
- Does IA have separate measures of success (i.e., distinct IA metrics, SLAs)? Is success defined by IA attributes? Is success defined by business attributes to which IA contributes?
- Do existing/emerging threats jeopardize meeting SLAs? How?
- Do emerging technologies enable meeting SLAs? How? What are the technical risks of emerging technologies? What are the business risks?

For example, the financial measurement area may look at how security and privacy enable revenue. FEA compliance may ensure agency funding; therefore, effective IA may preserve the budget revenue stream. How does IA enable cost savings or cost avoidance? Funds spent on core services are better than funds spent on recovering from loss of data due to poor backup process.

The above questions are exemplary and not exhaustive, but they do establish a mindset. Walking through each PRM attribute using the IA^2 Process and IA^2 Framework is a disciplined approach to identify, enumerate, articulate, and address risks in the PRM details. Do you really have to go to all this effort? The answer is an emphatic "it depends." How big is the project? How much investment is in the project? For a billion dollar solution, yes, there is tremendous benefit to exhaustive risk management. For a smaller project, scale the use of IA^2 to identify and address the relevant issues.

10.3.2.2 IA^2 Alignment with BRM

The process of developing a BRM identifies business areas, LOBs, and subfunctions relevant to the organization. The most granular level is the subfunction. Walk through the appropriate steps in the IA^2 P and consider the relevant aspects of IA^2 F to discern and address the business risks that include:

- Threats to the function of each business area
- Vulnerabilities of each business area

10.3.2.3 IA^2 Alignment with SRM

The SRM facilitates the discovery of services to support the business and performance objectives. Some services may already exist; others may be identified as necessary, but not in place. IA^2 facilitates identifying and addressing risks to service development and performance. The ECF (see chapter 12) assists in putting services in the context of the enterprise.

The enterprise consists of many business functions. Business functions consist of permutations of subsets of collectives (actors), systems (entities), and processes (actions). A service is the act of satisfying some demand (service as a verb); it is also the collective, system, or process that satisfies some demand (service as a noun). In general, a service requestor does not expect a response from a single, specific actor or entity; the service requestor expects a result. What, how, where, or who produces that results is not relevant to the requestor. For example, a service may follow the sun around the globe to provide the service to people during local work hours as well as to provide service globally 24 hours a day, every day. IA² helps identify risks in providing a service from multiple locations and multiple countries; communications handoff as work hours shift across time zones; the physical and technical infrastructure that varies among service producers; etc.

10.3.2.4   IA² Alignment with TRM

TRM aligns to business drivers defined in the PRM, BRM, and SRM. The IA services and mechanisms will address technology risks that in turn align with business risks. Distinguishing IA from IT prompts consideration of IA as support for both technical and business risks. The following provides some distinctions between IT and IA:

- IT infrastructure
  - Cables, wires, network interface, frequencies, wireless access, switches, routers
- IT services
  - Web services, service-oriented architecture (SOA), domain name service (DNS)
- IA policies
  - Identity and privilege management, access management
- IA infrastructure
  - Firewall, IDS, anti-malware, honeypot
- IA services
- CSIRT, forensics, risk assessment, security operating center (SOC)

Use the IA² F technology related views to discern risks associated with TRM details. Keep in mind that the focus of EA is align technology with business drivers. The focus of IA² is to align IA with business risks. Some of those business risks may be in terms of technical risks, but always the technical risks will align with a business risk.

10.3.2.5   IA² Alignment with DRM

IA addresses the security of data, data format, data structure, and data exchange. The IA² data/information view figures prominently in establishing an IA posture within the DRM. Data may be the focus of IA, or data about the data (metadata) may be the focus of IA. Metadata includes details about the data such as author, date of creation, last modification date, classification level, and source of data. Judgments on the quality and accuracy of the data may come in part from the metadata. IA² assists in identifying potential risks to metadata corruption (integrity), metadata disclosure (confidentiality), and access to metadata (availability). How does one ensure metadata integrity? Confidentiality? One method is to bind metadata with the data it belongs to and encrypt it (crypto-binding of metadata).

10.3.2.6 IA² Alignment Deliverables

As you can see, the complexities of FEA begin to emerge. The size and complexity may vary tremendously with permutations of details among PRM, BRM, SRM, TRM, and DRM. Moreover, the FEA artifacts (documents and diagrams) may be very lengthy and complex. IA² deliverables in support of FEA may include:

- A rather long narrative of the FEA IA² Process and findings
- Tables of reference models with IA² components in terms of:
  - Managing business risk, solution risk, project risk
  - CIA—confidentiality-integrity-availability
  - PAU—possession-authenticity-utility
  - PAN—privacy–authorized use–nonrepudiation
- Traceability matrix aligning business drivers to IA services and mechanisms via the many FEA RMs

The templates in the appendix provide a starting point. Rather than provide additional documents to the FEA set, insert the IA details to the PRM, BRM, SRM, TRM, and DRM as appropriate. This provides for IA integration from inception and carries the IA concepts throughout the inherent alignment of business to performance, service to business, technical to service and business, and data.

10.3.3 FEA Security and Privacy Profile

FEA Security and Privacy Profile, version 2.0, June 2006* (SPP) is a supplement to the FEA that addresses information security and privacy from a business enterprise perspective. The SPP is a methodology that uses the FEA framework; therefore, there it is not a distinct framework for security and privacy separate from the FEA itself.

SPP depends on the FEA reference models for structure and flow. SPP attempts to align the security controls specified in the NIST standards with the architectural components of FEA. If you are working on an FEA project, you should produce results consistent with the form and flow of FEA and the SPP as a supplement to FEA. The SPP is not nearly the breadth and depth of IA². IA² may be stand-alone

---

* www.cio.gov/documents/Security_and_Privacy_Profile_v2.pdf.

or support any enterprise architecture. Using IA² will provide better content than using SPP alone.

10.4   DoDAF Products Overview

The Department of Defense Architecture Framework (DoDAF) products are a series of documents under four families:

- All view (AV)
- Operational view (OV)
- System view (SV)
- Technical view (TV)

Table 10.1 elaborates on these views and presents an overview of IA integration using IA².

10.5   A List of EA Frameworks

Table 10.2 provides a list of major EA frameworks, references to further details, source of the framework, and a brief description. IA² is applicable to any EA framework as the IA² F and IA² P are designed as stand-alone tools, agnostic of any other standard or framework, and modular to select those parts applicable to the business risk at hand.

10.5.1   Enterprise Architecture Organizations

Table 10.3 provides a list of major EA organizations and respective Web addresses.

10.6   Commentary

The commercial building architect anticipates the business uses of the office building; the residential architect anticipates the uses of the house: number of children, number of bedrooms, size of play area, traffic patterns within the house, use of natural light, energy efficiency, etc. The enterprise architect discerns the business need and performance requirements and then aligns technical services and mechanisms to achieve them. The security architect anticipates risks, threats, and vulnerabilities to mission integrity, and safeguards to minimize business risk with the right harmony of security (restrictions) and empowerment (employee freedom to act) and budget. The enterprise architect may use an EA framework and model to produce and execute on an enterprise architecture. The IA architect uses IA² to identify, enumerate, articulate, and address business risk.

Table 10.1   DoDAF Products and IA² Relationship

Product Reference	Product Title	Product Description	IA Integration Using IA²
All view (AV)		The AV products provide overarching descriptions of the entire architecture (all three views) but do not present a distinct view of the architecture. The AV products define the scope, environment, and context of the architecture.	IA² provides for the addition of overarching description of organizational risk.
AV-1	Overview and summary information	Scope, purpose, intended users, environment depicted, analytical findings	Apply the IA² Process to determine the risks within scope, environment, purpose, and user group. Also, articulate the scope of the risks, as in what risks will be looked at (e.g., technical risk only versus business and technical).
AV-2	Integrated dictionary	Architecture data repository with definitions of all terms used in all products	Insert into the dictionary appropriate IA lexicon and definitions. Your organization may use a particular term with a specific meaning. Clarify the definitions in the AV-2 to ensure common and consistent use of the IA-related terms.

Operational view (OV)	The OV is a description of the tasks and activities, operational elements, and information exchanges required to accomplish the missions. Missions include both the core missions (fulfilling the core reason the organization exists) and business support processes that enable core mission execution. The OV contains graphical and textual products that comprise an identification of the operational nodes and elements, assigned tasks and activities, and information flows required between nodes. It defines the types of information exchanged, the frequency of exchange, which tasks and activities are supported by the information exchanges, and the nature of information exchanges.	IA² provides insight into risks from an operational view (not a systemic, technical view). The OV looks at the organization, organizational structure, organizational interactions, people, and policies driving behavior at the operational level.
OV-1	High-level operational concept graphic	High-level graphical and textual description of operational concept (organization structure, mission, physical proximity of locations, communications connectivity, etc.)	Supplement the graphics (perhaps an overlay) with references to risk. The textual description should also convey risks and how to address those risks.
OV-2	Operational node connectivity description	Operational nodes, functions/services at each node, internode connectivity, and information flow between nodes	An operational node (department, domain, service, function [not a system that is detail for later]) has an interface to communicate with other nodes. Identify and articulate the risks of the interfaces and the fact that communication occurs at all, with connectivity (e.g., other node may be weakest link) and with the information flow between the nodes.
OV-3	Operational information exchange matrix	Information exchanges that support the operational need; relevant attributes of the exchange	Identify risks with information exchanges (e.g., dependencies on information, information classification, and metadata).

Continued

Table 10.1   DoDAF Products and IA² Relationship (Continued)

Product Reference	Product Title	Product Description	IA Integration Using IA²
OV-4	Organizational relationships chart	Organizational hierarchy, roles, or other relationships among organizations; authority sources	The organization is a hierarchy of command and control, superior and subordinate relationships. There are risks in individual actions, group actions (departments), and intergroup actions (interdepartmental). Risks find root in no communication, miscommunication, office politics, and elected official politics. Authority sources touch on governance. The lack of governance is a risk, as is poorly defined governance.
OV-5	Operational activity model	Capabilities, operational activities, relationships among activities, inputs, and outputs. Overlays can show cost, performing nodes, or other pertinent information.	Operational activity touches on workflows and tasks within the ECF. All activities follow a systemic flow of input (dependencies, trigger events), process (performing tasks), and output (production, quality, external dependencies). Use the IA² Process to identify risks and how to address risks in operational activity.
OV-6a	Operational rules model	One of the three products used to describe operational activity—identifies business rules that constrain operation	Business rules touch on compliance requirements and the need for compliance management. IA² offers direction on compliance management and aligning (requirements engineering) IA with compliance requirements.

OV-6b	Operational state transition description	One of three products used to describe operational activity—identifies business process responses to events	These are the workflows and tasks. The response to events is response to inputs. Identify the risks associated with the inputs, input sources, input formats, input timeliness, input quality, input trust, etc.
OV-6c	Operational event-trace description	One of three products used to describe operational activity—traces actions in a scenario or sequence of events	The OV-6c is akin to a process map to convey a sequence of events to accomplish a task. OV-6a, OV-6b, and OV-6c describe operations in progressively more detail. IA² accommodates examining risks at these various detail levels. The IA² views apply at any level, and the ECF provides an enterprise context for entities (technology), actors (people and collectives), and actions (business functions, workflows, tasks).
OV-7	Logical data model	Documentation of the system data requirements and structural business process rules of the operational view	The IA² provides narrative regarding risks surrounding data and data requirements. The IA core principles provide a framework within which to articulate the business drivers for IA and how IA satisfies those business drivers.
Systems view (SV)		The SV is a set of graphical and textual products that describes systems and interconnections providing for, or supporting, organizational functions. Organizational functions include both the core mission and business support functions. The SV associates systems resources to the OV. These systems resources support the operational activities and facilitate the exchange of information among operational nodes.	IA² provides insight into risks from a systems view. The SV is a more technical focus than the OV. The SV looks at systems, systemic structure, system interactions, and policies driving systems. Note: Standards defining what to use for systems are the technical view, not the SV.

Continued

Table 10.1   DoDAF Products and IA² Relationship (Continued)

Product Reference	Product Title	Product Description	IA Integration Using IA²
SV-2	Systems communications description	Systems nodes, systems, and system items, and their related communications lay-downs	Interfaces are the public view of the system. Communications is the exchange of information or data through interfaces. The risks of the interfaces (access) are in SV-1. The risks of how the information exchange are in the SV-2.
SV-3	Systems–systems matrix	Relationships among systems in a given architecture; can be designed to show relationships of interest, e.g., system-type interfaces, planned versus existing interfaces, etc.	A system matrix examines the relationships among systems. Do the business requirements lead to integration, interoperability, federation, or a combination? Example risks include technical incompatibilities, costs of integrating systems, organizational politics that override technical capabilities, etc.
SV-4	Systems functionality description	Functions performed by systems and the system data flows among system functions	SV-4 looks at what the system does and the process it performs. Use IA² to identify the risks of performing the system functions. For example, has technical expediency ignored the reason to maintain privacy for employees? For customers?
SV-5	Operational activity to systems function traceability matrix	Mapping of systems back to capabilities or of system functions back to operational activities	Traceability matrix ensures alignment from business requirements to the technical mechanisms that fulfill the requirements. Use the IA², specifically the IA² LoS, to insert alignment of IA solutions to the business drivers that motivate them.

SV-6	Systems data exchange matrix	Provides details of system data elements being exchanged between systems and the attributes of that exchange	Similar to the above guidance, IA² provides the ability to insert IA details into each SV document. Use the IA² Process, the IA² Framework, the IA core principles, and the various frameworks as the current circumstances warrant. Record risks about the system as well as about the IA portion of the solution. Integrate IA into the enterprise architecture.
SV-7	Systems performance parameters matrix	Performance characteristics of systems view elements, for the appropriate timeframes.	See SV-6.
SV-8	Systems evolution description	Planned incremental steps toward migration of a suite of systems to a more efficient suite, or toward evolving a current system to a future implementation	See SV-6.
SV-9	Systems technology forecast	Emerging technologies and software/hardware products that are expected to be available in a given set of timeframes and that will affect future development of the architecture	See SV-6.
SV-10a	Systems rules model	One of three products used to describe systems functionality—identifies constraints that are imposed on systems functionality due to some aspect of systems design or implementation	See SV-6.
SV-10b	Systems state transition description	One of three products used to describe systems functionality—identifies responses of a system to events	See SV-6.

Continued

Table 10.1 DoDAF Products and IA² Relationship (Continued)

Product Reference	Product Title	Product Description	IA Integration Using IA²
SV-10c	Systems event-trace description	One of three products used to describe systems functionality—identifies system-specific refinements of critical sequences of events described in the operational view	See SV-6.
SV-11	Physical schema	Physical implementation of the logical data model entities, e.g., message formats, file structures, and physical schema	See SV-6.
Technical standards view (TV)		The TV is the minimal set of rules governing the arrangement, interaction, and interdependence of system parts or elements. Its purpose is to ensure that a system satisfies a specified set of operational requirements. The TV provides the technical systems implementation guidelines upon which engineering specifications are based, common building blocks are established, and product lines are developed. The TV includes a collection of the technical standards, implementation conventions, standards options, rules, and criteria organized into profiles that govern systems and system elements for a given architecture.	IA² addresses TV risks that include intrasystemic interdependencies (e.g., loss of a part of the system). Loss of any part of the system degrades the system; use IA² to identify levels of tolerance for degraded performance. Use IA² to examine the standards that describe what to use to implement and enforce policy. There are risks to not using standards, to using standards, to using certain products and vendors within standards. Use IA² to identify the trade-offs in performance, cost, and security.

TV-1	Technical standards profile	Listing of standards that apply to systems view elements in a given architecture	IA² looks at the risks in the list of standards. Do they reflect an appropriate level of guidance? Do they represent necessary compliance requirements? Do they sufficiently represent compliance requirements?
TV-2	Technical standards forecast	Description of emerging standards and potential impact on current systems view elements, within a set of timeframes	TV-1 looks at existing standards, TV-2 looks at emerging standards. Emerging standards may be all together new standards or revisions to existing standards. Use IA² to anticipate the risks of changes to standards. The innovation framework will assist in identifying the business reasons behind change, which also provide additional input to analyzing the risk posture.

Table 10.2 EA Frameworks

EA Framework (Reference)	Source	Description
AGATE (http://www.achats. defense.gouv.fr/ article33349)	Modeling for system architecture; French government	A French architecture framework with roughly the same intent as DoDAF
C4ISR	U.S. federal government (DoD)	Command, Control, Computers, Communications (C4); Intelligence, Surveillance, and Reconnaissance (ISR)
CIMOSA (cimosa.cnt.pl)	European consortium of approximately 30 vendors (AMICE); CIMOSA was developed for ESPRIT (European Strategic Program for Research and Development in Information Technology).	Common Information Model Open System Architecture(CIMOSA) defines a model-based enterprise engineering method. CIMOSA categorizes operations into generic and specific functions to promote process simulation and analysis.
DoDAF	U.S. federal government	Department of Defense Architecture Framework is based on FEA
E2AF (www.enterprise-architecture.info)	Institute for Enterprise Architecture Developments	Extended Enterprise Architecture Framework (E2AF); extends enterprise architecture beyond the enterprise boundaries to a more collaborative environment
EAP	U.S. commercial	Enterprise Architecture Planning by Steven Spewak

Table 10.2   EA Frameworks (Continued)

EA Framework (Reference)	Source	Description
IAF (http://www.capgemini.com/services/soa/ent_architecture/iaf/)	Commercial; Cap Gemini	Integrated architecture framework
ISO/IEC 14252	International Standards Organization	ISO 14252; a predecessor and influence on TOGAF, ISO 14252 is based on TAIFM.
TOGAF (http://www.opengroup.org/togaf/)	Commercial; The Open Group	The Open Group Architecture Framework
FEA	U.S. federal government	Federal Enterprise Architecture (FEA) is based on the Zachman Framework.
MODAF	Ministry of Defense Architecture Framework	A U.K. architectural framework with roughly the same intent as DoDAF
TAFIM (http://www.sei.cmu.edu/str/descriptions/refmodels.html)	U.S. federal government (DoD)	Technical Architectural Framework for Information Management (TAFIM); included for reference only, as the TAFIM was cancelled in January 2000
TEAF (http://www.treas.gov/offices/cio/egov/)	U.S. federal government	Treasury Enterprise Architecture Framework (TEAF) is based on the Zachman Framework.
Zachman Framework (http://www.zifa.com/)	Commercial; Zachman Institute for Framework Advancement	EA framework by John Zachman

Note: All URLs last accessed July 2007.

Table 10.3   EA Organizations Reference

Organization	Web Address
Association of Enterprise Architects	http://www.aeajournal.org/
Enterprise Architecture Interest Group	http://www.eaig.org/
System Architecture User Group	http://www.sa-user.com/default.asp
Enterprise Architect magazine	http://www.ftponline.com/mediakit/magazines/ea/editorial/
FEA	http://www.whitehouse.gov/omb/egov/
Global Enterprise Architecture Organization	http://www.etheryl.net/GEAO/
Netherlands Architecture Forum	http://www.naf.nl/
FEA Certification Institute	http://www.feacinstitute.org/
The Zachman Institute for Framework Advancement	http://www.zifa.com/
Enterprise Wide IT Architecture	http://www.ewita.com/
Enterprise Architecture Community	http://www.sharedinsights.com/networks/ea/

Note: All URLs last accessed in July 2007.

IA² ENTERPRISE CONTEXT

Chapter 11

The Framework Perspective

11.1 Introduction

The most important aspect of information assurance is *people*. Today, the most important person in this learning experience is *you*, the reader. You are today the product of everything that has gone into your mind up to this point. Your experiences provide you with mental models (a way to see and evaluate things), methodologies (a way to do something), and tools (a set of skills to apply in getting things done). Everyone's experiences are unique and include a combination of inherent talents and behaviors (nature, genetics) and learned skills and behaviors (nurture, environment). Nature provides the capacity and nurture realizes that capacity to varying degrees. Capacity and realization of that capacity are among the roots of differences among people.

These differences make us unique and provide richness to life. These differences also have the potential to cause conflict. People viewing the same thing often have varying interpretations according to their own experiences. Business people tend to see things from a business perspective and technical people from a technical perspective. Moreover, people tend to look at things from the perspective of their individual disciplines. Finance people see things and speak in terms of currency (e.g., dollars, euros, and pounds), balance sheets, and income statements. Network operators see things and speak in terms of bandwidth, throughput, and storage capacity. Although an increase in throughput often has economic benefit to the organization, rare is the formal articulation of alignment between an investment in an increase in network bandwidth and line items on a balance sheet. Even though financial managers and network operators intend, plan, and execute for the overall benefit of the organization, they are often frustrated with each other in discussing technology budgets, investments, and returns on investment. What they need is a process of *normalization* to create a common understanding, a common foundation on which to build a problem definition, develop a set of options, select a recommendation, plan a solution, and implement that solution. One normalization tool is the *framework*.

A framework is a basic conceptual structure that provides a common point of reference. This book uses a collection of frameworks to provide an enterprise perspective as well as to dive deeper into IA as it relates to the enterprise. The frameworks introduce concepts, not details. The frameworks are presented to provide the reader with awareness that such frameworks exist and a context in which to integrate IA into the business processes of governance, management, planning, and operations.

The frameworks in *Information Assurance Architecture* provide a way to look at the enterprise as a whole, break it down into constituent parts, examine the parts individually, and then sum up the parts for different views of the whole. There are many frameworks, and together they provide a variety of perspectives. Some frameworks overlap with others. As such, there is some redundancy, but a useful redundancy in that one perspective may not resonate with a particular manager, executive, general, admiral, colonel, or congressperson, yet another may. The IA architect must discern each audience's agenda and deliver the message accordingly. The frameworks help the architect make that discernment and clarify the IA message.

11.2   Frameworks as Decision Support Tools

We develop mental models to help ourselves deal with many aspects of our personal, social, and professional lives. The term *mental model* refers to cognitive archetypes, or the way the mind visualizes something. Mental models provide shortcuts for managing situations we are familiar with, or that we *perceive* we are familiar with. They save us time by reducing our need to repeatedly go through complex cognitive processes.

A negative aspect to mental models is prejudice, which is prejudging something. When our perceptions deceive us and we apply a tried-and-true solution to the wrong problem, out of habit we misapply that mental model. "Think out of the box" is one admonition that intends to make us aware that our mental models may not be serving us well in all situations. Frameworks provide a way to normalize our perceptions. Frameworks assist in decision making, first by helping us determine the appropriate question, then by guiding us toward finding the best answer. While frameworks facilitate effective use of our mental models, they also challenge our mental models to ensure their appropriate use.

11.2.1 Decision Making

Effective decision making results in action guided by knowledge. An effective security solution is complex at the system level. At the enterprise level, an effective security solution is overwhelming in terms of discerning the foundational issues, asking the appropriate questions, identifying options, making recommendations, and implementing the solution itself. IA^2 is a tool for the IA architect to apply in complexity management; IA^2 is a decision support system for information assurance.

So, why a decision support system? When the problem before you has a ready answer, move forward and execute; there is no decision to make because you have an answer—done, wrapped, sealed, and delivered. When the problem is vaguely defined, when conflicting alternatives are present, when contingencies must be considered, uncertainty emerges. To make a decision is to identify options and select the best option with the knowledge at hand; to make a decision means that there is some degree of uncertainty.

How do you know the knowledge you have is the best? How do you handle new knowledge? Are you asking the right questions? Are these the only options? Are these the best options? Are you looking for the best options, or are budget and time constraints driving you toward identifying adequate options. How do you determine if adequate is good enough? What factors must balance to result in good enough?

Figure 11.1 shows an increase in time and money as the solution moves from good enough to good to best. Unlimited time and money equate to option nirvana and ensure the status quo by fostering analysis paralysis. Limits on time and money mean a solution must be selected within the constraints of those resources. Selecting less than best should be a conscious decision and for the right reasons. Selecting a good enough solution should also be for justifiable business reasons. Justify your choice in terms of ROI or best available given schedule, staffing, and budget constraints. The key principle in decision making is *conscious choices with justification*.

11.2.2 Change

With respect to innovation, there are two change motivation principles:

■ Change motivation principle 1: If it ain't broke, don't fix it.
■ Change motivation principle 2: "Success in playing the game changes the game, tenacity in playing the old game turns success into failure."*

---

* Jamshid Gharajedaghi, *Systems Thinking—Managing Chaos and Complexity*.

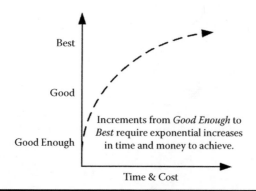

Figure 11.1 Best–good–good enough time and cost.

The intent of the first principle is to avoid allocating limited resources to improve something working adequately. Violating the first principle misallocates investment dollars. The intent of the second principle is not to ignore the need to invest in improvements just because something is working adequately. Too much tenacity in holding on to the old game may cause the organization to fear for its very existence as competition threatens the status quo. Change is necessary, but for the right reasons, reasons that support the core mission of the organization. The enterprise architect advises the organization on the appropriate balance between these change motivation principles.

The IA² focus is on identifying, enumerating, articulating, quantifying (when appropriate), and addressing business risk. Managing risk often leads to change. IA² addresses IA questions such as: What are the business risks of how we are doing business today? Is part of the new game an increase in security? As we move toward realigning the organization to address new competitive challenges, do we incorporate IA? How?

Frameworks provide guidance for *enterprise efficacy.** Frameworks facilitate an awareness of the need for change as well as the realization of change through identifying transformation activities, discerning the consequences of those actions, and identifying the costs, benefits, risks, and how to most effectively address those risks.

11.2.3 Simple System

Figure 11.2 shows a representation of a simple system; call this a system framework. IA² uses this and many other frameworks in simple and complex variations to provide the IA architect with an IA² Process to generate an IA architecture. That IA architecture may supplement a vastly complex solution on a national or international scale. The IA architecture may be for a relatively simple solution or application. Use the IA² Framework, the IA² Process, and the many frameworks herein in part or in whole where needed and as needed. Accomplishing an effective

---

* The power to produce a desired effect within the organization.

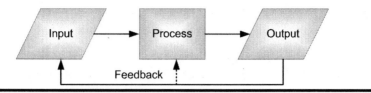

Figure 11.2 A simple system.

IA architecture, indeed any definition of an effective IA architecture, is contingent on business need, organizational need and risk tolerances, situational need, available knowledge, available resources, and time constraints.

11.2.4 Business versus Technical Perspectives

Business people convey their interests in business terms, e.g., customer service, marketing, balance sheets, and budgets. Technical people convey their interests in technical terms, e.g., network bandwidth, storage capacity, hits on a firewall, and the latest technology du jour (e.g., SOA*). Rarely does the twain meet on common ground. The bean counters on one side speak in terms of ledger entries, and bit-heads on the other side speak in techno terms of databases. Although they speak of the same thing and the seeds of agreement are plentiful, both sides often walk away frustrated because they cannot find the common ground. IA² is a tool that will help find this common ground by aligning security solutions (often technical, but not always) with business drivers.

Discovering this common ground begins with first distinguishing business from technical, and then linking or aligning the two. A business function may be *accounting*. A service within accounting may be expense reimbursements; another service may be accounts receivable. Each of these business functions and services is a collection of systems. The expense reimbursement service may consist of an automated system that accepts employee input and a manual system that reconciles employee claims against credit card receipts. This is the first link between business talk and techno-talk; that is, the enterprise consists of business functions that in turn consist of one or more systems, some of which are technical. The Enterprise Context Framework (ECF) (see chapter 12) aligns enterprise business functions with the components and subcomponents of systems, and to tasks in workflows.

11.3 Organizational Structure Context Framework

Organizations distinguish among people who *decide what to do*; those who *acquire, compile, and direct* the right people in what to do; and those people who *do*. This

---

* Service-oriented architecture (SOA).

leads to a hierarchy of superior–subordinate relationships that we are familiar with in commercial, government, military, and other organizations. The organizational structure is the environment of the hierarchical relationships within the enterprise. The following *Organizational Structure Context Framework* (OCF) presents hierarchies that distinguish governance, management, operations, and more.

- Governance
- Management
- Builders
- Operations
- Users
- Leaders

Each of the categories in the OCF may use a variety of frameworks specific to that category, or may look at the same framework from different perspectives. Many frameworks apply across governance, management, builders, operations, users, and leaders. The list of frameworks below barely dents the surface, but raises awareness that such frameworks exist. Each framework offers another tool in the architecture toolkit, a toolkit for use in developing enterprise architectures or IA architectures. Follow the principle of *using the right tool for the right job*.

11.3.1   Governance Frameworks

Examples of frameworks that support governance activities include:

- Innovation framework
- Enterprise management framework
- Enterprise architecture framework
- Future vision
- Creativity
- Critical thinking
- Stakeholder framework
  - Stakeholder identification
  - Stakeholder interests
  - Stakeholder currency
- Organizational effectiveness

11.3.2   Management Frameworks

Examples of frameworks that support management activities include:

- Decision making

- Change management
- Problem solving
  - Problem definition
  - Decision making
- Outreach framework (tie in with ATE framework)
  - Awareness
  - Understanding
  - Use
  - Effective use
  - Secure use
- Reality Check Framework (RCF)
  - Who
  - What
  - Why
  - When
  - Where
  - How

11.3.3   Builder Frameworks

Examples of frameworks that support builder activities include the following:

- Team building
- Relationship building
  - Individuals
    - Individual psychology, cognitive engineering
  - Organizations (e.g., agencies, departments, working groups, etc.)
    - Group psychology, industrial psychology
- System engineering
- Tools to support building efforts
  - Discovery
  - Analysis
  - Creating data repositories
    - Tracking details
  - Reporting details
- Communications
  - Communications protocols (person to person as well as technology to technology)
- Effective meetings
  - Engage operations to ensure smooth handoff.
- Vision, future casting
- Adjudication

- Facilitation
- Presentation
- System thinking
- System dynamics (decision support)
- Change management
  - Introduce innovation.
  - Introduce action.
- Decision making to keep moving toward the goal
- Work breakdown structure (WBS)
- Project management
- Physical infrastructure
  - Site selection
  - Facilities construction
- Stakeholder management
  - Engage stakeholders, executives, managers to ensure understanding of the goals.
- Transition management
  - Engage operations to ensure smooth handoff.

11.3.4   Operations Frameworks

Examples of frameworks that support operations activities include:

- IA operations cycle
  - Anticipate
  - Defend
  - Monitor
  - Respond
- Insider threat framework
- Operations center framework
  - Network operations center (NOC)
  - Security operations center (SOC)
  - System/application operations center (SyOC)
- Help desk
- Root cause analysis framework
- Computer security incident response team (CSIRT) framework (hierarchy and responsibilities)
- Incident response framework (process)

11.3.5   User Frameworks

User frameworks are not for users, but rather are to focus on users and user needs. Users perform tasks with or without the assistance of technology. Some users carry out the organizational mission. Some users support those executing the organizational mission. All contribute to organizational success. Those users that carry out the organizational mission include those who bring in the money (sales), perform the service (installers), produce the widget (assembly-line worker), fly the airplane, and face the enemy (war fighter).

Part of the challenge of operations is to make users aware of what to do (awareness) and to teach users what to do (understanding), how to perform the task at all (use), how to perform the task fluently (effective use), and how to perform the task to minimize business risk (secure use). Examples of frameworks that support user activities include:

- Objectives-based outcome framework
  - Awareness
  - Understanding
  - Use
  - Effective use
  - Secure use
- Accountability
  - Ownership of responsibilities
- User support
  - Various levels and perspectives of expertise
    - Help desk
    - SMEs
    - Operations
    - Management
    - Governance
- Workflow
  - Process
  - Task
    - Kinetic (physical) tasks
    - Cognitive (mental) tasks
      - Decision space
      - Decision events
      - Decision triggers

11.3.6   Leadership Frameworks

Leaders reside in every part of the organization and may draw upon the widest variety of frameworks. Examples of frameworks that support leadership activities include:

- Team building
- Relationship building

- Understanding individuals (e.g., personality profile framework)
- Understanding the organization (e.g., profiling agencies, departments, and working groups)
- Future vision
- Governance
- Adjudication
- Facilitation
- Presentation
- Innovation
- Decision making
- Change management
- Stakeholder engagement
- Organizational context
- Enterprise context

11.3.7   How to Use Frameworks

A framework is an outline, a guide, a cognitive tool. When faced with a situation, issue, problem, or challenge, consider which frameworks may apply. Create a document with sections for *introduction*, *background*, *scope*, *environment*, and *problem definition*, and then insert the appropriate framework outlines to guide brainstorming techniques.

The first round of inserting detail is an uninterrupted streaming effort. Go at it and let it go. Jump from topic to topic and let ideas flow. Often you will find that you add or rearrange the frameworks to fit the emerging method to address the situation at hand. This is fine. Actually, this is more than fine. Modifying the frameworks to fit your needs shows you are taking ownership of the problem and are gaining fluency with the idea of using a frameworks approach. Will you use every detail you create during the brainstorming sessions? Probably not; however, keep discarded ideas. The opportunity to use them may emerge later or in a different situation.

Following the initial rounds of brainstorming, walk through the frameworks methodically. Review each framework and critically consider if that framework applies to the situation at hand. Review the details under every section of each framework and critically consider if the details apply to the situation at hand. Ask yourself if the details are complete, and then revise according to need.

11.3.8   IA² Perspective of the Frameworks

The outline above includes business, technical, and security frameworks. The primary objective of IA² is to understand the business risk and then integrate IA into the business to address that risk. The role of the IA² architect is to maintain a holistic view and address every detail in the context of the whole. The core reason for the existence of the organization is not to be more secure; rather, being more secure increases the likelihood that the organization will fulfill the core reasons for its existence.

The IA^2 F presents various views and phases of identifying risk and addressing that risk. The IA^2 P demonstrates how to apply the IA^2 F in a business situation. The IA architect uses the frameworks along with the IA^2 F in a living, ever-evolving risk management process that establishes an IA baseline from which continual review and improvement proceed.

The ISO 9000 quality management standard uses a cycle of plan–do–check–act that roughly equates to idea conception, architect, and engineer (plan); implement, test, and deploy (do); verify accuracy and effectiveness by monitoring and reviewing operations (check); and maintain and improve according to emerging business needs and risks (act). To increase the effectiveness of your security management program, institute this or a similar quality management framework as an overarching guide to the effective application of IA^2 as an enterprise risk management tool.

Chapter 12

The Frameworks

12.1 Introduction

Frameworks both facilitate and challenge our mental models. Frameworks facilitate by providing guidelines, and challenge by providing an alternative perspective. Frameworks provide a disciplined approach to complexity management by decomposing the problem into manageable chunks. Frameworks help to ensure we address the right problem; little is worse than a multiyear investment to produce a brilliant solution to the wrong problem.

Frameworks distill complex issues into conceptual components. These conceptual components are often abstract, but need to be abstract to capture the essence of the issue. Many frameworks may seem elementary or oversimplified. This is not to trivialize the subjects that they deal with; rather, it is to identify the essence of those subjects for development of an IA architecture. For example, business accounting can be quite complex. The essence of business accounting boils down to revenues coming in and expenses going out.

IA^2 advocates the use of not one, but many frameworks to look at the problem from many perspectives. By outlining the problem from various perspectives, you have a greater opportunity to ensure the following:

- An accurate problem identification by taking into account all of the organization's significant operations
- A problem definition that covers all the relevant areas of the organization
- A solution definition that is enterprisewide
- Planning, testing, implementation, tracking, and reporting that involves every business area of the organization that is impacted

Frameworks help to identify fundamental patterns within business, people, behavior, technology, and information assurance. Frameworks help identify and isolate critical issues. For security, these include the *need* for security, the *fit* of security, and the *justification* for security; security justification will be explored in greater depth in chapter 13.

12.2 Objectives

The objectives of this chapter are to:

- Introduce the use of frameworks with respect to IA
- Enumerate a series of frameworks useful to the IA architect
- Articulate the details of frameworks useful to the IA architect

At the end of this chapter, you should be aware of a variety of frameworks as supplemental tools for information assurance architecture.

12.3 Enterprise Context Framework

The focus of the IA architect is information assurance. To integrate IA in the enterprise, the IA architect must interact with those in the roles of enterprise architect, systems engineer, business planner, business manager, technical manager, project manager, and operations manager, to name some. The responsibility of the IA architect is to integrate IA into the policies, standards, procedures, enterprise architecture, systems engineering, management, and operations. To achieve this, the IA architect needs an enterprise perspective on the business as well as the supporting technology within the enterprise.

There are many essential questions regarding the necessity for change and the focus of change. The first question is: Is change necessary at all? If change is necessary, where is it necessary? How do you decide what to change? Have you considered the local perspective, regional perspective, enterprise perspective, competitive perspective, marketplace perspective, and global perspective? What is the budget? Have you considered the solution perspective? What are the appropriate tools? How do you select the appropriate tools? How do you implement the solution to work at all? How do you implement the solution to work effectively? How do you implement the solution to work securely? IA^2 speaks of aligning security with the enterprise architecture.

To begin to address these questions, consider a work breakdown structure (WBS or WBS framework). A WBS is a method of refining a larger objective into smaller component parts. The following is a generic WBS framework:

- ■ System
  - – Subsystem
    - ■ Component
      - – Subcomponent
        - • Assembly
          - ■ Subassembly

The WBS framework is an outline within which to gradually refine a larger objective into smaller component parts. It presents an ever more granular breakdown of the system from system to subassembly. The WBS identifies smaller parts/tasks, which promote manageability and may allow many development activities to take place concurrently. Identifying individual components means that they can be designed to do one thing, do it well, and then be reused whenever there is need for the same function elsewhere. (The WBS above is from MIL-HDBK 881: *Department of Defense Handbook Work Breakdown Structures*.)

The WBS addresses entities (systems); however, the enterprise is more than just systems. The enterprise is the collection of all the business functions that support it. These business functions are themselves collections of systems; thus, a business function may be characterized as an aggregation of systems that interact to carry out the business function. An enterprise also consists of people, collections of people, activities, workflow, procedures, and more.

The following Enterprise Context Framework (ECF) abstractly accommodates all aspects of the enterprise:

- ■ Enterprise
  - – Business function
    - ■ System (**entity**, product, thing, deliverable)
      - – Subsystem
        - • Component
          - ■ Subcomponent
            - – Assembly
              - • Subassembly
    - ■ Business process (**action**)
      - – Workflow
        - • Process (procedure)
          - ■ Task
            - – Kinetic (manual)
            - – Cognitive (mental)
            - – Automated (service)
    - ■ Collectives
      - – Person (actor)
        - • Behavior
          - ■ Conscious
          - ■ Unconscious

In addition to systems, a business function may include many business processes. Each of these business processes may consist of a variety of workflows. Workflows in turn consist of processes, which in turn consist of tasks. People manually or mentally perform tasks either with or without the aid of technology. Technology may perform an automated service without the intervention of a person. For example, the accounting business function consists of business processes that include accounts receivable, employee expense reimbursement, and statements and ledgers. Accounts receivable workflows include inputs, trigger events for action, processing of inputs, production of some result, and the delivery of some output; procedures (formal representation of a process) assist with the performance of the workflow. Within procedures are prescribed tasks assigned to personnel or are automated tasks. A person may then perform a manual task (carry out a routine procedure) or a cognitive task (e.g., decide upon an action). An automated service may substitute for a person or enhance manual and cognitive tasks performed by a person.

Collectives are groups of people. Collectives may be teams, communities, working groups, departments, or other. People are the actors in the ECF and through their actions exhibit behavior. Behavior may be conscious in support of a task or unconscious, like the unwitting application of mental models that most of us are unaware we even have. Behavior motivations may include social, economic, political, moral, and many others. People will act within a business process or other social dynamic in the context of the enterprise. People may act upon or interact with entities (systems); entities may perform actions with other entities. The key attributes of the ECF that represent the enterprise dynamics are *entities*, *actors*, and *actions* (see Figure 12.1).

The ECF is a decomposition of the enterprise to its essential parts in terms of people (actors), processes (actions), and technology (entities). The ECF is a very powerful representation and provides an enterprise context for a system, for cog-

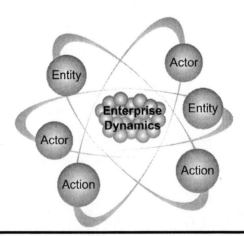

Figure 12.1   Enterprise dynamics of entities, actors, and actions.

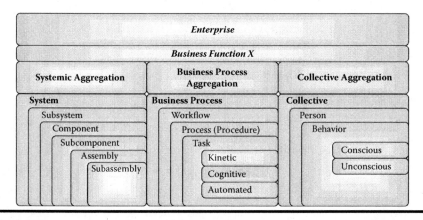

Figure 12.2 Enterprise Context Framework.

nitive tasks, for procedures (application of standards to implement and enforce policy), and for automated services (e.g., service-oriented architecture services). The ECF provides a broader context for specific details regarding the business, technology, risk, and integrating IA in the enterprise.

The enterprise consists of business functions that are themselves a collection of entities, actions, and actors (Figure 12.2). A collection of entities is a systemic aggregation (collection of systems) and systemic relationships (system interactions). A collection of actions is a business process aggregation and business process relationships. A grouping of actors is a collective or a collective aggregation (multiple groups).

The point of ECF and all frameworks is to prompt you to look at risk from many different perspectives and in many different contexts. The ECF provides a decomposition of enterprise components and constituents. The enterprise components and the relationships among them offer potential risk to the enterprise. Appendix B contains a matrix to capture details of cross sections between the ECF and the IA² views.

12.4 Enterprise Perspective of IA Framework

The enterprise represents the entirety of the organization. Even if the focus of an IA architecture is not the enterprise as a whole, the architect still defines the IA architecture in the context of the enterprise. Many frameworks help the IA architect determine the need for and the perspective for security measures. These frameworks start with a business focus that includes risk identification, and then work toward how to address those risks and whether there is a need for safeguards. The enterprise perspective of IA (EPIA) framework below presents a collection of frameworks useful across the enterprise; many have relevance to executive, management, development, operations, and business applications. Although these frameworks have many uses in addition to IA², the primary focus is on IA². These frameworks assist in identifying the essential questions surrounding the following, where X represents a business, technical, or security concern:

- Business perspective
  - The business need for X
  - The business fit of X
  - The business justification for X
- Technical perspective
  - The technical fit of X
  - The technical development and delivery of X
  - The technical mechanisms of X
  - The use of the technical mechanisms
- IA perspective
  - The business need for IA
  - The business fit for IA
  - The business justification for IA
  - The technical fit of IA
  - The technical acquisition/development and delivery of IA
  - The operations and maintenance of IA technical mechanisms
  - The use of IA (i.e., IA implications to the user community)

The frameworks are applicable to far more than just IA; therefore, we isolate IA as a special consideration for the IA architect. The EPIA framework is as follows:

- Business perspective
  - Business need—Innovation framework
  - Business fit—Enterprise architecture (EA) framework
  - Business justification—ROI framework
- Technical perspective
  - Technical fit—Systems engineering (SE) framework
  - Technical develop/delivery—Enterprise life cycle management (ELCM) framework, solutions life cycle management (SLCM)
  - Technical mechanisms—Standards framework
  - Communications/outreach—ATE framework
- IA perspective
  - Business security—Risk management framework
  - Technical security—Security standards framework
  - Security communications—SATE framework

The following sections elaborate upon these frameworks. The details for these frameworks are not comprehensive, but are enough to provide context for the information assurance architecture framework (IA^2 F) and to suggest areas of further research by the architect. Indeed, there are many books on innovation, hundreds of books on ROI, and thousands on risk management and security. The intent here is not to exhaustively cover the details.

12.5 Innovation Framework

The innovation framework assists to discern the business need for change.

What motivates business change? What motivates the need for innovation? What are the clues that the game has changed and it is time to change how your organization is playing in the game? There is first a need to know that the game has changed; second, to know what about the game has changed. These two factors drive innovation.

Recognizing when the game has changed requires a watch on such variables as market conditions, globalization, off-shoring, and competition. The authors of *Seeing What's Next** cite the introduction of voice communications over a wire, which was thought by Western Union Telegraph to be a novelty with only limited local use—the real money to them was in long-distance communications. However, the convenience of voice communications at a local level changed the game from exclusively long-distance service to include local service. Western Union's tenacity in playing the old game provided opportunity for AT&T to emerge and take over the communications marketplace by way of the new game (local service).

A useful innovation framework provides guidance on identifying the type of change as well as what to look at inside your organization in response to the type of change. Such an innovation framework looks like the following:

- Innovation type†
  - Disruptive—New market entry; creating a new market or new market need
  - Sustaining—Modification by an existing market player
- Innovation application
  - Product—Breadth, depth
  - Production—Vendor relationships, manufacturing
  - Sales and marketing—Marketplace relationships and tactics
  - Delivery—Customer relationships
  - Management—Employee relationships

The innovation type provides insight into the strategy of how to respond to the innovation. The application of innovation provides insight on where to focus inno-

---

* Paraphrased from the text *Seeing What's Next*, pp. xxii–xxvii.
† Ibid., p. xv.

vation. In many cases, there is not a need to modify the product itself. For example, with the introduction of the Internet and E-commerce, the music industry did not need to change radically how a song is created. Rather, the innovation is the delivery method and the pricing of the song. Previous distribution was via physical media (e.g., tape or CD) through a retail sales channel. Moreover, the purchase of the desired song often required purchasing a collection of other songs in which the buyer had little interest. The Internet provided the ability to sell instant downloading of a single song. Thus, the innovation was to create and support this new sales channel of instant downloading with an accompanying pricing structure to sell single songs or song collections.

IA^2 may use the innovation framework to address the evaluation of a new threat. A variation on a virus or worm may be thought of as a sustaining innovation developed by a *community of malicious intent* (COMI). The customary way to address viruses and worms is via anti-malware software. When a new strain of virus spreads faster than previous versions, the customary response is to introduce a faster, automated anti-malware signature file and disseminate to all organizational servers and desktops. A disruptive COMI innovation introduces a new and unanticipated type of threat. One such disruptive change to the U.S. federal government was the events of September 11, 2001; COMI activities are not restricted to the cyber-world. One consequence of these events was the introduction of legislation (e.g., Intelligence Reform and Terrorist Prevention Act of 2004) that requires government organizations to share information. Prior to this, the guiding principle in the intelligence world was *need-to-know*; now, *need-to-share* complements need-to-know. Much innovation on the part of many security professionals over the past several years is based upon attempts to balance between these two principles.

12.6   EA Framework

Enterprise architecture (EA) is a methodology that aligns business, technical, and operational solutions with the organization's core mission and strategic direction. The EA process is often stated in terms of:

- To-be—Target architecture
- As-is—Current architecture
- Transition—Migration plan from as-is to to-be

There are many EA frameworks to choose from according to the type of organization and organizational need. EA frameworks include:

- Department of Defense Architectural Framework (DoDAF)
- Zachman Framework

- The Open Group Architectural Framework (TOGAF)
- Federal Enterprise Architecture (FEA) Framework
  - For example, FEA Reference Models (RMs)
    - Performance Reference Model (PRM)
    - Business Process Reference Model (BRM)
    - Service Components Reference Model (SRM)
    - Technical Reference Model (TRM)
    - Data Reference Model (DRM)

12.7 ROI Framework

Return on investment boils down to two basic perspectives: *revenue* and *cost*. A business function, technology, security service, or IA mechanism contributes to either the sustainment or increase of revenue, or the decrease or avoidance of cost. Showing a positive ROI is an objective representation of business value. The IA instance of ROI is return on security investment (ROSI). Any business endeavor includes risk. Security addresses business risk. The challenges are to:

- Identify risk
- Quantify risk
- Manage risk via:
  - Share, e.g., interorganization cooperative (co-op)
  - Transfer, e.g., E-risk insurance
  - Accept,* e.g., cost of other options > cost of potential loss
  - Mitigate, e.g., invest in security services and mechanisms

The bottom line for most organizations is money. Even if there is a more altruistic motivation behind organizational mission, money is still a major driving factor. Organizational risks ultimately trace to revenue and cost. Security measures that address risk align with revenue benefits or cost benefits. The following ROI framework presents the revenue and cost benefits:

- Revenue
  - Revenue increase
    - Customer satisfaction; past performance leads to opportunities for new sales.

---

* Ignoring risk is implicit acceptance.

- Revenue sustainment
  - Mission realization/mission integrity
    - SLAs, e.g., uptime SLAs for E-commerce site
  - Customer satisfaction; contract renewal
- Cost
  - Cost reduction
    - Time spent chasing malware issues now spent on core service
  - Cost avoidance
    - Legislative compliance; SLA penalties

12.8 Awareness, Training, and Education (ATE) Framework

All people start at the point of not knowing that they do not know, that is, they lack awareness. Being aware means that you now know you do not know, or you now know about something but lack depth of knowledge. With depth of knowledge comes varying degrees of understanding, fluency, and skill. The depth of understanding is a combination of capability (capacity), desire, and practice. In the context of IA^2, this progression of learning follows a path to secure use:

- Awareness
- Understanding
- Use
- Effective use
- Secure use

Awareness arises from a foundation of not knowing what you do not know. After awareness, you know about something; there is a large difference between knowing about something and knowing that thing. Knowing that thing is in the realm of understanding. Knowledge precedes action and knowledge begets the capability for use. As someone begins to use a thing, he or she begins to inquire more into the nuances of that thing and incorporate this knowledge into ever more refined use. This iterative process results in increasing effective use. The discipline of information security or information assurance adds the notion of secure use. Secure use follows effective use on the presumption that to use something securely requires at least some level of effective use.

The ATE framework may apply to internal orientation of employees. Additionally, the ATE framework applies to outreach programs as part of a campaign to inform and persuade others with regard to security. Establishing objectives (desired outcomes) for each level of the ATE framework provides interim goals and milestones to measure progress toward those goals. With this premise in mind, let us proceed to define a series of objective categories:

- Enterprise objectives
- Programmatic objectives
- Personal objectives

Enterprise objectives include a desired state of operations, e.g., more cost effective, higher revenue generation, increase in customer service levels, or to reduce risk. From an IA perspective, the path to achieve this desired state includes overcoming that people do not know they do not know (IA awareness campaign), creating a level of understanding (IA training), creating a level of skill and fluency (IA training), and for some people a level of theoretical knowledge (IA education).

People generally have a natural resistance to change for fear of the unknown. Often, people must be persuaded to change. Persuasion may be negative or positive. Negative persuasion is purely for the benefit of the persuader and generally does not consider the interests of the person being persuaded. Examples include a con artist or even many marketing campaigns, advertisements, and commercials. Positive persuasion is win–win; the persuader (e.g., the organization) gets what it wants and the person (e.g., employee) gets what he or she wants. Organizational benefits may be greater profits, increased market share, or reduced risk exposure. Employee benefits may be a salary raise, recognition, promotion, or continued employment.

The goal of persuasion is to overcome inertia. It is not that people do not want to change; it is that people are not aware that change is necessary, or how to change, or why to change. Many people want to show up at work, do their assigned tasks, and go home to live their lives; it is not that they do not care, they just have other priorities. Executives and management have the responsibility to define and articulate why to change, the need for change, what to change, and how to change, and offer awareness, training, and education to facilitate change. A framework that captures *objective-centered outcomes* provides a guideline on how to address change. You may use this framework to discern and capture details of how to mitigate business risk by facilitating change via awareness, training, and education.

Employee objectives primarily include the *WIFM factor* (what's in it for me). Employees have vastly different personal goals, and the objective-based outcome details recognize and address these differences, e.g., in-house day care, new parent support, opportunity for leave without pay, and other personal benefits. Professional objectives for employees include those areas that benefit both the employee and the organization, e.g., increased productivity, salary increase, bonus, promotion, new assignment, higher visibility, opportunity to directly affect the bottom line.

12.8.1 Objective-Centered Framework

Table 12.1 provides a method to capture the details of the above objectives. The organization provides objectives where possible as a starting point. The employee is engaged in the process to complete his or her own objectives; this may be part of the annual employee review and planning process.

Table 12.1 Personal Objective-Centered Framework[a]

Objective Category	Awareness	Understanding	Use	Effective Use	Secure Use
Personal					
Professional					
Academic					

[a] Table purposely left blank.

12.9 SATE Framework

The security awareness, training, and education (SATE) framework is the ATE framework with a security-specific focus. The SATE framework is as follows:

- Security awareness
- Security training
- Security education

The same concepts apply as in the ATE framework, only with security-specific objectives. All members of the organization require some level of security awareness. Some members require broader awareness, that is, greater awareness of the breadth of security issues. Some members of the organization need security depth by way of training (e.g., system administrator, network engineers, firewall administrators, etc.). Security professionals require security education. The key difference between training and education is one of mechanism focus versus conceptual focus. Training provides the student with more mechanism skills, i.e., how to install and configure a firewall. Education provides the student with more conceptual or philosophical insight into the reasons for a firewall, including its fit in the greater technical scheme and the business drivers behind the need for a firewall.

12.10 SE Framework

Systems engineering (SE) is a discipline to assist with system development and delivery. The system framework (input, process, and output) provides a basis from which to define an SE framework:

- Input
  - Request
    - The acquisition of a capability, product, or service

- Process*
  - Technical management
    - Planning, scheduling, and oversight for the SE process
  - System design
    - Requirements engineering, solution definition (translation of stakeholder requirements into specifications for the solution)
  - Production
    - Realization of the solution
- Output
  - SE process work products
    - Systems engineering management plan (SEMP)
    - Requirements matrix via requirements engineering
    - Work breakdown structure (WBS) for scheduling and resource planning
  - SE process deliverable
    - The capability, product, or service; often in the form of a system or system of systems

There is much detail within the SE process. The above is a bare outline to provide an SE framework to raise awareness of SE as a discipline and as a useful tool for the IA architect.

12.11   Enterprise Life Cycle Management (ELCM) Framework

There are many life cycle management processes, including system life cycle management, solution life cycle management, and enterprise life cycle management (ELCM). These life cycles take on slightly different nuances, but all have the same objective of introducing a consistent, repeatable management process in furthering organizational interests and managing organizational resources. The ELCM framework consists of the following phases:

- Concept
- Architect
- Engineer
- Acquire/develop
- Implement
- Test
- Deploy

---

* A paraphrase of the systems engineering process as outlined by International Council of Systems Engineering (INCOSE) *Systems Engineering Handbook*.

- Train
- Operate and maintain
- Retire

12.11.1 Concept

Idea inception—when an idea is a good one, then what? There is need for a formal process within which new ideas may enter the organization and be considered in the context of the enterprise. Idea inception is innovation. The innovation framework comes into play here; a new concept attempts to introduce a new business need or satisfy an existing business need.

12.11.2 Architect

Assuming the idea is worth pursuing, the enterprise architect examines the business fit of the concept. The ensuing detail may include modifying existing EA artifacts (documents reflecting the EA) or the generation of new EA artifacts.

12.11.3 Engineer

An enterprise systems engineer examines the technical fit of the concept in the context of the enterprise. The term *technical* does not necessarily mean an automated solution. The term *technical* includes a new business service, technical service, a new task, or a task refinement. The result of applying the new concept may enhance a manual task, a cognitive task, or an automated service.

12.11.4 Acquire/Develop

The traditional question of build versus buy is less a question today. The guiding principle is buy COTS* first, buy custom second, build in-house third. Buying custom or building in-house will require exhaustive proof that such an approach is absolutely necessary, and even then expect volumes of questions and resistance. For example, if there is need to create a call center to increase customer service, this function can be outsourced to a company with the infrastructure and expertise to perform this business function. The call center service becomes a COTS solution easily obtained from a service provider.

---

* Commercial off-the-shelf, which includes software, managed services, and in some cases outsourcing.

12.11.5 Implement

Once a solution is developed or acquired, it must be made to work. Typically, implementation occurs as pilot or controlled introduction to ensure functionality and business fit. The general principle is that it is cheaper to work out the kinks early, on a smaller scale, than after a broad enterprise deployment. The desired result of the pilot is to predict the solution's effectiveness across the organization. Inherent in working effectively is working securely. Though inherent, there is still the need to highlight specific requirements for IA and to ensure those requirements are in the final solution.

12.11.6 Test

Once the solution demonstrates viability (works at all), there is need to test that solution to ensure that it works to fulfill the business need within specified operational parameters, that is, test that the solution works effectively. Testing a solution works effectively also includes testing that the solution works securely.

12.11.7 Deploy

Following successful testing, the solution must be deployed throughout the broader enterprise.

12.11.8 Train

The organization's personnel must learn how to use that solution to achieve the business objectives. Training (including awareness, training, and education) includes management, operations, and the user community. Training often precedes deployment, or is offered in conjunction with it, especially in a phased deployment.

12.11.9 Operate and Maintain

Solution architects, engineers, and builders control the solution up through deployment. During the deployment phase, there is a transition from building the solution to operating and maintaining that solution. In the operate and maintain phase, the builders move on to the next initiative and the operations group takes ownership of the solution.

12.11.10 Retire

All operations should align with organizational strategic objectives and policy. Recognizing when an operational process should be retired is problematic. The original rationale for the existence of a solution may have been lost (institutional memory can and does fail), and the consequences of removing a solution from operations are difficult to predict. In some circumstances, the only recourse is to remove the operation from production and wait to see who complains. However, there is never 100 percent certainty that someone actually does need the service, but does not know whom to contact to ask for it back. Moreover, failure to recognize the end of an operation's useful life means that the organization pays overhead to keep services running that may be vastly underutilized and have a negative operating ROI.

A formal enterprise architecture provides alignment from business drivers through to operations and maintenance. Such a formal alignment permits evaluation of the implications for removing a business service. Moreover, such a formal alignment provides the ability to identify business objectives that no longer exist. If the business objective is no more, then the business services that fulfill that business objective are no longer necessary either.

12.12 Security Framework

A security framework consists of the following nine IA core principles:

- Confidentiality—nondisclosure
- Integrity—accuracy
- Availability—usable on demand
- Possession—owner/custodian maintains custody
- Authenticity—conforms to reality
- Utility—accessible for use
- Privacy—individual rights
- Nonrepudiation—nondeniability
- Authorized use—appropriate access to services

Table 12.2 presents business risk motivations for the security framework.

More details on these core security principles are in chapter 2. This security framework finds basis in the traditional CIA triad—confidentiality, integrity, and availability—as well as in the Parker model, which adds possession, authenticity, and utility. The IA core principles include privacy, nonrepudiation, and authorized use because the risks they mitigate are not adequately covered by the other six. Personal privacy and civil liberties are of great concern to commercial organizations as well as government and the citizenry. Balancing personal privacy and civil liberties with security and safety of citizens is an ongoing difficult challenge.

Nonrepudiation means that a person or system cannot deny having performed an action or made a request. Online activities include commercial purchases, offers and acceptance (contracts), banking transactions, commercial

Table 12.2 Business Risk Motivations for security Framework

IA Core Principle	Risk	Mitigation Objective
Confidentiality	Disclosure of information	Nondisclosure
Integrity	Corruption of information or information technology	Accuracy
Availability	Loss of use	Usable on demand
Possession	Loss of physical possession; theft or misplacement	Owner/custodian maintains custody
Authenticity	Information does not reflect reality; although not corrupt, it is not accurate; deception violates authenticity.	Conforms to reality
Utility	Information or information technology may not be utilized for their intended purpose.	Accessible for use
Privacy	Violation of trust; legislative violation governing privacy rights	Protect individual rights; maintain trust levels
Nonrepudiation	Person initiating a communication or transaction may deny having done so.	Nondeniability; a communication or transaction is traceable to a particular person or entity (e.g., computer system or service)
Authorized use	Theft of service, e.g., toll fraud	Appropriate access to services

funds transfers, etc. Personal transactions often include a signature or other form of tangible representation of the agreement (e.g., store receipt). Subsequent disputes may examine the proof of those transactions. Disputes over online transactions, or virtual transactions, require definitive, unique representation of both parties. Nonrepudiation is part of the overall scheme to provide that definitive, unique representation.

Authorized use addresses theft of service, e.g., toll fraud. Toll fraud, or the theft of long-distance services, costs organizations worldwide billions of dollars per year. Theft of service may also be theft of CPU time in a multiprocessing environment, or theft of a service (unauthorized use of a service) in a service-oriented architecture (SOA).

12.13   Risk Management Framework

Any business endeavor includes risk, and the organization must address all risks. Addressing risk is not necessarily doing something about the risk; however, addressing risk does mean identifying, acknowledging, and formally stating the organizational position on that risk. The risk management framework is as follows:

- Identify risk
- Quantify risk
- Address risk via:
  - Accept, e.g., $ of other options > $ of potential loss
  - Ignore, i.e., implicit acceptance
  - Share, e.g., interorganization cooperative (co-op)
  - Transfer, e.g., E-risk insurance
  - Mitigate, e.g., invest in security services and mechanisms

12.14   Security Management Program Framework (SMP Framework)

Organizations concerned with security at all should identify those driving forces behind the need for security. The root drivers will be to manage business risk. Drivers directly affecting the form and content of a security management program (SMP) may include legislation, regulation, and business need (e.g., maintain operational SLAs of 99.9 percent uptime). These drivers influence both the form and content of the SMP. First, start by defining an SMP framework. The SMP framework will consist of security categories and security elements within each category. Which categories and elements are necessary is organization specific. If the organization is health care oriented, then HIPAA will have an influence on the SMP framework. If the organization is a publicly traded company in the United States, then Sarbanes–Oxley will have an influence on the SMP framework.

A good practice is to choose an industry standard on which to base the SMP framework, and then add, delete, or modify categories and elements to suit the needs of the organization. One industry standard is ISO 27002.* Another is NIST SP 800-53, and there are many others. Appendix D contains a sample SMP framework based on NIST SP 800-53.

Whichever SMP framework you choose provides a basis on which the entire organization looks at security. Any security-related task is done within the context of the SMP framework. The SMP framework provides a consistent and comprehensive view of security. It provides an outline for templates, tools, and guidelines for security planning, implementation, assessment, gap analysis, remediation analy-

---

* Formerly ISO 17799.

sis, regulatory reporting, management reporting, and much more. If a particular security element is not applicable to the organization or the organization chooses not to perform activities related to that security element, leave that element in the SMP framework and record the rationale as to why the organization chooses to accept the risks or chooses not to invest in a particular remediation. To record such rationale is to address each security element, and by extension address each risk. A legitimate manner of addressing risk is to consciously choose to accept it. Capturing these details in the context of the SMP framework provides a record that any omission of risk mitigation is a conscious omission and not omission by oversight.

The first enterprise product to develop within the context of the SMP framework is an interpretation guide. Define every term and provide a description of intent for each security element. This provides a consistent manner to think about security throughout the organization. This also provides interpretation of legislative or regulatory directions. Too often, the real intent of the legislation is lost to legalese or vague descriptions. Providing an interpretation ensures everyone thinks about security in common and consistent terms. Even if the interpretations are wrong, at least they are consistently wrong. Upon correcting an interpretation, there is a medium to disseminate a new interpretation guide—the SMP framework.

Security tasks include planning (to-be), discovery (as-is), risk management (accept, transfer, share, mitigate), implementation (transition), tracking progress, and reporting. The SMP framework provides an outline for tools, templates, and guidelines to assist with all enterprise security planning tasks. The IA^2 provides the ability to align security with business drivers. The SMP framework provides a foundation to execute on the information assurance architecture.

What if the SMP framework changes? The development of the SMP framework in the context of business need and using an industry standard as a basis for the SMP framework both provide a solid rationale behind the SMP framework format. If the business need changes or if there are updates to industry standard, modify the SMP framework accordingly. The new SMP framework provides a new foundation for the aforementioned tools, templates, and guidelines.

12.15 Reality Check Framework (RCF)

The RCF uses the classic who, what, why, when, where, and how as an approach to ask hard questions about a situation, proposed solution, architecture, etc. All aspects of business, technology, and security boil down to who, what, why, when, where, and how—these are the elements of the bottom line. The RCF provides a guide to examine a claim, document, system, solution, department, operation, etc., in context of who cares, who is using it, what they are using, what they are using it for, why they are using it, when they are using it, where they are applying it, and how. The RCF is an extremely flexible framework and assists in informative writing, investigative inquiry, and performing reality checks on policies, standards,

Table 12.3 Reality Check Framework Guide

Guide	Description	IA² Example
Who	Who uses X?	Who uses IA²? IA architect? Business planner? Enterprise architect? Other?
What	What parts of X are necessary? Sufficient?	What parts of IA² are necessary for the task at hand? What parts of IA² are sufficient?
Why	Why use X?	Why use IA²?
When	When should X be used?	When should IA² be applied?
Where	Where is X applicable?	Where in the enterprise does IA² apply?
How	How should X be used?	How does someone use IA²?

guidelines, procedures, workflows, services, and much more. Table 12.3 provides a guideline and examples with respect to IA².

The reality check assists to validate that the approach, solution, or artifact is practical for the intended purpose. Using the RCF early and often in the architecture, engineering, or development process provides clues to the need for corrective action.

12.16 Summary

The frameworks so far include:

- Work breakdown structure (WBS) framework
- Enterprise Context Framework (ECF)
- Enterprise perspective of IA (EPIA) framework
- Innovation framework
- Enterprise architecture (EA) framework
- Return on investment (ROI) framework
- Awareness, training, and education (ATE) framework
- Systems engineering (SE) framework
- Enterprise life cycle management (ELCM) framework
- Security framework
- Risk management framework
- Security management program (SMP) framework
- Security standards framework
- Security awareness, training, and education (SATE) framework
- Reality Check Framework (RCF)

The details of the frameworks are but a shadow of the depths to which each may extend. These frameworks play a role in organizational governance, management, and operations, including security governance, security management, and security operations. The IA² Framework is unique from the above frameworks, yet may include all of the above in various stages of the IA² Process. Each one of the frameworks is another tool for the IA practitioner, the business manager, and the IA architect. Choose the right tool for the right job. Modify the tool for the job at hand; scale it down or extend it according to your need.

12.17 IA² Framework Context

The complementary use of the frameworks in this chapter and the IA² Framework provides you with a set of tools to identify, enumerate, articulate, and address business risk in an enterprise context. Any particular element of the ELCM, ECF, ROI, and SATE will have details that pertain to each IA² view. Each IA² view for any particular element may have details of one or more IA core principles. The details may be quite complex and quite voluminous. The point of IA² is to provide tools, templates, and guidance to manage that complexity and focus on the relevant aspects within the volume of details. Appendix B contains a series of tables to capture IA details in terms of motivations behind IA, IA options, IA planning, and details of IA development, operations, maintenance, and performance.

Chapter 13

IA Justification

13.1   Introduction

There is great need to convey IA justification in the appropriate terms to executives, management, users, investors, etc. This chapter presents ideas for you to use as justification for IA in conversations, papers, and presentations. Table 13.1 provides a series of sample questions to consider when determining IA justification for the current project and your organization in general.

13.2   Objectives

The objective of this chapter is to prepare the IA architect to discuss IA justification in business terms from many different perspectives.

By the end of this chapter, you will be able to articulate justification for IA to many audiences. You may use the justification ideas in writing reports, developing presentations, and developing elevator speeches (concise, impactful vignettes) to convey the focus and benefits of IA.

13.3   ROI Justification

The business justification for IA may be in financial terms. The return on investment (ROI) framework provides guidance on determining IA justification in terms of revenue and cost:

Table 13.1 *RCF Guide* to IA Justification Questions

RCF	Questions
Who	Who benefits from IA? Who cares about IA? Who pays for IA? Who uses IA? Who wants to hear about IA directly? Who wants to hear about business value that IA may contribute to?
What	What terms will resonate with the audience of the justification message? ROI? Productivity? Risk mitigation? Stakeholder value? What will IA allow the organization to do that it cannot do already? What will IA allow the organization to do better that it is doing already?
Why	Why be concerned with IA at all? Is there a compliance requirement? Is this accepted good business practice?
When	When is IA important? At all times? During periods of high probability threat? Imminent threat?
Where	Where is IA applicable? What environment are you concerned with? What environment is the audience concerned with? Are the environments related? How?
How	How can the organization do business better tomorrow by introducing IA today? How do we identify risk? Assess risk probability? How do you convey the risk message in terms that the audience can identify with? How do you identify and convey the business benefit?

- Revenue
  - Increase revenue
  - Revenue acceleration
  - Sustain revenue
- Cost
  - Reduce cost
  - Avoid cost

13.3.1 Revenue

13.3.1.1 Increase Revenue

Producing revenue or increasing revenue production may include IA product/service offerings. If your organization offers IA services and products, then you have a direct effect on new revenue generation. More likely, IA will have an indirect effect on revenue as a marketing tool to increase market share; *our services are more secure than those of our competitors.* IA may enhance existing product offerings by adding security features or options; it may increase product sales due to security features (e.g., HIPAA-compliant product).

13.3.1.2   Revenue Acceleration

IA may decrease time to market of a product or service. The innovation, development, and manufacturing may be faster due to secure online processing of communications. IA features may add nonrepudiation (digital signatures) for faster processing of binding agreements, resulting in less delay due to paper processing, in-person meetings, and the need for pen signatures. IA may increase cash flow for similar reasons; customer payments are accelerated due to secure communications or online transaction processing. IA may contribute to secure automation of invoicing, collections, deposits, and electronic transfers.

13.3.1.3   Sustain Revenue

IA contributes to sustaining existing revenue streams. One example is a secure E-commerce site that protects the revenue realized by that site. IA contributes to customer retention due to high levels of security and privacy. IA contributes to market share retention due to IA features surrounding the customer use of your products and services. For example, a secure Web site is less likely to suffer from vandalism or hacker interference that may affect customer perceptions.

13.3.2   Cost

13.3.2.1   Reduce Cost

By ensuring secure online processing of transactions (e.g., E-commerce), IA contributes to the reduction of manual processes involving paper, printing, mailing, faxing, and the associated costs in labor and materials. Effective and provable application of IA contributes to the reduction of E-risk insurance premium costs. IA contributes to liability reduction via the *reasonable-man* review. *We put in place X, Y, and Z as prudent privacy safeguards. These are best industry practices. What more could we be expected to do?* There is also a reduction in liability exposure due to legislative compliance.

13.3.2.2   Avoid Cost

IA contributes to cost avoidance through legislative and regulatory compliance; i.e., avoid fines for noncompliance and avoid legal fees and court costs for defending corporate officers. IA helps to avoid penalties for failure to meet SLAs by preserving availability (uptime) of service.

IA contributes to cost avoidance by protecting assets, for example, safeguarding of intellectual property and availability of information and information technology resources. Productivity improvement is cost avoidance (hiring additional people when the same number of people can be more productive). Effective IA promotes greater uptime for mission-critical systems and business support systems, thus avoiding the cost of downtime due to security incidents.

You may use the IA quantification process and IA quantification framework to identify IA-related parameters in the ROI justification. The IAQP will align IA with the business scenario, and the quantification terms will correlate directly with revenue and cost.

13.4 IA Justification Based on Examining the Threat Space

IA is the protection of information and information technology assets. The need for protection presupposes some threat. The *threat space* to information technology includes threat sources, one of which is attackers. The nature of an attacker implies intelligence and intent; a natural phenomenon, by contrast, has no intelligence or intent. A taxonomy to address threats needs to accommodate the entire threat space, including acts of volition, naturally occurring threats, and genuine accidents.

13.4.1 Threat Sources and Types

A threat is "the potential for a threat-source to exercise (accidentally trigger or intentionally exploit) a specific vulnerability."[*] A threat source is "either (1) intent and method targeted at the intentional exploitation of a vulnerability or (2) a situation and method that may accidentally trigger a vulnerability."[†] A vulnerability is "a flaw or weakness in system security procedures, design, implementation, or internal controls that could be exercised (accidentally triggered or intentionally exploited) and result in a security breach or a violation of the system(s) security policy."[‡] Vulnerabilities are the doorways to mission entropy; threats are the keys that open those doors.

Threats are general categorizations of potential dangers. *Threat agents* are specific categories of potential dangers. *Kinetic threats* are imminent dangers. An *incident* occurs when a kinetic threat meets vulnerability. Table 13.2 presents examples of threats, threat agents, kinetic threats, and incidents.[§] For example, one threat category is a natural threat. One type of natural threat is weather. A threat agent under the natural threat of weather is a hurricane. A kinetic threat is the actual occurrence

---

[*] Defined in NIST SP 800-30.
[†] Defined in NIST SP 800-30.
[‡] Defined in NIST SP 800-30.
[§] The table represents only a small sampling of threats, threat agents, kinetic threats, and incidents.

Table 13.2   Threat Space Categories and Examples

Threat	Threat Agent	Kinetic Threat	Incident
Natural			
Weather	Tornado	Storms on July 7, 2007; tornado warning in effect from 16:00 to 20:00	July 7, 2007: Tornados develop and touch down in local area.Incident: July 7, 2007, tornado destroyed remote building on campus X housing server X; server lost completely along with backup tapes.
	Hurricane	Hurricane Isabelle formed in Atlantic with probable East Coast landing.	September 14, 2003: Hurricane Isabelle makes landfall and resulting flooding shuts down voice communications.
	Ice storm	January 22, 2008: Winter storm covering local area with 1/4 to 1/2 inches of ice	January 23, 2008: Ice storm affects Mid-Atlantic, essentially shutting down D. C.–Baltimore corridor, resulting in key personnel being kept from work; operations shut down for 36 hours.
	Lightening; fire	Severe thunderstorms predicted for August 5, 2008.	Lightening strike caused brush fire within proximity of data center and spread to roof. Firefighting efforts caused severe water damage to three key servers.

Continued

Table 13.2 Threat Space Categories and Examples (Continued)

Threat	Threat Agent	Kinetic Threat	Incident
Terrestrial	Earthquake, landslide, tsunami	Corporate data center is located near a known fault line.	Earthquake occurrence degrades service for 2 hours.
Cosmological	Comets, solar flare, etc.	Solar storm predicted for September 22, 2008	Solar storm interferes with communications; degrades service for 4 hours.
Nonhuman animal, insect, reptile, bird	Infestation	Known seasonal upswings in wasp population	Wasps invade HVAC and cause evacuation; degraded service for 30 minutes.
Human			
	Malicious, criminal, adversary	New virus traversing the Internet	SPAM carries virus onto organizational e-mail server.
		Destructive worm targeting Windows NT SP3 servers	Worm found on HR support server; minor impact to operations
		Biochemical agents appearing in USPS	Anthrax found in letter to COO
		Terrorist attack warning	IEDs found in two organizational locations
	Accidental, Employee	Data center is typically unmanned and openly accessible to all personnel during business hours.	Well-meaning but unknowledgeable employee reboots UNIX server by unplugging power cord.

		No e-mail or Internet use policy	Employees download unauthorized files to organizational PCs.
Civil infrastructure			
Civil transportation	Highway	Highway congestion creates permanent threat to operations due to personnel delays.	June 9, 2008: Truck struck bridge on 695 beltway, resulting in massive traffic delays, keeping key personnel from work; operations shut down for 4 hours.
	Mass transit	Building that contains operations resides on top of D.C. metro stop.	July 9, 2007: Metro fire causes evacuation of X; operations shut down for 3 hours.
	Federal Aviation Administration	Increase in air traffic threatens to overload current technical and employee capacity.	Congestion at major air hub on December 15, 2008, causes shipment delays and affects retail holiday revenues.
Utilities—government provided	Water	Heavy construction in surrounding area	April 2, 2008: Water-main break caused loss of water-cooled air conditioning; server farm shut down for 18 hours.
Technical			
Utilities—commercially provided	Electric	Local electric utility (power grid) is undersized for current demands.	September 22, 2007, brownout that turned into server room blackout; server farm down for 8 hours

Continued

Table 13.2 Threat Space Categories and Examples (Continued)

Threat	Threat Agent	Kinetic Threat	Incident
	Telephone; public switched telephone network (PSTN)	CO and IXC nonredundant service with many single points of convergence	March 14, 2008: T3-seeking backhoe finds its target; service lost for 6 hours.
Equipment			
	Server	Application server with no hard drive redundancy	Hard drive failure
	Router	No policy to keep router OS versions up to date	Route table corruption
	Ethernet switch	No component redundancy policy on critical LAN segments	Power supply failure
	Etc.		

of a hurricane within proximity of an organizational asset. A kinetic threat poses a real imminent risk. An incident is when the kinetic threat actually affects the organizational assets, that is, the hurricane rips the roof off the data center.

A risk assessment looks at both the asset space and the threat space. Knowledge of high-probability threats is valuable input to the decision-making process for assigning risk probabilities to assets. An asset vulnerability with a high threat probability is a higher priority for remediation than an asset vulnerability with no known or no expected threat.

13.4.2 IA² Threat Taxonomy

An *information assurance* (IA) *taxonomy* categorizes incidents by connecting threat agents to consequences through vulnerabilities.

Howard and Meunier's *Common Language* describes a lexicon and taxonomy for *computer-related crime*. The common language (CL) taxonomy is: an *attacker* uses a *tool* to exploit a *vulnerability* to perform some *action* on a *target* to achieve an *unauthorized result*. The CL categories are attacker, tool, vulnerability, action, target, and unauthorized result. Each CL category has many examples: attackers ∈ (hackers, spies, terrorists, insiders, competition, etc.); tool ∈ (hacker toolkit, physical attack, malware, etc.); vulnerability ∈ (design, configuration, implementation, etc.); action ∈ (probe, scan, spoof, etc.); target ∈ (account, process, system, data, etc.); unauthorized result ∈ (increased access, denial of service, theft, etc.). The CL taxonomy covers only malicious incidents, and though very useful, it is limited in scope. Malice implies intent that in turn implies human involvement—some volition; hence, CL is limited to computer crime. However, IA requires a broader lexicon and taxonomy.

A broader IA taxonomy is the IA² threat taxonomy, which is a threat agent either unaccompanied or through use of a tool that exploits a vulnerability to perform some action against an asset achieving some undesired result. Table 13.3 provides threat taxonomy examples. Using the threat taxonomy, you can read the first line in the table as "a hacker using a password cracker exploits the use of simple (noncomplex) passwords to gain unrestricted access to the R&D server, resulting in disclosure and loss of proprietary data. You can read the second line in the table as "a hurricane exploits poor roof construction, causing flooding in the data center, resulting in loss of all computing equipment."

The IA² threat taxonomy provides a method to describe the relationship between threat agents and vulnerabilities. This relationship is the intersection between the threat space and the asset space.

13.5 Expanding on the Adversary Threat Space

Adversaries have intelligence and intent and pose significant risk to the organization. Naturally occurring conditions are largely predictable; if not the actual

Table 13.3 IA² Threat Taxonomy

Threat Agent	Unaccompanied/ Tool	Vulnerability	Action	Target	Undesired Result
Hacker	Password cracker	Simple passwords	Unrestricted access	R&D server	Disclosure and loss of proprietary data
Hurricane	Unaccompanied	Construction (e.g., roof)	Flood	Data center	Loss of all computing equipment
Ice storm	Unaccompanied	Public services (highway administration)	Ice cover	Roads	Key personnel kept from critical operations
Venti caramel latte	Careless live-ware	Lack of a consumables policy	Spill	Unwitting laptop	Fried laptop and hard drive with critical data ($10K recovery cost)
	Etc.				

date and time, at least the potential for occurrence is known. Organizational assets are in a hurricane-prone area, earthquake zone, or floodplain or they are not. Adversaries are more difficult to predict. You may not even know your organization has an adversary; the adversary simply appears on your literal or virtual doorstep. You may be aware of an adversary but lack specific knowledge of its interest in your organization. Chapter 5 introduced a threat probability assessment (TPA). TPA evaluates adversary capability (means); tactical preferences (method); leadership, individual psychology, group and social dynamics, and political psychology (motivation, operations and interests); and potential adversarial objectives (mission).

If an adversary is well known to hate your organization or what it stands for (motivation), but has limited or no knowledge of how to execute a cyber-attack (low/no method), this gives you a clue how to characterize the risk. If an adversary is highly motivated and highly knowledgeable but lacks the funding to purchase the appropriate equipment or effectively use that equipment (no means), this gives you a clue how to characterize the risk.

If your assessment of the threat space finds a state-sponsored adversary with interest in your organization, a nation-state may easily have the means, method, and motivation to act. For example, consider a developing country with little indigenous technology to create an effective infrastructure (energy, roads, housing, water, etc.). If that country were to sponsor corporate espionage that sought after engineering designs and manufacturing process for, say, power tools, engines, or autos, it may accelerate its national growth by decades at a savings of billions of dollars by not having to purchase those same devices or capabilities. Given the potential payback of increased gross national product, increased quality of life for citizens, a broadened tax base, and emergence as a world player decades ahead of any previous expectations, this is a high motivation. The means comes from the power of government to collect and allocate tax revenues to the effort.

The following sections present IA justification in context of TPA elements means, method, motivation, and mission.

13.5.1 Adversary Means

Adversary means is the capability to carry out an attack—capability in terms of finances, equipment, and knowledge. IT attack means include:

- Finances
  - Private financing
  - State-sponsored financing
- Equipment
  - Common
  - Specialized

- Knowledge
  - Acquire directly
  - Hire expertise

The finances, equipment, and knowledge all contribute to the means of a potential attacker. The means contributes to the overall threat probability assessment (TPA). The TPA provides insight into justifying IA in cases of real, verifiable, highly probable threats. You may present IA justification in terms of a highly financed adversary, or an adversary that possesses specialized equipment known to exploit your organization's vulnerabilities.

13.5.1.1 Finances

Generally, state-sponsored financing provides much deeper pockets than private financing. A state-sponsored adversary is a government, or government-controlled group. Determining which government is providing financing also provides insight into motivation (political relationships) and method (prior history). Private financing may still be quite large. If a rival multi-billion-dollar organization wants your intellectual property, its finances, while not that of a government, are still substantial.

13.5.1.2 Equipment

Is the equipment necessary to carry out a successful attack common everyday equipment or highly specialized and expensive and hard to obtain? Common everyday equipment increases the threat probability due to its ease of acquisition. Some equipment is legitimately available only to a government. Therefore, the attacker must steal the equipment or purchase it on the black market. All of these add time, cost, and complexity to the attack means and thus lower the threat probability. Of course, all the characteristics of means, method, and motivation must be considered together, as each individually provides clues to the larger picture.

13.5.1.3 Knowledge

Does the attack require specialized knowledge or no particular knowledge at all? The plethora of canned cyber-attack tools provides moderate to high levels of sophisticated cyber-attacks that require minimal technical knowledge. A real-time adaptable attack with objectives of overcoming multiple defense-in-depth mechanisms may require a hands-on touch and quick adaptation on the fly. This is a high level of knowledge not easily acquired or purchased.

Standard IA defenses should safeguard against low-knowledge, easily available attack tools. Even if an attacker is not specifically your adversary, you may be an incidental victim. For example, anti-virus software is a standard IA mechanism that provides a safeguard against viruses traversing the Internet. Also, a firewall is a standard IA mechanism that provides safeguards against network-probing tools that require minimal knowledge to operate. A key data point here is that the sophistication of the attacks is increasing while the knowledge level of the attackers is not. This is due to the increasing availability of sophisticated attack tools that require little advanced technical knowledge; i.e., a point-and-click hacker toolkit.

13.5.2   Adversary Methods

An attack method is a systematic procedure employed by an attacker against information or information technology. Attack methods include computer system penetration and programmatic attacks of malicious code, mobile code, and denial of service. Programmatic attacks may be automated where they are set to initiate an attack without manual intervention. Programmatic attacks may also be interactive where intent and intelligence guide the systemic assaults. Interactive attacks provide opportunity to modify tactics on the fly as defenses are encountered or breached. Surveillance tools provide the ability for wiretapping, wireless tapping, and eavesdropping on live or transmitted communications.

13.5.2.1   Computer System Penetration

A security breach may result in information disclosure, resource theft, data corruption, forgery, denial of service, or rendering the resource unusable. There are two general methods for computer system penetration: *nontechnical* and *technical*. Nontechnical methods include social engineering, which is manipulating a person to gain access to the desired resources. Corporate espionage is another nontechnical penetration method. Corporate espionage may recruit existing employees or insert spies as new hires. Technical methods include wiretapping, data leaking, network sniffing, wireless signal interception, electrical pulse detection (e.g., fluctuations on an electrical line or video display updates), Trojans, and much more.

IA defense mechanisms are likewise nontechnical and technical; nontechnical includes preparation measures like security policies and employee awareness training. Technical includes defense-in-depth as appropriate to the technical infrastructure, for example:

- Perimeter network boundary
  - Boundary between public (e.g., Internet) and public servers (e.g., Web, e-mail)
- External boundary
  - Boundary between internal network (e.g., internal users) and unsecured external network (e.g., Internet)

- Community of interest (COI) boundary
  - Intraorganizational boundary between various logical COIs
  - For example, legal cannot access R&D, who cannot access payroll
- Host server boundary
  - Boundary between host server and intraorganizational, external, and COI
  - For example, server hardening or creating a bastion host
- Application boundary
  - Boundary between application and intraorganizational, COI
  - For example, session encryption

Included in defense-in-depth are protections against vulnerabilities (known system weaknesses) and system penetration. Proactive measures to test for weaknesses include vulnerability scans and penetration tests. Vulnerability scans check for obvious configuration flaws and up-to-date patches; penetration testing digs a little deeper by actually trying to break into the system. Vulnerability scans and penetration testing help answer the question: Are the security mechanisms in place actually working?

The *risk analysis* identifies high-probability threats and associated vulnerabilities in the asset space. Any association of a vulnerability with a highly probable threat is good IA justification.

13.5.2.2 Programmatic Attacks

In addition to system penetration, programmatic attacks are another IT attack method. Programmatic attacks include malicious code (malware), mobile code, and denial of service. Consider a recent occurrence of a programmatic attack where "zombies are fueling a new cyber crime wave."* Extortionists are hitting online casinos, retailers, and even the Port of Houston with zombie cyber-attacks not with the primary intent of performing any damage, but to extort money not to damage their sites and business operations.

The bottom line with respect to IT attack methods is twofold; first, there is a broad array of methods to penetrate cyber-security, and second, technical security is not enough. IA justification includes both technical and nontechnical IT attack methods with respect to the protection of information and information technology.

13.5.2.3 Computer, Automated

Many computer-based attacks may be automated. Automated attacks may be one-to-one attacker to target (e.g., system probing) or one-to-many (e.g., network map-

---

* http://www.usatoday.com/tech/news/computersecurity/2003-11-12-zombie-blackmail_x.htm.

ping) or many-to-one (e.g., distributed denial of service) or many-to-many (e.g., zombie attack on an IP address range). A ready supply of cyber-criminal tools and information is available on sites like the following:*

- http://www.phrack.org/
- http://www.iwar.org.uk/hackers/resources/harmless-hacking/index.html
- http://www.infosyssec.org/
- http://www.antionline.com/toplist.php
- http://www2.packetstorm.org:443/

13.5.2.4 Computer, Interactive

Computer systems may facilitate interactive attacks where computer criminals attempt security breaches in real-time. This type of attack is typically one to one with respect to attacker to target. The attacker may adjust technique depending on what is learned in real-time. Standard IA safeguards against known attack patterns, scripts, or tools are a start. If the threat space includes known adversaries with means, method, motivation, and mission for specific targets, you may justify sophisticated IA safeguards to monitor for, detect, and respond to real-time interactive attacks.

13.5.3 Adversary Motivations

Adversaries include hackers, computer criminals, terrorists, industrial spies, and insiders. Motivation implies volition, which narrows threat sources to human sources with malice. There are a plethora of computer crime motivations, ranging from simple vandalism through information warfare and asymmetrical adversarialism. Motivations include:

- Computer criminal psychology
- Personal
  - Monetary gain
  - Revenge
    - Disgruntled employees or estranged employees
- Industrial
  - Corporate espionage
    - Competitive advantage
- Political
  - Information warfare

---

* Note: Use caution when accessing Web sites; simply accessing the site may expose your computer to malware.

- Asymmetrical adversarialism
- Cyber-terrorism
  - Blackmail
  - Destruction

13.5.3.1 Computer Criminal Psychology

Criminal psychology has not changed, only now criminals have new tools and targets in information technology. Some tools facilitate the exploitation of computers and some tools use computers to facilitate non-computer-based crimes.

"Researchers have developed numerous classification systems that group hackers according to their skill levels, motivations, and goals into independent categories ranging from neophyte hackers to professional cyber-terrorists."* Dr. Ron Ross of NIST points out that cyberspace attacks are becoming more sophisticated, but the attackers are not. The reason for this is a repository of sophisticated cyber-attack tools available on the Internet that are readily available and easy to use. IA justification resides in the readily available repository of attack tools, readily available to both the concerted effort and the merely curious.

The *Hacker's Manifesto* was written in 1986, over 20 years ago. The hacker mentality has been around for a long time, and a whole hacker generation has grown up living the *Hacker's Manifesto*. In paraphrase,† the manifesto expresses lack of satisfaction and tolerance for a teaching system that does not give them what they want. There is a desire to take over the (cyber) world and general dissatisfaction with being labeled criminals for hacking: "You build atomic bombs, you wage wars, you murder, you cheat, and lie to us and try to make us believe it's for our own good, yet we're the criminals." They justify their actions saying that the principle of technical ability equates to the right to exercise that ability: "My crime is that of judging people by what they say and think, not what they look like. My crime is that of outsmarting you, something that you will never forgive me for." The manifesto ends with a resolute solidarity, "I am a hacker, and this is my manifesto. You may stop this individual, but you can't stop us all."

This manifesto is a straightforward proclamation that technical capability equates to the right to exercise that capability. Why do you climb Mt. Everest? Because it is there. Why does a hacker break into your system? Because he can. Door locks keep out the merely curious but do little to dissuade the burglar with a specific objective. Likewise, standard IA mechanisms do succeed in keeping out the casually curious. This is a valid justification for IA. For many companies, keeping out the merely curious is enough. For many more companies, keeping out the merely curious is just the beginning of more sophisticated IA.

---

* Campbell, Quinn, and Kennedy, David M., *The Psychology of Computer Criminals*, p. 6–18.
† http://www.technozen.com/manifesto.htm.

13.5.3.2   Personal Motivations

Much of personal motivation for computer criminals is found in criminal psychology. Motivations include money, revenge, the thrill, the challenge, because they can, because they believe they have a right to. "There is no simple explanation as to why computer criminals engage in hostile and destructive acts. The answer lies in a complex mixture of factors that depends on the social environment and individual personality factors."* The fact there are criminals is part of IA justification. Criminals used to go after physical assets like gold, currency, or jewels. This required physical presence and high risk on the part of the perpetrator. Now wealth exists as bits on hard drive. These bits are accessible from anywhere in the world with relatively low risk of discovery. Low risk on the part of the perpetrator equates to more attempts. This is a justification for IA safeguards and monitoring devices.

13.5.3.3   Industrial Motivations

In a world economy of interconnected competitors, it is reasonable to believe that corporate espionage has entered the information age. The status of economic power versus third world is at stake and the way of life for people in those economies. Consider a third-world country that desires in ten years to introduce a manufacturing facility that will create hundreds or thousands of jobs. Further, consider an out-of-work Cold War cyber-spy that offers his computer skills to accelerate time-to-market entry by eight years at a $1.5 billion reduction in start-up fees through stealing existing engineering documents and R&D data from a competitive company. A $150 million payment to this individual is 10 percent of the legitimate alternative with an 80 percent reduction in time to market. Moreover, even 1 percent of the legitimate alternative is $15 million. Although $15 million may not hire the best, it will still hire pretty darn good. These are strong motivations for industrial espionage. These are also strong justification for IA.

Other industrial motivations include competitive advantage through knowledge of competitor activities, discrediting a competitor, attempting to manipulate a competitor's stock price and valuation (e.g., bringing down the Web site of an online stock broker just as bad news hits the market), and many more.

13.5.3.4   Political Motivations

Political motivations include patriotism, rebellion, or power. Political motivations may fall under the state-sponsored category, independents acting out of love of their country or hatred of yours, or non-state-sponsored groups like Al Qaeda. A state-sponsored group has considerably more resources to draw upon than the oth-

---

* *The Psychology of Computer Criminals*, pp. 6–19.

ers do. Access to specialized tools and knowledge is difficult, but not impossible. As part of IA justification, you must ask if your organization is a potential target for a politically motivated action.

13.5.3.5 Information Warfare

Dr. Ivan Goldberg defines information warfare as "the offensive and defensive use of information and information systems to deny, exploit, corrupt, or destroy, an adversary's information, information-based processes, information systems, and computer-based networks while protecting one's own. Such actions are designed to achieve advantages over military or business adversaries."* "Business is war" is not a mere tongue-in-cheek aphorism, but rather a more literal reality. War is about business. Nation-states are formed in large to protect economic interests; these economic interests take form in commercial enterprises. There is a symbiotic relationship between commercial enterprise success and the success of the nation. The motivation of war is more often economics. The targets of war are often civilian and those that are of economic support to the nation. Targets of war have become more IT oriented as IT emerges as the center of trade and commerce.

There is justification for IA to protect information and information technology in a global environment where the paths of commerce are not limited by physical access. Virtual office fronts enable producers from across the globe to meet consumer demands. Discovering competitive secrets or subverting competition is but a few mouse-clicks away. Paranoid? Well, it can be. There is a distinction between paranoid and prudent. Prudent includes performing a risk assessment and risk analysis that addresses the threat space as well as the asset space. Act as reason and rationale about facts and assumptions prescribe.

13.5.3.6 Asymmetrical Adversarialism

Symmetrical warfare (adversarialism) means "both sides are (roughly) equally equipped. It is polite war to a fault, and both sides play by the rules."† The enemy is easy to spot—he is that guy lined up over there, across no-man's-land. Even the Cold War was symmetrical in the sense of a known enemy with rules of engagement, albeit somewhat clandestine.

Asymmetrical adversarialism is a new order of conflict engagement. Though not a new concept, it is a tactical philosophy adaptable to information technology. Traditional asymmetric adversarialism is the sniper killing anonymously from a distance, it is the terrorist striking innocents, and it is the use of an overwhelming

---

* http://www.psycom.net/iwar.2.html (accessed October 2007).
† Win Schwartau's *Asymmetrical Adversarialism in National Defense Policy.*

weapon of mass destruction (WMD) for which there is no defense available to the target country.

Information technology (IT) asymmetrical adversarialism includes the use of a single computer located across the world to launch denial-of-service attacks on government systems. It is the use of an e-mail virus to distribute a slave program to hundreds or thousand of computers across the Internet that lies dormant for years waiting for a single master command of "attack system 192.168.xxx.yyy." These attacks are very easy and inexpensive to launch; they are very difficult and very expensive to defend against.

IA justification is that we (global citizens) are playing by new warfare rules, rules that we do not even know about, perhaps even a game of unrestricted warfare where there are no rules. As previously mentioned, war is about business, about commerce, about economic success. A lack of arable land and potable water is a strong motivation to go take them from someone else. A desire for greater economic success, faster, with minimal cost is a strong motivation to take what you need from someone else. Traditional warfare required physical proximity of people and equipment. A cyber-combatant attacking an economic interest can do so from any Internet connection. Traditional warfare was one man, one weapon (e.g. one spear, one crossbow, one gun). A single cyber-combatant may control thousands of cyber-munitions from thousands of separate locations.

13.5.3.7 Cyber-Terrorism

Using any of thousands of readily available tools on the Internet, a cyber-terrorist may launch attacks against an industrial or political power's critical infrastructure that includes electrical grid(s), telecommunication service, air traffic control, water supply, food supply, transportation, and credit card service (transaction processing). "Advances in information technology and the necessity of improved efficiency, however, have precipitated a steadily and rapidly increasing amount of automation in, and interconnection among, these systems."* According to the USA PATRIOT Act, "America's critical infrastructures include energy (electric power, oil and gas), transportation (rail, air, merchant marine), finance and banking, information and telecommunications, public health, emergency services, water, chemical, government, defense industrial base, food, agriculture, and postal and shipping."

In terms of threats or threat space, one type of threat is people. People may exhibit adverse behavior with malicious intent. However, malicious intent is relative perception; one person's malice is another's patriotism or another's cause (religious or political). IA justification includes consideration of your organization as part of the critical infrastructure or in direct support of critical infrastructure. If your organization is not the target, it may be the weakest link. IA justification may come

---

* The President's Critical Infrastructure Protection Board, *National Strategy to Secure Cyberspace.*

in the name of national interest or in the interest of avoiding downstream liability by being the conduit for a successful attack.

This latter group may include hackers, that nebulous group of people that we spend so much time defending ourselves against. This latter group also includes state-sponsored adversaries and non-state-sponsored adversaries. State-sponsored adversaries include national armed forces or intelligence community. Non-state-sponsored adversaries may include terrorists.

13.5.4 Adversary Mission

An adversary *mission* is the focus of the means, method, and motivation. The mission is the segue from threat space (the adversary) to asset space (the adversary's target). The mission is the *target* and the *desired result* for that target. The target may be people, process, information, information technology, physical asset, or a pending business deal.

13.5.4.1 Targets

Example targets for an adversary mission include the following:

- Intellectual property
- E-commerce
- Physical infrastructure

13.5.4.2 Intellectual Property (IP)

Disclosure management is critical to maintain control of intellectual property. First, stop unauthorized access. Second, manage authorized access by creating IP categories governing access, for example:

- Global repository—Accessible globally
- Country-limited repository—Accessible within a country only
- Location-limited repository—Accessible within a particular location only
- Project-limited repository—Accessible only by individuals associated with the project

Additionally, publish and implement IP management policies that include items like:

- All traffic to/from knowledge repositories use a minimum of X-bit encryption, where X is at least the minimal safe key length of the day.

- All access is via username and password.
- Each individual accessing these repositories must have a unique username and password.
- User passwords meet minimum standards.
- Force password change every 30 days.

13.5.4.3   E-Commerce

E-commerce includes business-to-business and business-to-consumer. The number of Internet users continues to grow, as does their willingness to shop online.

13.5.4.4   Physical Infrastructure

Physical infrastructure may include facilities housing key operations critical to operations and revenue. Protection of physical infrastructure is important with respect to:

- Location
- Access
- Infrastructure

Factors relevant to physical location include local crime rates, building signage (e.g., XYZ corporate headquarters versus a more anonymous presence), surrounding buildings and businesses (e.g., closest corporate neighbor may manufacture or transport hazardous material), and exposure to natural elements (e.g., floodplain, tornado alley, or earthquake zone). Building access policies and implementation include monitoring for authorized access and creating audit trails of entry, and perhaps movement throughout the facilities. Access to lobby areas does not necessarily imply access permission to the general work area and data operations centers.

Building infrastructure includes electric, air conditioning, water, construction, phone service, and location of key infrastructure pieces (e.g., services demark locations). Known power interruptions may imply the need for UPS and building generators. Air conditioning units that are water cooled may be shut down in the event of a water-main break; if this building is located in an area where environmental conditions may increase the likelihood of water-main breaks, air-cooled backup units may be appropriate.

13.5.4.5   Desired Results of Target Attack

The desired result for the target may be any of the following:

- Knowledge—Gaining knowledge of information or information technology; gain personal knowledge
- Subvert—Subverting information or information technology; falsify; deceive
- Destroy—Destruction of asset
- Steal—Theft of asset; theft of service
- Render useless—Denial of service of assets; render unusable

The mission objectives correspond with the IA core principles. Mission objectives imply a target, a target that exists in the organization's asset space. The target may be physical (e.g., facilities, information technology, information [e.g., printed documents]) or virtual (e.g., information in transit).

The mission may be a general mission, as in a probe of all utility companies for access into their network. The mission may be specific, as when a known adversary wants your organization's fourth-quarter financial information from server X that resides at site Y. IA justification comes from examining the threat space, determining best information about the mission, and analyzing your asset space for vulnerabilities in light of the mission objective. The following sections elaborate on desired mission results.

13.5.4.6   Knowledge

An adversary may wish to gain knowledge from its target. The knowledge objective may be to discern the existence of a site, server, product, engineering design, or strategic plan. The objective may be details about any of these. Knowledge of a server may assist in deploying malware to exploit known vulnerabilities. Knowledge gathering may include social engineering, electronic listening devices, line of sight into executive boardrooms, or copying backup tapes stored off site.

13.5.4.7   Subvert

Subversion is more insidious than destruction. Destruction is obvious as the use of the asset ends. Subversion may be subtle changes to data, metadata, or documents. Slight misinformation may produce dramatically different end results from the original intent. A production line may produce products that will wear out sooner and result in high costs of honoring warranties. Slight shifts in navigation coordinates result in wide variances in travel paths and final destination (e.g., redirecting commercial airlines over restricted air space). Subtle deviations are also very difficult to discover.

13.5.4.8   Destroy

Destruction is the loss of an asset or the loss of use of an asset. Malware that causes a hard drive head crash is just as effective as physically smashing the drive.

13.5.4.9   Steal

Stealing involves the theft of information or information technology. This may be physical theft or virtual theft (e.g., copying via spyware).

13.5.4.10   Render Useless

Following the principle of least resistance, rendering something useless may be easier and cheaper than destroying it. Loss of use of a building may be just as devastating as loss of the building. For example, a biological agent (virus) or chemical in the ventilation system may render the building unsafe for human use.

Determining the means, method, motivation, and mission is not simple. There is a role for both deductive and inductive logic. Deductive conclusions from known facts are less likely than surmising possible outcomes from some facts and some assumptions. Assigning assumptions reliability and confidence levels helps to understand and manage uncertainty—reliability and confidence in information sources, method of process, authenticity of information (i.e., good source that may be misinformed), and conclusions.

Understanding the means, method, motivation, and mission assists you in determining appropriate safeguards and articulating justification for those safeguards to executives, management, operations, and users. All this seems like a lot for an IA professional. Well, it can be. IA is in part a science that requires applying known prudent safeguards in manners known to be effective. IA is also an art that takes creativity, thinking about organizational risk in new ways, and a constant vigil for showing the business value of IA.

13.6   Consequences

There are two perspectives on consequences: one is the consequence to your organization, and the other is the consequence to the adversary. The potential attack consequences to your organization and how they correlate to motivations include the following:*

- Level I—Interpersonal damages
- Level II—Intercorporate damages
- Level III—International damages

Like blood flow to a human and cash flow to an economy, the flow of information is important to the world economy; the secure flow of information is critical. Winn Schwartau's three information warfare levels—*interpersonal* damage, *intercorporate* damage, and *international* damage—best exemplify the potential consequences of poor information assurance.

---

* Winn Schwartau's three levels of information warfare.

13.6.1 Level I: Interpersonal Damage

IA architects and their customers' success are largely based on their respective abilities to deliver what they promise in the manner promised. Much of this includes secrecy about current work, secrecy based on trust and reputation. Disclosure of questionable or falsified personal information has the potential to interrupt or delay operations, and absolutely has the potential for long-term effects with regard to reputation of the individual and his or her organization.

13.6.2 Level II: Intercorporate Damage

IA architects may be involved with projects valued in the millions and even billions of dollars. The stakes are too high to take for granted that everyone else is playing by the rules. Corporate espionage or sabotage leading to theft of key intellectual property may lower barriers to competitive entry (e.g., source code); lower cost of entry implies lower costs and lower pricing when bidding against a competitor. Actual asset loss is a distant second concern to loss of intellectual property and contract award loss.

Sabotage may affect the integrity of product development, testing, or the certification and accreditation process. Any of these may delay a deliverable or raise questions about the quality of the deliverable. Compromise to a test lab may bring into question C&A work and may result in do-it-again demands, assuming the second-chance opportunity is even presented.

13.6.3 Level III: International Damage

IA architects may also be involved in domestic and foreign governments, and in businesses whose work or products have national or international importance. This leaves employees open to extortion, bribery, and other temptations to compromise the trust accorded them. Trust violations may result in disclosure, resource theft, or any other particular in the results taxonomy. The ultimate end could be economic destabilization (compromised government or commercial financial systems), back-door access to subversives, or intergovernment transport of secrets, including data providing insight on how to destabilize each other's infrastructures.

13.6.4 Adversary Consequences

Newton's first law of motion is that for every action there is an equal and opposite reaction. Adversary actions have consequences. In a nation-state situation, one cyber-attack may beget a response in kind. From a corporate perspective, launching counterattacks is more problematic. First and foremost, counterattacks are highly likely to be illegal. Second and almost as foremost, it is very difficult to discern who

Table 13.4   IA Justification in Potential Business Loss per IA Core Principle

IA Core Principle	IA Justification in Potential Business Loss
Confidentiality	Disclosure, interception, observed
Possession	Loss, theft of resources
Integrity	Modification, corruption
Authenticity	Forgery, fabrication
Availability	Denial of service, business interruption
Utility	Unusable
Authorized use	Theft of service, increased access
Nonrepudiation	Undeniable accountability for acts of commission and omission
Privacy	Compliance with privacy legislation (e.g., HIPAA Privacy Rule, Privacy Act)

the actual attacker is. The attack may look like it is coming from competitor Y, when in fact it is a third party using competitor Y resources. So, how do you impose consequences on the adversary?

There is IA justification in hiring IA professionals with the knowledge to capture appropriate logs and other evidence that is admissible in court. Learn how to use the existing laws to protect your organization. If appropriate laws do not exist, look into proposing new ones. Your organization may employ lobbyists with access to lawmakers. Your company may belong to a trade organization that has collective representation and access to lawmakers. Such activity is preemptive in nature to make adversary consequences painful so as to deter them from future attacks.

13.6.5   IA Core Principles as IA Justification

Table 13.4 provides IA justification as potential business losses against the IA core principles. These are useful justifications for IA that cover most potential organizational losses.

13.7   IA Operations Cycle as IA Justification

Justifying IA in terms of the IA operations cycle provides details in context of operations, administration, and maintenance. The IA operations cycle consists of anticipate, defend, monitor, and respond. The following sections elaborate on each phase in this cycle.

13.7.1 Anticipate

The IA operations cycle phase *anticipate* gives advance thought to business risk, threat space, asset space, vulnerabilities, and what they mean for organizational effectiveness, operations, and continued viability. Anticipation includes thought experiments, study of vicarious experiences (e.g., industry reports), and empirical evidence from the organizational environment. For example, a thought experiment is a device of the imagination, a purely hypothetical set of circumstances. A thought experiment may include using the threat taxonomies in this book to speculate on potential and probable threats to your organization, what impact those threats may have on your organization, and then considering how to best address those threats. Thought experiment details may come from the real experiences of others in magazine articles or Internet postings; again consider how the threats may impact your organization and how you already address them, how current IA projects will address them, or the need for new IA projects.

System or network penetration attempts are inevitable in a high-profile organization (e.g., U.S. military, Swiss bank). If monitoring detects no potential incidents, check the robustness of monitoring services and mechanisms. In the event of penetration, an analysis of this penetration is wise and should include how it was discovered, symptoms experienced, how it was reported, the triage steps to identify potential severity, and how it was escalated, investigated, and treated. Having resolved the issue at hand, root cause analysis (RCA) verifies that the resolution addressed the real cause, not just symptoms.

"Successful penetrations are typically the result of successive compromises, where two or more vulnerabilities are combined by the attacker to gain greater than authorized access. A lot of systems still assume that an attacker will not get to a certain point, and so they do not defend that point"*; anticipate the need for defense-in-depth.

Malware is a contraction of *malicious software* and includes virus, worm, Trojan horse, denial of service (DoS), distributed denial of service (DDoS), spyware, and many variations on a theme, including macro viruses, remote access Trojans (RATs), and spam. Malware may enter an organization via e-mail, Internet downloads, sneaker-net floppies and other removable/portable storage media, mobile code, and bugs in the operating system and application software.

Anticipated malware plus malware discovered through vulnerability analysis provide input to a defense-in-depth design. IA² includes defense-in-depth by defining a series of operational boundaries and trust relationships between boundaries.

---

* Cobb, Stephen, *Notes on System Penetration.*

Enforcement of trust relationships is achieved through a variety of security mechanisms appropriate to the organization, project, and business requirements.

13.7.2 Defend

The IA operations cycle phase *defend* is to oppose or ward off a danger or attack against information, information technology, or other organizational assets. Limitations on resources prevent the defense of 100 percent of assets from 100 percent of threats 100 percent of the time. Intelligent resource allocation provides insight into necessary and sufficient defenses. A principle of security is to make the cost of a successful attack high enough so as to prohibit the attempt and success of that attack. Defenses establish the cost level of a successful attack. For example, door locks will not deter a motivated attacker; however, they provide a sufficient safeguard against casual attacks (e.g., the merely curious). Additional safeguards like video cameras and security guards increase the defenses. The cost of a successful attack increases when there are safeguards to avoid or overcome. Then the attack is not an impossible feat, but is more difficult. Video cameras provide evidentiary records. The possibility of successful prosecution and jail time has now increased the cost of an attack even more.

The same principle applies in cyber-security. Absence of a firewall allows unrestricted access to all comers. A well-configured firewall prohibits entrance of the casually curious; however, the appropriate tools and knowledge allow entrance by those with the means (money to buy the tools), method (knowledge to use them), and motivation (reason for doing so). Adding additional safeguards, like a network intrusion detection system (NIDS), creates another safeguard to overcome, thus increasing the cost for a successful attack. Adding a host-based intrusion detection system (HIDS) is another safeguard. Configuring the host system to eliminate unnecessary applications and services, close down unnecessary ports, and use strong passwords for any access adds yet another layer. Defense-in-depth increases the attacker's cost of reaching the objective.

To reiterate, the objective is not to introduce airtight security measures with absolutely no chance of a successful attack. The objective is to introduce necessary security measures to sufficiently raise the cost of a successful attack to the point of being prohibitive. This takes us back to the threat space analysis. If the asset is a government installation and the potential attacker has state sponsorship from an unfriendly government, the means, method, and motivation may be high enough that complex defenses are necessary. On the other hand, small businesses that suffer more from incidental fallout than a focused attack are usually fine with the cyber-equivalent of door locks. A firewall and anti-malware cover most of the incidental threats. A sound backup and recovery plan provides adequate contingency planning for a potential incident. These claims are broad generalizations to make a point. Any particular organization must evaluate its own environment and prepare accordingly.

13.7.3 Monitor

The IA operations cycle *monitor* phase is to keep watch or observe people, processes, policy enforcement, systems, applications, information, and infrastructure, including IA defenses against anomalous behavior. With safeguards in place, monitoring the activity of the safeguards demonstrates they are working as intended. Monitoring activity logs may show signs of probing, a lesser activity that tests the environment prior to attack in earnest. Monitoring also provides insight into security awareness and understanding, e.g., ensure people are following security policy. Monitoring the effectiveness of operations, including IA operations, is the starting point to obtain the raw data.

Operational effectiveness reports are the first set of reports that show the value of IA. Operations reports may show number of intercepted attacks on the firewall, number and type of intrusion detections, number of probes on an E-commerce server, etc. *Management reports* refine operations reports into business function goals or tactical objectives, e.g., performance levels or SLAs. *Executive level reports* refine management reports in terms of revenue and costs. Although this is an oversimplified transition from operational data to executive reports, the goal is to provide the appropriate information and justification to the appropriate audience.

13.7.4 Respond

The IA operations cycle *respond* phase covers actions in response to a potential or verified security event or security incident. Responses may include standard responses to predictable events (e.g., help desk assistance on removing a known virus) and specialized responses, including tiger teams, subject matter experts, and digital forensics. Response is part of the larger computer security incident response center (CSIRC) activities: monitor, detect, notify, triage, escalate, isolate, resolve, restore, root cause analysis, and organizational feedback. The final response step is a review and modification of existing procedures in light of lessons learned through the root cause analysis. This completes the IA operation cycle, with response feeding information into more proactive anticipation, defense, and monitoring.

13.8 Empirical Evidence

Nothing speaks louder than empirical evidence, those lessons learned from personal experience, as well as vicarious lessons learned from the experiences of others.

13.8.1 Surveys

Empirical evidence regarding computer crime is found in a variety of surveys found worldwide:

- Australian Federal Police, Australian Computer Crime and Security Survey
- FBI, FBI Computer Crime and Security Survey
- UK Department of Trade and Industry, Information System Security Breaches Survey
- Japan's Information Security Survey
- The Information Technology Association of America (ITAA) and Brain-bench™ Global Cyber Security Survey
- Many more

All surveys show an increase in computer crime over the past year, though it is difficult to conclude with confidence if incidents are increasing or the ability to detect and willingness to report are increasing. The likely reality is that all three are influencing findings and conclusions. Worldwide concerns about cyber-security have prompted national surveys to determine the breadth and depth of these threats. Interestingly, according to a Digital Research survey, "disgruntled employees are the biggest threat to computer security in the United States than external hackers," says a research firm survey. The second biggest problem reported were those created by user accounts left active after employees have quit the company."*

13.8.2   Recent Media Coverage

Whether the increase in cyber-security incidents is a result of actual increase in attacks, better detection methods, or a willingness to share information, there is no doubt that IA is critical for an E-commerce economy. The IA experiences of other organizations provide justification for IA within your own. Real and recent accounts of attempted attacks, successful or otherwise, provide business rationale for investing in IA.

13.9   Compliance Requirements

Many federal laws and regulations describe compliance requirements for information assurance. Noncompliance may result in financial penalties and jail time. Even if not a direct requirement of the law, there remain executive responsibilities of due diligence and due care, a violation of which may result in shareholder or other lawsuits. Information technology introduces many new concerns with respect to legal obligations, including, but certainly not limited to, protection of information assets, contract definitions, intellectual property management, and defamation protection.

---

* http://www.ciol.com/content/news/trends/101062102.asp.

13.9.1 Cyberspace Law

There are many technology-focused laws, regulations, and policies requiring the attention of commercial and government organizations. A small sampling of U.S. laws is:

- Homeland Security Act of 2002
- USA PATRIOT Act
  - Pertains to protection of U.S. critical commercial infrastructure
- Electronic Communications Privacy Act
- Sarbanes–Oxley Act of 2002
  - Pertains to executive responsibilities for accurate portrayal of organizational finances
- Gramm–Leach–Bliley Act
  - Pertains to financial institutions
- Health Insurance Portability and Accountability (HIPPA) Act of 1996
  - Insured privacy issues
- Federal Information Security Management Act (FISMA) 2002
  - Implications for NIST security categorizations and certification and accreditation (C&A)
- National Strategy to Secure Cyberspace
  - Although not a compulsory compliance requirement, this does provide insight into national concern for cyber-security.

Legislative and regulatory compliance to avoid monetary fines and avoid jail time for organizational officers is strong justification for investing in IA. A formal compliance management program identifies all relevant compliance requirements and decomposes the requirements into actionable items. These actionable items are prioritized according to risk, budget, schedule, and effect on overall operations.

13.9.2 Legal Obligations

Legal obligation management includes:

- Contract definition
- Intellectual property management
- Defamation protection against acts *by* others and against unauthorized actions taken *toward* others
- Objectionable materials or speech
- Corporate policy on intellectual property rights and privacy

The IA architect considers legal obligations from various perspectives, including:

- Employees
  - Employment contracts
  - Employee behavior, including defamation and objectionable materials and speech
  - Ownership of end products or parts of products (intellectual property management)
- Customers
  - Reselling agreements (selling products/services to a customer)
  - Advisor agreements (usually in the form of limited liability disclaimers)
    - For example, interpretation of cyber-laws, assessing these laws for customers, and providing recommendations on compliance actions
- Vendors
  - For example, software licensing for Company X use as well as its customers
- Strategic partnerships
  - Co-development projects and intellectual property management

The same compliance management program that addresses legislative and regulatory compliance may also address legal obligations. A contract or an SLA is a compliance obligation. The organization must maintain a list of these compliance obligations and decompose them into terms understandable by management and operations. Compliance management is a justification for IA.

13.10   IA Justification Summary

There are many sound business arguments for the acquisition and ongoing operations of information assurance measures. Given the premise that security can never protect 100 percent of assets against 100 percent of threats 100 percent of the time, risk assessment must determine what assets to protect, and IA must select the right tools for the right job and the right safeguards for the risk level.

To be accepted, IA must be justified in real business terms. There are many real threats the organization needs to recognize and deal with to maintain viable operations. The credibility of the IA professional depends on identifying the real threats and dealing with them in a way that promotes the organization's success.

The following are some useful aphorisms to help deliver the IA message:

- Security is no longer a nice-to-have, it is a legislative mandate.
- Security is a process, not a destination.
- Corporate executives do not buy security; they invest in solutions for business risk management.
- IA's primary goal is to maintain mission integrity within acceptable service levels.

- Optimize stakeholder (e.g., shareholder, constituent, corporate officer) value.
- Security is not to keep people out so much as it is to let the right people in.
- Security is a prudent business enabler.
- Security may be an investment in revenue generation or preserving revenue streams.
- Security is a cost of doing business.
- Business need drives the acquisition of technology; information assurance aligns with technology and business process. Corollary: Security for its own sake is not good business.
- The objective of safeguards is not to protect 100 percent of the assets 100 percent of the time from 100 percent of the threats; rather, the objective of safeguards is to make a successful attack cost prohibitive.
    - The cost of safeguards should be less than the value of assets they protect.
    - The cost of breach should be greater than the probable payoff.
- Consequences add to the cost of an attack: capturing evidence and pursuing prosecution make it painful for adversaries.

Chapter 14

Future of IA and IA²

14.1 Introduction

Douglas N. Dickson in *Using Logical Techniques for Making Better Decisions* states: "1) Few people can intuitively forecast the future even in the short term without building biases of the present; 2) Without a rigid structure to force human beings into more logical frames of mind, they will continue to believe that what exists now will exist in the future." So, how does one think about the future in a credible, disciplined manner that avoids overtones of divination, fortune telling, superstition, or just plain blind luck? A framework of course! In this case, a future vision framework (FVF).

14.2 Objectives

The objectives for this final chapter are:

- Introduce a future vision framework.
- Discuss the future of IA.
- Discuss the future of IA².

By the end of this chapter, you should be able to consider the future in objective terms using the future vision framework. Moreover, you will have some ideas regarding the future of IA and the future of IA².

Figure 14.1   IA divination.

14.3   Future Vision

A serious discussion of the future touches many aspects of higher thought, including natural sciences, mathematical sciences, psychology, and philosophy. Consideration of the future as something humanity has control over is not a globally accepted premise. The concept of progress, that is, the universe, the world, and humanity are actually going somewhere, is largely a Western thought. Many Eastern philosophies are based on determinism or predestiny: the outcome already exists, actions have no effect on consequences, and we merely become aware of the outcome as it unfolds. The idea of control—or lack of it—over one's own environment and destiny has profound psychological implications on how people frame and address problems.

Controls over the future aside, most cultures do have an interest in predicting the future, or at the least thinking about the future and what it may bring. The challenge is to provide a process that avoids the more esoteric (Figure 14.1). The FVF provides a rational, consistent, repeatable process to consider the future. The narrative interweaves IA² applicability in the interest of producing IA architectures that are extensible and agile to accommodate predictable as well as unpredictable future needs of managing business risk. The FVF is not hard science, but is rather a rational guide for focusing thought on the future.

14.3.1   General Bounds

Jay Forrest suggests that the future can be seen like a:*

- Train—Albeit with ups and downs, following a defined track
- Glider—Some individual control, but the winds determine direction and distance with gravity dictating the inevitable
- River raft—Some individual control from left to right bank but still within confines of the banks
- Sailboat—Individual control uses the winds to guide in generally a desired direction, albeit with many tacks and tides causing delays and sidetracks

---

* Paraphrase from *Systems Dynamics, Alternative Futures, and Scenarios*, p. 1.

Personal preference is the sailboat analogy albeit with the addition of rolling swells, crashing waves, perfect breezes, plodding shade clouds passing overhead, and many other variations that make the trip precariously fascinating.

14.3.2 Future Vision Framework

Where does the future begin? Is it a result of today? Yesterday? Everything that has come before? Is the future a nested set of ever-repeating patterns of vast complexity? Considerations can become quite philosophical. However, in the interest of pragmatism, consider the following seven processes through which to consider the future:*

- Drivers—Influences and motivations to action
- Extension—Looking forward from the present
- Extrapolation—Looking forward from the past
- Pendulum—What is old is new again
- Patterns—Discernable coherence from an aggregation of discrete actions
- Connections—Butterfly effect and pinball effect; the subtle and sometimes frantic results from seemingly innocuous actions
- Chaos—An attempt to bound and explain the complexities of random behavior

These processes apply from a variety of perspectives, including industry, organizational, departmental, group, group dynamics, business, and technical. The IA architect applies these processes and perspectives to the situation at hand, whether to predict the future of IA, predict the future of business/technology that may influence IA, or predict the future organizational impact of the current project and IA constraints. The following sections provide an expansion on these future vision processes and provide examples through a look at the future of IA.

14.3.2.1 Drivers

Drivers behind IA architectural concerns include those in the Table 14.1.

14.3.2.2 Extension

The executive boardroom has little interest in information assurance per se; *executives want to manage business risk.* They do not want to buy firewalls and anti-malware software; *executives want to invest in risk management solutions.* As an extension of this requirement, there will be an increase in demand to align and justify IA

---

* Inspired by *Thinking in the Future Tense.*

Table 14.1   IA Architectural Influences

Driver	Description
Economy	Economic competitiveness; employers/ employees; distributed workforce; off-shoring
Ecology	Natural resources and global implications
Legislation	Additional legislative compliance requirements similar to Sarbanes–Oxley, HIPAA
Litigation	Notable court cases surrounding security legislation will provide insight to the corporate concern du jour.
Society	[Intra- | inter-] Group dynamics; increasing gap between have and have-nots adds to the potential for crime
Globalization	Increasing awareness of global dependencies; intercountry and intereconomy dynamics
Competition	Necessity may be the mother of invention; competition is the catalyst for innovation. Is your game changing? Has it changed? Are you still playing the old game? Principle: Playing the old game harder just gets you to the same end faster, tired, and poorer.
Domestic politics	Elections may result in change of people or change of party; new personal and political agendas change the playing ground and perhaps some of the fundamental architectural principles.
World politics	State-sponsored adversaries (e.g., national armies); non-state-sponsored adversaries (e.g., organized crime, terrorists)
Geographic boundaries versus geopolitical boundaries	Physical border versus virtual border
Technology	Advances; rate of change (e.g., Moore's law)

with business operations from an ROI perspective to justify both initial investment and ongoing IA operations. Information assurance extends to business assurance, business functionality assurance, capability assurance, or mission assurance. Align IA with the business functionality it enables or safeguards. Current concerns that by extension will drive future IA activities include compliance management. Legislative compliance now dictates the need for IA (e.g., Sarbanes–Oxley, HIPAA Privacy Rule, HIPAA Final Security Rule, etc.). Look for increasing legislation to protect the personal data and financial transaction data now almost ubiquitously online. Compliance management includes legislation management, litigation management, compliance assessments, gap analysis, remediation planning, policy development, awareness training, tracking, and reporting; look for increasing service offerings and automation in these areas.

14.3.2.3 Extrapolation

One way to look at the future is to extrapolate the future from past events. Extrapolation may take a heuristic path with basis in judgment or a rational path with basis in mathematics/statistics.

The Internet provides the ability to reach local, regional, national, and worldwide customers in manners never before possible. The result is mass competitiveness where economies of scale rule and high-volume business can push margins to razor-thin levels. For example, the independent insurance agent can no longer compete in personal lines (i.e., auto and homeowner's insurance) with regional or national direct writers. The Internet provides the necessary knowledge for the consumer to determine appropriate insurance levels, search engines provide the lowest-cost provider, and there is little or no competitive differentiation other than price.

Technology pushes and continues to push commoditization of many product and service areas, and this will change the independent insurance agent business. This is but one example of many where commoditization will change the face of small-business America that must compete in an ever-encroaching world economy where less expensive labor, and therefore less expensive products/services, is but a mouse-click away.

Such commoditization will drive further investments in technology to reach a broader customer base; competitive differentiators in the market share battle will accommodate consumer security and privacy demands to protect customer information and technology-driven revenue streams.

The time is past when a computer scientist could be an expert across the range of computing technology. The increasing spread of technology and the depth of knowledge required to use a particular technology effectively drive the need for specialization, and so it goes for IA. One specialized discipline in particular is the need for security architects, those who guide the complexities of IA projects and align business drivers and compliance requirements with security services and mechanisms. The focus on highly specialized expertise will drive the need for outsourcing and IA specialist contractors.

14.3.2.4 Pendulum

Business *cycles* are repetitive on varying timescales, *trends* are movements more or less in a distinct direction, and *pendulums* swing from one predictable end to the other. One business pendulum swing is whether to build in-house or buy externally. A more recent pendulum involves managed security service providers (MSSPs) versus performing security in-house. The current complexity of security is causing focus on MSSP solutions. With complexity reduction through COTS and other in-house configurable solutions, the pendulum is likely to swing back to in-house for mid-range companies (less expensive in-house solutions); larger, distributed organizations are likely to stay with outsourcers to take advantage of their cost effectiveness due to economies of scale.

Many MSSPs use *off-shoring* to reduce labor costs for MSS operations. Off-shoring uses foreign workers; *foreign* is a relative term applicable to any country. Consider the risk and cost benefits of trusting the security of your organization to foreign nationals whose best interests may not include your organization's success or the success of your country. The prediction is that growing awareness of this, heightened by security incidents that negatively affect business performance and national interests, will push the security field to the top percentiles of the domestic service industry.

14.3.2.5 Patterns

Going the way of industrial technology, the telephone, and fax machine, computing technology is no longer new and novel, but a business tool to provide support for business operations. IA superimposes operational restrictions on technology to provide secure business operations. There will be an increasing need to formally align technology and security with business operations for many reasons, including compliance management (i.e., align operations with legislative requirements), and to justify technical and security infrastructure as part of ROI justification as both an initial investment and ongoing operations.

14.3.2.6 Connections

Event relationships provide insight into event occurrence, with one event causing or predicting another. If we assume event A has some relation to event B, the following provide some insights regarding the potential relationship between them:

- Causal—The relation between cause and effect; a predictable result or flow from one action or event (A) to the next (B); an occurrence of event A *causes* the occurrence of event B.

- Coincidence—The occurrence of events that chance to happen at the same time but seem to have some connection.
- Correlation—A relation existing between actions or events that occur together in such a way not attributable only to chance. Event A may not cause event B, but other events or circumstances may result in events A and B occurring together.
- Contribution—The occurrence of one event (A) is not causal but contributory to event B; event A is necessary but not sufficient to cause or predict event B.
- Control—Event A has power or control over event B; event A is not the cause of event B, but influences it. Given the absence of event A, event B would still exist, but in a different state or behavior.
- Cultural—The relationship between events A and B is a cultural relationship such that the relationship is specific to a particular culture or society, but not to another.
- Convention—The relationship between events A and B is one of convention or social expectation; there is no cause and effect outside the conventional expectation for the fulfillment of the relationship.
- Conditioned—The cause and effect is not a natural occurrence, but one that is conditioned, e.g., Pavlov's dog (B) salivates at the ring of a bell (A).

IA addresses risks. The process of discerning and understanding risk comes from historical details. Similar unfolding of events today that correspond to previous events may predict a pending security incident. One of the many benefits of a root cause analysis (RCA) is to understand the relationship between events. Does the occurrence of one event indeed cause another or predict another?

14.3.2.7 Chaos

In the future thought framework, there must be consideration to unpredictability. There is always the opportunity for the random factor of a natural event, the unpredictable action of a person or of a group. Random influences inherent in chaos include political events (e.g., election, terrorist event, war), natural events (e.g., tsunami), or an opportunity to exercise personal control or pursue personal advancement of position or cause (e.g., office politics).

The organization cannot control chaos and cannot even influence chaos. However, the organization may control its response to chaotic events. For example, the results of the December 2004 tsunami include increased awareness of such events and the need for coastline safeguards against natural occurrences. The tsunami is the result of an earthquake, the root cause of which is available via seismic research. A seismic early-warning system is one of many natural-risk early-warning services that may feed into a NOC or SOC.

14.3.3 Increase in Decision-Making Complexity

Over the years, competition has grown from down the street, to across town, to regional, to national, and now to global. As implications of a world market with virtual Internet storefronts continue to emerge, decision-making factors grow exponentially in volume, complexity, and contradiction. Organizations face conundrums, oxymorons, and paradoxes on a daily basis. Securing intellectual property in the organization protects jobs and gross national product (GNP) in a cutthroat world economy where any opportunity for competitive advantage is exploited. Customer information, intellectual property, R&D data, finances, accounting transactions, etc., are all online. An Internet connection implies a virtual doorway for the world to walk through and look around the corporate information repositories. As the Internet continues to provide ease of market entry for world competitors, local economies will grow to depend on the success of these economic ventures. Increased competitiveness will drive increasing sophistication of attack methods, which will in turn drive the need for IA advances. Welcome to the new battleground of cyberspace where virtual munitions have very real economic affects—IA is here to stay.

14.3.4 Systems Dynamics

Consider the effects of the future on technology and information assurance versus effects of technology and information assurance on the future—what comes first, the chicken or the egg? Enter systems thinking and the discipline of systems dynamics and dynamic feedback loops, where causes produce effects that in turn influence or become causes in complex arrays of recursive loops. Many factors go into a systems dynamics model for predicting the future, including:

- Awareness factor—Any model may only reflect known constants and variables. Even allowing for a random, unexpected event includes bounds on awareness with respect to the type of event, the time of occurrence, the duration, and impact.
- Control factor—This is the organization's scope of control over inputs to organizational operations; many inputs will happen and the organization has no control.
- Influence factor—Often a lack of control may not imply a lack of influence. Probability looks at hard numbers from historical experience (empirical and vicarious) or speculative future.
- Response factor—In the absence of control or influence, prepare appropriate contingent responses. An organization cannot stop a hurricane from hitting its main operation facility, but it can control how it responds to a hurricane hitting through continuity and contingency planning.

- Certainty factor—Or conversely, the uncertainty factor is a heuristic for dealing with the fact that things do not always happen as expected.
- Confidence factor—A mathematical/statistical representation of certainty.

Table 14.2 presents IA² application of systems dynamics factors.

Figure 14.2 provides an example of the systems dynamics of risk using a stock and flow model. Each box represents a stock, something that may accumulate or reduce. The double arrows represent flows in and out of the stocks. The single arrows identify influences on the flows. As shown, the threat means, method, motivation, and mission influence the flow of new threats into threat space. Actions influence what is considered a priority risk. Consequences of those actions affect the flow of viable threats, e.g., a consequence of reprisal or jail time will affect a threat's actions. Risk analysis and determination of certainty and confidence levels affect the flow of new priority risks. Priority risks receive IA budget according to IA budget priorities. This method of modeling considers the dynamic relationship of enterprise entities, actors, and actions. The model in the figure is but a partial model of the overall enterprise dynamics of risk. IA² provides a lexicon and foundational concepts to expand on the use of systems dynamics as a modeling tool for IA and predicting the application of IA within the enterprise.

Table 14.2   Systems Dynamics Factors

Factor	IA Application
Awareness factor	Awareness is the first step to specific accommodation; otherwise, provide contingency plans and a default plan to cover unknowns.
Control factor	If the organization can control an event, provide a plan.
Influence factor	If the organization cannot control an event, consider if it can influence the event or the causes. If so, provide a plan.
Response factor	If the organization cannot control or influence the event, it can at least control its response to it.
Probability factor	An attempt at hard representation of reality that takes on the form of probability calculations; conditional probability (the Bayesian probability of X given Y); and compound conditional probability (probability of X given Y and Z)
Certainty factor	Soft heuristic for the organization to determine the likelihood of an event; this is more akin to gut feel.
Confidence factor	Hard statistic in determining the likelihood of an event; careful not to quantify a gut feel solely to add statistical credibility

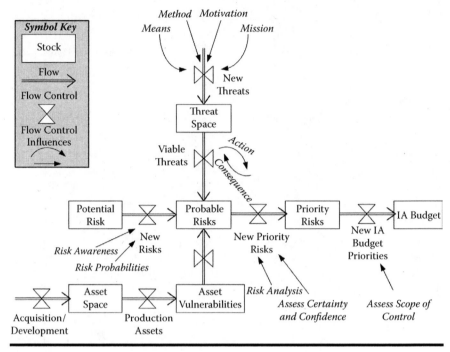

Figure 14.2 Systems dynamics of risk.

14.3.5 Constants and Variables

Complexity management is a major constraint in considering the future, especially in terms of architecture. Architecture produces tangible results that quickly show the accuracy of future considerations. Distinguishing constants and variables promotes complexity reduction. Constants include laws of physics, laws of nature (though stretchable with genetic engineering), human psychology, and human behavior, the latter falling into predictable patterns. Variables include specific technical mechanisms that may be popular or useful today, but are replaced quickly with new developments.

14.3.6 Summary of IA Future Vision

Any prediction has a degree of uncertainty from the start, as Figure 14.3 shows. Uncertainty increases exponentially as time increases. There is a tremendous amount of money spent on attempting to minimize uncertainty. We pay a fortune to professional investment managers because they must have more accurate methods to predict the financial performance of companies and markets—don't they? Governments invest under the assumption that more knowledge equals better decisions; therefore, let us have bigger, better, faster networks to exchange information.

Does a faster exchange of information really decrease uncertainty? Because there is no way to eliminate uncertainty, the best we can hope for is to manage our own biases and fallibilities. This is no small feat and well worth pursuing, as it is in the realm of our personal control and influence. Nonetheless, there is always the external random factor that we have no control over and no way of predicting—despite the claims of media 20/20 hindsight.

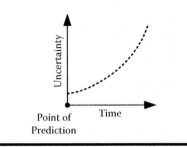

Figure 14.3 Prediction uncertainty over time.

At best, a framework for future thought may provide insight into where current circumstances are leading, although certainty decreases as time increases from the point of prediction. The best approach is to build a modular, agile framework where specifics come and go in the larger, more constant architectural abstraction. At its core, architecture considers the wants and needs of the user. Architecture also attempts to be flexible, agile, and adaptable. A future thought framework allows architects to consider the future in an objective manner. Is it perfect? No. Is it useful? Yes, in the right context, and taken with salt of varying grain sizes.

Whatever the future holds, our ability to predict that which we can, and cope with that which we cannot, finds foundation in the richness of philosophy. C. S. Lewis defines chronological snobbery as the uncritical acceptance of the intellectual climate of our own age and the assumption that whatever has gone out of date is on that count discredited. The knowledge of our time is not the best by exclusive virtue of merely belonging to our time. Patterns abound in nature, human activity, individual psychology, group dynamics, organizational behavior, political behavior, and technology. The cycles of repetition and the trigger events for pattern changes are difficult to identify, but not impossible—look far enough in the past and you find a point that is today; look a little ahead of that point, and perhaps you find tomorrow.

Much sound thought goes into analyzing future events. Actuarial mathematics support insurance loss predictions and thus determine premiums. Astronomy predicts the position of planets through past orbital observances. Most predictive methods are imperfect to one degree or another, and all are subject to unforeseen influences. Likewise, looking forward in business, technology, and information assurance has great benefits for planning and designing effective solutions. Developing a viable framework in which to consider the future helps, but nothing provides definite answers. Therefore, avoid analysis paralysis. Consider the information at hand, separate fact from speculation, determine confidence level in facts, identify constraints, clearly state assumptions, and go for it; an educated jump in partial light beats a reflexive leap in the dark.

14.4   The Future of IA

Table 14.3 provides a summary of how to consider IA in context of the FVF. Following the table are elaborations on the future of IA.

Drivers for the IA future find root in business need. The traditional and mostly current technical environment is point-to-point solutions that require specific connectivity between users and applications (e.g., client/server). Business drivers demand an environment in which old applications (legacy) and new applications can communicate. Indeed, not only communicate, but also find each other without user or administrator intervention. IA solutions today address this point-to-point environment. As the concept of services evolves into real business solutions, the paradigm of point to point (one to one) is replaced with a paradigm of many to many. Service-oriented architecture (SOA) provides a design philosophy for Web services. In an SOA environment, a new service advertises itself to a service registry. A service request looks at the service registry and finds a service provider to fulfill the request. The service requestor does not necessarily know what service provider fulfills the request, and does not really care so long as the request is fulfilled within an acceptable schedule and budget and provides satisfactory quality. Moreover, a service requestor may advertise the kinds of services it wants. A new service provider may begin sending information to the requestor without the requestor knowing that a new service even exists.

SOA, or more generically the concept of Web services, provides an environment in which service providers and service requestors come and go. This service environment, the services themselves, and service consumers provide a new operating paradigm and a whole new set of challenges for IA. IA services and mechanisms that adequately address this new paradigm will continue to emerge in coming years.

The theme of this book is the need for more formality behind IA and IA justification. Additional research in enterprise architecture, enterprise systems engineering, systems engineering, and other enterprise perspective tools will integrate IA as part of the enterprise, operations, and workflow. IA is still largely an after-the-fact bolt-on today; the future holds more integration of IA as part of doing business. Business will regard firewalls and anti-malware as it does door locks. You do not think much about them after you use them, and you establish the state according to need—open up in the morning and lock up at night.

There is an increasing desire for situational awareness that provides a real-time or near-real-time snapshot of organizational risk environment and security posture addressing that risk. With increases in situational awareness, there will be the need for dynamic adjustment to security posture according to changes in the risk environment. For example, an increase in U.S. terrorist threat level may modify the risk environment for all or part of the U.S. critical infrastructure. Situational awareness services/mechanisms will evaluate the potential organizational impact and provide suggestions for manual adjustment (or automatically adjust) the respective security posture to accommodate the new risks.

Table 14.3   Future Vision of IA

FVF	Description	IA Future
Drivers	Influences and motivations to action	Global economy; virtual assets and enterprise wealth (e.g., intellectual property, knowledge); new technologies in support of business demands introduce new risks (e.g., Web services). Legislative and regulatory complexities to protect information and information technology. Emerging technologies (e.g., Web services).
Extension	Looking forward from the present	The $100 laptop (http://laptop.media.mit.edu/); E-commerce
Extrapolation	Looking forward from the past	Internet, relatively unknown to pervasive inside 20 years; implications of this medium in education, world politics, global economy
Pendulum	What is old is new again	Build versus buy; in-house versus outsource
Patterns	Discernable coherence from an aggregation of discrete actions	Patterns in a threat space that includes solitary hackers, non-state-sponsored adversaries, and state-sponsored adversaries. A pattern of organizational loss produces increases in cyber-legislation.
Connections	Butterfly effect and pinball effect; the subtle and sometimes frantic results from seemingly innocuous actions	Discerning connections, influences, relationships, and implications via systems thinking and modeling via systems dynamics
Chaos	An attempt to bound and explain the complexities of random behavior	There is always a random factor; you cannot predict it, you should not ignore it, but you can expect it and prepare a response.

Many information systems provide for user identification and assigning of users to groups. Another way to think of groups is not in terms of individuals but in terms of roles. Roles have certain privileges by default, usually tied to job responsibilities. The organization defines a finite number of roles, and the roles and privileges are managed and enforced according to policy. Individual users may be associated with roles without reframing their identities.

Attribute management provides for attributes (characteristics) and attribute values for a person or entity. Attributes provide a more dynamic method of privilege management with regard to awareness (know something exists), access, read, write/ modify, features for use, etc.

Metadata is a subset of attributes. Attributes apply to people, entities (information technology), and information (data). Metadata provides data about the data. Metadata may include the creator of the data, the date and time created, relevant cross-indexing of the data, source of the data, etc. The Dublin Core Metadata Initiative (http://dublincore.org/) is one effort to develop metadata standards for online information. IA concerns with metadata include the accuracy of the metadata: Is it trustworthy, from a trusted source, passed through trusted hands to get to the consumer of the metadata? Does the metadata indeed belong to the data? Has the metadata been modified in transit? Prior to transit or otherwise, has the integrity of the metadata-to-data relationship been compromised? Look for emerging work in the cryptobinding of metadata that ensures the confidentiality, integrity, and nonreputable association of metadata with the data to which it belongs.

An *avatar* is a virtual representation of a person. A person uses an avatar in virtual worlds to interact with other avatars representing other people. Virtual worlds are simulated online environments that avatars may inhabit and live. The duration of the online environment may be as long as a game (a few minutes or few hours), or it may persist and allow interaction for months and years. Virtual worlds include fantasy gaming as well as serious games that simulate real-life situations and promote real-time interactions, like an education or social environment. IA issues already include protecting online identities, online identity theft, and adjudication between game players and game administrators when adverse decisions affect an online persona. Moreover, virtual worlds add the ever-blurring distinction between reality and entertainment. There are questions of how much personal details (and perhaps professional details) enter the online environment.

Look for an emerging realization of the changing face of war. There are difficult questions to ask with regard to war. What defines war? What defines a warrior? What defines a combatant? Who and what are the targets of war? The changing face of war includes a changing understanding of the conventions of war, the purpose of war, the manifestation of war, and the motivation for war.

Despite such questions, wars are real and affect lives and livelihoods. Actually, livelihood, the means of subsistence, is the greatest motivation for war. Famine in one region incites desire for another's bounty. If trade does not work, then taking by force will. The traditional attack by a country's military is a means to an end, where that end is economic advancement. Attacking a country's infrastructure has economic impact. Attacking a country's commerce has economic impact. Attacking perceptions and instilling fear in the population has economic impact. The IA architect considers organizational exposure in light of threat space interest in the organization as an objective of war and as an objective of economic interest.

Cyber-warfare is not exclusively a military activity. There is no need to confront a strong military when the same economic objective can be accomplished by attacking the economic entity directly. Who is the enemy? A state-sponsored combatant in uniform and with a gun? A non-state-sponsored terrorist? An independent cyber-mercenary with a PhD in computer science? Your competition in the marketplace? A buck-toothed antisocial teenager with nothing better to do than scope out weaknesses in corporate networks? Is it one enemy? Are they all enemies? The future of IA considers the changing face of the threat space, including threat means, methods, motivations, and missions.

The threat space is constantly evolving. The sophistication of cyber-attacks is increasing while the sophistication level of the cyber-attackers themselves is not. Readily available attack tools on the Internet are configurable and adaptable to take advantage of new vulnerabilities. There is the possibility (dare we say probability) of a cyber-Pearl Harbor where the U.S. economy (not exclusively the military) suffers overwhelming attack completely by surprise. This will likely come from many different directions in many different forms with very little direct connection or attribution to the actual source.

14.5   The Future of IA²

Table 14.4 provides a summary of how to consider IA² in context of the FVF. Following the table are elaborations on the future of IA².

The future of IA² includes refinement of the IA² Framework and IA² Process. These refinements will occur as practical application of IA² provides additional insights. There will be substantial expansion on the IA quantification, especially in modeling IA enterprise dynamics. There will also be more formal alignment of IA² constructs with the disciplines of systems engineering and enterprise systems engineering.

Situational awareness is a challenge for any operation. Relative to current objectives, situational awareness discerns what the current circumstances are, who the players are, who is in motion, and what they are doing. Situation awareness asks: Are we making progress toward objectives, are operations effective, are operations secure? Situational awareness applies to commercial organizations, government organizations, and the military. Situational awareness applies to network operations as well as IA operations. IA² provides frameworks within which to define situation awareness attributes, acceptable operation levels, warning thresholds, and business context.

Table 14.4   Future Vision of IA²

FVF	Description	IA Future
Drivers	Influences and motivations to action	The complexity of risk management and the business expense of IA are strong influences on the continual refinement of IA as a discipline for risk management.
Extension	Looking forward from the present	The current IA provides an IA framework, an IA process, and many supporting frameworks. These are foundational to defining areas of further research in IA quantification and IA modeling.
Extrapolation	Looking forward from the past	The past of IA resides in enterprise architecture and the need to formalize IA in context of an enterprise architecture. IA will evolve as EA evolves in support of business activity, aligning technology with business drivers, and aligning IA with business risk.
Pendulum	What is old is new again	Einstein looked at Hume's philosophy of epistemology for opinions/insight while formulating his relativity theories. Many IA insights find root in classical philosophy. Philosophies that attempt to build a foundation on principles with the application of those principles left up to the IA architect.
Patterns	Discernable coherence from an aggregation of discrete actions	IA provides a lexicon and reference as a way forward to define methods for identifying threat patterns and how to address those patterns in risk management.

Table 14.4 Future Vision of IA² (Continued)

FVF	Description	IA Future
Connections	Butterfly effect and pinball effect; the subtle and sometimes frantic results from seemingly innocuous actions	IA may assist to distinguish correlations in emerging events. The nature of these correlations provides insight in how to address the trigger event (e.g., cause) and the resulting event (e.g., effect). Models will emerge to represent complex behavior for IA as a method to reduce business risk. Models that include direct cause and effect as well as indirect and more subtle relationships of trigger events and resulting events, e.g., systems dynamics models.
Chaos	An attempt to bound and explain the complexities of random behavior	IA provides a foundation to develop more sophisticated uncertainty management models to anticipate and accommodate the random factor of events. The objective will not be uncertainty elimination (this is unrealistic), but rather heightened awareness of issues for contingency planning to manage uncertainty.

Bayesian probability is a mathematical concept that applies a *degree of belief* factor to the probability calculations. This is an overlap with the concept of managing uncertainty, where Bayesian probability provides a variable with which to insert uncertainty (or certainty) into a probability calculation. The use of Bayesian probability will contribute to the modeling of risk and how to address risk. These formal risk models will use the IA² Frameworks to define the problem space as well as to formulate solution options.

Operations research (OR) is a mathematical tool to assist in generating optimal solutions to complex problems. OR is a decision support tool for many complex business problems. It focuses on specific elements of the problem at a static point in time; that is, OR does not factor in time delays inherent in a complex system.

Systems dynamics is a methodology for studying complex feedback systems where the results of one process (A) affect another process (B) that is also affected by processes C and D, and then the results of process B affect process E, which in turn affects process A. The results of process E take time to reach process A, but as they do the new results of process A kick off another set of dynamic feedback.

Studying snapshots of A, B, C, D, and E over time provides a systemic picture of their relationships and the eventual outcome of the system.

IA^2 provides a foundation with which to define and understand systems dynamics models of risk. A generic representation of this type of model is the mission integrity boundary model in chapter 1. The quantification of IA operations provides thresholds (upper and lower limits) that define mission integrity. IA systems dynamics models may show the effects of an evolving threat space, status of IA services and mechanisms, and organizational risk posture on mission integrity. The model will show effects over time with other aspects feeding a dynamic threat space, including random factors and factors representing uncertainty (e.g., Bayesian probability).

A practical theme is the need to align IA with business drivers. This alignment needs to extend from operations to the core drivers of executive decision making, which are the income statement and the balance sheet. The IA^2 Framework provides an IA^2 LoS that enables the aligning of IA operations to business line items and shows direct relationships of IA to financial statements and financial ratios. It is possible to extend this modeling concept to real-time, which shows the effects of fluctuating risk levels on the financial posture of the organization.

The objectives of IA^2 are to provide a lexicon and a set of standards and frameworks to identify, enumerate, articulate, and address business risk. This foundation provides the ability to pursue many nuances of IA, including quantification and business modeling. Future work on IA^2 includes quantification models for situational awareness, financial models that align IA with income statement and balance sheet, a maturity model to gauge the effectiveness of the organization's IA posture, systems dynamics models of risk, and the Bayesian representation of risk in terms of conditional probabilities and compound conditional probabilities. IA^2 provides an IA^2 Framework, IA^2 Process, and a useful set of frameworks to think about IA in an enterprise context.

Norman Cousins states, "Wisdom is the anticipation of consequences." Architecture is applied wisdom. IA architecture is wisdom applied to the security of information and information technology to maintain mission integrity.

Appendix A: IA² Process Template

IA² Process Template
DD Month CCYY

Introduction

The IA² Process (IA² P) (Figure A.1) guides the use of the IA² Framework. This IA² P template provides you with a guide to apply IA² P.

Intent

Define what the solution is and what it is for—a statement of intent defines what it is for as well as what it is. Describe the intent of the IA² P. The intent may be to augment an enterprise architecture, a systems engineering focus, systems development, or requirements engineering. Table A.1 provides a template to make notes in context of enterprise dynamics; Table A.2 provides a template in context of the IA² views. Appendix B provides additional templates for IA² views that may help you during application of the IA² Process. Determine what works best for the situation at hand. The templates provide a guide to capture details. Following use of the templates to gather details, write a narrative of the intent. This narrative may transfer to the official enterprise architecture documents.

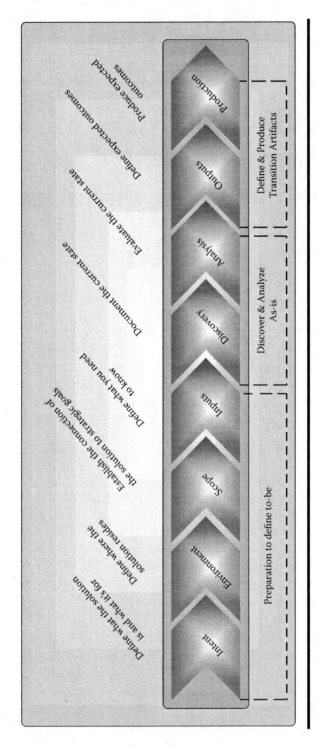

Figure A.1 IA² Process.

Table A.1 Enterprise Dynamics: Intent Details

Enterprise Dynamics Category	What the Solution Is	What the Solution Is for	Comments
Entities			
Actors			
Actions			

Table A.2 IA² F Views: Intent Details

IA² F Views	What the Solution Is	What the Solution Is for	Comments
People			
Policy			
Business process			
Systems and applications			
Data/information			
Infrastructure			

Intent Narrative

TBD

Environment

Define where the solution resides. Tables A.3 and A.4 provide alternative templates to identify the components of the environment. For the sake of simplicity, the template uses the IA² F views for the remainder of the IA² Process. Review Appendix B for other applicable templates and use according to your judgment.

Table A.3   Environment Details

Category	Details	Comments
Geography		
Organization		
Business		
Technical		

Table A.4   IA² F Views: Environment Details

IA² F Views	Details	Comments
People		
Policy		
Business process		
Systems and applications		
Data/information		
Infrastructure		

Environment Narrative

TBD

Scope

Establish the connection of the solution to strategic goals.

Table A.5   IA² F Views: Scope Details

IA² F Views	Details	Comments
People		
Policy		
Business process		
Systems and applications		
Data/information		
Infrastructure		

Scope Narrative

TBD

Inputs

Define what you need to know.

Table A.6   IA² F Views: Input Details

IA² F Views	Details	Comments
People		
Policy		
Business process		
Systems and applications		
Data/information		
Infrastructure		

Inputs Narrative

TBD

Discovery

Document the current state.

Table A.7   IA² F Views: Discovery Details

IA² F Views	Details	Comments
People		
Policy		
Business process		
Systems and applications		
Data/information		
Infrastructure		

Discovery Narrative

TBD

Analysis

Evaluate the current state.

Table A.8   IA² F Views: Analysis Details

IA² F Views	Details	Comments
People		
Policy		
Business process		
Systems and applications		
Data/information		
Infrastructure		

Analysis Narrative

TBD

Outputs

Define expected outcomes.

Table A.9   IA² F Views: Output Details

IA² F Views	Details	Comments
People		
Policy		
Business process		
Systems and applications		
Data/information		
Infrastructure		

Outputs Narrative

TBD

Production

Produce expected outcomes.

Table A.10   IA² F Views: Production Details

IA² F Views	Details	Comments
People		
Policy		
Business process		
Systems and applications		
Data/information		
Infrastructure		

Production Narrative

TBD

Summary and Conclusion

TBD

Appendix B:
Templates of IA² F Views

Table B.1 provides a template to capture details for the 6 IA² views by the 9 IA core principles, or 54 granular views of IA. This table may capture insights with regard to governance, management, building, operations, use, and leadership (the Organizational Context Framework [OCF]). If the table is applied to all six layers in the OCF, there will 324 views of IA with an organizational context. One instance of the table may capture governance insights with regard to compliance requirements and strategic objectives. Another instance of the table may capture management insights that convert strategic objectives to strategic plans, tactical objectives, and tactical plans. Are 324 views too many? A better question for you, the IA architect, is how many views are enough to satisfy the needs of the situation?

The other tables provide templates for variations on IA² F views. Which apply? You know your situation best. This book provides many tools to draw upon. The use and application of the tools is situation dependent. The details from these tables provide input to the application of the IA² Process of defining intent for the IA (e.g., governance, strategic objectives); defining the environment for the IA application (e.g., physical infrastructure, safety and comfort of people); and defining the scope (e.g., business processes and the systems and applications that support them). Define however many views are necessary to identify the risks, enumerate the risks, articulate the risks, and address those risks.

Use of these tables is *not* a massive fill-in-the-blank exercise. Use these tables as a guide to think about the situation in smaller parts, from various perspectives, and in various contexts. Use these tables to discern the right questions about risk, capture the answers, articulate options, and determine how to convey recommendations in terms that will resonate with the audience.

Table B.1   IA² Views by IA Core Principles

IA² View →/IA Core Principle	People	Policy	Process	Systems and Applications	Data/Information	Infrastructure
Confidentiality						
Integrity						
Availability						
Possession						
Authenticity						
Utility						
Nonrepudiation						
Authorized use						
Privacy						

Table B.2   IA² Views by Reality Check Framework

IA² View →/RCF Element	People	Policy	Process	Systems and Applications	Data/Information	Infrastructure
Who						
What						
Why						
When						
Where						
How						

Table B.3 IA² Views by Organizational Context Framework

IA² View →/OCF Element	People	Policy	Process	Systems and Applications	Data/Information	Infrastructure
Governance						
Management						
Builders						
Operations						
Users						
Leaders						

Table B.4   IA² Views by ELCM Phase

IA² View →/ ELCM Phase	People	Policy	Process	Systems and Applications	Data/Information	Infrastructure
Concept						
Architect						
Engineer						
Acquire/develop						
Implement						
Test						
Deploy						
Train						
O&M						
Retire						

Table B.5   IA² Views by the IA² LoS Elements

IA² View →/IA² LoS Elements	People	Policy	Process	Systems and Applications	Data/Information	Infrastructure
Business requirements						
IA architecture						
IA CONOPS						
IA PfM[a]						
IA enterprise systems engineering						
IA design						
IA services						
IA mechanisms						
Vendor selection						
Product selection						
Implementation						
O&M						

[a] Portfolio management (PfM).

Table B.6   IA² Views by the ECF Elements

IA² View →/ECF Elements	People	Policy	Process	Systems and Applications	Data/Information	Infrastructure
Business function						
Entity						
System						
Subsystem						
Component						
Subcomponent						
Assembly						
Subassembly						
Action						
Business process						

Continued

Table B.6 IA² Views by the ECF Elements (Continued)

IA² View →/ECF Elements	People	Policy	Process	Systems and Applications	Data/Information	Infrastructure
Workflow						
Process						
Task						
Kinetic task						
Cognitive task						
Automated task						
Actor						
Collectives						
Person						
Behavior						
Conscious						
Unconscious						

Table B.7 IA² Views by Risk Management

IA² View →/Risk Management Elements	People	Policy	Process	Systems and Applications	Data/Information	Infrastructure
Accept/ignore						
Share						
Transfer						
Mitigate						

Appendix C: IA Quantification Process Template

IA Quantification Process (IAQP) Template
DD Month CCYY

Introduction

There is much activity in industry to quantify results with metrics and measures. The challenge is how to do so at all, and then how to do so accurately such that results actually represent reality and have useful business meaning. The IAQP provides a methodology to quantify IA with the intent of showing useful business meaning to IA. The IAQP consists of the following steps: generate a *narrative* of the problem, identify *parameters* from the narrative, identify the metrics and measures of the parameters through *quantification*, describe how to *discover* the measures, describe through *analysis* what to do with the measures, describe how to *report* the findings, and, lastly, describe how to provide *feedback* to the organization for an enterprise benefit from the quantification process.

For purposes of the example in the IAQP template, the Organizational Context Framework presents *governance, management, builders, operations, use,* and *leaders*. From the perspective of creating a solution, governance drives management, management provides direction to builders, builders create and turn over to operations, and operations provides for user demands. From the perspective of ongoing operations and showing business value, users provide feedback to operations, operations provides reports to management, and management provides reports to governance. IAQP helps discern what metrics and measures to capture from users that provide meaningful operational feedback in terms of *does operations work at all, does it work effectively,* and *does it work securely*. Operations refines user input to generate reports

405

to management in terms of how operational performance contributes to meeting tactical objectives that align with strategic plans. Management refines operations input to generate reports to the executive level (governance) in terms of meeting strategic objectives.

Narrative

Provide a narrative of the problem. If necessary, use the problem assertion document (appendix I) to assist in identifying and articulating the problem narrative. The narrative will evolve in an iterative process as understanding of the situation at hand translates into better articulation. Do not wait to understand the situation before attempting to generate a narrative; more often than not, articulating the situation will help you to understand it.

Example Narrative

Techno Wonder Widgets, Inc. is subject to Sarbanes–Oxley Act of 2002 (SOX). How do we track the effectiveness of a security awareness and training program as part of an overall SOX compliance program? *Note*: The problem narrative below uses X to represent all possible numeric values. The actual values come later.

Techno Wonder Widgets, Inc. desires to have SOX *awareness* level (AL) for X% of the enterprise population. An additional objective is for X% of the population to have an acceptable level of *understanding* of SOX (UL).

There is an enterprise population (EP) of X distributed among X sites (S). Enterprise population consists of X direct employees (E) and X contractors (C). X% of the enterprise population have computer access (CA) on a regular basis. The potential mediums for distributing awareness and training material include e-mail, live training, printed material, video training, and audio. An effective awareness program provides at least X opportunities to see and hear the message (M) within an X month timeframe (TF).

Commentary: *The generation of the above narrative occurred in multiple iterations. The first iteration did not include the abbreviations of potential parameters. The point is, IAQP is an iterative process.*

Parameters

Use the frameworks described in this book to assist in identifying key entities in the narrative. Consider what parameters may represent characteristics or states of the key entities. Enterprise dynamics and Enterprise Context Framework (ECF) present *entities*, *actors*, and *actions*. Use these as a potential guide to identify parameters. Then consider each parameter's *relevant* characteristics and states. A characteristic is something about the parameter that may be useful to know. A state describes the various postures for each characteristic.

Focus on identifying the parameters, characteristics, and states in this step. The quantification step (the next step) determines the values that represent the posture of the entity by way of its characteristics and states.

Table C.1 Parameters and Their Characteristics and States

Parameter	Characteristics	States	Comments
Entities			
Actors			
Actions			

Table C.2 Parameters and Their Characteristics and States (Example)

Parameter	Characteristics or Components	States	Comments
Entities			
Computers	NA	NA	TBD
Video terminals (e.g., televisions)	NA	NA	TBD
Sites	NA	NA	TBD
Actors			
Enterprise population (EP)	Employee	Unaware, aware, lack of understanding, understanding[a]; computer access	Awareness level (AL), understanding level (UL), CA
EP	Contractor	Unaware, aware, lack of understanding, understanding; computer access	Awareness level (AL), understanding Level (UL), CA
Actions			
Disseminate awareness and training material.	NA	NA	TBD
View awareness and training material.	NA	NA	TBD
Study and internalize training material (understanding).	NA	NA	TBD
Track awareness (measure).	NA	NA	TBD
Track understanding (measure).	NA	NA	TBD

Table C.2   Parameters and Their Characteristics and States (Example) (Continued)

Parameter	Characteristics or Components	States	Comments
IA aspects			
AL	Target	NA	Define the target AL.
	Actual	NA	Measure the EP quantity with some awareness level; measure the number of awareness encounters for the given timeframe (TF).
UL	Target	NA	Define the target UL.
	Actual	NA	Measure the EP quantity with some understanding level; measure the level of understanding for each EP member.
Other			
TF	NA	NA	Define timeframe.

[a] An employee starts out as unaware; an awareness video takes him from a state of unaware to a state of being aware. Now he is aware, he still may lack understanding. Additional training takes him from a state of lack of understanding to a state of understanding.

Quantification

Table C.3 presents all relevant parameters and their respective metric and measure. *Note*: A metric is a standard of measure (e.g., meters), and a measure is an amount; e.g., there are 1,000 meters in 1 kilometer. The metrics are meters and kilometers, the measures are 1,000 and 1, respectively.

Table C.3　Parameter Quantification

Parameter	Metric	Measure	Comments

Table C.4　Parameter Quantification (Example)

Parameter	Metric	Measure	Comments
EP	Qty	50,000	There are 50,000 total employees.
E	Qty	45,000	45,000 are direct employees.
C	Qty	5,000	5,000 are contractor employees; all contractors have access to Techno Wonder Widgets facilities on a regular basis (not less than weekly) as part of their regular duties.
S	Qty	125+	125 actual organizational sites; plus a large number of customer sites where most people work full-time
CA	Percentage	85%	Corollary: 15% of EPs do not have regular access to a computer.
M	Qty	3	3 SOX awareness/training message encounters
TF	Months	12	12-month timeframe
AL	Qty/%		This value requires discovery.
UL	Qty/%		This value requires discovery.

Key Parameters

Key parameters are those that represent the details necessary to report on the objective as stated in the narrative. The key parameters in the example are awareness level and understanding level. Awareness level is measured as the number of employee and contractor awareness message encounters within a 12-month period. The understanding level is measured as a retention level of awareness details as presented in the awareness messages. Measuring understanding requires a survey or quiz to discern the retention level.

Discovery

In the discovery section, describe how to obtain the measures for each key parameter. The measure in the quantification table (Table C.5) represents the totals for the enterprise; the discovery method is how to obtain measures of key parameters (actuals) to compare against these totals. For example, discovery is how to obtain the quantity of people within the enterprise population that are aware of the new security policy. That quantity compared to the total enterprise population (EP) yields the percentage of the EP aware of the new security policy.

Table C.5   Parameter Quantification

Parameter	Source	Discovery Method

Example

The key parameters are awareness level (AL) and understanding level (UL). AL is the number of message encounters. How is the message encountered? Given there are 50,000 people to track, live training is cost prohibitive. Printed material is also cost prohibitive given cost of printing and mailing via USPS.* All employees and contractors have an e-mail address, and most by far use e-mail on a regular basis (multiple times per week). All employees have a corporate intranet account for

---

* United States Postal Service.

access to organizational news, documents, and other information as appropriate to access permissions.

The awareness and training campaign consists of sending out e-mail notification to all employees regarding an online awareness and training program. This program will take place in four quarterly installments throughout the next 12 months.

Table C.6 Parameter Quantification (Example)

Parameter	Source	Discovery Method
AL	E-mail logs, training Web site logs	Track number of people who receive e-mail; track return receipts; track access to online awareness and training program (require use of employee accounts to access)
UL	Quiz/survey results database or reports	Each quarterly awareness and training encounter presents a short quiz (3 questions) that asks questions regarding the details; track correct responses. The total UL correct answers is (3 questions (50,000 employees) or 150,000 as the maximum UL.

Analysis

Describe how to analyze the measures for each parameter. Also, describe the holistic consideration of all the parameters together.

Table C.7 Analysis

Parameter	Target measure	Timeframe	Analysis

Example

Table C.8   Analysis (Example)

Parameter	Target Measure	Timeframe	Analysis
AL	100%	Initial awareness campaign + 12 months, or 1 September 2008	Track quantity and percentage of EP per quarter.
UL	90%+	Ditto	Track quantity and percentage of EP per quarter.

Report

Describe how to report the analysis results. Describe if reports go to the executive/ governance level, management level, or operations level. Each will have a different level of detail and a different focus for the message. Executive and governance reports focus on business value of awareness and understanding. Management reports show if they have to address issues with their subordinates reading e-mail and complying with organizational requests. Operations show if the tactical execution of the awareness and training endeavor was successful.

Example

The example provides a mockup of the final results for awareness level (AL) and understanding level (UL). Figure C.1 provides a graph of the final AL results, and Figure C.2 provides a graph of the final UL results.

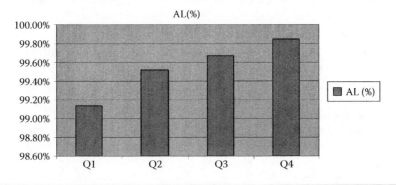

Figure C.1   Mockup of AL%.

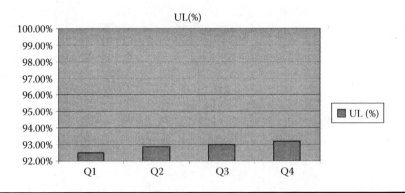

Figure C.2   Mockup of UL%.

Table C.9   Mockup of Final Results

AL	50,000	49,567	49,758	49,834	49,923
AL (%)		99.13%	99.52%	99.67%	99.85%
UL	150,000	138,788	139,322	139,535	139,784
UL (%)		92.53%	92.88%	93.02%	93.19%

Feedback

The organizational feedback is also relative to the reporting level (governance, management, or operations). *Executives* focus on the bottom line and look to affect balance sheet and income statement line items with investments in compliance management, as well as awareness and training to achieve organizational compliance. *Management* focuses on performance and wants to measure personnel carrying out strategic plans and meeting tactical objectives. In this example, the organizational goals include awareness and understanding of how to be compliant with SOX. *Operations'* focus is on the tactical execution of making employees aware and understand in a cost-effective manner. Lessons for operations include determining the effectiveness of e-mail and Web-based training versus some other method.

So, what is the focus for improvement? Well, that depends on what the objective is. Moreover, it depends on what you really find during the IAQP and during the discovery and analysis process.

Lastly, review the details of the IAQP with respect to final results and consider ways to improve the IAQP itself.

Appendix D: Security Management Program Framework

National Institute of Standards and Technology (NIST) standards are available free of charge at www.nist.gov; the NIST security standards are available at csrc.nist.gov. The information herein does not intend to duplicate the excellent work of these standards, but rather use these standards as a basis to develop organizational-specific tools to use during the planning and execution of a security management program (SMP). The same organizational-specific tools may find foundation in the International Standards Organization (ISO) security standards (e.g., ISO 27002 [formerly ISO 17799]) or other industry security standards. The book *How to Achieve ISO 27001 Certification—An Example of Compliance Management* by Sigurjon Thor Arnason and Keith D. Willett introduces the concept of an SMP framework. This book uses the same concept, but uses NIST SP 800-53 as a basis for the SMP framework.

Table D.2 displays an SMP framework that uses NIST SP 800-53, *Recommended Security Controls for Federal Information Systems*, as a basis. The abbreviations in the "Control Reference" column are those used in the NIST standards. The categories and elements are verbatim from the NIST SP 800-53 standard. The reason for this is to support the claim that the organization's security program is consistent and compliant with the NIST standards. If the organization is better served through compliance with ISO 27002 or in achieving ISO 27001 certification, then use the ISO standards as a basis for the SMP instead of NIST.

There are many uses and benefits for an SMP framework; these benefits include:

- A standard outline in which to define organizational security.
- A security outline with basis in an industry standard.

- This example of an SMP uses the NIST standard, another SMP may find basis in ISO 27002, and another SMP may find basis in COBIT practices (Control Objectives for Information and Related Technology).
- The SMP framework provides the ability to generate tools and templates all with the same outline.
- One such tool is an SMP interpretation guide that records the organizational-specific definitions of each security category and element.
- The same SMP framework as in Table D.2 may have additional columns, like:
    - Baseline findings
    - Assessment findings for DD Month CCYY (e.g., Assessment Findings 13 May 2009)
    - Gap analysis
    - Remediation analysis
    - Fiscal year (FY) CCYY plans; note that CC = century, YY = year (e.g., 2009)
    - FY CCYY accomplishments

Not all columns need to be in the same table or even in the same document. Indeed, create as many documents as necessary, only use exactly the same framework, outline, and table structure in every document. Even if the element is not applicable, label the element N/A and express a rationale as to why the element is N/A. This will provide a record of thought process behind why certain elements are not in the security management plan. Business drivers may change and a new manager without organizational history may want to know why X is not in the SMP—you will have an answer. Business drivers may change and upon annual review of the SMP, you notice the old rationale no longer holds true—you will have a reference.

Another important reason to use exactly the same framework in every document is so personnel may easily compare plans, accomplishments, findings, gaps, remediation, and progress reporting. Even though all these details may be in different documents, they will have the same form and flow by virtue of using the same framework and table structure. Another important reason to use exactly the same framework is if you decide to insert a quantification scheme (IA metrics) in the SMP. You may copy the framework from a word processing document to a spreadsheet document and devise a clever quantification scheme with respect to SMP planning, SMP accomplishments (implementations), compliance assessments (baseline and subsequent snapshots), etc. Maintaining the same framework in an IA metrics tool provides the ability to easily copy the results back to a word processing file to generate management reports.

The Web site www.ia2.info contains many useful downloads and supplemental information regarding IA². Have the book at hand when accessing this site to find and enter any password requirements for access.

Table D.1 presents SMP categories, and Table D.2 presents an SMP framework and an interpretation guide template based on NIST SP 800-53. The control summary verbiage is almost verbatim from the NIST document. The actual NIST SP 800-53 document contains much more detail. The interpretation column provides an organizational-specific summary of what the control means to the organization. Often, security professionals within the same organization will interpret guidance differently. The interpretation guide provides a consistent, organizationally accepted interpretation.

Table D.1   SMP Categories (Based on SP 800-53)

Control Reference	Category	Summary	Interpretation
AC	Access control technical	Intentionally left blank	Intentionally left blank
AT	Awareness and training		
AU	Audit and accountability		
CA	Certification, accreditation, and security assessments		
CM	Configuration management		
CP	Contingency planning		
IA	Identification and authentication		
IR	Incident response		
MA	Maintenance		
MP	Media protection		
PE	Physical and environmental protection		
PL	Planning		
PS	Personnel security		
RA	Risk assessment		
SA	System and services acquisition		
SC	System and communications protection		
SI	System and information integrity		

Table D.2 Security Management Plan Framework (SMP Framework)

Control Reference	Category/ Subcategory/ Element	Control Summary	Interpretation
AC	**Access Control Technical**		
AC-1	Access control policy and procedures	The organization develops, disseminates, and periodically reviews/updates: (i) a formal, documented access control policy that addresses purpose, scope, roles, responsibilities, management commitment, coordination among organizational entities, and compliance; and (ii) formal, documented procedures to facilitate the implementation of the access control policy and associated access controls.	Intentionally left blank
AC-2	Account management	Addresses the processes with which to request, adjudicate, grant/deny, create, maintain, revoke, and delete system accounts.	
AC-3	Access enforcement	The organization manages information system accounts, including establishing, activating, modifying, reviewing, disabling, and removing accounts. The organization reviews information system accounts [assignment: organization-defined frequency, at least annually].	
AC-4	Information flow enforcement	The information system enforces assigned authorizations for controlling access to the system in accordance with applicable policy.	
AC-5	Separation of duties	The information system enforces separation of duties through assigned access authorizations.	
AC-6	Least privilege	The information system enforces the most restrictive set of rights/privileges or accesses needed by users (or processes acting on behalf of users) for the performance of specified tasks.	

Control Reference	Category/ Subcategory/ Element	Control Summary	Interpretation
AC-7	Unsuccessful login attempts	The information system enforces a limit of [assignment: organization-defined number] consecutive invalid access attempts by a user during a [assignment: organization-defined time period] time period. The information system automatically locks the [selection: account/node] for an [assignment: organization-defined time period] and delays next login prompt according to [assignment: organization-defined delay algorithm] when the maximum number of unsuccessful attempts is exceeded.	
AC-8	System use notification	The information system displays an approved, system use notification message before granting system access informing potential users: (i) that the user is accessing a U.S. government information system; (ii) that system usage may be monitored, recorded, and subject to audit; (iii) that unauthorized use of the system is prohibited and subject to criminal and civil penalties; and (iv) that use of the system indicates consent to monitoring and recording. The system use notification message provides appropriate privacy and security notices (based on associated privacy and security policies or summaries) and remains on the screen until the user takes explicit actions to log on to the information system.	
AC-9	Previous logon notification	The information system notifies the user, upon successful logon, of the date and time of the last logon, and the number of unsuccessful logon attempts since the last successful logon.	

Control Reference	Category/ Subcategory/ Element	Control Summary	Interpretation
AC-10	Concurrent session control	The information system limits the number of concurrent sessions for any user to [assignment: organization-defined number of sessions].	
AC-11	Session lock	The information system prevents further access to the system by initiating a session lock after [assignment: organization-defined time period] of inactivity, and the session lock remains in effect until the user reestablishes access using appropriate identification and authentication procedures.	
AC-12	Session termination	The information system automatically terminates a remote session after [assignment: organization-defined time period] of inactivity.	
AC-13	Supervision and review—access control	The organization supervises and reviews the activities of users with respect to the enforcement and usage of information system access controls.	
AC-14	Permitted actions without identification or authentication	The organization identifies and documents specific user actions that can be performed on the information system without identification or authentication.	
AC-15	Automated marking	The information system marks output using standard naming conventions to identify any special dissemination, handling, or distribution instructions.	
AC-16	Automated labeling	The information system appropriately labels information in storage, in process, and in transmission.	
AC-17	Remote access	The organization authorizes, monitors, and controls all methods of remote access to the information system.	

Control Reference	Category/ Subcategory/ Element	Control Summary	Interpretation
AC-18	Wireless access restrictions	The organization: (i) establishes usage restrictions and implementation guidance for wireless technologies; and (ii) authorizes, monitors, and controls wireless access to the information system.	
AC-19	Access control for portable and mobile devices	The organization: (i) establishes usage restrictions and implementation guidance for organization-controlled portable and mobile devices; and (ii) authorizes, monitors, and controls device access to organizational information systems.	
AC-20	Use of external information systems	The organization establishes terms and conditions for authorized individuals to: (i) access the information system from an external information system; and (ii) process, store, and transmit organization-controlled information using an external information system.	
AT	**Awareness and Training**		
AT-1	Security awareness and training policy and procedures	The organization develops, disseminates, and periodically reviews/updates: (i) a formal, documented security awareness and training policy that addresses purpose, scope, roles, responsibilities, management commitment, coordination among organizational entities, and compliance; and (ii) formal, documented procedures to facilitate the implementation of the security awareness and training policy and associated security awareness and training controls.	

Control Reference	Category/ Subcategory/ Element	Control Summary	Interpretation
AT-2	Security awareness	The organization provides basic security awareness training to all information system users (including managers and senior executives) before authorizing access to the system, when required by system changes and [assignment: organization-defined frequency, at least annually] thereafter.	
AT-3	Security training	The organization identifies personnel who have significant information system security roles and responsibilities during the system development life cycle, documents those roles and responsibilities, and provides appropriate information system security training: (i) before authorizing access to the system or performing assigned duties; (ii) when required by system changes; and (iii) [assignment: organization-defined frequency] thereafter.	
AT-4	Security training records	The organization documents and monitors individual information system security training activities, including basic security awareness training and specific information system security training.	
AT-5	Contacts with security groups and associations	The organization establishes and maintains contacts with special interest groups, specialized forums, professional associations, news groups, or peer groups of security professionals in similar organizations to stay up to date with the latest recommended security practices, techniques, and technologies and to share the latest security-related information, including threats, vulnerabilities, and incidents.	

Control Reference	Category/ Subcategory/ Element	Control Summary	Interpretation
AU	**Audit and Accountability**		
AU-1	Audit and accountability policy and procedures	The organization develops, disseminates, and periodically reviews/updates: (i) a formal, documented audit and accountability policy that addresses purpose, scope, roles, responsibilities, management commitment, coordination among organizational entities, and compliance; and (ii) formal, documented procedures to facilitate the implementation of the audit and accountability policy and associated audit and accountability controls.	
AU-2	Auditable events	The information system generates audit records for the following events: [assignment: organization-defined auditable events].	
AU-3	Content of audit records	The information system produces audit records that contain sufficient information to establish what events occurred, the sources of the events, and the outcomes of the events.	
AU-4	Audit storage capacity	The organization allocates sufficient audit record storage capacity and configures auditing to reduce the likelihood of such capacity being exceeded.	
AU-5	Response to audit processing failures	The information system alerts appropriate organizational officials in the event of an audit processing failure and takes the following additional actions: [assignment: organization-defined actions to be taken (e.g., shut down information system, overwrite oldest audit records, stop generating audit records)].	

Control Reference	Category/ Subcategory/ Element	Control Summary	Interpretation
AU-6	Audit monitoring, analysis, and reporting	The organization regularly reviews/ analyzes information system audit records for indications of inappropriate or unusual activity, investigates suspicious activity or suspected violations, reports findings to appropriate officials, and takes necessary actions.	
AU-7	Audit reduction and report generation	The information system provides an audit reduction and report generation capability.	
AU-8	Time stamps	The information system provides time stamps for use in audit record generation.	
AU-9	Protection of audit information	The information system protects audit information and audit tools from unauthorized access, modification, and deletion.	
AU-10	Nonrepudiation	The information system provides the capability to determine whether a given individual took a particular action.	
AU-11	Audit record retention	The organization retains audit records for [assignment: organization-defined time period] to provide support for after-the-fact investigations of security incidents and to meet regulatory and organizational information retention requirements.	
CA	**Certification, Accreditation, and Security Assessments**		
CA-1	Certification, accreditation, and security assessment policies and procedures	The organization develops, disseminates, and periodically reviews/updates: (i) formal, documented security assessment and certification and accreditation policies that address purpose, scope, roles, responsibilities, management commitment, coordination among organizational entities, and	

Control Reference	Category/ Subcategory/ Element	Control Summary	Interpretation
		compliance; and (ii) formal, documented procedures to facilitate the implementation of the security assessment and certification and accreditation policies and associated assessment, certification, and accreditation controls.	
CA-2	Security assessments	The organization conducts an assessment of the security controls in the information system [assignment: organization-defined frequency, at least annually] to determine the extent to which the controls are implemented correctly, operating as intended, and producing the desired outcome with respect to meeting the security requirements for the system.	
CA-3	Information system connections	The organization authorizes all connections from the information system to other information systems outside of the accreditation boundary through the use of system connection agreements and monitors/controls the system connections on an ongoing basis.	
CA-4	Security certification	The organization conducts an assessment of the security controls in the information system to determine the extent to which the controls are implemented correctly, operating as intended, and producing the desired outcome with respect to meeting the security requirements for the system.	

Control Reference	Category/ Subcategory/ Element	Control Summary	Interpretation
CA-5	Plan of action and milestones	The organization develops and updates [assignment: organization-defined frequency] a plan of action and milestones for the information system that documents the organization's planned, implemented, and evaluated remedial actions to correct deficiencies noted during the assessment of the security controls and to reduce or eliminate known vulnerabilities in the system.	
CA-6	Security accreditation	The organization authorizes (i.e., accredits) the information system for processing before operations and updates the authorization [assignment: organization-defined frequency, at least every three years] or when there is a significant change to the system. A senior organizational official signs and approves the security accreditation.	
CA-7	Continuous monitoring	The organization monitors the security controls in the information system on an ongoing basis.	
CM	**Configuration Management**		
CM-1	Configuration management policy and procedures	The organization develops, disseminates, and periodically reviews/updates: (i) a formal, documented configuration management policy that addresses purpose, scope, roles, responsibilities, management commitment, coordination among organizational entities, and compliance; and (ii) formal, documented procedures to facilitate the implementation of the configuration management policy and associated configuration management controls.	

Control Reference	Category/ Subcategory/ Element	Control Summary	Interpretation
CM-2	Baseline configuration	The organization develops, documents, and maintains a current baseline configuration of the information system.	
CM-3	Configuration change control	The organization authorizes, documents, and controls changes to the information system.	
CM-4	Monitoring configuration changes	The organization monitors changes to the information system conducting security impact analyses to determine the effects of the changes.	
CM-5	Access restrictions for change	The organization: (i) approves individual access privileges and enforces physical and logical access restrictions associated with changes to the information system; and (ii) generates, retains, and reviews records reflecting all such changes.	
CM-6	Configuration settings	The organization: (i) establishes mandatory configuration settings for information technology products employed within the information system; (ii) configures the security settings of information technology products to the most restrictive mode consistent with operational requirements; (iii) documents the configuration settings; and (iv) enforces the configuration settings in all components of the information system.	
CM-7	Least functionality	The organization configures the information system to provide only essential capabilities and specifically prohibits or restricts the use of the following functions, ports, protocols, and/or services: [assignment: organization-defined list of prohibited and restricted functions, ports, protocols, and services].	

Control Reference	Category/ Subcategory/ Element	Control Summary	Interpretation
CM-8	Information system component inventory	The organization develops, documents, and maintains a current inventory of the components of the information system and relevant ownership information.	
CP	**Contingency Planning**		
CP-1	Contingency planning policy and procedures	The organization develops, disseminates, and periodically reviews/updates: (i) a formal, documented contingency planning policy that addresses purpose, scope, roles, responsibilities, management commitment, coordination among organizational entities, and compliance; and (ii) formal, documented procedures to facilitate the implementation of the contingency planning policy and associated contingency planning controls.	
CP-2	Contingency plan	The organization develops and implements a contingency plan for the information system addressing contingency roles, responsibilities, assigned individuals with contact information, and activities associated with restoring the system after a disruption or failure. Designated officials within the organization review and approve the contingency plan and distribute copies of the plan to key contingency personnel.	
CP-3	Contingency training	The organization trains personnel in their contingency roles and responsibilities with respect to the information system and provides refresher training [assignment: organization-defined frequency, at least annually].	

Control Reference	Category/ Subcategory/ Element	Control Summary	Interpretation
CP-4	Contingency plan testing and exercises	The organization: (i) tests and exercises the contingency plan for the information system [assignment: organization-defined frequency, at least annually] using [assignment: organization-defined tests and exercises] to determine the plan's effectiveness and the organization's readiness to execute the plan; and (ii) reviews the contingency plan test/exercise results and initiates corrective actions.	
CP-5	Contingency plan update	The organization reviews the contingency plan for the information system [assignment: organization-defined frequency, at least annually] and revises the plan to address system/ organizational changes or problems encountered during plan implementation, execution, or testing.	
CP-6	Alternate storage site	The organization identifies an alternate storage site and initiates necessary agreements to permit the storage of information system backup information.	
CP-7	Alternate processing site	The organization identifies an alternate processing site and initiates necessary agreements to permit the resumption of information system operations for critical mission/business functions within [assignment: organization-defined time period] when the primary processing capabilities are unavailable.	

Control Reference	Category/ Subcategory/ Element	Control Summary	Interpretation
CP-8	Telecommunications services	The organization identifies primary and alternate telecommunications services to support the information system and initiates necessary agreements to permit the resumption of system operations for critical mission/ business functions within [assignment: organization-defined time period] when the primary telecommunications capabilities are unavailable.	
CP-9	Information system backup	The organization conducts backups of user-level and system-level information (including system state information) contained in the information system [assignment: organization-defined frequency] and protects backup information at the storage location.	
CP-10	Information system recovery and reconstitution	The organization employs mechanisms with supporting procedures to allow the information system to be recovered and reconstituted to a known secure state after a disruption or failure.	
IA	**Identification and Authentication**		
IA-1	Identification and authentication policy and procedures	The organization develops, disseminates, and periodically reviews/updates: (i) a formal, documented identification and authentication policy that addresses purpose, scope, roles, responsibilities, management commitment, coordination among organizational entities, and compliance; and (ii) formal, documented procedures to facilitate the implementation of the identification and authentication policy and associated identification and authentication controls.	

Control Reference	Category/ Subcategory/ Element	Control Summary	Interpretation
IA-2	User identification and authentication	The information system uniquely identifies and authenticates users (or processes acting on behalf of users).	
IA-3	Device identification and authentication	The information system identifies and authenticates specific devices before establishing a connection.	
IA-4	Identifier management	The organization manages user identifiers by: (i) uniquely identifying each user; (ii) verifying the identity of each user; (iii) receiving authorization to issue a user identifier from an appropriate organization official; (iv) issuing the user identifier to the intended party; (v) disabling the user identifier after [assignment: organization-defined time period] of inactivity; and (vi) archiving user identifiers.	
IA-5	Authenticator management	The organization manages information system authenticators by: (i) defining initial authenticator content; (ii) establishing administrative procedures for initial authenticator distribution, for lost/compromised or damaged authenticators, and for revoking authenticators; (iii) changing default authenticators upon information system installation; and (iv) changing/refreshing authenticators periodically.	
IA-6	Authenticator feedback	The information system obscures feedback of authentication information during the authentication process to protect the information from possible exploitation/use by unauthorized individuals.	

Control Reference	Category/ Subcategory/ Element	Control Summary	Interpretation
IA-7	Cryptographic module authentication	The information system employs authentication methods that meet the requirements of applicable laws, executive orders, directives, policies, regulations, standards, and guidance for authentication to a cryptographic module.	
IR	**Incident Response**		
IR-1	Incident response policy and procedures	The organization develops, disseminates, and periodically reviews/updates: (i) a formal, documented incident response policy that addresses purpose, scope, roles, responsibilities, management commitment, coordination among organizational entities, and compliance; and (ii) formal, documented procedures to facilitate the implementation of the incident response policy and associated incident response controls.	
IR-2	Incident response training	The organization trains personnel in their incident response roles and responsibilities with respect to the information system and provides refresher training [assignment: organization-defined frequency, at least annually].	
IR-3	Incident response testing and exercises	The organization tests and exercises the incident response capability for the information system [assignment: organization-defined frequency, at least annually] using [assignment: organization-defined tests and exercises] to determine the incident response effectiveness and documents the results.	
IR-4	Incident handling	The organization implements an incident handling capability for security incidents that includes preparation, detection and analysis, containment, eradication, and recovery.	

Control Reference	Category/ Subcategory/ Element	Control Summary	Interpretation
IR-5	Incident monitoring	The organization tracks and documents information system security incidents on an ongoing basis.	
IR-6	Incident reporting	The organization promptly reports incident information to appropriate authorities.	
IR-7	Incident response assistance	The organization provides an incident response support resource that offers advice and assistance to users of the information system for the handling and reporting of security incidents. The support resource is an integral part of the organization's incident response capability.	
MA	**Maintenance**		
MA-1	System maintenance policy and procedures	The organization develops, disseminates, and periodically reviews/updates: (i) a formal, documented information system maintenance policy that addresses purpose, scope, roles, responsibilities, management commitment, coordination among organizational entities, and compliance; and (ii) formal, documented procedures to facilitate the implementation of the information system maintenance policy and associated system maintenance controls.	
MA-2	Controlled maintenance	The organization schedules, performs, documents, and reviews records of routine preventative and regular maintenance (including repairs) on the components of the information system in accordance with manufacturer or vendor specifications and organizational requirements.	

Control Reference	Category/ Subcategory/ Element	Control Summary	Interpretation
MA-3	Maintenance tools	The organization approves, controls, and monitors the use of information system maintenance tools and maintains the tools on an ongoing basis.	
MA-4	Remote maintenance	The organization authorizes, monitors, and controls any remotely executed maintenance and diagnostic activities, if employed.	
MA-5	Maintenance personnel	The organization allows only authorized personnel to perform maintenance on the information system.	
MA-6	Timely maintenance	The organization obtains maintenance support and spare parts for [assignment: organization-defined list of key information system components] within [assignment: organization-defined time period] of failure.	
MP	**Media Protection**		
MP-1	Media protection policy and procedures	The organization develops, disseminates, and periodically reviews/updates: (i) a formal, documented media protection policy that addresses purpose, scope, roles, responsibilities, management commitment, coordination among organizational entities, and compliance; and (ii) formal, documented procedures to facilitate the implementation of the media protection policy and associated media protection controls.	
MP-2	Media access	The organization restricts access to information system media to authorized individuals.	

Control Reference	Category/ Subcategory/ Element	Control Summary	Interpretation
MP-3	Media labeling	The organization: (i) affixes external labels to removable information system media and information system output indicating the distribution limitations, handling caveats, and applicable security markings (if any) of the information; and (ii) exempts [assignment: organization-defined list of media types or hardware components] from labeling so long as they remain within [assignment: organization-defined protected environment].	
MP-4	Media storage	The organization physically controls and securely stores information system media within controlled areas.	
MP-5	Media transport	The organization protects and controls information system media during transport outside of controlled areas and restricts the activities associated with transport of such media to authorized personnel.	
MP-6	Media sanitization and disposal	The organization sanitizes information system media, both digital and nondigital, prior to disposal or release for reuse.	

Control Reference	Category/ Subcategory/ Element	Control Summary	Interpretation
PE	**Physical and Environmental Protection**		
PE-1	Physical and environmental protection policy and procedures	The organization develops, disseminates, and periodically reviews/updates: (i) a formal, documented physical and environmental protection policy that addresses purpose, scope, roles, responsibilities, management commitment, coordination among organizational entities, and compliance; and (ii) formal, documented procedures to facilitate the implementation of the physical and environmental protection policy and associated physical and environmental protection controls.	
PE-2	Physical access authorizations	The organization develops and keeps current a list of personnel with authorized access to the facility where the information system resides (except for those areas within the facility officially designated as publicly accessible) and issues appropriate authorization credentials. Designated officials within the organization review and approve the access list and authorization credentials [assignment: organization-defined frequency, at least annually].	

Control Reference	Category/ Subcategory/ Element	Control Summary	Interpretation
PE-3	Physical access control	The organization controls all physical access points (including designated entry/exit points) to the facility where the information system resides (except for those areas within the facility officially designated as publicly accessible) and verifies individual access authorizations before granting access to the facility. The organization controls access to areas officially designated as publicly accessible, as appropriate, in accordance with the organization's assessment of risk.	
PE-4	Access control for transmission medium	The organization controls physical access to information system distribution and transmission lines within organizational facilities.	
PE-5	Access control for display medium	The organization controls physical access to information system devices that display information to prevent unauthorized individuals from observing the display output.	
PE-6	Monitoring physical access	The organization monitors physical access to the information system to detect and respond to physical security incidents.	
PE-7	Visitor control	The organization controls physical access to the information system by authenticating visitors before authorizing access to the facility where the information system resides other than areas designated as publicly accessible.	

Control Reference	Category/ Subcategory/ Element	Control Summary	Interpretation
PE-8	Access records	The organization maintains visitor access records to the facility where the information system resides (except for those areas within the facility officially designated as publicly accessible) that include: (i) name and organization of the person visiting; (ii) signature of the visitor; (iii) form of identification; (iv) date of access; (v) time of entry and departure; (vi) purpose of visit; and (vii) name and organization of person visited. Designated officials within the organization review the visitor access records [assignment: organization-defined frequency].	
PE-9	Power equipment and power cabling	The organization protects power equipment and power cabling for the information system from damage and destruction.	
PE-10	Emergency shutoff	The organization provides, for specific locations within a facility containing concentrations of information system resources, the capability of shutting off power to any information system component that may be malfunctioning or threatened without endangering personnel by requiring them to approach the equipment.	
PE-11	Emergency power	The organization provides a short-term uninterruptible power supply to facilitate an orderly shutdown of the information system in the event of a primary power source loss.	
PE-12	Emergency lighting	The organization employs and maintains automatic emergency lighting that activates in the event of a power outage or disruption and that covers emergency exits and evacuation routes.	

Control Reference	Category/ Subcategory/ Element	Control Summary	Interpretation
PE-13	Fire protection	The organization employs and maintains fire suppression and detection devices/systems that can be activated in the event of a fire.	
PE-14	Temperature and humidity controls	The organization regularly maintains, within acceptable levels, and monitors the temperature and humidity within the facility where the information system resides.	
PE-15	Water damage protection	The organization protects the information system from water damage resulting from broken plumbing lines or other sources of water leakage by providing master shutoff valves that are accessible, working properly, and known to key personnel.	
PE-16	Delivery and removal	The organization authorizes and controls information system-related items entering and exiting the facility and maintains appropriate records of those items.	
PE-17	Alternate work site	The organization employs appropriate management, operational, and technical information system security controls at alternate work sites.	
PE-18	Location of information system components	The organization positions information system components within the facility to minimize potential damage from physical and environmental hazards and to minimize the opportunity for unauthorized access.	
PE-19	Information leakage	The organization protects the information system from information leakage due to electromagnetic signal emanations.	

Control Reference	Category/ Subcategory/ Element	Control Summary	Interpretation
PL	**Planning**		
PL-1	Security planning policy and procedures	The organization develops, disseminates, and periodically reviews/updates: (i) a formal, documented security planning policy that addresses purpose, scope, roles, responsibilities, management commitment, coordination among organizational entities, and compliance; and (ii) formal, documented procedures to facilitate the implementation of the security planning policy and associated security planning controls.	
PL-2	System security plan	The organization develops and implements a security plan for the information system that provides an overview of the security requirements for the system and a description of the security controls in place or planned for meeting those requirements. Designated officials within the organization review and approve the plan.	
PL-3	System security plan update	The organization reviews the security plan for the information system [assignment: organization-defined frequency, at least annually] and revises the plan to address system/organizational changes or problems identified during plan implementation or security control assessments.	

Control Reference	Category/ Subcategory/ Element	Control Summary	Interpretation
PL-4	Rules of behavior	The organization establishes and makes readily available to all information system users a set of rules that describes their responsibilities and expected behavior with regard to information and information system usage. The organization receives signed acknowledgment from users indicating that they have read, understand, and agree to abide by the rules of behavior, before authorizing access to the information system and its resident information.	
PL-5	Privacy impact assessment	The organization conducts a privacy impact assessment on the information system in accordance with OMB policy.	
PL-6	Security-related activity planning	The organization plans and coordinates security-related activities affecting the information system before conducting such activities to reduce the impact on organizational operations (i.e., mission, functions, image, and reputation), organizational assets, and individuals.	
PS	**Personnel Security**		
PS-1	Personnel security policy and procedures	The organization develops, disseminates, and periodically reviews/updates: (i) a formal, documented personnel security policy that addresses purpose, scope, roles, responsibilities, management commitment, coordination among organizational entities, and compliance; and (ii) formal, documented procedures to facilitate the implementation of the personnel security policy and associated personnel security controls.	

Control Reference	Category/ Subcategory/ Element	Control Summary	Interpretation
PS-2	Position categorization	The organization assigns a risk designation to all positions and establishes screening criteria for individuals filling those positions. The organization reviews and revises position risk designations [assignment: organization-defined frequency].	
PS-3	Personnel screening	The organization screens individuals requiring access to organizational information and information systems before authorizing access.	
PS-4	Personnel termination	The organization, upon termination of individual employment, terminates information system access, conducts exit interviews, retrieves all organizational information system-related property, and provides appropriate personnel with access to official records created by the terminated employee that are stored on organizational information systems.	
PS-5	Personnel transfer	The organization reviews information systems/facilities access authorizations when personnel are reassigned or transferred to other positions within the organization and initiates appropriate actions.	
PS-6	Access agreements	The organization completes appropriate signed access agreements for individuals requiring access to organizational information and information systems before authorizing access and reviews/updates the agreements [assignment: organization-defined frequency].	

Control Reference	Category/ Subcategory/ Element	Control Summary	Interpretation
PS-7	Third-party personnel security	The organization establishes personnel security requirements, including security roles and responsibilities for third-party providers, and monitors provider compliance.	
PS-8	Personnel sanctions	The organization employs a formal sanctions process for personnel failing to comply with established information security policies and procedures.	
RA	**Risk Assessment**		
RA-1	Risk assessment policy and procedures	The organization develops, disseminates, and periodically reviews/updates: (i) a formal, documented risk assessment policy that addresses purpose, scope, roles, responsibilities, management commitment, coordination among organizational entities, and compliance; and (ii) formal, documented procedures to facilitate the implementation of the risk assessment policy and associated risk assessment controls.	
RA-2	Security categorization	The organization categorizes the information system and the information processed, stored, or transmitted by the system in accordance with applicable laws, executive orders, directives, policies, regulations, standards, and guidance and documents the results (including supporting rationale) in the system security plan. Designated senior-level officials within the organization review and approve the security categorizations.	

Control Reference	Category/ Subcategory/ Element	Control Summary	Interpretation
RA-3	Risk assessment	The organization conducts assessments of the risk and magnitude of harm that could result from the unauthorized access, use, disclosure, disruption, modification, or destruction of information and information systems that support the operations and assets of the agency (including information and information systems managed/ operated by external parties).	
RA-4	Risk assessment update	The organization updates the risk assessment [assignment: organization-defined frequency] or whenever there are significant changes to the information system, the facilities where the system resides, or other conditions that may impact the security or accreditation status of the system.	
RA-5	Vulnerability scanning	The organization scans for vulnerabilities in the information system [assignment: organization-defined frequency] or when significant new vulnerabilities potentially affecting the system are identified and reported.	
SA	**System and Services Acquisition**		
SA-1	System and services acquisition policy and procedures	The organization develops, disseminates, and periodically reviews/updates: (i) a formal, documented system and services acquisition policy that includes information security considerations and that addresses purpose, scope, roles, responsibilities, management commitment, coordination among organizational entities, and compliance; and (ii) formal, documented procedures to facilitate the implementation of the system and services acquisition policy and associated system and services acquisition controls.	

Control Reference	Category/ Subcategory/ Element	Control Summary	Interpretation
SA-2	Allocation of resources	The organization determines, documents, and allocates as part of its capital planning and investment control process the resources required to adequately protect the information system.	
SA-3	Life cycle support	The organization manages the information system using a system development life cycle methodology that includes information security considerations.	
SA-4	Acquisitions	The organization includes security requirements and security specifications, either explicitly or by reference, in information system acquisition contracts based on an assessment of risk and in accordance with applicable laws, executive orders, directives, policies, regulations, and standards.	
SA-5	Information system documentation	The organization obtains, protects as required, and makes available to authorized personnel adequate documentation for the information system.	
SA-6	Software usage restrictions	The organization complies with software usage restrictions.	
SA-7	User-installed software	The organization enforces explicit rules governing the installation of software by users.	
SA-8	Security engineering principles	The organization designs and implements the information system using security engineering principles.	
SA-9	External information system services	The organization: (i) requires that providers of external information system services employ adequate security controls in accordance with applicable laws, executive orders, directives, policies, regulations, standards, guidances, and established service level agreements; and (ii) monitors security control compliance.	

Control Reference	Category/ Subcategory/ Element	Control Summary	Interpretation
SA-10	Developer configuration management	The organization requires that information system developers create and implement a configuration management plan that controls changes to the system during development, tracks security flaws, requires authorization of changes, and provides documentation of the plan and its implementation.	
SA-11	Developer security testing	The organization requires that information system developers create a security test and evaluation plan, implement the plan, and document the results.	
SC **System and communications protection**			
SC-1	System and communications protection policy and procedures	The organization develops, disseminates, and periodically reviews/updates: (i) a formal, documented system and communications protection policy that addresses purpose, scope, roles, responsibilities, management commitment, coordination among organizational entities, and compliance; and (ii) formal, documented procedures to facilitate the implementation of the system and communications protection policy and associated system and communications protection controls.	
SC-2	Application partitioning	The information system separates user functionality (including user interface services) from information system management functionality.	
SC-3	Security function isolation	The information system isolates security functions from nonsecurity functions.	
SC-4	Information remnance	The information system prevents unauthorized and unintended information transfer via shared system resources.	

Control Reference	Category/ Subcategory/ Element	Control Summary	Interpretation
SC-5	Denial-of-service protection	The information system protects against or limits the effects of the following types of denial of service attacks: [assignment: organization-defined list of types of denial-of-service attacks or reference to source for current list].	
SC-6	Resource priority	The information system limits the use of resources by priority.	
SC-7	Boundary protection	The information system monitors and controls communications at the external boundary of the information system and at key internal boundaries within the system.	
SC-8	Transmission integrity	The information system protects the integrity of transmitted information.	
SC-9	Transmission confidentiality	The information system protects the confidentiality of transmitted information.	
SC-10	Network disconnect	The information system terminates a network connection at the end of a session or after [assignment: organization-defined time period] of inactivity.	
SC-11	Trusted path	The information system establishes a trusted communications path between the user and the following security functions of the system: [assignment: organization-defined security functions to include, at a minimum, information system authentication and reauthentication].	
SC-12	Cryptographic key establishment and management	When cryptography is required and employed within the information system, the organization establishes and manages cryptographic keys using automated mechanisms with supporting procedures or manual procedures.	

Control Reference	Category/ Subcategory/ Element	Control Summary	Interpretation
SC-13	Use of cryptography	For information requiring cryptographic protection, the information system implements cryptographic mechanisms that comply with applicable laws, executive orders, directives, policies, regulations, standards, and guidance.	
SC-14	Public access protections	The information system protects the integrity and availability of publicly available information and applications.	
SC-15	Collaborative computing	The information system prohibits remote activation of collaborative computing mechanisms and provides an explicit indication of use to the local users.	
SC-16	Transmission of security parameters	The information system reliably associates security parameters with information exchanged between information systems.	
SC-17	Public key infrastructure certificates	The organization issues public key certificates under an appropriate certificate policy or obtains public key certificates under an appropriate certificate policy from an approved service provider.	
SC-18	Mobile code	The organization: (i) establishes usage restrictions and implementation guidance for mobile code technologies based on the potential to cause damage to the information system if used maliciously; and (ii) authorizes, monitors, and controls the use of mobile code within the information system.	

Control Reference	Category/ Subcategory/ Element	Control Summary	Interpretation
SC-19	Voice-over-Internet protocol	The organization: (i) establishes usage restrictions and implementation guidance for Voice-over-Internet Protocol (VoIP) technologies based on the potential to cause damage to the information system if used maliciously; and (ii) authorizes, monitors, and controls the use of VoIP within the information system.	
SC-20	Secure name/ address resolution service (authoritative source)	The information system that provides name/address resolution service provides additional data origin and integrity artifacts along with the authoritative data it returns in response to resolution queries.	
SC-21	Secure name/ address resolution service (recursive or caching resolver)	The information system that provides name/address resolution service for local clients performs data origin authentication and data integrity verification on the resolution responses it receives from authoritative sources when requested by client systems.	
SC-22	Architecture and provisioning for name/address resolution service	The information systems that collectively provide name/address resolution service for an organization are fault tolerant and implement role separation.	
SC-23	Session authenticity	The information system provides mechanisms to protect the authenticity of communications sessions.	

Control Reference	Category/ Subcategory/ Element	Control Summary	Interpretation
SI	**System and Information Integrity**		
SI-1	System and information integrity policy and procedures	The organization develops, disseminates, and periodically reviews/updates: (i) a formal, documented system and information integrity policy that addresses purpose, scope, roles, responsibilities, management commitment, coordination among organizational entities, and compliance; and (ii) formal, documented procedures to facilitate the implementation of the system and information integrity policy and associated system and information integrity controls.	
SI-2	Flaw remediation	The organization identifies, reports, and corrects information system flaws.	
SI-3	Malicious code protection	The information system implements malicious code protection.	
SI-4	Information system monitoring tools and techniques	The organization employs tools and techniques to monitor events on the information system, detect attacks, and provide identification of unauthorized use of the system.	
SI-5	Security alerts and advisories	The organization receives information system security alerts/advisories on a regular basis, issues alerts/advisories to appropriate personnel, and takes appropriate actions in response.	

Control Reference	Category/ Subcategory/ Element	Control Summary	Interpretation
SI-6	Security functionality verification	The information system verifies the correct operation of security functions [selection (one or more): upon system startup and restart, upon command by user with appropriate privilege, periodically every [assignment: organization-defined time period] and [selection (one or more): notifies system administrator, shuts the system down, restarts the system] when anomalies are discovered.	
SI-7	Software and information integrity	The information system detects and protects against unauthorized changes to software and information.	
SI-8	Spam protection	The information system implements spam protection.	
SI-9	Information input restrictions	The organization restricts the capability to input information to the information system to authorized personnel.	
SI-10	Information accuracy, completeness, validity, and authenticity	The information system checks information for accuracy, completeness, validity, and authenticity.	
SI-11	Error handling	The information system identifies and handles error conditions in an expeditious manner without providing information that could be exploited by adversaries.	
SI-12	Information output handling and retention	The organization handles and retains output from the information system in accordance with applicable laws, executive orders, directives, policies, regulations, standards, and operational requirements.	

Appendix E: Security Management Program Template Outline

The SMP outline in this appendix is based on the SMP framework; both are based on NIST SP 800-53. All tools, templates, and guidelines in support of the organization's SMP are based on exactly the same framework to provide a common form and flow to all SMP-related documents. A common form and flow promotes comprehensiveness and consistency for all IA efforts. *Comprehensiveness* is relative to the SMP framework because this framework provides categories and elements to *capture all IA relevant to the organization*. Consistency comes from addressing all security elements. Addressing a security element is not necessarily the provision of a safeguard. A sufficient manner to address a security element may be to provide a rational explanation as to why the organization chooses not to provide that safeguard; a statement to the affect of "We choose to accept the risk this safeguard would mitigate for the following reasons: expense (purchase and operations), complexity for user base, etc."

The main topics in the outline are in header format (bold and larger font). The subtopics or the elements are in normal format. Potential document titles using the SMP framework and SMP outline include:

- SMP As-Is Baseline (discovery templates, reporting templates)
- SMP As-Is Snapshot; ongoing review, tracking, and trending
- SMP To-Be (Target Security Posture for ABC Company)
- SMP Gap Analysis
- SMP Remediation Analysis
- SMP Project Planning
- SMP Operations Plan
- SMP Performance Reporting

Use of exactly the same SMP framework and SMP outline provides a common look and feel for discovery tools (questionnaires, assessment guides, audit guides), analysis tools, reporting templates, and tracking templates. Analysis tools may compare as-is discovery against to-be plans. Reporting includes gap analysis, remediation analysis, what should be done (good business practice), what may be done (authority), and what can be done (resource restrictions; budget, people, knowledge, time). Tracking templates provide the ability to record progress in what is done to address business risks. Using the same SMP framework for all tools, templates, and guides provides consistency, the ability to compare apples to apples from discovery through analysis and reporting.

If additional details are necessary to reflect your organization's particular needs, by all means modify the framework and outline accordingly. Once the framework is finalized, stick with it to ensure consistency across all efforts. If at some future point there is need to modify the SMP framework, be sure to disseminate updated versions of templates and tools.

For IA², the IA architect may use the SMP outline as a transition tool from IA architecture to IA planning, implementation, and operations. The IA architect may use Table E.1 to capture IA² details for relevant security controls in context of the SMP outline. This same table appears in chapter 9.

The Web site www.ia2.info contains many useful downloads and supplemental information regarding IA². Have the book at hand when accessing this site to find and enter any password requirements for access.

Table E.1 IA² Details of Security Controls

IA² Topic	Description
Section header	<Insert description of security control.>
Drivers	Describe drivers behind IA. IA addresses business risk and technical risk. Root drivers are generically to further organizational and stakeholder interests, ensure organizational viability, and support, empower, protect, and facilitate the fulfillment of the organizational mission.
IA² views	Describe applicable IA² views: People, policy, business process, systems and applications, information/data, infrastructure (technical, physical)
IA core principles	Describe applicable IA core principles: Confidentiality-integrity-availability (CIA), Possession-authenticity-utility (PAU), Privacy–authorized use–nonrepudiation (PAN)
Compliance requirements	Legislative, policy, guidelines, executive order, presidential directive, or other requirement specifically calling out or implying the use of specific standards
ELCM application	Describe applicable ELCM elements: Concept, architect, engineer, develop/acquire, implement, test, deploy, train, O&M, retire
Verification	Describe applicable verification methods, e.g., system test and evaluation (ST&E), certification and accreditation (C&A), others.
Operations	List applicable IA ops cycle elements: Anticipate, defend, monitor, respond

SMP Outline

1. Access control technical

1.1 Access control policy and procedures

1.2 Account management

1.3 Access enforcement

1.4 Information flow enforcement

1.5 Separation of duties

1.6 Least privilege

1.7 Unsuccessful login attempts

1.8 System use notification

1.9 Previous logon notification

1.10   Concurrent session control

1.11   Session lock

1.12   Session termination

1.13   Supervision and review—access control

1.14   Permitted actions without identification or authentication

1.15   Automated marking

1.16   Automated labeling

1.17   Remote access

1.18   Wireless access restrictions

1.19   Access control for portable and mobile devices

1.20   Use of external information systems

2. Awareness and training

2.1 Security awareness and training policy and procedures

2.2 Security awareness

2.3 Security training

2.4 Security training records

2.5 Contacts with security groups and associations

3. Audit and accountability

3.1 Audit and accountability policy and procedures

3.2 Auditable events

3.3 Content of audit records

3.4 Audit storage capacity

3.5 Response to audit processing failures

3.6 Audit monitoring, analysis, and reporting

3.7 Audit reduction and report generation

3.8 Time stamps

3.9 Protection of audit information

3.10   Nonrepudiation

3.11   Audit record retention

4. Certification, accreditation, and security assessments

4.1 Certification, accreditation, and security assessment policies and procedures

4.2 Security assessments

4.3 Information system connections

4.4 Security certification

4.5 Plan of action and milestones

4.6 Security accreditation

4.7 Continuous monitoring

5. Configuration management

5.1 Configuration management policy and procedures

5.2 Baseline configuration

5.3 Configuration change control

5.4 Monitoring configuration changes

5.5 Access restrictions for change

5.6 Configuration settings

5.7 Least functionality

5.8 Information system component inventory

6. Contingency planning

6.1 Contingency planning policy and procedures

6.2 Contingency plan

6.3 Contingency training

6.4 Contingency plan testing and exercises

6.5 Contingency plan update

6.6 Alternate storage site

6.7 Alternate processing site

6.8 Telecommunications services

6.9 Information system backup

6.10　Information system recovery and reconstitution

7. Identification and authentication

7.1 Identification and authentication policy and procedures

7.2 User identification and authentication

7.3 Device identification and authentication

7.4 Identifier management

7.5 Authenticator management

7.6 Authenticator feedback

7.7 Cryptographic module authentication

8. Incident response

8.1 Incident response policy and procedures

8.2 Incident response training

8.3 Incident response testing and exercises

8.4 Incident handling

8.5 Incident monitoring

8.6 Incident reporting

8.7 Incident response assistance

9. Maintenance

9.1 System maintenance policy and procedures

9.2 Controlled maintenance

9.3 Maintenance tools

9.4 Remote maintenance

9.5 Maintenance personnel

9.6 Timely maintenance

10. Media protection

10.1 Media protection policy and procedures

10.2 Media access

10.3 Media labeling

10.4 Media storage

10.5 Media transport

10.6 Media sanitization and disposal

11. Physical and environmental protection

11.1 Physical and environmental protection policy and procedures

11.2 Physical access authorizations

11.3 Physical access control

11.4 Access control for transmission medium

11.5 Access control for display medium

11.6 Monitoring physical access

11.7 Visitor control

11.8 Access records

11.9 Power equipment and power cabling

11.10   Emergency shutoff

11.11   Emergency power

11.12   Emergency lighting

11.13   Fire protection

11.14   Temperature and humidity controls

11.15   Water damage protection

11.16   Delivery and removal

11.17   Alternate work site

11.18   Location of information system components

11.19   Information leakage

12. Planning

12.1 Security planning policy and procedures

12.2 System security plan

12.3 System security plan update

12.4 Rules of behavior

Appendix F: NIST Document Applicability Template

The details of the first two columns in Table F.1 are from the *Guide to NIST Information Security Documents*.* The use of the NIST standards is not ubiquitous, but notable in anticipation of its growing popularity as a baseline for developing information assurance solutions in the U.S. government, U.S. critical infrastructure, and use by many commercial organizations in the United States. Table F.1 presents NIST standards within the SMP framework. You may use this table to record standards relevant to your organization along with a description of applicability. Be sure to cover who, what, why, when, where, and how the standards apply. If you prefer different standards than NIST, the SMP framework is still a good organizing tool to record applicable standards in context of the area they address.

The Web site www.ia2.info contains many useful downloads and supplemental information regarding IA^2. Have the book at hand when accessing this site to find and enter any password requirements for access.

---

* csrc.nist.gov (last accessed July 2007).

Table F.1   NIST References by SMP Categories (as Based on SP 800-53)

Control Reference	Category/Document	Description of Applicability[a]
AC	**Access Control Technical**	
AC	FIPS 201-1: *Personal Identity Verification for Federal Employees and Contractors*	Note: Use this column to record organizational applicability and specific references within the standard/guidance that are applicable to the organization.
AC	FIPS 200: *Security Controls for Federal Information Systems*	Intentionally left blank
AC	FIPS 188: *Standard Security Labels for Information Transfer*	
AC	SP 800-100: *Information Security Handbook for Managers*	
AC	SP 800-97: *Guide to IEEE 802.11i: Robust Security Networks*	
AC	SP 800-96: *PIV Card/Reader Interoperability Guidelines*	
AC	SP 800-87: *Codes for the Identification of Federal and Federally Assisted Organizations*	
AC	SP 800-83: *Guide to Malware Incident Prevention and Handling*	
AC	SP 800-81: *Secure Domain Name System (DNS) Deployment Guide*	
AC	SP 800-78: *Cryptographic Algorithms and Key Sizes for Personal Identity Verification*	
AC	SP 800-77: *Guide to IPSec VPNs*	
AC	SP 800-76: *Biometric Data Specification for Personal Identity Verification*	
AC	SP 800-73, Rev 1: *Integrated Circuit Card for Personal Identification Verification*	

Control Reference	Category/Document	Description of Applicability[a]
AC	SP 800-68: *Guidance for Securing Microsoft Windows XP Systems for IT Professionals: A NIST Security Configuration Checklist*	
AC	SP 800-66: *An Introductory Resource Guide for Implementing the Health Insurance Portability and Accountability Act (HIPAA) Security Rule*	
AC	SP 800-58: *Security Considerations for Voice Over IP Systems*	
AC	SP 800-57: *Recommendation on Key Management*	
AC	SP 800-48: *Wireless Network Security: 802.11, Bluetooth, and Handheld Devices*	
AC	SP 800-46: *Security for Telecommuting and Broadband Communications*	
AC	SP 800-45: *Guidelines on Electronic Mail Security*	
AC	SP 800-44: *Guidelines on Securing Public Web Servers*	
AC	SP 800-43: *Systems Administration Guidance for Securing Microsoft Windows 2000 Professional System*	
AC	SP 800-41: *Guidelines on Firewalls and Firewall Policy*	
AC	SP 800-36: *Guide to Selecting Information Technology Security Products*	
AC	SP 800-28: *Guidelines on Active Content and Mobile Code*	
AC	SP 800-24: *PBX Vulnerability Analysis: Finding Holes in Your PBX before Someone Else Does*	
AC	SP 800-19: *Mobile Agent Security*	

Control Reference	*Category/Document*	*Description of Applicability*[a]
AC	SP 800-14: *Generally Accepted Principles and Practices for Securing Information Technology Systems*	
AC	SP 800-12: *An Introduction to Computer Security: The NIST Handbook*	
AT	**Awareness and Training**	
AT	FIPS 200: *Security Controls for Federal Information Systems*	
AT	SP 800-100: *Information Security Handbook for Managers*	
AT	SP 800-66: *An Introductory Resource Guide for Implementing the Health Insurance Portability and Accountability Act (HIPAA) Security Rule*	
AT	SP 800-50: *Building an Information Technology Security Awareness and Training Program*	
AT	SP 800-40: *Procedures for Handling Security Patches*	
AT	SP 800-31: *Intrusion Detection Systems (IDSs)*	
AT	SP 800-16: *Information Technology Security Training Requirements: A Role- and Performance-Based Model*	
AT	SP 800-14: *Generally Accepted Principles and Practices for Securing Information Technology Systems*	
AT	SP 800-12: *An Introduction to Computer Security: The NIST Handbook*	
AU	**Audit and Accountability**	
AU	FIPS 200: *Security Controls for Federal Information Systems*	
AU	FIPS 198: *The Keyed-Hash Message Authentication Code (HMAC)*	

Control Reference	Category/Document	Description of Applicability[a]
AU	SP 800-100: *Information Security Handbook for Managers*	
AU	SP 800-92: *Guide to Computer Security Log Management*	
AU	SP 800-89: *Recommendation for Obtaining Assurances for Digital Signature Applications*	
AU	SP 800-86: *Guide to Integrating Forensic Techniques into Incident Response*	
AU	SP 800-83: *Guide to Malware Incident Prevention and Handling*	
AU	SP 800-72: *Guidelines on PDA Forensics*	
AU	SP 800-68: *Guidance for Securing Microsoft Windows XP Systems for IT Professionals: A NIST Security Configuration Checklist*	
AU	SP 800-66: *An Introductory Resource Guide for Implementing the Health Insurance Portability and Accountability Act (HIPAA) Security Rule*	
AU	SP 800-57: *Recommendation on Key Management*	
AU	SP 800-52: *Guidelines on the Selection and Use of Transport Layer Security*	
AU	SP 800-49: *Federal S/MIME V3 Client Profile*	
AU	SP 800-45: *Guidelines on Electronic Mail Security*	
AU	SP 800-44: *Guidelines on Securing Public Web Servers*	
AU	SP 800-42: *Guideline on Network Security Testing*	
AU	SP 800-19: *Mobile Agent Security*	

Control Reference	Category/Document	Description of Applicability[a]
AU	SP 800-14: *Generally Accepted Principles and Practices for Securing Information Technology Systems*	
AU	SP 800-12: *An Introduction to Computer Security: The NIST Handbook*	
CA	**Certification, Accreditation, and Security Assessments**	
CA	FIPS 200: *Security Controls for Federal Information Systems*	
CA	SP 800-100: *Information Security Handbook for Managers*	
CA	SP 800-85: *PIV Middleware and PIV Card Application Conformance Test Guidelines*	
CA	SP 800-79: *Guidelines for the Certification and Accreditation of PIV Card Issuing Organizations*	
CA	SP 800-76: *Biometric Data Specification for Personal Identity Verification*	
CA	SP 800-66: *An Introductory Resource Guide for Implementing the Health Insurance Portability and Accountability Act (HIPAA) Security Rule*	
CA	SP 800-65: *Integrating Security into the Capital Planning and Investment Control Process*	
CA	SP 800-55: *Security Metrics Guide for Information Technology Systems*	
CA	SP 800-53A: *Guide for Assessing the Security Controls in Federal Information Systems*	
CA	SP 800-47: *Security Guide for Interconnecting Information Technology Systems*	
CA	SP 800-42: *Guideline on Network Security Testing*	

Control Reference	Category/Document	Description of Applicability[a]
CA	SP 800-37: *Guidelines for the Security Certification and Accreditation of Federal Information Technology Systems*	
CA	SP 800-36: *Guide to Selecting Information Technology Security Products*	
CA	SP 800-35: *Guide to Information Technology Security Services*	
CA	SP 800-30: *Risk Management Guide for Information Technology Systems*	
CA	SP 800-26: *Security Self-Assessment Guide for Information Technology Systems*	
CA	SP 800-23: *Guideline to Federal Organizations on Security Assurance and Acquisition/Use of Tested/Evaluated Products*	
CA	SP 800-22: *A Statistical Test Suite for Random and Pseudorandom Number Generators for Cryptographic Applications*	
CA	SP 800-20: *Modes of Operation Validation System for the Triple Data Encryption Algorithm (TMOVS): Requirements and Procedures*	
CA	SP 800-18: *Guide for Developing Security Plans for Information Technology Systems*	
CA	SP 800-17: *Modes of Operation Validation System (MOVS): Requirements and Procedures*	
CA	SP 800-14: *Generally Accepted Principles and Practices for Securing Information Technology Systems*	
CA	SP 800-12: *An Introduction to Computer Security: The NIST Handbook*	

Control Reference	Category/Document	Description of Applicability[a]
CM	**Configuration Management**	
CM	FIPS 200: *Security Controls for Federal Information Systems*	
CM	SP 800-100: *Information Security Handbook for Managers*	
CM	SP 800-86: *Guide to Integrating Forensic Techniques into Incident Response*	
CM	SP 800-83: *Guide to Malware Incident Prevention and Handling*	
CM	SP 800-81: *Secure Domain Name System (DNS) Deployment Guide*	
CM	SP 800-70: *Security Configuration Checklists Program for IT Products*	
CM	SP 800-68: *Guidance for Securing Microsoft Windows XP Systems for IT Professionals: A NIST Security Configuration Checklist*	
CM	SP 800-48: *Wireless Network Security: 802.11, Bluetooth, and Handheld Devices*	
CM	SP 800-46: *Security for Telecommuting and Broadband Communications*	
CM	SP 800-45: *Guidelines on Electronic Mail Security*	
CM	SP 800-44: *Guidelines on Securing Public Web Servers*	
CM	SP 800-43: *Systems Administration Guidance for Securing Microsoft Windows 2000 Professional System*	
CM	SP 800-40: *Procedures for Handling Security Patches*	
CM	SP 800-37: *Guidelines for the Security Certification and Accreditation of Federal Information Technology Systems*	

Control Reference	Category/Document	Description of Applicability[a]
CM	SP 800-35: *Guide to Information Technology Security Services*	
CM	SP 800-14: *Generally Accepted Principles and Practices for Securing Information Technology Systems*	
CM	SP 800-12: *An Introduction to Computer Security: The NIST Handbook*	
CP	**Contingency Planning**	
CP	FIPS 200: *Security Controls for Federal Information Systems*	
CP	SP 800-100: *Information Security Handbook for Managers*	
CP	SP 800-86: *Guide to Integrating Forensic Techniques into Incident Response*	
CP	SP 800-83: *Guide to Malware Incident Prevention and Handling*	
CP	SP 800-81: *Secure Domain Name System (DNS) Deployment Guide*	
CP	SP 800-66: *An Introductory Resource Guide for Implementing the Health Insurance Portability and Accountability Act (HIPAA) Security Rule*	
CP	SP 800-57 *Recommendation on Key Management*	
CP	SP 800-56A: *Recommendation for Pair-Wise Key Establishment Schemes Using Discrete Logarithm Cryptography*	
CP	SP 800-50: *Building an Information Technology Security Awareness and Training Program*	
CP	SP 800-45: *Guidelines on Electronic Mail Security*	
CP	SP 800-44: *Guidelines on Securing Public Web Servers*	

Control Reference	Category/Document	Description of Applicability[a]
CP	SP 800-43: *Systems Administration Guidance for Securing Microsoft Windows 2000 Professional System*	
CP	SP 800-41: *Guidelines on Firewalls and Firewall Policy*	
CP	SP 800-34: *Contingency Planning Guide for Information Technology Systems*	
CP	SP 800-25: *Federal Agency Use of Public Key Technology for Digital Signatures and Authentication*	
CP	SP 800-24: *PBX Vulnerability Analysis: Finding Holes in Your PBX before Someone Else Does*	
CP	SP 800-21, Rev 1: *Guideline for Implementing Cryptography in the Federal Government*	
CP	SP 800-14: *Generally Accepted Principles and Practices for Securing Information Technology Systems*	
CP	SP 800-13: *Telecommunications Security Guidelines for Telecommunications Management Network*	
CP	SP 800-12: *An Introduction to Computer Security: The NIST Handbook*	
IA	**Identification and Authentication**	
IA	FIPS 201-1: *Personal Identity Verification for Federal Employees and Contractors*	
IA	FIPS 200: *Security Controls for Federal Information Systems*	
IA	FIPS 190: *Guideline for the Use of Advanced Authentication Technology Alternatives*	
IA	FIPS 140-2: *Security Requirements for Cryptographic Modules*	

Control Reference	Category/Document	Description of Applicability[a]
IA	SP 800-100: *Information Security Handbook for Managers*	
IA	SP 800-97: *Guide to IEEE 802.11i: Robust Security Networks*	
IA	SP 800-96: *PIV Card/Reader Interoperability Guidelines*	
IA	SP 800-87: *Codes for the Identification of Federal and Federally Assisted Organizations*	
IA	SP 800-86: *Guide to Integrating Forensic Techniques into Incident Response*	
IA	SP 800-81: *Secure Domain Name System (DNS) Deployment Guide*	
IA	SP 800-78: *Cryptographic Algorithms and Key Sizes for Personal Identity Verification*	
IA	SP 800-77: *Guide to IPSec VPNs*	
IA	SP 800-76: *Biometric Data Specification for Personal Identity Verification*	
IA	SP 800-73, Rev 1: *Integrated Circuit Card for Personal Identification Verification*	
IA	SP 800-72: *Guidelines on PDA Forensics*	
IA	SP 800-68: *Guidance for Securing Microsoft Windows XP Systems for IT Professionals: A NIST Security Configuration Checklist*	
IA	SP 800-66: *An Introductory Resource Guide for Implementing the Health Insurance Portability and Accountability Act (HIPAA) Security Rule*	
IA	SP 800-63: *Recommendation for Electronic Authentication*	
IA	SP 800-52: *Guidelines on the Selection and Use of Transport Layer Security*	

Control Reference	Category/Document	Description of Applicability[a]
IA	SP 800-48: *Wireless Network Security: 802.11, Bluetooth, and Handheld Devices*	
IA	SP 800-46: *Security for Telecommuting and Broadband Communications*	
IA	SP 800-45: *Guidelines on Electronic Mail Security*	
IA	SP 800-44: *Guidelines on Securing Public Web Servers*	
IA	SP 800-36: *Guide to Selecting Information Technology Security Products*	
IA	SP 800-32: *Introduction to Public Key Technology and the Federal PKI Infrastructure*	
IA	SP 800-25: *Federal Agency Use of Public Key Technology for Digital Signatures and Authentication*	
IA	SP 800-24: *PBX Vulnerability Analysis: Finding Holes in Your PBX before Someone Else Does*	
IA	SP 800-14: *Generally Accepted Principles and Practices for Securing Information Technology Systems*	
IA	SP 800-12: *An Introduction to Computer Security: The NIST Handbook*	
IR	**Incident Response**	
IR	FIPS 200: *Security Controls for Federal Information Systems*	
IR	SP 800-100: *Information Security Handbook for Managers*	
IR	SP 800-92: *Guide to Computer Security Log Management*	
IR	SP 800-83: *Guide to Malware Incident Prevention and Handling*	

Control Reference	Category/Document	Description of Applicability[a]
IR	SP 800-66: *An Introductory Resource Guide for Implementing the Health Insurance Portability and Accountability Act (HIPAA) Security Rule*	
IR	SP 800-61: *Computer Security Incident Handling Guide*	
IR	SP 800-50: *Building an Information Technology Security Awareness and Training Program*	
IR	SP 800-36: *Guide to Selecting Information Technology Security Products*	
IR	SP 800-31: *Intrusion Detection Systems (IDSs)*	
IR	SP 800-14: *Generally Accepted Principles and Practices for Securing Information Technology Systems*	
IR	SP 800-12: *An Introduction to Computer Security: The NIST Handbook*	
MA	**Maintenance**	
MA	FIPS 200: *Security Controls for Federal Information Systems*	
MA	SP 800-100: *Information Security Handbook for Managers*	
MA	SP 800-88: *Media Sanitization Guide*	
MA	SP 800-77: *Guide to IPSec VPNs*	
MA	SP 800-34: *Contingency Planning Guide for Information Technology Systems*	
MA	SP 800-24: *PBX Vulnerability Analysis: Finding Holes in Your PBX before Someone Else Does*	
MA	SP 800-14: *Generally Accepted Principles and Practices for Securing Information Technology Systems*	

Control Reference	Category/Document	Description of Applicability[a]
MA	SP 800-12: *An Introduction to Computer Security: The NIST Handbook*	
MP	**Media Protection**	
MP	FIPS 200: *Security Controls for Federal Information Systems*	
MP	SP 800-100: *Information Security Handbook for Managers*	
MP	SP 800-92: *Guide to Computer Security Log Management*	
MP	SP 800-88: *Media Sanitization Guide*	
MP	SP 800-86: *Guide to Integrating Forensic Techniques into Incident Response*	
MP	SP 800-72: *Guidelines on PDA Forensics*	
MP	SP 800-66: *An Introductory Resource Guide for Implementing the Health Insurance Portability and Accountability Act (HIPAA) Security Rule*	
MP	SP 800-57: *Recommendation on Key Management*	
MP	SP 800-36: *Guide to Selecting Information Technology Security Products*	
MP	SP 800-24: *PBX Vulnerability Analysis: Finding Holes in Your PBX before Someone Else Does*	
MP	SP 800-14: *Generally Accepted Principles and Practices for Securing Information Technology Systems*	
MP	SP 800-12: *An Introduction to Computer Security: The NIST Handbook*	
PE	**Physical and Environmental Protection**	
PE	FIPS 200: *Security Controls for Federal Information Systems*	

Control Reference	Category/Document	Description of Applicability[a]
PE	SP 800-100: *Information Security Handbook for Managers*	
PE	SP 800-96: *PIV Card/Reader Interoperability Guidelines*	
PE	SP 800-92: *Guide to Computer Security Log Management*	
PE	SP 800-86: *Guide to Integrating Forensic Techniques into Incident Response*	
PE	SP 800-78: *Cryptographic Algorithms and Key Sizes for Personal Identity Verification*	
PE	SP 800-76: *Biometric Data Specification for Personal Identity Verification*	
PE	SP 800-73, Rev 1: *Integrated Circuit Card for Personal Identification Verification*	
PE	SP 800-66: *An Introductory Resource Guide for Implementing the Health Insurance Portability and Accountability Act (HIPAA) Security Rule*	
PE	SP 800-58: *Security Considerations for Voice Over IP Systems*	
PE	SP 800-24: *PBX Vulnerability Analysis: Finding Holes in Your PBX before Someone Else Does*	
PE	SP 800-14: *Generally Accepted Principles and Practices for Securing Information Technology Systems*	
PE	SP 800-12: *An Introduction to Computer Security: The NIST Handbook*	
PL	**Planning**	
PL	FIPS 199: *Standards for Security Categorization of Federal Information and Information Systems*	

Control Reference	Category/Document	Description of Applicability[a]
PL	SP 800-100: *Information Security Handbook for Managers*	
PL	SP 800-89: *Recommendation for Obtaining Assurances for Digital Signature Applications*	
PL	SP 800-81: *Secure Domain Name System (DNS) Deployment Guide*	
PL	SP 800-66: *An Introductory Resource Guide for Implementing the Health Insurance Portability and Accountability Act (HIPAA) Security Rule*	
PL	SP 800-65: *Integrating Security into the Capital Planning and Investment Control Process*	
PL	SP 800-64: *Security Considerations in the Information System Development Life Cycle*	
PL	SP 800-58: *Security Considerations for Voice Over IP Systems*	
PL	SP 800-57: *Recommendation on Key Management*	
PL	SP 800-48: *Wireless Network Security: 802.11, Bluetooth, and Handheld Devices*	
PL	SP 800-46: *Security for Telecommuting and Broadband Communications*	
PL	SP 800-45: *Guidelines on Electronic Mail Security*	
PL	SP 800-44: *Guidelines on Securing Public Web Servers*	
PL	SP 800-42: *Guideline on Network Security Testing*	
PL	SP 800-41: *Guidelines on Firewalls and Firewall Policy*	

Control Reference	Category/Document	Description of Applicability[a]
PL	SP 800-40, Ver 2: *Creating a Patch and Vulnerability Management Program*	
PL	SP 800-40: *Procedures for Handling Security Patches*	
PL	SP 800-37: *Guidelines for the Security Certification and Accreditation of Federal Information Technology Systems*	
PL	SP 800-34: *Contingency Planning Guide for Information Technology Systems*	
PL	SP 800-33: *Underlying Technical Models for Information Technology Security*	
PL	SP 800-32: *Introduction to Public Key Technology and the Federal PKI Infrastructure*	
PL	SP 800-31: *Intrusion Detection Systems (IDSs)*	
PL	SP 800-30: *Risk Management Guide for Information Technology Systems*	
PL	SP 800-27: *Engineering Principles for Information Technology Security (A Baseline for Achieving Security)*	
PL	SP 800-26: *Security Self-Assessment Guide for Information Technology Systems*	
PL	SP 800-25: *Federal Agency Use of Public Key Technology for Digital Signatures and Authentication*	
PL	SP 800-21, Rev 1: *Guideline for Implementing Cryptography in the Federal Government*	
PL	SP 800-19: *Mobile Agent Security*	
PL	SP 800-18: *Guide for Developing Security Plans for Information Technology Systems*	

Control Reference	Category/Document	Description of Applicability[a]
PL	SP 800-14: *Generally Accepted Principles and Practices for Securing Information Technology Systems*	
PL	SP 800-12: *An Introduction to Computer Security: The NIST Handbook*	
PS	**Personnel Security**	
PS	FIPS 200: *Security Controls for Federal Information Systems*	
PS	SP 800-100: *Information Security Handbook for Managers*	
PS	SP 800-66: *An Introductory Resource Guide for Implementing the Health Insurance Portability and Accountability Act (HIPAA) Security Rule*	
PS	SP 800-14: *Generally Accepted Principles and Practices for Securing Information Technology Systems*	
PS	SP 800-12: *An Introduction to Computer Security: The NIST Handbook*	
RA	**Risk Assessment**	
RA	SP 800-83: *Guide to Malware Incident Prevention and Handling*	
RA	SP 800-66: *An Introductory Resource Guide for Implementing the Health Insurance Portability and Accountability Act (HIPAA) Security Rule*	
RA	SP 800-65: *Integrating Security into the Capital Planning and Investment Control Process*	
RA	SP 800-63: *Recommendation for Electronic Authentication*	
RA	SP 800-60: *Guide for Mapping Types of Information and Information Systems to Security Categories*	

Control Reference	Category/Document	Description of Applicability[a]
RA	SP 800-59: *Guideline for Identifying an Information System as a National Security System*	
RA	SP 800-53A: *Guide for Assessing the Security Controls in Federal Information Systems*	
RA	SP 800-51: *Use of the Common Vulnerabilities and Exposures (CVE) Vulnerability Naming Scheme*	
RA	SP 800-48: *Wireless Network Security: 802.11, Bluetooth, and Handheld Devices*	
RA	SP 800-46: *Security for Telecommuting and Broadband Communications*	
RA	SP 800-45: *Guidelines on Electronic Mail Security*	
RA	SP 800-44: *Guidelines on Securing Public Web Servers*	
RA	SP 800-42: *Guideline on Network Security Testing*	
RA	SP 800-40, Ver 2: *Creating a Patch and Vulnerability Management Program*	
RA	SP 800-40: *Procedures for Handling Security Patches*	
RA	SP 800-37: *Guidelines for the Security Certification and Accreditation of Federal Information Technology Systems*	
RA	SP 800-36: *Guide to Selecting Information Technology Security Products*	
RA	SP 800-34: *Contingency Planning Guide for Information Technology Systems*	
RA	SP 800-32: *Introduction to Public Key Technology and the Federal PKI Infrastructure*	

Control Reference	Category/Document	Description of Applicability[a]
RA	SP 800-31: *Intrusion Detection Systems (IDSs)*	
RA	SP 800-30: *Risk Management Guide for Information Technology Systems*	
RA	SP 800-28: *Guidelines on Active Content and Mobile Code*	
RA	SP 800-26: *Security Self-Assessment Guide for Information Technology Systems*	
RA	SP 800-25: *Federal Agency Use of Public Key Technology for Digital Signatures and Authentication*	
RA	SP 800-24: *PBX Vulnerability Analysis: Finding Holes in Your PBX before Someone Else Does*	
RA	SP 800-23: *Guideline to Federal Organizations on Security Assurance and Acquisition/Use of Tested/Evaluated Products*	
RA	SP 800-19: *Mobile Agent Security*	
RA	SP 800-14: *Generally Accepted Principles and Practices for Securing Information Technology Systems*	
RA	SP 800-13: *Telecommunications Security Guidelines for Telecommunications Management Network*	
RA	SP 800-12: *An Introduction to Computer Security: The NIST Handbook*	
SA	**System and Services Acquisition**	
SA	FIPS 200: *Security Controls for Federal Information Systems*	
SA	SP 800-100: *Information Security Handbook for Managers*	

Control Reference	Category/Document	Description of Applicability[a]
SA	SP 800-97: *Guide to IEEE 802.11i: Robust Security Networks*	
SA	SP 800-85: *PIV Middleware and PIV Card Application Conformance Test Guidelines*	
SA	SP 800-83: *Guide to Malware Incident Prevention and Handling*	
SA	SP 800-76: *Biometric Data Specification for Personal Identity Verification*	
SA	SP 800-66: *An Introductory Resource Guide for Implementing the Health Insurance Portability and Accountability Act (HIPAA) Security Rule*	
SA	SP 800-65: *Integrating Security into the Capital Planning and Investment Control Process*	
SA	SP 800-64: *Security Considerations in the Information System Development Life Cycle*	
SA	SP 800-36: *Guide to Selecting Information Technology Security Products*	
SA	SP 800-35: *Guide to Information Technology Security Services*	
SA	SP 800-34: *Contingency Planning Guide for Information Technology Systems*	
SA	SP 800-33: *Underlying Technical Models for Information Technology Security*	
SA	SP 800-31: *Intrusion Detection Systems (IDSs)*	
SA	SP 800-30: *Risk Management Guide for Information Technology Systems*	
SA	SP 800-27: *Engineering Principles for Information Technology Security (A Baseline for Achieving Security)*	

Control Reference	Category/Document	Description of Applicability[a]
SA	SP 800-23: *Guideline to Federal Organizations on Security Assurance and Acquisition/Use of Tested/Evaluated Products*	
SA	SP 800-21, Rev 1: *Guideline for Implementing Cryptography in the Federal Government*	
SA	SP 800-14: *Generally Accepted Principles and Practices for Securing Information Technology Systems*	
SA	SP 800-12: *An Introduction to Computer Security: The NIST Handbook*	
SC	**System and Communications Protection**	
SC	FIPS 201-1: *Personal Identity Verification for Federal Employees and Contractors*	
SC	FIPS 200: *Security Controls for Federal Information Systems*	
SC	FIPS 198: *The Keyed-Hash Message Authentication Code (HMAC)*	
SC	FIPS 197: *Advanced Encryption Standard*	
SC	FIPS 190: *Guideline for the Use of Advanced Authentication Technology Alternatives*	
SC	FIPS 186-3: *Digital Signature Standard (DSS)*	
SC	FIPS 180-2: *Secure Hash Standard (SHS)*	
SC	FIPS 140-2: *Security Requirements for Cryptographic Modules*	
SC	SP 800-100: *Information Security Handbook for Managers*	
SC	SP 800-97: *Guide to IEEE 802.11i: Robust Security Networks*	

Control Reference	Category/Document	Description of Applicability[a]
SC	SP 800-90: *Recommendation for Random Number Generation Using Deterministic Random Bit Generators*	
SC	SP 800-89: *Recommendation for Obtaining Assurances for Digital Signature Applications*	
SC	FIPS 201-1: *Personal Identity Verification for Federal Employees and Contractors*	
SC	FIPS 200: *Security Controls for Federal Information Systems*	
SC	FIPS 199: *Standards for Security Categorization of Federal Information and Information Systems*	
SC	SP 800-100: *Information Security Handbook for Managers*	
SC	SP 800-83: *Guide to Malware Incident Prevention and Handling*	
SC	SP 800-81: *Secure Domain Name System (DNS) Deployment Guide*	
SC	SP 800-78: *Cryptographic Algorithms and Key Sizes for Personal Identity Verification*	
SC	SP 800-77: *Guide to IPSec VPNs*	
SC	SP 800-73, Rev 1: *Integrated Circuit Card for Personal Identification Verification*	
SC	SP 800-70: *Security Configuration Checklists Program for IT Products*	
SC	SP 800-68: *Guidance for Securing Microsoft Windows XP Systems for IT Professionals: A NIST Security Configuration Checklist*	
SC	SP 800-67: *Recommendation for the Triple Data Encryption Algorithm (TDEA) Block Cipher*	

Control Reference	Category/Document	Description of Applicability[a]
SC	SP 800-66: *An Introductory Resource Guide for Implementing the Health Insurance Portability and Accountability Act (HIPAA) Security Rule*	
SC	SP 800-58: *Security Considerations for Voice Over IP Systems*	
SC	SP 800-57: *Recommendation on Key Management*	
SC	SP 800-56A: *Recommendation for Pair-Wise Key Establishment Schemes Using Discrete Logarithm Cryptography*	
SC	SP 800-52: *Guidelines on the Selection and Use of Transport Layer Security*	
SC	SP 800-49: *Federal S/MIME V3 Client Profile*	
SC	SP 800-46: *Security for Telecommuting and Broadband Communications*	
SC	SP 800-45: *Guidelines on Electronic Mail Security*	
SC	SP 800-44: *Guidelines on Securing Public Web Servers*	
SC	SP 800-41: *Guidelines on Firewalls and Firewall Policy*	
SC	SP 800-38D: *Recommendation for Block Cipher Modes of Operation: Galois/Counter Mode (GCM) for Confidentiality and Authentication*	
SC	SP 800-38C: *Recommendation for Block Cipher Modes of Operation: The CCM Mode for Authentication and Confidentiality*	
SC	SP 800-38B: *Recommendation for Block Cipher Modes of Operation: The RMAC Authentication Mode*	

Control Reference	Category/Document	Description of Applicability[a]
SC	SP 800-38A: *Recommendation for Block Cipher Modes of Operation—Methods and Techniques*	
SC	SP 800-36: *Guide to Selecting Information Technology Security Products*	
SC	SP 800-32: *Introduction to Public Key Technology and the Federal PKI Infrastructure*	
SC	SP 800-29: *A Comparison of the Security Requirements for Cryptographic Modules in FIPS 140-1 and FIPS 140-2*	
SC	SP 800-28: *Guidelines on Active Content and Mobile Code*	
SC	SP 800-25: *Federal Agency Use of Public Key Technology for Digital Signatures and Authentication*	
SC	SP 800-22: *A Statistical Test Suite for Random and Pseudorandom Number Generators for Cryptographic Applications*	
SC	SP 800-21, Rev 1: *Guideline for Implementing Cryptography in the Federal Government*	
SC	SP 800-20: *Modes of Operation Validation System for the Triple Data Encryption Algorithm (TMOVS): Requirements and Procedures*	
SC	SP 800-19: *Mobile Agent Security*	
SC	SP 800-17: *Modes of Operation Validation System (MOVS): Requirements and Procedures*	
SC	SP 800-15, Ver 1: *Minimum Interoperability Specification for PKI Components (MISPC)*	

Control Reference	Category/Document	Description of Applicability[a]
SC	SP 800-14: *Generally Accepted Principles and Practices for Securing Information Technology Systems*	
SC	SP 800-12: *An Introduction to Computer Security: The NIST Handbook*	
SI	**System and Information Integrity**	
SI	FIPS 200: *Security Controls for Federal Information Systems*	
SI	SP 800-100: *Information Security Handbook for Managers*	
SI	SP 800-92: *Guide to Computer Security Log Management*	
SI	SP 800-86: *Guide to Integrating Forensic Techniques into Incident Response*	
SI	SP 800-85: *PIV Middleware and PIV Card Application Conformance Test Guidelines*	
SI	SP 800-83: *Guide to Malware Incident Prevention and Handling*	
SI	SP 800-66: *An Introductory Resource Guide for Implementing the Health Insurance Portability and Accountability Act (HIPAA) Security Rule*	
SI	SP 800-61: *Computer Security Incident Handling Guide*	
SI	SP 800-57: *Recommendation on Key Management*	
SI	SP 800-51: *Use of the Common Vulnerabilities and Exposures (CVE) Vulnerability Naming Scheme*	
SI	SP 800-48: *Wireless Network Security: 802.11, Bluetooth, and Handheld Devices*	

Control Reference	Category/Document	Description of Applicability[a]
SI	SP 800-45: *Guidelines on Electronic Mail Security*	
SI	SP 800-44: *Guidelines on Securing Public Web Servers*	
SI	SP 800-43: *Systems Administration Guidance for Securing Microsoft Windows 2000 Professional System*	
SI	SP 800-42: *Guideline on Network Security Testing*	
SI	SP 800-36: *Guide to Selecting Information Technology Security Products*	
SI	SP 800-31: *Intrusion Detection Systems (IDSs)*	
SI	SP 800-28: *Guidelines on Active Content and Mobile Code*	
SI	SP 800-19: *Mobile Agent Security*	
SI	SP 800-14: *Generally Accepted Principles and Practices for Securing Information Technology Systems*	
SI	SP 800-12: *An Introduction to Computer Security: The NIST Handbook*	

[a] All NIST security documents are available on csrc.nist.gov (last accessed July 2007).

Appendix G: IA Standards Best Practices References

Most people like the concept of *best practices*; the phrase has a nice sound and rings of perfection as well as a *Ka-Ching!* price tag. As one executive put it as he interrupted a presentation on best practices, "Stop right there! I can't afford best practices! I don't want best practices! I want *good enough* practices!" Although not likely to build a successful marketing campaign with the tagline of "Buy our services 'cause they're darn well good enough!" one does understand the executive's position. So, talk about best practices, but understand that in many situations *adequate practices* are the compromise between cost and benefit.

Like so many popular buzz phrases, the meaning of *best practices* is vague. A mention of best practices is the same as saying *they, he, she,* or some other indefinite reference. The question is: What are best practices? Where does one find them? Who else thinks they are best practices? The table below provides some references to best practices and their sources. Each is a best practice according to the beholder. ISO does not carry a lot of weight in the U.S. defense arena; they look more to DoD Instructions and Directives. U.S. DoD Instructions do not carry a lot of weight with an Australian company doing business on three continents.

Table G.1 provides the beginning of an IA standards best practices reference. There are many IA standards; the applicability of any particular one is organizational and situational dependent. Commercial organizations tend toward internationally accepted standards like ISO or legislatively driven standards like COBIT.

Table G.1   Best Practice References

Source Country	Institution	Best Practice	Online Source
International	International Standards Organization (ISO)	ISO 15408—Common Criteria	www.iso.org
International	International Standards Organization (ISO)	ISO 27000—a series of information technology standards; also the glossary of terms used in the ISO 27000 series	www.iso.org
International	International Standards Organization (ISO)	ISO 27001—an information security management system (ISMS) certification standard (published)	www.iso.org
International	International Standards Organization (ISO)	ISO 27002—code of practice for information security techniques; note: the current version of ISO 27002:2005 is ISO 17799:2005 renamed	www.iso.org
International	International Standards Organization (ISO)	ISO 27003—a new ISMS implementation guide (pending)	www.iso.org
International	International Standards Organization (ISO)	ISO 27004—a standard for ISMS metrics and measures (pending)	www.iso.org
International	International Standards Organization (ISO)	ISO 27005—a standard for risk management (pending)	www.iso.org

International	International Standards Organization (ISO)	ISO 27006—a guide to the accreditation of organizations offering certification (pending)	www.iso.org
International	International Standards Organization (ISO)	ISO 27799—a guide to ISO 27001 for health sector organizations	www.iso.org
International	International Standards Organization (ISO)	ISO 11770-[1–3]—key management	www.iso.org
International	International Standards Organization (ISO)	ISO 13335-[1–5]—IT security management guidelines	www.iso.org
International	International Standards Organization (ISO)	ISO/IEC 18403—guidelines for implementation, operation, and management of IDS	www.iso.org
International	International Standards Organization (ISO)	Many more	www.iso.orgInternational Organization on Computer Evidence (IOCE) Guidelines for Best Practice in the Forensic Examination of Digital Technology
International	International Organization on Computer Evidence (IOCE)	*Guidelines for Best Practice in the Forensic Examination of Digital Technology*	http://ncfs.org/home.html
International	International Organization on Computer Evidence (IOCE)	*Digital Evidence: Standards and Principles*	http://www.ioce.org/index.php?id=9
International	Information Technology Infrastructure Library (ITIL)	Service management	http://www.itil-officialsite.com/home/home.asp

Source Country	Institution	Best Practice	Online Source
Canada	Communications Security Establishment (CSE)	Publications include IT Security Handbook, Threat and Risk Assessment Working Guide, and many more	http://www.cse.dnd.ca/index-e.html
Europe	European Telecommunications Standards Institute (ETSI)	Many security standards	http://www.etsi.org/
United States	Center for Emergency Response (CERT)	*Guide to System and Network Security Practices*	http://www.cert.org/
United States	Center for Emergency Response (CERT)	Security improvement modules	http://www.cert.org/
United States	Center for Emergency Response (CERT)	CSIRT development	http://www.cert.org/csirts/
United States	ISACA	COBIT security baseline	http://www.isaca.org/
United States	Office of Management Budget (OMB)	OMB Circular A-130 Appendix III—"Security of Federal Automated Resources"	http://www.whitehouse.gov/omb/circulars/a130/appendix_iii.pdf
United States	Carnegie Mellon University	System Security Engineering (SSE) Capability Maturity Model (CMM)	http://www.sse-cmm.org/index.html
United States	Purdue University	CERIAS	http://www.cerias.purdue.edu/
United States	DoD issuances	DoD directives (e.g., 8500.01E IA), DoD instructions (8500.2 IA implementation)	http://www.dtic.mil/whs/directives/

United States	IETF	RFC 2196: Site Security Handbook	http://www.ietf.org/rfc/rfc2196.txt
United States	Information Assurance Technical Framework Forum (IATFF)	Many guides to IT security	http://www.iatf.net/
United States	National Institute of Standards and Technology (NIST) Computer Security Resource Center (CSRC)	Many guides to IT security	http://csrc.nist.gov/
United States	Federal Enterprise Architecture Program Management Office	Federal Enterprise Architecture (FEA)	http://www.feapmo.gov/
United States	Department of Defense	Department of Defense Architecture Framework (DoDAF)	jitc.fhu.disa.mil/jitc_dri/pdfs/dodaf_v1v1.pdf
United States	Institute for Enterprise Architecture Developments	Enterprise architecture (EA)	http://www.enterprise-architecture.info/
United States	IEEE	IEEE 1362-1998: Guide for Information Technology—System Definition Concept of Operation Document	http://standards.ieee.org/reading/ieee/std_public/description/se/1362-1998_desc.html
United States	U.S. Department of Justice (DoJ)	*Forensic Examination of Digital Evidence: A Guide for Law Enforcement*	http://ncfs.org/digital_examination_guide.pdf
United States	Scientific Working Group for Digital Evidence (SWGDE)	"Best Practices for Digital Evidence Laboratory Programs"	http://ncfs.org/swgde/documents/swgde2003/BestPractices.pdf
United States	Forum of Incident Response and Security Teams (FIRST)	Best practice library	http://www.first.org/resources/guides/

Note: All URLs last accessed July 2007.

Appendix H: Root Cause Analysis Template

Root Cause Analysis (RCA) Report for
Company Name
DD Month CCYY

Introduction

Provide a brief introduction that includes event details resulting in the need for an RCA, imminent activity in support of the RCA, etc. An RCA is about identifying connections between events and ultimately determining *cause and effect*. The RCA process separates cause and effect from other event relationships as shown in the list below. For the descriptions in the list, assume an event (A) has some relation to event (B); the following provide some insights regarding the potential relationship between (A) and (B):

- Causal: The relation between cause and effect; a predictable result or flow from one action or event (A) to the next (B); an occurrence of (A) *causes* the occurrence of (B).
- Coincidence: The occurrence of events that chance to happen at the same time but seem to have some connection.
- Correlation: A relation existing between actions or events that occur together in such a way not attributable only to chance. (A) may not cause (B), but other events or circumstances may result in (A) and (B) occurring together.
- Contribution: The occurrence of one event (A) is not causal but contributory to even (B); event (A) is necessary but not sufficient to cause or predict event (B).
- Control: (A) has power or control over (B); (A) is not the cause of (B), but influences (B); given the absence of (A), (B) would still exist, but in a different state or behavior.

- Cultural: The relationship between events (A) and (B) is a cultural relationship such that the relationship exists in a particular culture or society, but not another.
- Convention: The relationship between (A) and (B) is one of convention or social expectation; there is no cause and effect outside the conventional expectation for the fulfillment of the relationship.
- Conditioned: The cause and effect is not a natural occurrence, but one that is conditioned, e.g., Pavlov's dog (B) salivates at the ring of a bell (A).

The need for an RCA presumes the occurrence of an undesirable event and the need to determine the cause of that event. The purpose of the RCA is to identify the *root cause* of that undesirable event. The RCA examines incident details, determines the facts surrounding the incident, and distinguishes the causal events and circumstances versus other types of event relations that may be more symptomatic or even unrelated despite appearances. The RCA results provide feedback to the organization to reduce or eliminate the likelihood of incident recurrence. If event recurrence cannot be eliminated with certainty, at the least the RCA contributes to reducing the effect of any recurrence on the organization.

Root Cause Analysis (RCA) Methodology

The root cause methodology consists of the following processes:

- Discovery
- Analysis
- Reporting
- Resolution

The discovery process consists of a series of interviews, phone conferences, and documentation to discern the details of the incident and details surrounding the incident that may have contributed to incident occurrence. The analysis process evaluates the details and makes conclusions regarding event relations. The analysis may or may not identify a root cause with 100 percent certainty. The reporting process consists of presenting the details of the analysis. This template provides one template for RCA reporting. The resolution process consists of organizational feedback to reduce or eliminate the potential for incident recurrence.

RCA Summary

Table H.1 provides a summary of the RCA findings.

Table H.1   RCA Summary

RCA Consideration	Component	Comments
Equipment/material		
Procedure		
Personnel		
Design		
Training		
Management		
External phenomenon		

Conclusions

The [likely]* root cause of this incident is TBD.

1. The incident is [not] due to an equipment/material issue.
2. The incident is [not] due to a procedure issue.
3. The incident is [not] due to a personnel issue.
4. The incident is [not] due to a design issue.
5. The incident is [not] due to a training issue.
6. The incident is [not] due to a management issue.
7. The incident is [not] due to an external phenomenon issue.

Further Considerations and Open Issues

TBD

Recommendations

TBD

---

* If the root cause is not 100 percent determinable, attempt to identify the most likely cause with justification and explanation regarding why root cause is indeterminable.

Mitigation Plan

TBD

Organizational Feedback

TBD

Table H.2 Organizational Feedback

Area	Component	Organizational feedback
Equipment/material		
Procedure		
Personnel		
Design		
Training		
Management		
External phenomenon		

Supporting Details

TBD

Organization Perspective

TBD

The details in the following section provide more information on the discovery and analysis that support the conclusions regarding the RCA.

Root Cause Analysis (RCA) Details

Include a summary narrative that includes the following details:

- Discovery
  - Information necessary for investigation
  - Available information; unavailable information and why
- Sources of discovery information
  - Documents, logs, people, etc.

The RCA details are provided in the context of the following outline:

- Players—people involved in the incident as well as the RCA investigation and reporting
- Incident—incident details
- Examine each of the following and their relevant contributions (if any) to the incident:
    - Equipment/material
    - Procedure
    - Personnel
    - Design
    - Training
    - Management
    - External phenomenon

Players

The table below provides a summary of the people involved in the incident, RCA investigation, and RCA reporting.

Table H.3   Players

Role	Assignment	Organization	Comments

Incident

Identify and articulate details of the incident in terms of the following:

- **Who**: Who was involved, affected.
- **What**: What was involved, affected.

- **Why**: Why activity was occurring during which the incident happened (e.g., routine maintenance, production service running as usual, new software installation, etc.).
- **When**: Date, time; include significance (e.g., end of quarter, end of month, holiday season).
- **Where**: Address, building, floor, room, system/technology.
- **How**: Describe the symptoms surrounding the incident (e.g., testing of new application brought down the production server).

Activity Sequence/Chronology Leading to Event

Table H.4 presents a chronology of significant events leading up to and beyond the event.

Table H.4   Event Sequence

Activity	Date	Time	Comments

Note in the "Comments" column whether the activity is contributory, noncontributory, or of indeterminate relationship to the event.

Information Gathered during RCA Process

TBD

People Interviewed during RCA Process

TBD

Equipment/Material

Was equipment/material a cause? If so, why was equipment/material a cause?
TBD

Table H.5   Equipment/Material Analysis

Cause Code	Subcategories	Cause Degree	Description
1A	Defective or failed part		
IB	Defective or failed material		
IC	Defective weld, braze, or soldered joint		
ID	Error by manufacturer in shipping or marking		
IE	Electrical or instrument noise		
IF	Contamination		

Cause degree: D = direct cause, C = contribution, R = root cause, NA = not applicable,

Comments

TBD

Procedure

Was procedure a cause? If so, why?
TBD

Table H.6   Procedure Analysis

Cause Code	Subcategories	Cause Degree	Description
2A	Defective or inadequate procedure		
2B	Lack of procedure		

Cause degree: D = direct cause, C = contribution, R = root cause, NA = not applicable.

Comments

TBD

Personnel

Were personnel a cause? If yes, why?
TBD

Table H.7   Personnel Analysis

Cause Code	Subcategories	Cause Degree	Description
3A	Inadequate work environment		
3B	Inattention to detail		
3C	Violation of requirement or procedure		
3D	Verbal communication problem		
3E	Other human error		

Cause degree: D = direct cause, C = contribution, R = root cause, NA = not applicable.

Comments

TBD

As point of explanation for "inadequate work environment," consider the following excerpt from the DoE *RCA Guide*, 1992:

> Facility and equipment operability, procedures and documentation, and management attitudes are all part of the work environment that needs to be evaluated for each of these steps. Common problems that need to be considered are:

- Cognitive overload
- Cognitive underload/boredom
- Habit intrusion
- Lapse of memory/recall
- Spatial misorientation
- Mindset/preconceived idea
- Tunnel vision or lack of big picture
- Unawareness
- Wrong assumptions made
- Reflect/instinctive action
- Thinking and actions not coordinated
- Insufficient degree of attention applied
- Shortcuts evoked to complete job

- Complacency/lack of perceived need for concern
- Confusion
- Misdiagnosis
- Fear of failure/consequences
- Tired/fatigued*

Design

Was design a cause? If so, why was design a cause?
TBD

Table H.8   Design Analysis

Cause Code	Subcategories	Cause Degree	Description
4A	Inadequate man–machine interface		
4B	Inadequate or defective design		
4C	Error in equipment or material selection		
4D	Drawing, specification, or data errors		

Cause degree: D = direct cause, C = contribution, R = root cause, NA = not applicable.

Comments

TBD

---

* DoE, *RCA Guide*, 1992, p. H-1.

Training

Was training a cause? If so, why?
TBD

Table H.9 Training Analysis

Cause Code	Subcategories	Cause Degree	Description
5A	No training provided		
5B	Insufficient practice or hands-on experience		
5C	Inadequate content		
5D	Insufficient refresher training		
5E	Inadequate presentation or materials		

Cause degree: D = direct cause, C = contribution, R = root cause, NA = not applicable.

Comments

TBD

Management

Was management a cause? If so, why?
TBD

Table H.10 Management Analysis

Cause Code	Subcategories	Cause Degree	Description
6A	Inadequate administrative control		
6B	Work organization/planning deficiency		
6C	Inadequate supervision		
6D	Improper resource allocation		
6E	Policy not adequately defined, disseminated, or enforced		
6F	Other management problem		

Cause degree: D = direct cause, C = contribution, R = root cause, NA = not applicable.

Comments

TBD

External Phenomenon

Was external phenomenon a cause? If so, why?
TBD

Table H.11   External Phenomenon Analysis

Cause Code	Subcategories	Cause Degree	Description
7A	Weather or ambient condition		
7B	Power failure or transient		
7C	External fire or explosion		
7D	Theft, tampering, sabotage, or vandalism		

Cause degree: D = direct cause, C = contribution, R = root cause, NA = not applicable.

Comments

TBD

References

U.S. Department of Energy (DoE). 1992. *Root cause analysis guidance document*, 1992.

Appendix I: Problem Assertion Document Template

Problem Assertion Document (PAD) for
Company Name
DD Month CCYY

Introduction

Insert a brief introduction that includes pending activity and motivation for the PAD. *The objective of a formal problem assertion document (PAD) is to ensure the identification and articulation of the right problem.* The subsequent solution will then address and resolve the real problem.

In brief, a problem is the experience of an undesirable state or outcome. The PAD provides assistance to think about, identify, and articulate the problem. The benefits of the PAD include a standard approach to problem assertions that is consistent, comprehensive, and repeatable. The formality of the PAD methodology provides the ability to capture lessons learned from each experience and to evolve the PAD template to incorporate these learned lessons.

In producing a solution to a problem, there are four possible outcomes:

1. Right solution to the right problem (RSRP)
2. Right solution to the wrong problem (RSWP)
3. Wrong solution to the right problem (WSRP)
4. Wrong solution to the wrong problem (WSWP)

The target result is RSRP; even so, this is just the beginning. An additional factor is the degree of the problem that the solution resolves. If indeed we end up with the right solution to the right problem, that solution may resolve less than 100 percent of the problem. The residual problem may need a separate solution. The residual problem may be irresolvable, e.g., *if we repeal the law of gravity, we have a solution*. The residual problem may be perfectly acceptable. The best possible outcome is RSRP with 100 percent resolution.

The RSWP outcome may produce a brilliant solution. Brilliant solutions to the wrong problem produce wonderful results that are of no use to anyone because the solution has no problem to resolve. Another characterization of this type of result is "build it and they will come" or "technology for technology's sake." While at times academically interesting, the investments in these types of solutions are a waste of limited resources.

The WSRP may be a failure in any number of areas. A root cause analysis (RCA) will assist in discovering personnel issues, process issues, technology issues, etc., that contributed to the development of the wrong solution. Resolving the environment that permits WSRP is absolutely critical to ensure such poor results do not repeat themselves. The explanation for such results may be quite subtle in organization culture, individual psychology, mental maps, decision making, etc. The formality of an RCA may assist with uncovering these nuances.

The WSWP is the worst of all situations with resource investments doomed from the outset.

The Problem Space

There is a difference between the problem and the problem space. The problem is what we are trying to identify and resolve. The problem space includes all the aspects of and around the problem, including the environment within which the problem occurs, the people and technology affected by the problem, and the people and technology causing the problem.

PAD Methodology

The intent of the PAD methodology is to discover and record the details that comprise the problem space. Using the tables and guideline in this template, the PAD methodology consists of:

- Defining the problem space
  - Brainstorming
- Problem statement
- Reality check
- Recommendation

Brainstorming consists of generating ideas without criticism or evaluation—free flow with anything that comes to mind. During brainstorming, there is nothing that is ridiculous, unrelated, off the wall, or that warrants any other pejorative label. All ideas are fair game and recorded during brainstorming. What may finally end up as a discarded idea may indeed be the catalyst to the final solution. Apply brainstorming to the guideline herein to define the problem space.

Having gathered, enumerated, and articulated the **problem space**, there remains the critical evaluation of the details to discard supposition and keep facts. The **problem statement** section provides a guideline for problem definition. Having stated the problem, perform a **reality check** on the problem statement to see if it makes sense. Finally, make **recommendations** on how to proceed with addressing the problem. Similar to addressing risk, there may be a need to fix the problem, or the problem resolution may be impractical or impossible. The formal process in this template provides a manner to reach an intelligible conclusion with facts and rationale to back up the final decision.

Define the Problem Space

The PAD process consists of a careful review of available information regarding the specifics of the problem, research into possible causes of the problem, and analysis of evidence as it pertains to the possible problem characteristics. Sources consulted in the course of this PAD include:

- Business experts with the areas of:
  - TBD
- Technical experts with the areas of:
  - TBD

Table I.1 presents problem space categories and a guideline to think about each. Reuse the outline in Table I.1 as a guide to record findings, thoughts, comments, issues, and questions in the following sections. Then, record details in context of what may be in scope and out of scope with respect to the problem space.

Table I.1   Problem Space Category Descriptions

Problem Space Category	Guide
Personnel	Intraorganizational people and their relationship with the problem. Include whether they are (or may be) contributors to the problem or recipients of the problem, the latter being a state of having to deal with the problem or the problem situation.
Players	Record any other players and their relationship with the problem. These include any people outside the organization or immediate problem environment. Note that complex systems have many times removed cause-effect relationships.
Process (business process)	Consider policy that drives standards and process. Consider the execution of the process, cognitive understanding, manual ability/dexterity to execute. Are there design issues with the process? Is it a training issue? Is it a management issue?
Organization	Consider organizational structure: hierarchical, matrix, chain of command, communications protocol, culture, organizational reward structure. Is the problem with governance (policy, strategic objectives)? Is the problem with management (strategic plans, tactical objectives)? Is the problem with operations (tactical execution)? Is the problem with use (awareness, understanding, ability)?
Environmental	Consider intraorganizational as well as interorganizational environments. Is the problem internal? Is the problem external?
Data/information	What data surrounds the problem space? Is it adequate in content? Understandable in form? Available for use?
Applications/business functions	What business functions and applications surround the problem space?
Technology/ Infrastructure	Technology includes far more than just computers. Consider any tool that assists a person to perform a task effectively as technology. Consider any aspect that supports a person in performing a task effectively as infrastructure. Infrastructure may be a computer network infrastructure (i.e., routers, cables, wireless) or utilities (i.e., water, HVAC).

When considering each problem space category in the following sections, Table I.2 provides sample questions to ask in the context of each problem category.

Table I.2   Problem Statement Guide

Perspective	Guide
Who	Whom does the problem affect? Who contributes to the problem?
What	What does the problem affect? What contributes to the problem?
Why	Why is the effect what it is? Why do the contributors contribute to the problem?
When	When does the problem occur?
Where	Where does the problem occur?
How	How does the problem occur? How is the problem realized (known)? How is the problem encountered?

Personnel and Players

Table I.3 provides a summary of the people involved in or around the problem space. Who wants change? Whom does the problem affect? Who may contribute to the problem? Who may be causing the problem?

Table I.3   Personnel and Player's List

Name	Role	Organization/ Department	Comments
TBD			

Is a person or people part of the problem space? State why or why not. Common contributions to the problem may include the following:*

- Cognitive overload
- Cognitive underload/boredom
- Habit intrusion
- Lapse of memory/recall
- Spatial misorientation
- Mindset/preconceived idea
- Tunnel vision or lack of big picture
- Unawareness
- Wrong assumptions made
- Reflect/instinctive action
- Thinking and actions not coordinated
- Insufficient degree of attention applied
- Shortcuts evoked to complete job
- Complacency/lack of perceived need for concern
- Confusion
- Misdiagnosis
- Fear of failure/consequences
- Tired/fatigued

Table I.4 provides for an analysis of the players to identify problem areas, traits, and relevancy for each player in the problem space.

Table I.4 People Analysis

Subcategories	Problem Involvement	Description
Work environment		
Inattention to detail		
Violation of policy		
Violation of requirement or procedure		
Communication problem		
Other human error		

Problem involvement: D = direct, C = contributing, P = root problem, NA = not applicable.

---

* Excerpt from DoE *RCA Guide*, 1992, p. H-1.

Additional Commentary

TBD

Training

Is training (poorly designed, delivered, or nonexistent) part of the problem space? State why or why not.

Table I.5   Training Analysis

Subcategories	Problem Involvement	Description
No training provided		
Insufficient practice or hands-on experience		
Inadequate training content		
Insufficient refresher training		
Inadequate presentation or materials		

Problem involvement: D = direct, C = contributing, P = root problem, NA = not applicable.

Additional Commentary

TBD

Management

Is management part of the problem space? State why or why not.

Table I.6 Management Analysis

Subcategories	Problem Involvement	Description
Inadequate administrative control		
Work organization/ planning deficiency		
Inadequate supervision		
Improper resource allocation		
Policy not adequately defined, disseminated, or enforced		
Other management problem		

Problem involvement: D = direct, C = contributing, P = root problem, NA = not applicable.

Additional Commentary

TBD

Process

Is process part of the problem space? State why or why not.

Table I.7   Process

Subcategories	Problem Involvement	Description
Business function		
Workflow		
Procedure		
Task		
Kinetic task		
Cognitive task		

Problem involvement: D = direct, C = contributing, P = root problem, NA = not applicable.

Additional Commentary

TBD

Evaluation of process will benefit from distinguishing inputs, process, and outputs as in the following outline:

- Inputs
  - Dependencies, requirements, interface, format
- Process
  - Internal procedures
- Outputs
  - Expectations, requirements, interface, format

Equipment/Material (including Information Technology)

Is equipment or material part of the problem space? State why or why not.

Table I.8   Equipment/Material Analysis

Subcategories	Problem Involvement	Description
System		
Subsystem		
Inherent flaw (e.g., software bug)		
Malfunction flaw (e.g., power brownout)		

Problem involvement: D = direct, C = contributing, P = root problem, NA = not applicable.

Additional Commentary

TBD

Design

Is design part of the problem space? State why or why not.

Table I.9   Design Analysis

Subcategories	Problem Involvement	Description
Inadequate human–machine interface		
Inadequate or defective design		
Error in equipment or material selection		
Drawing, specification, or data errors		

Problem involvement: D = direct, C = contributing, P = root problem, NA = not applicable.

Additional Commentary

TBD

Environmental

Is the environment part of the problem space? State why or why not.

Table I.10   Environmental Analysis

Subcategories	Problem Involvement	Description
Weather		
Cosmological		
Terrestrial		
Power failure or transient		
External fire or explosion		
Theft, tampering, sabotage, or vandalism		

Problem involvement: D = direct, C = contributing, P = root problem, NA = not applicable.

Additional Commentary

TBD

Data

Is data part of the problem space? State why or why not.

Table I.11   Data Analysis

Subcategories	Problem Involvement	Description
Structure of data		
Categorization or classification		
Metadata		

Problem involvement: D = direct, C = contributing, P = root problem, NA = not applicable.

Additional Commentary

TBD

Applications

Is the application part of the problem space? State why or why not.

Table I.12 Applications Analysis

Subcategories	Problem involvement	Description
Software quality assurance (SQA) issue		
Malfunction		
Inherent design flaw (e.g., adheres to RFC, RFC design is flawed)		

Problem involvement: D = direct, C = contributing, P = root problem, NA = not applicable.

Additional Commentary

TBD

Discerning Details of the Problem

Use Table I.13 to define the discrete parts of the problem. For each problem attribute, describe the desired outcome, the end state. Describe the current state and highlight the roadblocks to reaching the end state. State the necessary actions to address and overcome the roadblocks. Following are some sample questions to discern the roadblock details:

- Who
  - Who is in the way?
  - What about them is in the way?
    - Authority, desire, personality, personal control, etc.
- What
  - What is in the way?
    - Process (business process)
    - Organization

- ■ Environmental
- ■ Data/information
- ■ Applications/business functions
- ■ Technology/infrastructure
- ■ Why
  - – Why is the roadblock a roadblock? What about it makes it in the way of problem resolution? A cause or contributor to the problem?
  - – Is there a conflict of policy or procedure?
- ■ When
  - – When is the roadblock a roadblock? Is there an issue with timing (e.g., conflict with other daily, weekly, monthly, quarterly, or annual event)?
- ■ Where
  - – Where does the roadblock emanate from? Where does the roadblock manifest as a roadblock? For example, is this a corporate mandate without full knowledge of the local operating environment (i.e., an exception is warranted)?
- ■ How
  - – How does the roadblock become a roadblock? How is it in the way of problem resolution?

Expressing the discrete parts of the final problem also includes expressing a problem perspective. Problem perspectives include:

- ■ Governance—Mission, policy, strategic objectives
- ■ Management—Strategic plans, tactical objectives, tactical plans, building, implementing
- ■ Operations—Operating and maintaining
- ■ Use—Workflow, process, tasks

Problem resolution recommendations need to go to the appropriate organizational level for executive backing, policy modifications, management oversight, operations execution, and user awareness and understanding. Stating details of each perspective as applicable will assist in making the problem statement actionable.

Table I.13   Final Problem: The Discrete Parts

Problem Characteristics	Desired Outcome/ End State	Current State	Roadblocks	Required Actions
Attribute				
Who				
What				
Why				
When				
Where				
How				
Perspective				
Governance				
Management				
Operations				
Use				
Category				
Personnel				
Players				
Process (business process)				
Organization				
Environmental				
Data/information				
Applications/business functions				
Technology/infrastructure				

Problem Statement

Compile a narrative from the above that states the problem in three paragraphs (or sections):

- Desired outcome
- Current state and associated roadblocks
- Required actions to overcome roadblocks and achieve desired outcome

Problem Statement Checks/Balance

Having produced a final problem statement, Table I.14 prompts for details regarding the problem statement and the effects of a solution (whatever that solution may be); remember the goal is to identify the problem, the correct problem. The objective is to ensure an investment of resources actually produces a solution to the correct problem.

Note: The objective of the PAD is to produce a clearly stated problem, not a solution. Do not get caught up in discussing solution details. We are not looking to define a problem that fits a solution. We are looking to identify and clearly articulate the correct problem.

Table I.14 provides a template to perform a reality check on the problem statement. The reality check questions are only guidelines to spark thought; by all means, add questions. Record answers, comments, and conclusions regarding the questions in the table as well. Maintaining a record of thought process and rationale is extremely valuable for personal, team, and organizational learning.

Table I.14   Problem Statement Checks/Balance

Checkpoint	Reality Check	Comments
Who	Who does the problem affect? Who benefits from a solution?	
What	What is the environment of the problem? The scope (breadth and depth)? What will be changed as a result of a solution?	
Why	Why is the problem a problem? Why will a solution resolve the problem?	
When	When does the problem cause the effect? Is the problem pervasive (exists all the time) or only sometimes? If only sometimes, what circumstances bring about the problem? When will a solution resolve the problem?	Circumstances may include people (culture, conditioning), process (actions), technology, etc.
Where	Where does the problem occur? Is it localized? Is it enterprisewide?	
How	How does the problem manifest? How does the problem affect expected outcomes?	

Further Considerations

As a result of the checks and balances phase, the following details warrant consideration:

- Premises
  - TBD
- Assumptions
  - TBD
- Open issues
  - TBD

- Questions
  - TBD
- Expected residual problem
  - TBD

Recommendations

Given the problem as stated, the results of the checks and balances, and the further considerations, the recommendations at this time are:

- [Not to] Proceed with TBD
- TBD

References

U.S. Department of Energy (DoE). 1992. *Root Cause Analysis Guidance Document*, 1992.

Appendix J: Privacy Management Program Outline

The content of this appendix is an outline for a privacy management program. Privacy is one of the IA core principles as well as a concern in legislation and civil liberties. Creating a privacy management program using the outline herein will assist in isolating those privacy issues that may present risk to the organization as well as how to address those risks.

Privacy Management Program for
CompanyName
DD Month CCYY

1 Introduction

A key phrase in privacy is *protected information* (PI); one example of PI is personally identifiable information (PII). Compliance requirements provide input to determine what protected information is, and circumstances determine when information becomes protected. The privacy issue with regard to personal privacy, protection from identity theft, protection of health details and financial details, and resulting legislation and regulation forces organizational executives to deal with privacy as part of their due diligence and fiduciary responsibility to stakeholders. In recognition of organizational responsibilities with regard to privacy, the privacy management program (PMP) is a supplement to the security management program. The purpose of the PMP is to address privacy as a distinct but cohesive complement to the SMP.

2 PMP Scope

PMP scope consists of environment and content. The environment is the business and technical environment. The PMP content scope is the breadth and depth of privacy concerns with respect to the environment scope. The PMP content scope addresses facilities, technology, and personnel aspects within the environment scope.

2.1 Environment Scope

2.2 Content Scope

3 Privacy Compliance Requirements

3.1 Legislative, Regulatory, and Other Authoritative Compliance Requirements (Must-Dos)

Articulate the authoritative privacy requirements and what the organization must do to comply with those requirements.

3.2 Policy and Internally Imposed Compliance Requirements (Should-Dos)

Articulate what the organization should do in the name of good business practice with regard to privacy.

4 Privacy Architecture

4.1 Protected Information: Definition, Scope, Bounds, and Qualifications

Include sources that influence the determination of what is protected information and when information becomes protected.

4.2 Privacy Architectural Principles, Constraints, and Assumptions

4.2.1 PI Business and Technical Principles

4.2.2 PI Business and Technical Constraints

4.2.3 PI Business and Technical Assumptions

5 Privacy Architecture Views

5.1 People

5.2 Policy

5.3 Business Process

5.4 Systems and Applications

5.5 Data/Information

5.6 Infrastructure

5.6.1 Physical

5.6.2 Technical

6 Privacy: A Workflow Perspective

There are many perspectives with which to view privacy. One perspective is a work-flow. A generic workflow consists of a front office (customer interactions), back office (processing), and data transmission, in this case the transmission of protected information.

6.1 Front Office

6.1.1 Protected Information (PI) Creation and Acceptance

6.1.2 PI Owners and Custodians

6.2   *Protected Information (PI) Transmission*

6.2.1   PI in Transit

6.2.2   Real-Time Processing

6.2.3   Batch Processing

6.3   *Back Office*

6.3.1   PI at Rest (Storage)

6.3.2   Local

6.3.2.1   Backup

6.3.2.2   Archive

6.3.3   Attribute-Based Access Controls (ABACs)

6.3.4   PI Sharing (Inter- and Intraorganizational)

6.3.5   PI Destruction and Discard

6.3.5.1   Destruction

6.3.5.2   Discard

7   PMP Implementation

7.1   *Protected Information Management Policy and Practice*

7.2   *Privacy Rights Management*

7.3   *Stakeholder Trust Management*

7.4   *Privacy Services*

7.5   *Privacy Mechanisms*

7.6   *Privacy Vendors and Products*

7.7   *Operations and Maintenance*

7.8   *Best Practices*

8 Privacy Impact Assessment (PIA)

A U.S. government–related requirement for some programs to assess the privacy impact of a new application, system, or service.

9 Privacy Compliance Verification Process

9.1 Initial

9.1.1 Certification and Accreditation

9.1.2 System Test and Verification

9.1.3 Compliance Assessment

9.2 Ongoing

9.2.1 Compliance Assessment

10 Privacy Awareness, Training, and Education

10.1 Personnel

10.2 Business Associates

10.2.1 Partners

10.2.2 Vendors

10.2.3 Contractors

10.2.4 Other

11 Privacy Outreach Program

12 Glossary

From a privacy perspective, it is particularly important to define privacy, personally identifiable information (PII), and other supporting terms. Reference or produce a common IA glossary that conveys your organization's definition and use of IA-related terms. People will think about privacy and use the term *privacy* in different ways. A glossary will provide a set of common definitions that will promote consistent use.

Appendix K: E-Insurance

E-insurance plays a role in organizational risk management; the following sections expand on E-insurance details of business benefits, an E-insurance model, and possible E-insurance coverage.

Business Benefit

"By writing policies for network security exposures, the insurance industry is providing:

- Vital risk transfer for network security exposures;
- Incentives for network security best practices, including lower insurance premiums; and
- Improved cyber-risk management and education."*

Risk prevention services are available as part of the application process; some insurance carriers offer an online or on-site security assessment free of charge,† regardless of whether the applicant purchases the insurance. This is helpful to the underwriting process and provides extremely valuable analysis/information to the company's chief technology officer, risk manager, and other senior executives.

E-Insurance Model

A comprehensive E-insurance framework includes:

---

* Insurance Information Institute, *Most Companies Have Cyber-Risk Gaps in Their Insurance Cover Coverage*, 2003.
† Remember, you get what you pay for.

- Business/technical drivers
  - BIA and risk analysis to determine appropriate application of risk transference and risk sharing, including which business areas and tolerable percentage of risk acceptance
- Roles and responsibilities
  - Decision makers: central versus local versus business line
- Coverage levels
  - What and to what extent
- Cost
  - Corporate overhead
  - Business line expense
- Security insurance providers
  - Who
  - Evaluation
    - Underwriting ability
    - Fiscal viability
- Claims process
  - Have policies been used?
  - If so, how did insurance investigation go? Claim process? Claim payment?
- Affects of risk mitigation investments on insurance premiums
  - Optimize investment in security measures to achieve desirable amount of residual risk that may be cost effectively shared or transferred to insurance carrier.
- Monitoring and track results
  - Monitoring results provides:
    - Insight into the business benefit of E-insurance
    - Insight into the uses of alternative risk management practices
      - For example, accepting risk via self-insurance
  - Insurance makes a prediction of losses
    - Track projections against actual.
    - Use data to determine value of E-insurance as an investment in risk management.
- Lessons learned and organizational feedback
  - E-insurance is integral in the risk management process
    - Risk governance considerations include insurer input into risk management.
    - Empirical evidence from actual experiences; track appropriate coverage, appropriate coverage levels, and need for supplemental risk mitigation or additional risk sharing.
    - Organizational benefits from underwriting and other actuarial quantification of risk increases organizational insight into risk.

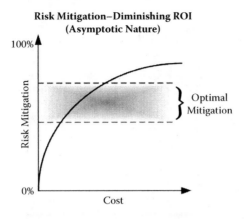

Figure K.1   Risk mitigation.

Policy

Although a separate security policy* for E-insurance is overkill, a risk management policy may state something to the effect of: *Company X proactively identifies and manages risks to our organization and the services we provide our customers while balancing the expense with the interest of our stakeholders (e.g., investors). Effective risk management includes defining risk that we will accept, risk that we will mitigate, and risk we will share or transfer.* This policy statement is generic, but provides the foundation for exploring risk management options that include insurance and E-insurance.

IA² Perspective

Risk mitigation gets closer to 100 percent with each increase in security investment, but never quite reaches 100 percent; there is always residual risk. Therefore, part of the architectural challenge (your challenge) is to optimize mitigation investments via security measures and share or transfer the residual risk by some other means—one of those means is insurance coverage. Figure K.1 shows the asymptotic nature of risk mitigation investment. The question is what to do with residual risk—accept, share, or transfer?

Risk Sharing/Transfer

Insurance coverage is one method to share or transfer risk. Transferring all risk may appear an attractive option and a way to avoid risk mitigation investment; however,

---

* "Policy" in the sense of policy-procedure-standard, not insurance policy.

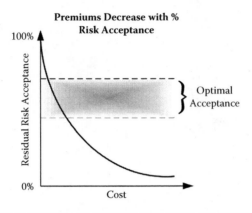

Figure K.2   Risk acceptance.

the premium cost for transferring all risk is likely to be exorbitant even if this option is available at all (Figure K.2). Use E-insurance as part of a comprehensive risk management program that balances risk mitigation and sharing.

Balancing Risk Management

Figure K.3 shows a balance of risk mitigation and residual risk sharing to provide an optimal investment in risk management. Work with insurance providers to determine the best method to optimize E-insurance premiums:

- Insuring for less than residual risk
- Increasing deductible and using E-insurance for catastrophic losses and absorbing nuisance losses in-house

Figure K.3   Balance of risk mitigation and risk acceptance.

There are prices and costs associated with risk mitigation, sharing, transfer, and acceptance. The prices include the expense of mitigation services and mechanisms as well as insurance premiums. The costs include the addition of ongoing operations, maintenance, and upgrades. The initial price of risk acceptance is zero; however, the final cost for accepting all risk may be the most expensive option, with the ultimate price being going out of business. Your job as an IA architect includes finding the right balance in addressing all risk.

Appendix L: Reading List

The following sections contain some interesting and useful references by subject area. These contain additional details of many aspects presented herein and generally provide good reading for a current or aspiring IA architect.

Enterprise Architecture

- *Introduction to Enterprise Architecture* by Scott A. Bernard
- *Enterprise Architecture Planning* by Steven H. Spewak

Systems Engineering

- *The Art of Systems Architecture* by Mark W. Maier and Eberhardt Rechtin
- *Systems Engineering Principles and Practice* by Alexander Kossiakoff and William N. Sweet
- *The Systems View of the World* by Ervin Laszlo
- *INCOSE Systems Engineering Guide* (www.incose.org)

Information Assurance

- *Norwich University Journal of Information Assurance* (NUJIA) (nujia.norwich.edu/)
- *Computer Security Handbook, 4th Edition* by Seymour Bosworth and Michel E. Kabay

Compliance Management

- *How to Become ISO 27001 Certified—An Example of Compliance Management* by Sigurjon Thor Arnason and Keith Willett

Innovation

- *Seeing What's Next* by Clayton M. Christensen, Erik A. Roth, and Scott D. Anthony
- *Thinking in the Future Tense* by Jennifer James
- *Five Minds for the Future* by Howard Gardner

Leadership

- *Visualizing Project Management* by Kevin Forsberg, Hal Mooz, and Howard Cotterman
- *The Prepared Mind of a Leader* by Bill Welter and Jean Egmon
- *Leading With Questions* by Michael J. Marquardt

Change Management

- *Change* by Paul Watzlawick

Cognitive Science

- *Pragmatics of Human Communication* by Paul Watzlawick
- *Mind—Introduction to Cognitive Science* by Paul Thagard
- *Working Minds—A Practioner's Guide to Cognitive Task Analysis* by Beth Crandall, Gary Klein, and Robert R. Hoffman

Critical Thinking and Decision Making

- *Wharton on Making Decisions* by Robert E. Gunther, Stephen J. Hoch, and Howard C. Kunreuther
- *The Psychology of Judgment and Decision Making* by Scott Plous
- *Frameworks for Thinking* by David Moseley, Vivienne Baumfield, Julian Elliott, and Steven Higgins
- *Adaptive Thinking* by Gerd Gigerenzer
- *Mistakes Were Made (but not by me)* by Carol Tavris and Elliot Aronson
- *Don't Believe Everything You Think* by Thomas Kida
- *Sources of Power—How People Make Decisions* by Gary Klein

Information Warfare

- *Information Warfare and Security* by Dorothy E. Denning
- *Strategic Warfare in Cyberspace* by Gregory J. Rattray
- *Unrestricted Warfare* by Qiao Liang and Wang Xiangsui

Systems Thinking and Systems Dynamics

- *Systems Thinking* by Jamshid Gharajedaghi

Glossary

Term	Description
Address, addressing	Formulating and articulating a response; e.g., to address a risk is to formulate and articulate a response to that risk in terms of accept, ignore, share, transfer, or mitigate.
Adjudication	A formal process to resolve conflicts or disputes.
Align	Establish a direct link to or correlation with.
Architect	One who applies the discipline of architecture.
Architectural add-on	Architectural constructs added to the architectural baseline during a project, or otherwise, until adopted as part of the architectural framework and included in a future architectural baseline.
Architectural baseline	A snapshot of the architectural framework at a point in time. An architectural framework is a living construct. However, to be useful, a baseline provides a "line in sand" that states, for the moment, this is what the architectural framework looks like.
Architectural component	A generic term referring to the discrete items comprising an architectural framework or architectural process.
Architectural driver	A motivation behind the architecture. Examples include business, technical, and architectural principles.

Term	Description
Architectural phases	The three high-level phases of producing an architecture plan: to-be, as-is, and transition; much detail goes into each phase to produce an architecture plan.
Architectural principle	A fundamental edict or underlying faculty with regard to architecture as a practice or the architecture of the solution at hand.
Architectural process	Provides a disciplined methodology to promote repeatability, consistency, high quality, and complexity management in producing an architecture.
Architectural view	A perspective on the architecture that isolates and focuses attention on a specific class of concerns.
Architecture	1. A product of the architecture process, e.g., an IA architecture document. 2. The art of consciously forming a coherent structure.
Artifact	A practical creation; may be a document or device; many EA standards specify "EA artifacts" that are documents with specific form, flow, and content as specified by the EA standard.
Asset	An object of value owned by the organization.
Asset space	A collective term referring to all organizational assets, all attributes of assets, and the environment containing assets.
Assumption	A quality, fact, or statement taken to be true.
Attribute	A naturally occurring or inherent characteristic.
Availability	Information or information resource is ready for immediate use.
Authenticity	Information or information source conforms to reality.
Authorized use	Cost-incurring services are available only to authorized personnel (e.g., toll-fraud prevention).

Term	Description
Builder	One who compiles pieces into a coherent whole; the term here applies in context of governance, management, builders, operations, users, and leaders where a builder establishes a business or technical service and transfers the end product to operations to oversee ongoing use.
Business capability	A state of being where the enterprise (the organization) is able to perform an activity, or the ability to perform an action.
Business driver	A motivation that finds root in the core reasons for the existence of the organization; an expression of motivation to further stakeholder interests.
Business need	The lack of something within the organization; a condition requiring something to fill a void, e.g., a new service, a new product, a new product feature, the business to sustain a revenue stream.
Business objective	A purpose to be achieved to further organizational progress.
Cause	To bring on the occurrence of something; i.e., the performance of X leads to the occurrence of Y in a consistent manner, and therefore X is the cause of Y.
Certification and accreditation (C&A)	A formal process to validate the presence and effectiveness of security controls.
Characteristic	A distinguishing trait or property.
Chief information officer (CIO)	A CIO has responsibility for organizational information. Note: the title is not chief information technology officer; the CIO responsibilities are for information, not just information technology.
Class	A group consisting of entities with the same or similar characteristics.
Classification	The act of assigning entities to a class.
Coincidence	To occur at the same time without causal connection; i.e., the occurrence of X and the occurrence of Y, but each is not the cause or a reliable predictor of the other.

Term	*Description*
Compliance assessment	The formal process to discern the organizational policy and practice as compared against a compliance requirement at a given point in time.
Compliance management	The formal tactical process to identify, understand, assess, analyze, and address organizational compliance requirements.
Compliance management program (CMP)	An initiative to identify, enumerate, and decompose compliance requirements into organizational directives.
Compliance requirements	Qualifications, often in the form of restrictions, to operations and organizational actions; compliance requirements may be external (e.g., legislative) or internal (e.g., mission statement).
Community of interest (COI)	A group of entities (a.k.a. domains) defined by logical relationship; physical proximity may be dispersed.
Community of malicious intent (COMI)	Pronounced *co-me*; COMI is a collective term that represents all persons that purposely set out to do damage to the organization or organizational information. COMI includes hackers, spies (corporate and government), non-state-sponsored adversaries, etc.
Confidentiality	Information is disclosed and observable only by authorized personnel or information resources.
Conservancy principle	A fundamental edict or underlying faculty of maintaining a quantity.
Constraint	A restriction or bounds.
Construct (noun)	The term *construct* refers generically to a tool, template, methodology, or framework that contributes to the development, operation, or understanding of something; e.g., an O&M construct is the network operations center (NOC) or the IA ops cycle.
Context	The environment within which something exists or resides.

Term	*Description*
Continuity of operations plan (COOP)	A plan to sustain key business functions at acceptable service levels during an event that may otherwise prevent the execution of these business functions.
Contributory	To add to the whole; i.e., the occurrence of X is necessary but not sufficient for the occurrence of Y.
Correlation	To occur at the same time with predictable simultaneous occurrence, but without causal connection; i.e., the occurrence of X may be a predictor of the occurrence of Y, but is not the cause of the occurrence of Y.
COTS (1)	Common off-the-shelf software.
COTS (2)	Common off-the-shelf solution; this book uses this definition for the implication that a common off-the-shelf solution may include software, hardware, or a service (e.g., outsourcing or managed service).
Deliverable	An obligation in the form of a document, artifact, system, system aggregation, enterprise solution, or other as specified.
Domain	A self-contained entity or collection of related artifacts that may consider a self-contained entity (e.g., PC and peripherals).
Domain component	An artifact that comprises a domain.
Domain interaction	Communication between domains; communication occurs between domain interfaces.
Domain interface	The visible part of a domain.
Dynamic remediation	Closure of a security gap on the fly; e.g., an IDS detects an intruder and remediates (corrects) the vulnerability automatically.
Dynamics	A state of action, e.g., entity interactions; may result in change.
Endogenous	Occurring within the organization.
Enterprise	An aggregation of people, process, and technology for purposeful activity.

Term	Description
Enterprise architecture	A unifying discipline using a set of design artifacts and descriptive representations to describe an entity or function such that it can be produced to requirements and be maintained over its life cycle.
Enterprise Context Framework (ECF)	A representation of the enterprise in terms of people, process, and technology.
Enterprise dynamics	A representation of the enterprise activity through the interrelation of actors (people), actions (process), and entities (technology).
Enterprise efficacy	The power to produce a desired effect within the organization.
Enterprise life cycle management (ELCM)	An approach to guiding a product or service from creation through discarding. ELCM is a phased approach for idea conception, architecture, engineering, development or acquisition, implementation, testing, deployment, training, operations and maintenance, and retirement.
Enterprise system engineering (ESE)	A discipline to evaluate, plan, and ultimately produce a system in context of the enterprise, including overall fit of the system, dependencies, expectations, relationships, and effect on other systems.
Entity	A person or thing, or something that has existence; entities may include person, process, application, system, daemon, thread, device, etc.
Exogenous	Occurring outside the organization.
Framework	A conceptual structure that provides order.
Federal Information Security Management Act of 2002 (FISMA)	A U.S. federal law to increase computer and network security within the federal government and affiliated parties like government contractors.
Governance	A process of strategic decision making that provides direction.
Harmony	To reach a state of optimality by way of integration.

Term	Description
Hierarchy	A top-down structure that denotes superior–subordinate relationships; may represent a control structure or a classification structure (e.g., bullet and subbullet, where the subbullet is subcategory to the superior bullet).
IA adjudication	A formal process to resolve conflicts or disputes in context of information assurance; e.g., resolve disputes of local policy versus enterprise policy, or resolve conflicts between legislative directives (state law says X and federal law says Y and foreign law says Z).
IA architect	One who applies the discipline of architecture to information assurance.
IA core principles	The collection of fundamental edicts or underlying faculties providing motivation for risk mitigation activities, services, and mechanisms to maintain mission integrity; the IA core principles are confidentiality, integrity, availability, possession, authenticity, utility, nonrepudiation, authorized use, and privacy.
IA mechanism	Equipment, tool, or component to mitigate business risk.
IA operational construct	The combining of parts for a practical purpose involving the application of processes in support of IA operations.
IA^2 applied taxonomy	The formal categorization of the IA^2 LoS.
IA^2 architect	One who applies the discipline of IA^2 to information assurance.
IA^2 artifact	A practical creation in support of the IA^2 Process or resulting IA architecture.
IA^2 drivers	Motivations behind the information assurance architecture: its design, look, feel, process, and application; IA^2 drivers include business and technology.
IA^2 instantiation	To represent an IA^2 abstraction by concrete instance.
IA^2 Framework	The basic conceptual structure for defining and describing an IA^2 solution.

Term	Description
IA^2 LoS	The formal linking of IA business requirements to IA operations and maintenance.
IA^2 meta-view	Viewing the whole of IA^2 with the intent of deriving a broader perspective and overall order (e.g., viewing the business rationale versus getting caught up in IA^2 for its own sake).
IA^2 model	The representation or blueprint of an IA^2 instance (IA^2 instantiation).
IA^2 operational construct	The combining of parts for a practical purpose involving the application of processes in support of the IA^2 development process.
IA^2 principle	A fundamental edict or underlying faculty of information assurance architecture.
IA^2 Process	The steps required to generate an information assurance architecture.
IA quantification framework (IAQF)	A conceptual structure that provides an orderly way to examine, discover, plan, and use objective representations of IA.
IA quantification process (IAQP)	A methodology to produce a scheme for objective representation of IA.
IA^2 view	A representation of an IA system from the perspective of related concerns or issues; a collection of logically related IA models.
IA^2 work product	A document or other artifact that assists in the development or production of the final IA architecture.
Influence (general use)	The production of an effect by subtle means; influence may include direct causation, but is typically more subtle.
Influence (in scope of control)	In terms of scope of control, influence is distinct from direct control.
Information assurance (IA)	Defining and applying a collection of policies, methodologies, security services, and security mechanisms to maintain mission integrity with respect to people, process, technology, information, and supporting infrastructure.

Term	*Description*
Information assurance architecture (IA²)	1. The art of consciously forming a coherent structure of information assurance services and mechanisms. 2. The documentation resulting from the IA architect applying the IA² Framework.
Information assurance management program (IAMP)	The initiative to formally define the organizational approach to information assurance; similar to an SMP.
Innovator	One who creates or enhances; an introducer of something new.
Instance	An example of a category.
Integrate	To blend, coordinate, or unite with; e.g., the purpose of IA² is to provide tools, templates, and methodology to integrate IA with the enterprise by way of integrating IA with EA and other business perspectives.
Integrity	Information remains unchanged from source to destination and has not been accidentally or maliciously modified.
Interface	A place of interaction; a communication point.
Management	A process of tactical decision making and execution using governance directives as guidance.
Measure	A numeric amount (e.g., 100, 50,000, 12). A metric specifies the standard of measure. A measure is how many of the metric (e.g., 100 yards is the length of an American football field; yards is the metric, 100 is the amount of that metric).
Mechanism	Equipment, tool, or component.
Metadata	Data about data; e.g., creator, date of creation, date of last modification, classification, data owner.
Meta-view	Viewing the whole with the intent of deriving a broader perspective and overall order (e.g., viewing the forest versus the trees).
Methodology	A set of formal procedures.
Metric	A standard of measure (e.g., quantity [or count], yards, meters, inches, liters, etc.).

Term	Description
Mission	A specific task or set of tasks given to an individual or collection of individuals or entities, e.g., organization.
Mission entropy	When operations exceed acceptable deviation parameters, operations have entered a state of mission entropy.
Mission integrity	Mission integrity is maintained when all relevant operations are working toward the fulfillment of the mission within an acceptable level of deviation.
Mitigate (mitigation)	To make less harmful.
National Institute of Standards and Technology (NIST)	As stated on NIST's Web site (http://www.nist.gov/), NIST is a nonregulatory federal agency within the U.S. Department of Commerce. NIST's mission is to promote U.S. innovation and industrial competitiveness by advancing measurement science, standards, and technology in ways that enhance economic security and improve our quality of life.
Nonrepudiation	The inability for a message sender to later deny having sent the message.
Object	A logical or physical something that may be viewed, sensed, or otherwise receive focus; a subject may act upon an object.
Ontology	The philosophical definition is a discipline concerned with nature, categories, and relations of being; in context of technology, an ontology is a specification of concepts to establish common meaning to promote effective communications.
Operational construct	The combining of parts for a practical purpose involving the application of processes.
Operations	Practical application of processes. Alternatively, consider that policy describes the functional parameters of business or mission, standards describe what to use to enforce policy, and procedures describe how to use the standards to enforce policy; operations is the practical application of procedures.

Term	Description
Parsimony	The least complex explanation; taking great care with resources.
Perspective	A point of view.
Policy	A document stating bounds and qualifications for organizational behavior; they may reflect external compliance requirements like legislation, and internal compliance requirements like organizational mission or values.
Possession	Information or information resource remains in the custody of authorized personnel.
Principle	A fundamental edict or underlying faculty.
Privacy	Personal privacy is protected and relevant privacy compliances are adhered to (e.g., Privacy Act 1974); to be free from observation or intrusion.
Procedure	How to apply the standards to implement and enforce policy; formal representation of a process.
Region	A group of entities (a.k.a. domains) whose relationship is defined by physical proximity. Domains may be grouped within a region (physically grouped) or COI (logically grouped).
Relationship	Connecting or communicating; e.g., two entities may have a relationship via their respective interfaces.
Remediation	The process of providing a remedy; correcting or counteracting a gap in security, e.g., between compliance requirement and policy or between policy and practice.
Risk	The possibility of loss or injury.
Risk governance	Strategic decision making with respect to risk and risk management.
Risk management	Tactical decision making and implementation of safeguards with respect to minimizing risk.
Risk mitigation	To reduce risk.
Schema	A diagram of a framework.
Scheme	A systematic representation.

Term	Description
Security	A service or mechanism that provides a safeguard; preserve functional intent; preserve mission integrity.
Security domain	A domain when viewed for purposes of information assurance consideration.
Security education, training, and awareness (SETA)	The conveyance of security throughout the enterprise in varying detail. The intent of awareness is to let the audience know about something. Training conveys how to use that something. Education conveys the theory behind, the why about that something.
Security event	A noteworthy occurrence; an event that may be of significance from a mission integrity perspective.
Security incident	An event confirmed to be of significance from a mission integrity perspective.
Security management program (SMP)	The initiative to formally define the organizational approach to security.
Security region	A collection of security domains grouped by physical proximity.
Security service	In context of IA^2, a security service is a set of processes to maintain confidentiality, integrity, and availability; the main purpose is to distinguish from mechanisms.
Service	The act of satisfying some demand (verb) or the entity that satisfies some demand (noun); a service may be a business service or a technical service; the provision of a service may be manual (via person) or automated (via technology).
Service-oriented architecture (SOA)	SOA is a design philosophy that enables the ability to add, modify, and remove services from an enterprise environment; SOA is more specific than Web services or technical services.
Solution	In context of IA^2, consider the solution to be the final result to the customer that solves the business problem at hand; the solution may be product, system, systemic aggregation, service, functional operation, etc.

Term	Description
Solution life cycle management (SLCM)	A formal process to manage an organizational solution across inception, creation, implementation, operations, and termination.
Standard	Describes what to use to implement and enforce policy.
Subject	An initiator or executor of action; a subject may be sentient, cyber, or another inanimate tool; a subject may act upon an object.
System	A collection of entities (real or virtual) that interact to produce an objective or result. These entities may be stand-alone or aggregated in various collections of subsystems, components, subcomponents, or other breakdown.
System development life cycle (SDLC)	A formal process to development systems consisting of phases:[a] initiation, acquisition/development, implementation, operations/maintenance, and retirement.
System engineering	A discipline to evaluate, plan, and ultimately produce a system.
System framework	Input → process → output → feedback.
Systems architecture	Refers to the way in which a system vision is expressed in the structure and dynamics of the system and often in context of a collection of systems. It provides, on various architecture abstraction levels, a coherent set of models, principles, guidelines, and policies, used for the translation, alignment, and evolution of the components that exist within the scope and context of a system.
Technical services	A term referring to the generic provision of automated tasks within the enterprise.
Taxonomy	An orderly classification; an alignment of classes in a particular relationship.

[a] Generic phases adopted from NIST SP 800-64. *Security Considerations in the Information System Development Life Cycle.*

Term	*Description*
Threat	An expression of intent to inflict damage, or circumstances that provide opportunity for unintended damage.
Threat agent	An entity capable of introducing threat.
Threat space	A collective term referring to all organizational threats, all attributes of threats, and the environment containing threats.
Traceability	A formal link from one element to another; often used in IA^2 in reference to requirements and establishing formal traceability from business drivers through a series of tables to operations and maintenance (O&M).
Transactional nonrepudiation	The nondeniability of an individual or service performing a particular activity (e.g., logon, monetary transfer, database update).
Utility	Information is fit for a purpose and in a usable state.
Vulnerability	A weakness that may be exploited to cause loss or injury.
Web services	A term referring to the generic provision of automated tasks within the enterprise where those automated tasks are invoked and provided via Web technologies.
Work breakdown structure (WBS)	A method for organizing the entire scope of a project.
Work product	A document or other artifact that assists in the development or production of the final solution; a deliverable is a contractual obligation where a work product is a nice-to-have, or often an essential-to-have, but not explicitly called out contractually.

References

Arnason, Sigurjon Thor and Willett, Keith D., 2008, *How to Achieve ISO 27001 Certification—An Example of Compliance Management*, Auerbach Publications, Boca Raton, FL.

Booth-Butterfield, Steve, *Steve's Primer of Practical Persuasion and Influence*, 1996, West Virginia University, Morgantown. (http://www.as.wvu.edu/~sbb/comm221/primer.htm, accessed July 2004

Bosworth, Seymour, and Kabay, M.E., Eds., 2002, *Computer Security Handbook 4th Edition*, John Wiley & Sons, Hoboken, NJ.

The Business Continuity Institute, 2002, *Business Continuity Management – Good Practice Guide*, (www.thebci.org, last accessed February 2008)

Campbell, Quinn, and Kennedy, David M., 2002, "The Psychology of Computer Criminal" in the *Computer Security Handbook 4th Edition*, Bosworth, Seymou,r and Kabay, M.E., Eds., John Wiley & Sons, Hoboken, NJ.

Carnegie Mellon University, February 2002, *INFOSEC Assessment Capability Maturity Model (IA-CMM) v2.1*, Pittsburgh, PA.

Carnegie Mellon University, June 15, 2003, *Systems Security Engineering – Capability Maturity Manual, Model Description Document, v3.0*, Pittsburgh, PA.

Christensen, Clayton M., Anthony, Scott D., and Roth, Erik A., 2004, *Seeing What's Next*, Harvard Business School Press, Cambridge, MA.

Cobb, Stephen, 2002, *Notes on System Penetration as included in lecture notes in Norwich University Masters Program in Information Assurance (MSIA)*, Northfield, VT.

Diamond, Jennifer, 2003, *Aligning the Organization for IT Project Success: Improving Customer Acceptance and ROI*, Management Agility, Inc.

Dickson, Douglas N., 1983, *Using Logical Techniques for Making Better Decisions*, John Wiley & Sons, Hoboken, NJ.

Federal Enterprise Architecture Documents (http://www.whitehouse.gov/omb/egov/a-1-fea.html, accessed March 2008)
- Business Reference Model, v. 2.0
- Performance Reference Model, v. 1.0
- Technical Reference Model, v. 2.0
- Data and Information Reference Model, v. 1.0

Forrest, Jay, 2007, *Systems Dynamics, Alternative Futures, and Scenarios,* The Strategic Decision Simulation Group (http://www.systemdynamics.org/conferences/1998/PROCEED/00095.PDF, accessed October 2007)

Gharajedaghi , Jamshid, 1999, *Systems Thinking—Managing Chaos and Complexity,* Butterworth-Heinemann, New York.

Haley, Charles, 2003, *Using Trust Assumptions in Security Requirements Engineering,* The Open University, London, U.K.

Hallberg, Carl, Hutt, Arthur E., and Kabay, M.E., 2002, "Management Responsibilities and Liabilities," in the *Computer Security Handbook 4th Edition,* Bosworth, Seymour and Kabay, M.E., Eds., John Wiley & Sons, Hoboken, NJ.

Howard, John D., and Longstaff, Thomas A., 1998. *A Common Language for Computer Security Incidents,* Sandia National Laboratories, Sandia, NM.

Howard, John D., and Meunier, Pascal, 2002, "Using a 'Common Language' for Computer Security Incident Information, in the *Computer Security Handbook 4th Edition* Bosworth, Seymour, and Kabay, M.E., Eds., John Wiley & Sons, Hoboken, NJ.

Hunter, Richard, 2002, *World Without Secrets,* Gartner Press, Stamford, CT.

Insurance Information Institute, August, 2003, *Most Companies Have Cyber-Risk Gaps in Their Insurance Cover Coverage.*

Kruse II, Warren G., and Heiser, Jay G., 2001, *Computer Forensics: Incident Response Essentials,* Addison-Wesley, United Kingdom.

Maier, Mark W., and Rechtin, Eberhardt, 2002, *The Art of Systems Architecting, 2d Ed.,* CRC Press, Boca Raton, FL.

Marks, Richard D., 2004, *Enterprise Liability for Information Security.*

National Institute of Standards & Technology (NIST) (http://csrc.nist.gov/publications/nistpubs/, accessed July 2007)
- Various Special Publications (SP)
- Various Federal Information Processing Standards (FIPS)

OECD Guidelines for the Security of Information Systems and Networks: Towards a Culture of Security, OECD Council, July 25, 2002.

Parker, Donn B., 2002, "Toward a New Framework for Information Security," in the *Computer Security Handbook 4th Edition* Bosworth, Seymour and Kabay, M.E., Eds., John Wiley & Sons, Hoboken, NJ.

Practical Guide to Federal Enterprise Architecture v. 1.0, Chief Information Officer Council, February 2001. (http://www.enterprise-architecture.info/Images/Documents/Federal%20Enterprise%20Architecture%20Guide%20v1a.pdf, accessed February 2008)

The President's Critical Infrastructure Protection Board, *National Strategy to Secure Cyberspace,* February 2003, USA

Schneier, Bruce, 1999, *Attack Trees,* CounterPane Systems (www.counterpane.com, last accessed March 2008), presentation to SANS Network Security.

Schwartau, Winn, 2003, *Asymmetrical Adversarialism in National Defense Policy.*

Spewak, Steven H., 1992, *Enterprise Architecture Planning,* John Wiley & Sons, Hoboken, NJ.

Spitzner, Lance, 2003, *Honeypots – Tracking Hackers,* Addison Wesley, United Kingdom.

Systems Engineering Handbook, International Council on Systems Engineering (INCOSE) v2a, 2004, USA

Trygstad, Ray, 2004, *Security Policy*, Illinois Institute of Technology, (www.itm.iit.edu/578/lesson7/lesson07.ppt), accessed June 2004.

U.S. Department of Energy (DoE), 1992, *Root cause analysis guidance document.*

Whitcomb, Carrie Morgan, Spring 2002 , "An Historical Perspective of Digital Evidence: A Forensic Scientist's View," *International Journal of Digital Evidence,* Volume 1, Issue 1 (www.ijde.org, last accessed March 2008).

Willett, Keith D., and Gardner, Robert K., *Risk Analysis and Assessments: Focus on Intelligent, Coordinated, Non-State Adversary*, Computer Sciences Corporation, June 2004

Willett, Keith D., July 2000, *Applied IP Telephony* course developed by Keith D. Willett, Avaya, Inc.

Willett, Keith D., April 2002, *IP Telephony – The Business Case*, CTN Technologies, Inc.

List of Figures

List of Tables

INDEX

Index